# www.wadsworth.com

wadsworth.com is the World Wide Web site for Wadsworth and is your direct source to dozens of online resources.

At wadsworth.com you can find out about supplements, demonstration software, and student resources. You can also send email to many of our authors and preview new publications and exciting new technologies.

**wadsworth.com**
Changing the way the world learns®

*In memory of Janice Jordan (1947–1998),
a warm and gifted colleague, whose
excellent choices touched many people.*

# Life's Choices

## PROBLEMS AND SOLUTIONS

**RICHARD S. SHARF**
*University of Delaware*

**Brooks/Cole**
Thomson Learning™

*Australia • Canada • Mexico • Singapore • Spain • United Kingdom • United States*

*Counseling Editors:* Eileen Murphy/Julie Martinez
*Assistant Editor:* Jennifer Wilkinson
*Editorial Assistant:* Marin Plank
*Marketing Manager:* Caroline Concilla
*Signing Representative:* Ron Shelly
*Project Editor:* Matt Stevens
*Print Buyer:* Mary Noel
*Permissions Editor:* Joohee Lee
*Production Service:* Forbes Mill Press
*Text Designer:* Adriane Bosworth

*Photo Researcher:* Terri Wright
*Copy Editor:* Robin Gold
*Cover Designer:* Roger Knox
*Cover Image:* © Tony Stone Images
*Compositor:* Wolf Creek Press
*Printer:* Custom Printing/Von Hoffmann Press
*Photo Images:* (Part I) © John A. Rizzo, PhotoDisc;
(Part II) © Esbin-Anderson/PhotoNetwork PNI;
(Part III) © John Coletti/Stock Boston/PNI

For permission to use material from this
text, contact us by
   **Web:** www.thomsonrights.com
   **Fax:** 1-800-730-2215
   **Phone:** 1-800-730-2214

Library of Congress
Cataloging-in-Publication Data

Sharf, Richard S.
  Life's choices : problems and solutions / Richard S. Sharf.
    p. cm.
  Includes bibliographical references and index.
  ISBN 0-534-35933-7
   1. College students—Psychology. 2. College students—Conduct of life.
3. Choice (Psychology) I. Title.

LB3609.S554 2001
378.198—dc21                                        00-025258

For more information, contact
**Wadsworth/Thomson Learning**
**10 Davis Drive**
**Belmont, CA 94002-3098**
**USA**
**www.wadsworth.com**

**International Headquarters**
Thomson Learning
International Division
290 Harbor Drive, 2nd Floor
Stamford, CT 06902-7477
USA

**UK/Europe/Middle East/South Africa**
Thomson Learning
Berkshire House
168-173 High Holborn
London WC1V 7AA
United Kingdom

**Asia**
Thomson Learning
60 Albert Street, #15-01
Albert Complex
Singapore 189969

**Canada**
Nelson/Thomson Learning
1120 Birchmount Road
Toronto, Ontario M1K 5G4
Canada

# Contents

## Part One

## LEARNING AND WORKING    21

### Chapter 2

### *Learning and Studying*    22

### Chapter 3

### *Choosing Careers*    53

## Chapter 4

## Adjusting to Work    82

## Chapter 8

## Gender Roles      182

## Part Three

## PERSONAL CHOICES AND SOLUTIONS   273

## Chapter 13

## Coping Strategies    328

## Appendix A

## Life's Choices: Journal Pages    342

## Glossary    355

## References    369

## Index    381

# Preface

I believe that students want to be able to solve problems in their own lives that deal with personal choices and relationships. Currently, there is no text that is both practical for students in their everyday decision making, yet also is grounded in psychological and social science theory. Unlike other texts, this text gives students suggestions for solutions to problems in their lives and shows them, through the use of case studies, how others have handled these problems.

The text is directed at a broad audience, including students in four-year colleges, community colleges, and high schools. Also, when writing this book, I have kept the needs of returning adult college students in mind. Case examples include students in their twenties and thirties, as well as traditional college age students. This book will be useful for typical courses in human relations, psychology of adjustment, personal growth, life choices, and current problems in living.

## Goals

Basic goals of the text are for students to learn how they can solve their own problems by applying knowledge from psychological and social science research. Students should appreciate the case material that makes the information in the text come alive. Questions about the cases and psychological research related to them should be of interest to many students. The "Problems and Solutions" feature will help students focus on the purpose of the material and see the relevance for their own lives. Instructors should find that students will be interested in the text and will be more open to discussing issues related to personal growth and the psychology of adjustment than when reading other texts. The use of questions, both in the text and in the instructor's manual, provides an opportunity for instructors to discuss issues in class that are raised in the text. This text is likely to be particularly helpful for use with students who are practical and resist material that seems theoretical or not related to their own personal needs.

My rationale for selection of chapters is based on their relevance to student issues. In Part I, "Learning and Working," I have included a chapter on learning using a somewhat different approach than in many books (although still including many practical suggestions) because a good proportion of students have had a course on study skills or an introduction to college. Also, I have provided two chapters on career issues: one on career choice, the other on work adjustment. Part II, "Relationships," addresses relationships with family and romantic partners and friends. Gender issues, sexual relationships, and cultural diversity deal with other relationship issues, as do problems dealing with mourning and bereavement. Part III, "Personal Choices and Solutions," focuses on personal solutions to difficult problems such as substance abuse and dealing with stress, anxiety, and anger. The last chapter in this section describes coping in a broad sense.

An instructor's manual accompanies this text and provides examination questions as well as exercises and transparencies that instructors may use in class. The instructor's manual includes multiple choice questions and essay questions that can be used for examinations. The multiple choice questions were developed using Bloom's taxonomy. In addition to the questions in the text that can be used for class discussion, other questions and classroom exercises are described for each chapter. In addition, transparency masters will help instructors present the material for student note taking.

## *Features*

This text includes several features designed to increase student interest. These include "Problems and Solutions" boxes, questions at the beginning and throughout each chapter, and useful recommended readings and Web sites. The "Problems and Solutions" boxes that run throughout the chapters help students focus on the usefulness of the material and remind students that information from psychological and social science research can help them in dealing with life issues. Questions at the beginning of the chapter help students think about what is coming and what questions in their lives will be answered. The questions are based on chapter outlines. Questions that follow major sections of the text can be used in several ways: They can be assigned for homework or be discussed in class, or both. These questions should help students think about the relevance of the material that they are studying. Definitions of concepts are provided for students in the margins where the concept is first discussed; these are also collected in the glossary at the end of the book. The case studies used to illustrate important concepts in each chapter are more thorough than in most other texts. Occasionally, dialog is presented between the client and myself to show how certain concepts can be useful in solving problems. This emphasis on demonstration and application is unique to this text. I have also provided recommended readings for students. Most of these are self-help books that are based on psychological research and have been written by prominent researchers. Others are texts that describe issues such as sex and drug abuse in more detail than is possible in this text. Because many students now have access to the Internet, I have provided Web sites that I feel will interest students because these sites relate to specific topics in the chapters. Students should be warned that Web addresses do change and that those listed might not be current.

A frequent problem for instructors teaching a basic course in psychology of adjustment or human relations is making the material relevant to student needs and involving them in discussion of the material. This text seeks to help instructors with that concern. The practical focus of the text toward use of "Problems and Solutions" and questions and case examples should help instructors get increased enthusiasm and class participation from students. Students who are focused on "What does this do for me?" are likely to find the application of psychology and social science to be useful for them. This practical focus differentiates this text from others that are currently available.

## *Acknowledgments*

I would like to thank Mr. Nick Simons and Dr. Sharon Mitchell of the University of Delaware for reading portions of the manuscript. I especially appreciate the help and skill that Lisa Sweder provided in typing the manuscript. And, I would like to thank Vincent W. Hevern of Le Moyne College, who helped provide the Web sites for this text.

I would also like to thank the following reviewers for helping make this a better book:

John Brennecke, Mt. San Antonio College
James F. Calhoun, University of Georgia
D. Jean Christy, Delaware Technical and Community College
Stephen S. Coccia, Orange County Community College
Susan Coffey, Central Virginia Community College
Carmen N. Colón, Community College of Philadelphia
Diane Hodson, University of Georgia
Chris Moore, Claremont Graduate University

Richard Morehouse, Viterbo College
Linda Petroff, Central Community College
Patricia A. Ramone, Delaware Technical and Community College
Deborah Weber, University of Akron

*Richard S. Sharf*

# CHOICES AND SOLUTIONS

Throughout life, individuals make numerous significant choices. The choices discussed in this book are learning, work, love and friendship, raising a family, sex, gender roles, stress (worry, anxiety, depression, anger management), alcohol and drugs, dying, and cultural diversity. All these issues require thought and choice. With the growth from childhood to adolescence and into adulthood comes an increasing responsibility for one's choices. As individuals (rather than their parents) become more responsible for their own decisions, the need to make choices that are going to affect the direction of their lives become greater and greater. In adulthood, individuals make choices that affect not only their own lives, but also those of their partners, children, and co-workers.

Researchers (psychologists, sociologists, and educators) and therapists (counselors, psychiatrists, and psychologists) have developed a number of strategies for dealing with problems. For each of the many problems people encounter in life, I will describe some of the concerns and show solutions for dealing with them. In addition to showing the approaches of researchers and psychotherapists, I will discuss my own work as a counselor. I have had the privilege during the last 25 years to work with a great number of college students with a very wide variety of concerns. By sharing their approaches to dealing with problems which are consistent with those developed by experts, you can develop new ways to deal with concerns that you encounter in your own life that may upset you or cause you to think about your own future.

People sometimes wonder, Am I well adjusted? Am I normal? How can I tell if I'm making the right decision? Can I ever be happy? And if I am happy, will I know it? Such questions are difficult to answer, but there are ways of viewing them so they don't seem too vague and overwhelming. Let's look first at issues related to "psychological adjustment."

## ADJUSTMENT AND DEVELOPMENT

Four major concepts that help to describe a person's development are discussed here: adjustment, choices, change, and growth. Adjustment has a variety of meanings for people. How individuals make choices in their lives is often a function of how "well-adjusted" they are. With choices come changes and responsibility in our lives. Some of these decisions are more difficult to make than others are. With change can come growth in psychological development that can affect our relationships with others.

## Adjustment

**adjustment** Ways in which people cope with their lives, and the problems and challenges that they face; refers to all areas of life.

**Adjustment** is usually used when discussing human behavior to describe how people cope with their lives, and the problems and challenges that they face. This broad term refers to all areas of life. For example, we might describe adjusting to school, adjusting to a new job, adjusting to being newly divorced, or adjusting to the death of a family member. Sometimes the phrase "get adjusted" or "adjust to it" means "get over it" or "stop complaining." This implies that there is an appropriate way to be "adjusted." This can be seen in the term "well-adjusted," which has come to mean that people can handle their problems well, do not worry too much, or are easy to get along with.

Each person has his or her own style of coping and dealing with problems and crises. When I work with students who have problems, I want to learn about their style of dealing with crises and what are problems for them. How others solve the problem can help a little, but usually what is important is that a person can solve a problem in a way that works best for him or her. It is usually not helpful to listen to the judgments of others about your own adjustment unless they come from professionals or from people who consider your concerns carefully. For example, you might be told you should go to college directly from high school. For many reasons, however, some people go to work after high school before they go to college or never go to college at all. Some people say it is wrong for married couples not to have children, but married couples can lead fulfilling lives whether or not they have children. What seems appropriate for a person or a couple might seem abnormal or "not adjusted" to others.

## Choices

**choices** Selecting from alternatives; choices cover all areas of life.

As individuals enter high school and deal with choices of friends, romantic partners, courses, and events that they attend, they start to realize that they have **choices.** During adolescent years, a common source of friction between parents and their children is that of choice and independence. Parents have different approaches to child raising and how much independence they feel is appropriate for their son or daughter (discussed in Chapter 5). It is likely that you and your parents have disagreed about topics such as how late to stay out at night, your friends, your course of study, and your activities. If you have children of your own, you are likely to see the development of independence from a different point of view. As individuals mature, they are increasingly responsible for their own choices. Other people, such as supervisors and teachers might or might not like their choices. As we grow in independence, however, we have more and more opportunities to choose our own work and our relationships and fewer people to advise us. In this book, we will discuss some choices that you might have and how to deal with problems that can accompany them.

Most choices, particularly those that involve human relationships, are not totally irreversible. For example, if you choose between two jobs and the one that you choose doesn't work out, you might not be able to have the second job, but other opportunities still await you. In relationships, some choices are reversible. For example, a relationship continues until one partner wishes to stop it. Sometimes, one partner wants to resume it and the other doesn't. Dating relationships commonly have several break-ups and reconciliations. At other times, one or both partners will agree to stop the relationship. Of course, some choices are irreversible. Choosing to vacation in Alaska and going there can't be changed. But, the effect of the choice on you can be changed. Other choices are very difficult to reverse. The choice to stop using heroin or to stop smoking is a difficult one that might require continued work. In this book, I have provided suggestions for helping yourself or others when you make difficult choices.

## *Change*

**change** To make different or to alter; individuals have the ability to make many changes in their lives.

Choices allow you to **change,** to change how you live your life. Often, it is difficult to tell whether you want a change. For example, it may be hard to decide whether you want to stay in a course before the drop period ends. You might think about staying in a relationship for hours at a time. Being aware of the choices you have and the reasons for them is not easy. For example, if Arlene is in a relationship with David who acts in a nasty way toward her, she might want to stop the relationship. If she finds it hard to be independent and to be alone, however, she might resist making such a change. Being aware of your own needs and the difficulties you have in making changes of various types is one purpose of this book. The more you know about how you make changes and choices, the more control you can have over the events in your life.

Although making personal changes can be frightening, it can also be exhilarating. When a person decides he or she wants to get out of an abusive relationship and feels the strength or power that comes with making that decision, he or she can experience a positive feeling, along with the uncertainty that comes with making a difficult life choice. Making a career choice that feels right, or fixing an unpleasant job situation at work can bring about a sense of accomplishment and control over situations and events. As you make changes, these changes can affect how you feel about yourself and other decisions that you make.

## *Growth*

**growth** A process that continues throughout one's lifetime; can be in several areas: physiological, emotional, and intellectual.

**Growth** comes from making choices and changes. Rather than a goal, growth is a process that goes on throughout our lifetime. As we get new information and make new choices, we are growing. We learn about the consequences of each new decision. Few individuals stick with an original career choice. If you think about what you wanted to do when you were six and what you want to do now, these choices are probably quite different. You have much more new information now, more information about your interests, abilities, and values than you did many years ago.

Likewise, it is rare for individuals to meet in the ninth grade and then become partners for life. Although it does occur, it usually requires that individuals grow in compatible ways so that as each person matures, the other does too. Because this is so rare, many people have romantic relationships with several people in their lives before settling down to one person, if in fact they choose to do that. In relationships, individuals learn about themselves and others. In family relationships that are usually quite stable, people keep up contact with their brothers and sisters, as well as parents, throughout life. Although this is not always true, individuals often work hard to keep difficult relationships with parents and siblings going. One way they do this is by making choices about when to give in to another person, when to become more distant, when to separate in some ways (but not all ways) from others, and when to be assertive. Thus many relationships, such as those with parents, grow or change, even though the feeling of closeness might not diminish.

In almost every chapter of this book, issues of adjustment, choice, change, and growth are implicit. Rather than discuss each of these concepts for each chapter, my focus is on different ways to change what you do if you want to and ways to help others change. When you are changing a situation, you are making choices, coping or adjusting to a situation, and growing. Through the growth process, you can increase your satisfaction with your life. Defining satisfaction or what makes you happy is difficult. Psychologists have examined this subject, and the findings are somewhat complex.

## HAPPINESS

**happiness** A feeling of pleasure or satisfaction; can last an instant or months or years.

Summaries of research (Myers & Diener, 1997) indicate that there is general agreement among people about what is important in bringing about happiness. Although there are large individual differences and exceptions, the variables that seem to contribute most to overall **happiness** are love and marriage, work, and personal views. In general, married people tend to be happier than those who are single or divorced. This could mean that people who are experiencing good intimate relationships are more likely to be happy than those who are not. Another contributor to overall happiness is job satisfaction. When people are unemployed or dissatisfied with their jobs, this seems to have a negative effect on being generally happy or content.

Another major factor is that of people's attitude toward themselves. Those who have high self-esteem, are optimistic, and feel in control of their lives are more likely to be happy than those who are not. More than a century ago, Sigmund Freud observed that love and work are core characteristics of a healthy person. His observations would seem to apply today, as individuals rate these variables as significant in their subjective perception of happiness.

Other factors also contribute to happiness: religion, social activity, and health. In general, those who are religious tend to identify themselves as being happier, to a moderate degree, than those who are not. This may be because for many people religion provides meaning and a sense of purpose. Moral values that are implicit in religion give individuals a sense of relationship to family and community. Although it would appear that being healthy would be essential to feeling happy, those who are in poor health are often able to deal with their situation, and while being uncomfortable, might be able to experience happiness in other areas of life. In general, those who have many friends and are active with family, acquaintances, and community are much more likely to feel happy than those who are alone. Religion, social activity, and health have been found to be important to the perception of happiness, but not as important as love, work, and attitude towards self.

Probably what is least important in determining happiness are physical variables that describe individuals. For example, age and gender do not seem to be related to happiness. People can feel happiness at any age, and men and women tend to be equally happy. There is little relationship between intelligence or educational attainment and a feeling of happiness. Nor do people in one section of the country, in cities, suburbia, or rural areas, report differences in happiness. More money does not necessarily mean more happiness. Once individuals' earnings exceed the poverty level, more money does not appear to bring about more happiness. Many people, even those who earn more than $100,000 a year, complain about not having enough money to meet their needs. Often this is due to observing what friends within a similar financial bracket own.

Social comparison theory (Fiske & Taylor, 1991) suggests that what is important is the subjective feeling of happiness rather than objective determinants. For example, what is important is how you feel about how much money you make, how healthy you are, how old you are, and your current work, rather than the actual amount you make, your actual physical condition, your age, or the prestige level of your job. Researchers also point out that how we make subjective judgments about our happiness is based on those who are around us, and the people who are similar to us, friends, and neighbors. For example, if your life seems more settled than that of your friends, and you have fewer economic problems, you might perceive yourself as happy. But if your friends seem to have happier family relationships, better jobs, or more money, then you might perceive yourself as more dissatisfied and less happy. If individuals have expectations and goals for themselves that they meet, they are likely to feel happier than if they do not meet these goals. Because happiness is a subjective state, the search for it is valuable, and people continually do things or make changes to bring about a sense of happiness.

**Q 1.1** Considering the variables described above that contribute to happiness, which seem most important to you and why?

## RESPONSIBILITY

A focus on happiness can sound selfish or self-centered. William Glasser (Glasser, 1965, 1998; Sharf, 2000; Wubbolding, 1988) has developed a theory of psychotherapy that focuses on control over one's life and responsibility to oneself and others. Glasser applied his concepts of reality therapy to helping people with problems and also applied them to schools and industry. His approach is to help people see choices where previously they thought they had none. By taking control of one's life, individuals can make choices and assume responsibility for their choices. As a way of understanding the types of choices that individuals need to make, Glasser describes the needs that individuals strive to meet to be happy in their lives.

**belonging** The need to love, to share, and to cooperate with others; defined by William Glasser.

**power** The need to control others and be better than others; defined by William Glasser.

**freedom** How we wish to live our lives, express ourselves, and worship; defined by William Glasser.

Glasser believes there are four basic psychological needs that are essential for human beings: belonging, power, freedom, and fun. The need for **belonging** includes the need to love, to share, and to cooperate. Friends, family, or pets can meet this need. The need for **power** often conflicts with our need for belonging. For example, our need to be powerful in a marriage conflicts with the need to be loved by one's spouse. Glasser believes that it is not insufficient love that destroys relationships but, rather, the power struggle between husbands and wives and their difficulties in negotiating and compromising. The need for **freedom** refers to how we want to live our lives, how we want to express ourselves, with whom we choose to associate, what we want to read or write, how we want to worship, and other areas of human experience. In a dictatorship, the ruler's need for power conflicts with other individuals' need for freedom. If an individual has a need for freedom that is so strong that she has no significant relationship with others, then the need for belongingness is

**fun** Hobbies and things
we do for amusements
such as sports, reading,
collecting, laughing,
and joking; defined by
William Glasser.

not met and the individual is likely to feel lonely. Although the need for fun is not as strong a need as those for power, freedom, or belonging, it is still an important one (Glasser, 1998). **Fun** may be laughing, joking, sports activities, reading, collecting, and many other areas of one's life. To be happy, individuals should meet these needs (belonging, power, freedom, fun) and balance them so that one need does not totally dominate another.

Glasser believes that individuals try to control their world and themselves so that they can meet their needs. Often individuals make choices to try to control their world, without being aware of these choices. Many would consider Glasser extreme in his emphasis on choice. He does not use words such as *depressed, angry, anxious,* or *panicky.* Instead, he uses a verb form of these words to emphasize action and the choice implied in taking an action. Thus, he uses words such as *depressing, angering, anxietizing,* and *phobicing.* For example, if a grandparent dies, we might feel sad or depressed. After a brief period, Glasser says we choose to depress, that is, to maintain the feeling of depression. Glasser believes that when people say, "I am choosing to depress" rather than "I am depressed," they are less likely to choose to depress and less likely to feel depressed. Thus, Glasser believes that individuals, usually without awareness, choose to get nervous before an exam, choose to get angry at a parent, or choose to be late for class. Essentially, Glasser believes that individuals make choices such as these to satisfy other needs. The choice to be late to class might be made to satisfy some other need, for example getting an assignment done on time. In this sense, an individual chooses among needs. To use another example, if you cut class, you might be meeting a need for freedom, while not meeting a need for belongingness or power. If you were in class, you would be with other students and working on mastery of a subject.

Glasser believes that individuals can meet their own needs while respecting the needs of others. For example, a high school student is suspended for smoking, thus upsetting her parents and affecting their needs concerning her. The student can be shown that by choosing to smoke, she might not be meeting her needs for fun and power because she will not be able to do some after school activities and will not be able to get many things that she wants. The choice of smoking rather than going to school will limit her ability to meet needs for belonging (socialize with other students), for power (go to college), and freedom (make other choices based on schooling). Glasser, who has worked with juvenile offenders, believes that they have made choices that place them in a restricted environment (juvenile home). He asked people not only to look at their current choice, but at the possible outcomes of the choice. In this sense, he is emphasizing individuals' responsibilities for their decisions.

**Q 1.2** Do you agree with Glasser that you choose to depress or to anxietize? Explain and give an example.

**Q 1.3** Give an example of a choice that you made that had impact on your life, that you were not aware of at the time, but later became aware of.

# LIFE ROLES

**life roles** Different behaviors displayed in different types of situations.

Whereas Glasser emphasized choice, needs, and responsibility, Super (1990) described important life roles that individuals encounter. His view gives a different perspective on choices by describing types of choices and ways that individuals behave depending on their **life roles.** Individuals differ in the degree to which they emphasize major life roles that include studying, working, community service, home and family, and leisure activities. Also, some roles are more important than others at any given point in time. For example, for adolescents, studying is likely to be more important than working or community service. For individuals who are 35 years old, home and family and working might be more important than study or leisure activities are. Although these are not the only roles that individuals play, they are important roles because they constitute major activities that individuals are involved in during their lifetimes. The chapters in this book will, to varying degrees, cover one or more of these roles described in more detail here (Super, 1970; Super & Nevill, 1986, 1989).

*Studying* Studying includes a number of activities that can take place throughout the life span. During the school years, these include taking courses, going to school, and studying in a library or at home. We know that people may choose to continue education at any time during their lifetime. Newspapers show pictures of 80-year-old men and women receiving their high school diplomas or college degrees. Many people continue their education on a part-time basis throughout their lives for pleasure or to improve their chances of advancing in their job. This role is the focus of Chapter 2, "Learning and Studying."

*Working* Working can start in childhood, when children help their parents around the home, mow the lawn, or take jobs such as baby-sitting and delivering newspapers. It is common for adolescents to take a part-time job after school or during the summer. Many adults get one or more jobs at various times during their lives. During retirement, jobs for pay or profit might be for fewer hours than they were during a person's younger years. Important in this role are choosing a career (Chapter 3) and being satisfied with work (Chapter 4).

*Community Service* Community service includes a broad range of voluntary service groups that can be social, political, or religious. Young people often participate in Boy or Girl Scouts, Indian Guides, or Boy's or

Girl's Clubs, which have as a part of their purpose either direct service to others or indirect service through the collection of money or goods. These groups, along with service fraternities and sororities, are available in various forms to adolescents. Activities can include literacy projects, environmental clean-up, or assistance in hospitals. Activity in these service groups along with participation in political parties and trade unions is available to adults throughout the life span.

Community service is an opportunity for individuals to express their **social interest.** Alfred Adler (1964), a contemporary of Sigmund Freud, believed that a basic human value that individuals should strive for was social interest, which meant being concerned with other people in the world and helping to build a better future for others. Adler felt that social interest was so important that it could be viewed as an indicator of positive mental health. If people had little social interest, then they were likely to be self-centered, put down others, and not have constructive goals. On the other hand, if they were concerned about others, and worked to help others, then they were likely to be more satisfied in their own lives. When individuals can identify and empathize with others, they are more likely to develop a feeling of happiness and success because of experiencing a feeling of belongingness or social connectedness. By being concerned about others, we can make courageous decisions that other people as well as ourselves face. Those who stand up against discrimination or defend people who have been unjustly accused, are putting themselves in a difficult position, but are also expressing their own sense of responsibility and social interest. Whether service to the community is through formal organizations or through informal involvement in social issues, the opportunity to be concerned about others can contribute to one's own sense of well-being. Although not discussed directly in one particular chapter, the concepts of community service and social interest are implicit in Chapter 5, "Family Relationships," Chapter 6, "Love and Friendship," Chapter 8, "Gender Roles," and Chapter 9, "Cultural Diversity." These chapters in particular focus on how individuals view themselves in relationship to others.

***Home and Family*** This role can vary greatly depending on the age of the individual. A child can help at home by taking care of his or her room or by doing the dishes or mowing the lawn. Adolescents can take on more obligations by doing tasks that are more complex or that have more responsibility, such as baby-sitting. For adults, responsibility for children and a home becomes much more important than it was in earlier years. Adults might have to take care not only of their own children but also their

**social interest** The sharing and concern for the welfare of others that can guide people's behavior throughout their lives.

aging parents. As adults enter their later years, their responsibility for home and family can increase or markedly decrease. For example, grandparents might live with their children, or grandchildren, or both, live in adult communities, or live alone. Chapter 5, "Family Relationships," Chapter 6, "Love and Friendship," and Chapter 10, "Dying and Living," are specifically related to this role.

**lifetime sports** Less physically demanding and requiring fewer participants than other sports.

*Leisure Activities*  The nature and importance of leisure are likely to vary considerably throughout the lifetime. Leisure is a particularly important and valued activity of children and adolescents. Often this includes both active participation in sports and more sedentary activities, such as watching television and reading. The term **lifetime sports** refers to sports that are less physically demanding and that require fewer participants so that they are easier for adults to participate in at various points in their lifetimes. Contrast football and basketball with golf, tennis, and bowling. For adults, leisure activities might become more sophisticated and intellectual, such as attending a play, going to a museum, or joining groups that discuss books, stocks and bonds, or religious issues. One specific activity sometimes referred to as "recreational" that is discussed in this book, is the use of alcohol and drugs (Chapter 11). Although alcohol and drugs can give pleasurable sensations—and in some cases, alcohol, when used in moderation, can have beneficial health effects—drugs and alcohol can have a variety of other effects that create problems for individuals and those close to them.

**Q 1.4** Which life roles are most important to you? Explain your participation, commitment to, and knowledge of the life roles.

These roles can be examined from three different perspectives, how much individuals participate in them, how committed they are, and how much they know about them. Participation in a role can include doing something, being active in an organization, observing people, or reading about an activity. Whereas participation refers to what you actually do, commitment refers to your future plans, what you plan to do. But commitment also can include the present, such as feeling committed to campaigning politically. Participation and commitment are quite different. For example, a person may say that he is committed to his religion but never pray or go to church (participate). Knowledge refers to how much you know about a particular role. Children's knowledge of the "working role" is often limited to what they see on television and hearing their parents talk about jobs. Likewise, a child's knowledge of the "home and family" role is very different than the knowledge that an adult has when she is a parent. These three concepts, participation, commitment, and knowledge provide different ways of viewing the importance of the five life roles that have been discussed here.

**Q 1.5** In the future, which life roles do you expect will change relative to your participation, commitment, and knowledge? Explain.

# COPING WITH LIFE ROLES AND PROBLEMS

**primary appraisal**
Applied to problem solving, the process of determining whether there is a problem or danger.

**secondary appraisal**
Applied to problem solving, the process of determining the best way to deal with the problem.

Many strategies can be used in coping with problems that people encounter in a variety of life's roles. In this chapter, I will discuss some general suggestions or approaches to life problems. In the later chapters, I will describe some specific ways of handling different types of problems. In understanding or appraising problems, there are two general steps (Lazarus & Folkman, 1984; Kleinke, 1998). The first step (**primary appraisal**) is to determine whether there is a problem or danger. Is there something to be concerned about? The next step (**secondary appraisal**) is to determine what, if anything, can be done about the problem. For example, if parents observe their son or daughter coming home drunk, then they might assess (without consciously asking), Is this something to be upset about? If it is, then they determine how best to deal with it. How individuals deal with or cope with a situation can be classified into two types: problem-focused and emotion-focused.

## *Problem-Focused Coping*

**outer-directed solution**
Changing the behavior of others or in some way managing the environment or parts of a problem.

**inner-based solution**
Changing attitudes toward events or people or learning new skills to cope with problems.

Problem-focused approaches are often used for problems that have a possible solution. Solutions can be outer directed or inner directed. An **outer-directed solution** is to try to change or affect the behavior of others or in some way manage the environment. In contrast, an **inner-based solution** deals with our own values and individuals might change their own attitudes toward events or people. In other instances, individuals develop new skills, such as learning to successfully interact with a person of a different race or learning a new language. In this book, problem-focused strategies are particularly appropriate for studying (Chapter 2, "Learning and Studying"), choosing a career (Chapter 3, "Choosing Careers"), and problems at work (Chapter 4, "Adjusting to Work"). Problem-focused strategies also occur in all of the other chapters, along with emotion-focused problems and strategies.

## *Emotion-Focused Solutions*

Often, we react emotionally to a problem. This is particularly true when dealing with concerns that are out of our control. For example, dealing with the death of a friend, or hearing that a parent has been diagnosed with cancer, are problems for which we might have a deep emotional reaction, but no solution. When coping with emotional issues, individuals focus on ways to manage emotional distress. Two of the more important ways are to seek support from others and to express feelings to others. Taking a break from a situation, meditation, and physical exercise are other ways that people deal with emotion-focused problems. Emotion-focused solutions, along with some problem-focused solutions are discussed in Chapters 5 through 12, which deal, to varying degrees, with relationships with other people. In addition, further coping strategies for dealing with a variety of problems will be given in Chapter 13. Regardless of whether the situation requires a problem-focused, emotion-focused solution, or both, several attitudes toward adapting to problems are helpful in coping with difficulties.

## *Adaptive Attitudes*

**openness** Flexible, problem-solving attitude; looking for new ideas.

**orientation toward others** Indicating an interest in being with others.

**agreeableness** Making an effort to agree with others.

**conscientious** Being reliable, taking pride in activities that one does.

Attitudes that help individuals cope with a variety of problems tend to emphasize flexibility with self and others. I will discuss four attitudes that are effective in dealing with problem and emotion-focused concerns (Kleinke, 1998): Openness, orientation toward others, agreeableness, and conscientiousness. **Openness** refers to looking for new ideas and new ways to solve problems. Being curious about our world and the people in it is an example of openness. **Orientation toward others** refers to enjoying being around people, laughing and joking, and being cheerful, talkative, and energetic. Most problems relate to other people in one way or another, so enjoying being with people and appreciating them helps in dealing with problems. Being agreeable rather than contentious is another useful attitude. People who feel they get along with others, don't get into arguments often, and try to be courteous with others, tend to solve problems relatively easily. **Agreeableness** does not mean that individuals must agree all the time with others, but that they make an effort to do so where appropriate. Being **conscientious** means being reliable and taking pride in the activities that one does, and being responsible for what we say and do. Having these attitudes helps individuals deal with virtually any life problem.

**blaming oneself** Being critical of oneself for causing a problem.

**avoiding a problem** Not trying to solve a problem by not thinking about it or by doing a neutral activity.

**self-critical beliefs** General beliefs that interfere with coping with problems.

In contrast, some attitudes are not helpful in dealing with problems (Kleinke, 1998) such as avoiding problems, blaming oneself, and being self-critical. Taking responsibility for a problem and trying to deal with it can be helpful, but **blaming oneself** for having caused it is ineffective. Focusing on how bad the problem is and not focusing on the ways to deal with it are not helpful. **Avoiding a problem** by not thinking about it, by doing self-destructive activities such as drinking or neutral activities such as watching television that do not deal with the problem, are not beneficial. **Self-critical beliefs** interfere with coping with problems. Beliefs such as "I am a failure," "I'm no good," and "I'm useless" all interfere with coping with problems because they distract from the issues.

Let's look at an example of a problem that will further explain some of these concepts.

> Jennie, a 21-year-old college freshman, has been on Christmas vacation. While at home, she rear-ended a car when coming out of a shopping center with her boyfriend. She was driving her roommate's minivan and dented the bumper and hood of the car along with damaging the radiator. The trunk and rear bumper of the other car were also damaged. Jennie was afraid about telling her roommate about what had happened.

> Jennie's dilemma has both problem-focused and emotion-focused components. By talking to her boyfriend about the situation she was able to manage her fear of the situation and was able to get support from him in dealing with Karen. Jennie was able to take a problem-focused approach by discussing ways to deal with the anger she anticipated that Karen would show (an outer-directed strategy). Jennie also thought about ways that she could remain calm in the presence of Karen's anger (an inner-directed solution). In the past, she had just yelled back.

**Q 1.6** Think of a situation you have been in that was somewhat similar to Jennie's. Show how adaptive attitudes such as openness, orientation toward others, agreeableness, and conscientiousness might have helped you in this situation, or would have.

In the rest of the book, we will be looking at more specific strategies for dealing with a variety of problems and issues. Some of the proposed solutions will reflect the adaptive attitudes of openness, orientation toward others, agreeableness, and conscientiousness rather than non-adaptive attitudes such as avoidance, self-blame and self-defeating comments.

## CONFIDENTIALITY AND PRIVACY

**confidentiality** Keeping a secret and not telling others what has been told to you in confidence.

This book deals with personal questions that vary greatly in how intimate and private they are. Most issues that deal with the life roles of studying, working, community service, and leisure are relatively easy to talk about with other people. However, many issues having to do with home and family are quite private, and **confidentiality** is very important. Interactions with parents, brothers and sisters, and romantic partners can include issues you want to discuss only with very few people. Other examples of issues discussed in this book that are highly personal are sexual behavior and drug use. In deciding whom to talk about such issues with, individuals are concerned about trust and privacy. When you talk about a topic that feels deeply personal, you are probably very careful about whom you choose to speak with. One of the concerns that you are likely to have is trust. You want to know that the person you talked to will not tell anyone else. Rumors about individuals' sexual behavior or drug use can be quite harmful to their relationships with others.

In writing this book, I am sharing much of my experience in counseling college students of all ages during the past 25 years. Examples of how individuals deal with problems and resolve them can be very helpful. Therefore, I have presented a number of case studies or examples of how people have coped with a variety of issues and problems. In doing so, I have been very careful to protect their identities. I have changed several facts about their backgrounds to respect their confidentiality such that someone very close to them would not be able to recognize them. I very much value the individuals who have shared their lives with me and who have taught me so much about dealing with life's choices and problems. Because I think that actual problems make abstract or complex issues come to life, I feel that it is important to give real examples of how people cope with life's problems and choices.

Often, I describe a situation that individuals have encountered. Sometimes I do this from my viewpoint, at other times from theirs. When I describe a discussion between a student and myself, I use my initials (RS) to indicate when I am talking.

You have already noticed that in this chapter I have asked you questions about your own life. I will continue this throughout the book. In choosing the questions, I have tried to select those that are important, but not so personal as to intrude on your privacy. I tried to select questions such that if you lost your book, you would not be uncomfortable if someone else read your answers. If you write answers to your questions in this book, keep the concept of confidentiality in mind. Others might see your notes. If you write the names of other people when answering questions in this book, you might choose to use initials or to change their names.

**Self-disclosure** Describing personal aspects of yourself to others.

Many of the questions that are in this book could be discussed in class. When talking about your choices in your life and related concerns in class, it is important to consider carefully which events or situations you are comfortable talking about and which you are not. **Self-disclosure,** describing personal aspects of yourself to others, is valuable in that it builds a sense of closeness with others. On the other hand, describing parts of your life to others also requires trust. Assuming confidentiality in a classroom is very difficult, as individuals vary in how well they keep secrets and in their memory of what material is secret and what material is not. You will learn more from this book by sharing your own experiences, but only if doing so feels comfortable to you. "Comfortable" is a subjective feeling about what will not be hurtful to you and people that you talk about.

## Types of Problems and Solutions

The topics that are covered in this book cover the five life roles discussed and can be grouped into three categories: learning and working, relationships, and personal choices and solutions. In each chapter, we will examine the types of problems that individuals encounter in their lives and then evaluate solutions for them. The following paragraphs explain the grouping of life's choices, resulting problems, and possible solutions.

Part I, "Learning and Working" focuses on two of the most important and time-consuming activities in the lives of individuals. Chapter 2, "Learning and Studying," describes both the way people learn and techniques for improving time management, organization, studying, and preparing for exams. Chapter 3, "Choosing Careers," explains the importance of understanding your personality, interests, values, and abilities to make appropriate career choices. Strategies for looking for a job, writing a résumé, and conducting job interviews are also covered. When individuals start to work, they can encounter a variety of problems as they adjust to a new job. Chapter 4, "Adjusting to Work," describes issues of work satisfaction as well as ways of dealing with difficulties such as losing a job or encountering discrimination on the job.

Part II includes six chapters, each devoted to different types of relationships or relationship issues. (Chapter 5, "Family Relationships," includes discussion of relationships between children and their parents, as well as brothers and sisters from both a child's and parent's perspective. Included is a discussion of divorce and its impact on families. Developing caring for others that can lead to friendship and love is the subject of Chapter 6, "Love and Friendship." A part of romantic relationships, sexuality, is discussed in Chapter 7, "Sexuality and Intimacy." Other issues include avoiding pregnancy and sexually transmitted diseases as well as dealing with unwanted sexual contact. In almost all societies, people expect others to behave depending on their gender. Chapter 8, "Gender Roles," explains different expectations that people experience in childhood, adolescence, and adulthood depending on their gender. Suggestions are given for ways that people can relate more easily to the other gender. Chapter 9, "Cultural Diversity," discusses prejudice and discrimination and ways to improve relationships with people who are culturally different from ourselves. How to cope with the death of a friend or family member is one of the most difficult crises that people face. Chapter 10, "Dying and Living," discusses ways of understanding grieving, as well as ways in which people deal with their own dying when they have a terminal illness. Although problems and their solutions are discussed in each of these chapters, ways of handling one's own problems is the specific focus of the next part.

Part III, "Personal Choices and Solutions," describes ways of handling a variety of problems in managing stress. One specific problem that can be a major concern for some individuals and their families is that of substance abuse. Chapter 11, "Abusing Substances," includes discussion of problems resulting from abuse of cigarettes, alcohol, marijuana, and other drugs, as well as treatment strategies. How to deal with stress that results from traumatic events, crises, or a variety of frustrations is the subject of Chapter 12, "Managing Stress." Strategies for dealing with anxiety, depression, and anger are given. The final chapter, "Coping Strategies," describes five strategies that can be used for a variety of problems including those that are discussed in Parts I and Part II.

Questions occur at several points in each chapter. The questions at the very beginning of the chapter provide a way to think about the topics that are going to be discussed. These questions can help you understand each of the major sections within the chapter. The questions that are found in the margin next to the text are designed to help you think about how the information in the text can be applied to situations that concern you or people you care about.

## PROBLEMS AND SOLUTIONS

There are "Problems and Solutions" boxes throughout this book. In most cases, these boxes summarize the material that is discussed in the text. They are included to emphasize types of problems and strategies that will work in solving the problems. By including them, I hope to show that there are solutions or approaches to even the most difficult problems. The solutions that are given are more fully described in the text.

I have also included three other features to help you learn more about the topics in this text: definitions, recommended readings, and Web sites. Definitions are given for important terms in the margins near where they are first discussed. All the definitions appear in the glossary at the end of this book. Recommended readings (listed at the end of each chapter after this one) are books on topics related to each chapter. Many are self-help books that are well written and nontechnical. Most are based on psychological research. A few books, particularly those on sexuality and drug-abuse, explore the subject in more depth than this book does. Web sites listed at the ends of the chapters provide a variety of resources such as information from experts and links to other Web sites. Although I have provided the Web addresses, these might have changed by the time you read this book.

## SUMMARY

These chapters cover a variety of personal issues. Examining how you cope with your own choices and problems and finding out about new strategies for doing so can help you look at your concerns and relationships from different points of view. I have written this book so that you can draw practical information from it to help you deal with your own choices.

## RECOMMENDED READINGS

*The Pursuit of Happiness: Who is Happy and Why?*
David G. Meyers (Morrow, 1992)
> The search for happiness, described on pages 5 and 6, has been important for many people. Meyers provides both suggestions as well as research dealing with The Pursuit of Happiness. The subjective assessments of their own lives, rather than objective circumstances, affect people's happiness. Meyers makes suggestions about comparing ourselves with others. He describes how such comparisons can make us feel dissatisfied. His suggestions help people to enhance their senses of happiness and satisfaction. In this book, Meyers does not focus on the individual alone but, rather, on the individual in relationship to other people.

*Learned Optimism: How to Change Your Mind and Your Life*
Martin E. Seligman (Pocket Books, 1990)
> Seligman is a researcher who has studied learned helplessness and depression. In this clearly written book, he focuses on optimism and its role in people's lives. He compares pessimism and optimism as outlooks on life. He describes how these views affect performance in work, school, and sports, describing how optimism can positively affect individuals' emotional and physiological health. Suggestions are given for enhancing performance and behaviors through optimistic thinking.

*What You Can Change & What You Can't*
Martin E. Seligman (Knopf, 1994)
> Coping with life roles and problems has been a focus of this first chapter of this text (see page 9). This section assumes that you are able to make changes in all areas of your life. Seligman studies topics such as learned helpless, depression, and optimism. He also examines research in biological psychiatry that suggests that some areas of human functioning cannot be changed. These areas include our physique, intelligence, and aspects of our personality. Examining both the viewpoints that individuals can change and that they cannot, Seligman suggests ways to alter those aspects of human behavior that can be changed. In this discussion, he includes methods for treating alcoholism, anxiety, depression, overeating, sexual problems, and posttraumatic stress. His reading style is enjoyable and readable.

# RECOMMENDED WEB SITES

*American Self-Help Clearinghouse Source Book*
http://www.cmhc.com/selfhelp/

>This online clearinghouse provides contact information for more than 800 self-help groups and organizations across the United States. In learning to cope with specific problems or challenging life situations, some of these groups might be helpful in providing suggestions to you.

*American Psychological Association (APA)*
http://www.apa.org/

>The largest professional organization of psychologists, the APA publicizes the latest research findings for many topics discussed in this book. Students should consider using this as a source for information for topics related to adjustment or other psychological issues.

# one

# LEARNING AND WORKING

*Part I describes activities that you are likely to spend much of your time doing. Studying and working are time consuming, and they can present a number of difficult problems. Chapter 2 explains how people learn and gives suggestions for how to learn and study effectively. Career choice is the focus of Chapter 3. Finding work that is interesting, that you are good at, and that you value can be difficult. Chapter 3 helps with the process of reviewing your current career choice or finding new options. When you are working, whether part-time or full-time, a variety of concerns can arise. Chapter 4 explains the work adjustment process and how to cope with work related problems.*

# LEARNING AND STUDYING

VERBAL-LINGUISTIC . . . . . . . . . . . . . . . . . . . . _____

LOGICAL-MATHEMATICAL. . . . . . . . . . . . . . . . . . . _____

VISUAL-SPATIAL. . . . . . . . . . . . . . . . . . . . . . . _____

MUSICAL-RHYTHMIC. . . . . . . . . . . . . . . . . . . . . _____

BODILY-KINESTHETIC. . . . . . . . . . . . . . . . . . . . _____

INTERPERSONAL . . . . . . . . . . . . . . . . . . . . . . _____

INTRAPERSONAL . . . . . . . . . . . . . . . . . . . . . . _____

## STUDYING

LEARNING FROM TEXTBOOKS . . . . . . . . . . . . . . . . *Describe the strategy that you use to learn material for an English or history course.*

LEARNING FROM LECTURES . . . . . . . . . . . . . . . . . *What style of note taking if any do you use?*

STUDY GROUPS . . . . . . . . . . . . . . . . . . . . . . . *What are the pros and cons of studying with 2 or 3 other people?*

## TIME MANAGEMENT . . . . . . . . . . . . . . . . . . . *When is time management the biggest problem for you?*

PERSONAL PLANNERS . . . . . . . . . . . . . . . . . . . . *How do you plan your week?*

HOURLY SCHEDULES . . . . . . . . . . . . . . . . . . . . *How do you plan your day?*

PROCRASTINATION. . . . . . . . . . . . . . . . . . . . . *When is this a problem for you?*

EXAMS. . . . . . . . . . . . . . . . . . . . . . . . . . . *What is the best way to prepare?*

---

After examining the monetary reward for education, this chapter will look at how children learn and the role of enjoyment and curiosity in early learning. This will lead to learning about attitudes people have toward learning and their strategies for studying. Learning styles often affect the way individuals learn different material. This can affect what you think about strategies that are given here for studying from text books, learning from lectures, and learning from study groups. All these offer potential help in your course work. Another aspect of learning is how you manage your time and deal with procrastination. Tips are given for working with these issues and preparing for exams.

## DOES LEARNING PAY?

Why bother to get more education? Will it make much difference over a lifetime in the amount of money people make? Learning pays. Certainly the amount of learning that people do in a lifetime can help them develop

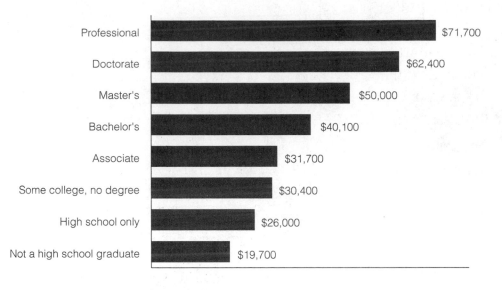

FIGURE **2.1  MEAN ANNUAL EARNINGS FOR PEOPLE AGED 18 AND OVER BY HIGHEST LEVEL OF EDUCATION, 1997.**

(From *Occupational Outlook Quarterly,* U.S. Department of Commerce, Bureau of the Census, Washington, DC, 1999, p. 40.)

interests that they have, lead to increased self confidence, and lead to more satisfaction with life. Further, learning as measured by the amount of education that a person has, is also closely related to income. When the annual income of those who have not graduated from high school, or who have graduated from high school but do not have any education after high school, is compared with those who have a doctorate or professional degree (such as in law or medicine), the comparisons are quite dramatic. Figure 2.1 shows the vast differences in annual salaries in 1997 between those without a high school education ($19,700) and those with a doctorate ($62,400) or professional degree ($71,700). In 1997, the earnings of those with a bachelor's degree were about 54 percent higher than the earnings of those with a high school education. These data emphatically show how the amount of education people have greatly affects their lifetime earnings (Chart: Education, 1999). Pryor and Schaffer (1997) point out that students who graduate from college without college-level reading and quantitative skills have more difficulty getting college-level jobs than do students with higher level skills. Thus, an interest in learning throughout the life span can pay off financially and in enjoyment.

---

## Problems and Solutions

---

### How can I make learning more enjoyable?

- Be curious about the subject
- Explore the content

---

# HOW CHILDREN LEARN

In this section, we cover three broad concepts that are important in how children (and college students) learn: curiosity, exploration, and the learning of information. Curiosity is a basic need that has been observed in animals as well as in human infants; it is a need to find out about the environment. Whereas curiosity is a need, exploration is a behavior. By exploring their environment, children meet their needs for curiosity. Basically, play and playful activities are expressions of exploratory behavior. As children play and explore, they learn information that helps meet their curiosity need, and puts them in a position of feeling more self confident and more in control of the environment around them. Although learning as a child and learning as a college student seem to be very different processes, some elements of early childhood learning are helpful to review when discussing learning in college.

## Curiosity

**curiosity** The desire for something new or unusual; the tendency among people to explore their environment for its own sake.

**Curiosity** is basic to our being and survival (Berlyne, 1960). When basic needs are interfered with, such as when a child is hungry, thirsty, or lonely, curiosity can develop as a way of meeting these needs. When a child is uncertain or confused, the child might decide to resolve his or her confusion by meeting a need for curiosity. Also, boredom, a wish for excitement, or a desire for stimulation can produce curiosity. Curiosity can be observed in very young children when they are playing with new objects, new people, and new concepts. Being exposed to puzzling new toys or situations, the child must try to understand them or try out new behaviors. For example, a child seeing a toy horse might try to ride it, fantasizing that he is riding a real horse. Another child might pick up a stick, pretending that it is a baseball bat and that she is a professional baseball player. This type of fantasized thinking can stimulate the learning process, as children try to interpret and learn about the world around them. Fantasizing about being a doctor or nurse and using information that you used in biology class can help you learn biological information.

## *Exploration*

**exploration** The act of searching for something or examining something.

Being curious can lead to children's exploring their environment, home, school, and parental relationships. Whereas curiosity refers to the desire for knowledge or for something new or unusual, **exploration** is the act of searching or examining. Several complex activities make up exploratory behavior, and I will describe some here (Jordaan, 1963). Exploratory behavior can be intentional and systematic, or it can be accidental. For example, children might want to find out how a clock works by carefully disassembling the pieces and putting them back together (intentional), or they might find a broken clock and just start to play with it (accidental). Sometimes exploratory behavior occurs when someone asks a child to do something, other times because a child seeks something out on his or her own. Thus, sometimes a teacher requests that a child put a puzzle together, or the child might take the initiative to do it. In exploring, a child can use either current or past experience. Having played with a puzzle three weeks ago, a child might decide to play with a similar one now. Some exploratory behavior can benefit a child and help the child learn. Other behavior can just be for the enjoyment of the activity, such as writing one's name backward. Some exploratory behavior that is required can later turn out to be enjoyable. For example, being required to read does not mean that reading will always be a chore. Once the skill is partially mastered, children are likely to read on their own initiative. These types of exploratory behaviors are learning activities, even though the child would not be able to label them as such. They set the stage for the more formal learning that comes with attending school.

When exploration is interfered with, however, a child can experience conflict and have less to do with peers, adults, and subjects that might be related to school. When exploration is stifled, a child might lose the motivation to explore or learn. His or her work might become less imaginative. For example, if a child is criticized for breaking toys, hiding them under the bed, or putting them under a sofa pillow, and if this type of criticism is continual, the child is less likely to explore or to try to get information. A truly withdrawn child might have difficulty trying new activities and learning new things. Naturally, most children are not at one end or the other of the exploration-withdrawal continuum. Rather, they choose to explore some activities but not others.

Exploratory behavior builds on other exploratory behavior. For example, a third-grader might learn, in very general terms, how a phone works. Such learning will develop in sophistication, both at a teacher's request and also perhaps on the child's own initiative in later years. As a fifth-grader, the child might draw on past experience with the phone, as he or she learns more about the details of its operation. In high school, a student might learn more about electricity and communication systems in physics or general science classes. If this exploratory behavior continues in college, it might turn into taking electrical engineering courses to understand communication systems. In general, early learning or exploratory behaviors are often remembered as being fun and enjoyable, whereas exploration that is less self-initiated, such as that which takes place in school might be viewed more negatively. Seeing biology as an opportunity to explore living beings provides motivation that memorizing terms does not.

## Learning Information

Being motivated to learn information is an essential part of the child's growing process. Well-known psychologist Erik Erikson (1963) has developed an eight-stage model of psychosocial development. The third stage, *initiative versus guilt,* and the fourth stage, *industry versus inferiority,* particularly focus on the importance of attitudes toward learning during the childhood years. Starting at about the age of 4 or 5, the initiative versus guilt stage highlights the importance of play. Erikson believes that children should take the initiative to make up games, to pretend, and to play in a variety of ways. If children feel that they are doing something wrong, they might become fearful or feel guilty. In this stage, the child should be motivated to try new things and to explore. The concept is rather similar to that described earlier in the Exploration section.

Between the ages of 6 and 11, children experience the industry versus interiority stage when they have the freedom to make things and to organize objects and plans. Children can get a sense of industriousness if they are successful, yet feel inferior if they are unsuccessful. Particularly during their school time, but also outside, children develop a sense of achievement by organizing, developing, and applying information. Children who are successful in their school work tend to feel independent, competent, and adequate. A sense of inferiority develops when one cannot perform well in school or in other tasks. If the child has difficulty reading, or is picked last for sports teams, that child might feel less skilled than others. A sense of inferiority can hinder an individual from trying to learn. Such feelings can affect attitudes toward school in high school and college. Students who are returning to college after years in the workforce

**Q 2.1** How did your early exploratory activities and play affect your attitude toward learning?

**Q 2.2** To what degree is your enjoyment of a subject related to your ability to learn it? Explain.

can find themselves in challenging situations that can bring about feelings of inferiority. Furthermore, if an individual continues to feel that he or she cannot learn very well and does not experience much success at school, this can affect later success on a job and lifetime earnings.

## LEARNING AND REMEMBERING

Learning, by studying for an exam or trying to remember material for some other related use, is more than just cognitions (thinking); other factors are also important. Being active in your thinking while studying helps you stay motivated as does interest in the subject that you are learning. Learning takes practice and how you practice, or memorize is important. When you are learning, it is helpful to have as little interference as possible and be able to concentrate as much as possible. Having an organizational system for learning helps because it is much easier to learn related information than to learn information that is not connected to other information. Later, to make it easier to connect information, I will describe a few tricks (mnemonic devices) that make information easier to learn.

### Attitude

To learn requires that the learner pay attention to the material to be learned. One of the best ways to do that is to find a way to be interested in the material. Before you entered elementary school, you probably had some choice about what you learned and what you could fantasize about. As you got older, more structure was put into the learning process. It is still possible, however, to create interest in a subject. Trying to apply the information to a real-life situation or problem that you have is one example. If you are studying history, think about how reading about the Second World War relates to some current political events. By being active and paying attention to what you are learning, you can become more aware of the details. This is why an upright position, even slightly uncomfortable, allows you to remember material more easily than you can in a slouched position. Being relaxed is helpful, but being too relaxed makes it difficult to attend or remember.

The feeling of being lost or overwhelmed by the material is not only uncomfortable, it also makes it difficult to concentrate. One problem with falling behind in assignments is that maintaining a positive attitude about a course becomes much more difficult. When this happens, a feeling of frustration often replaces interest that might have been there previously. To remedy this, students may change plans to do leisure activities so that they can schedule time to read and take notes.

---

## *Problems and Solutions*

---

### *How can I remember what I study?*

- Make it interesting—be active
- Reduce interference
- Visualize material
- Use a "mind map"
- "Mnemonics"

---

## *Practice*

**overlearning** Going over material after you already know it; a useful technique for improving memory.

Going over material several times helps you to retain it. By continuing to rehearse information, the chances of you remembering it are increased, as are the chances of you fully understanding the material. Just as athletes and musicians must practice, so does anyone else who wants to learn information. A useful technique to improve your memory is to **overlearn.** If you continue to go over material after you already know it, you are overlearning it. Your chances of remembering the material are increased.

**massed practice** A technique of learning in which the lessons or periods of practice follow each other without a break; a technical description of "cramming."

If it is good to overlearn material, is it also good to "cram" for an exam? Psychologists have studied the efficiency of cramming (**massed practice** versus spreading studying out over a few days) (Hettich, 1998). In general, researchers have found that it is better to spread studying out rather than do it all at once. For example, rather than study for an exam for ten hours straight, it would be better to study for three hours one day, three hours the next, and four hours the following day. Cramming tends to take too much energy and to make it too difficult to memorize a great deal of material. Also, if the cramming is done right before an exam, an individual is more likely to feel anxious and that can interfere with learning.

## *Minimizing Interference*

Because attention to the material that is to be learned is so important, anything that distracts from that can make it more difficult for you to retain information. Studying several courses during a day can make it difficult to learn the material, especially if the courses are similar, such as two history courses or two chemistry courses. On the day of an exam, it is probably better to study only for that course, so that other information will not interfere with learning material for the test. In fact, a review of material that will be on the exam right before the test can help to avoid forgetting material. When there are two or more exams on the same day, a brief review before each exam can be helpful.

Not all distractions or interferences are from other material. If you've ever taken an exam when you had a fever, you know that some health problems can interfere with remembering and thinking clearly. Trying to study when loud music is playing or taking an exam in a room next to a class where a loud movie is being shown can be quite distracting. Individuals vary in their ability to tolerate distractions. Some can tolerate noise, poor lighting, or crowded conditions for some courses more than others can. If you are depressed or upset, you will have more difficulty concentrating. Being worried about how you will do on an exam and what grade you will get detracts from learning about the content. Worrying about your grade or trying to guess your grade as you're taking an exam interferes with being able to recall the material and answer questions. Visualizing the material, such as charts or lists, or reciting material to yourself can keep you active and minimize interference.

## *Organizing Information*

**mind map** A method of outlining material by grouping information in large or small amounts on one piece of paper.

When a text book is easy to follow or a lecture seems organized, there is usually a relationship between topics. Going back over lecture notes to reorganize them or to make sure that the organizational system is clear can be quite helpful. If you have time when you are reading a textbook, it can be helpful to outline the reading, even if it is in a broad or general way. A **mind map** is a method of outlining. You can write small or large amounts of material on one piece of paper, make lists of basic information, and then draw arrows from one list to another. For example, if you were studying economics, you might find it helpful to make a list of supply features and demand features and then draw arrows from one feature of "demand" that is related to another feature or features of "supply." Learning is usually improved when material can be associated to other material. If you understand the chain of events that takes place in photosynthesis or if you know how a math formula works, you will do better than if you just memorize the information.

Figure 2.2 shows a "mind map" for this chapter up to this section. How children learn is related to Erikson's initiative stage and to tips for remembering. Note that the student has related Erikson's concept of "Initiative" to "2. Are curious," and his concept of "Inferiority" to "4. Exploration stifled." You might try a mind map for the rest of this chapter.

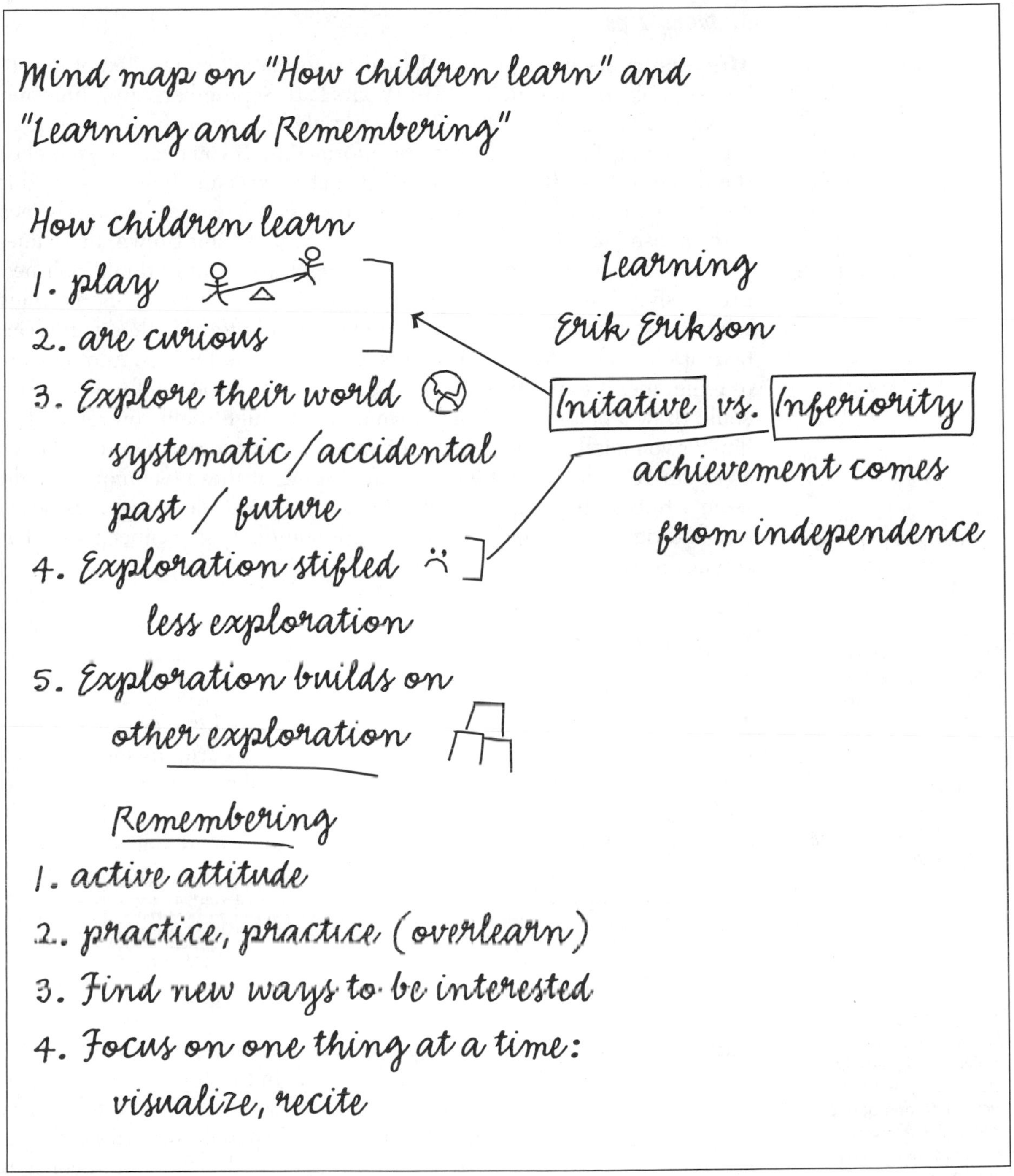

Mind map on "How children learn" and
"Learning and Remembering"

How children learn
1. play
2. are curious
3. Explore their world
        systematic/accidental
        past / future
4. Exploration stifled
        less exploration
5. Exploration builds on
        other exploration

Learning
Erik Erikson
[Initative] vs. [Inferiority]
achievement comes
    from independence

Remembering
1. active attitude
2. practice, practice (overlearn)
3. Find new ways to be interested
4. Focus on one thing at a time:
        visualize, recite

FIGURE 2.2  MIND MAP

## *Memory Tips*

**mnemonics** Strategies to help remember information by making it more relevant. Acronyms are an example of a mnemonic device.

**acronym** Words that are created from the first letter of other words. They are used to help remember a series of words and are a type of mnemonic device.

**Q 2.3** Why do you learn better from some courses than from others?

**Q 2.4** How can you improve your practice of memorization skills?

**Q 2.5** How do you cope with outside interference when you are studying?

**Q 2.6** What are other ways you can overcome interferences that affect your studying?

**multiple intelligence** A view that suggests that individuals have different learning styles or different ways of remembering material. Gardner lists seven forms of intelligence.

**Mnemonics** are strategies to help make information more relevant to you. For example, rhymes such as "Thirty days hath September, April, June and November . . ." and "In 1492, Columbus sailed the ocean blue" are ways of remembering dates or other specific information. If you need to remember the name of John Brown and the fact that he was an abolitionist, and it helps to wear polished brown shoes to the exam because "bolish" rhymes with "polish" and the color brown reminds you of John Brown, that's fine. But rather than wear brown shoes, you might just want to think "polished brown shoes" to remember John Brown, the abolitionist. Sometimes **acronyms,** words that are created from the first letters of other words, can be helpful, such as MADD, Mothers Against Drunk Drivers. Another way to remember is to use pictures or diagrams of what you want to learn. You could draw a picture of John Brown and that might help you remember him, or you might make a picture of a mad mother so that you would have a cue for remembering them. Although some of these techniques might seem artificial, they require active thinking and provide a way of associating material to other material, or to common objects or concepts so that you can remember them more easily.

## LEARNING STYLES

Although certain approaches to learning are helpful for everyone to use—such as being active, practicing what you need to learn, organizing information, and avoiding interferences—not everyone learns the same way. Some people learn best by watching others, and others learn more easily by listening to others. Yet others might learn best by doing. In addition, some activities require certain types of learning styles. For example, to learn to type or word process, you need to do it, not watch somebody do it, or listen to a lecture on typing. Making use of the best learning style for you and for the course or the type of information that you are trying to learn is a flexible way to approach learning.

A helpful way of viewing differences in learning styles is Howard Gardner's (1983) theory of **multiple intelligences.** Gardner views intelligence not in terms of math and verbal skills, but in terms of a variety of styles in which people learn. He has identified seven forms of intelligence: verbal-linguistic, logical-mathematical, visual-spatial, musical-rhythmic, bodily-kinesthetic, interpersonal, and intrapersonal. Schools and colleges do not emphasize each of these styles equally. Many courses fit a verbal-linguistic style, such as English, history, communications, and philosophy.

## Gardner's Multiple Intelligences

- Verbal-linguistic
- Logical-mathematical
- Visual-spatial
- Musical-rhythmic
- Bodily-kinesthetic
- Interpersonal
- Intrapersonal

Others fit the logical-mathematical style, such as math, engineering, and accounting. Some courses fit both the verbal and the logical, such as economics, psychology, and business. Relatively few fit the visual-spatial (architecture, film, art, and geography), and musical-rhythmic (music). You can have opportunities to use a variety of styles of learning in many different disciplines and courses. Each of these multiple intelligences are described in more detail in the following sections.

### Verbal-Linguistic

Verbal-linguistic persons listen well and have a good memory for discussions and lectures. They are likely to want to read and write; they like to tell stories and to remember dates and facts. This style of learning is very helpful for game shows such as *Jeopardy*. Teachers, lawyers, and politicians are apt to be good at and enjoy this style of learning.

### Logical-Mathematical

Figuring things out and working with numbers are skills that logical-mathematical learners possess. They like to solve problems and use logical reasoning, so they like problems that have answers, rather than vague questions such as "What is the meaning of life?" These learners are likely to do well on math and accounting courses and courses where categorizing and classifying is needed. The types of occupations that they like and do well in include engineering, accounting, physics, mathematics, biology, and geology.

### Visual-Spatial

Building, drawing, doodling, and watching films are typical activities of people who are primarily visual-spatial. Whereas some people get overwhelmed by charts and diagrams (such as those found in biology and chemistry), visual-spatial learners enjoy them, as well as maps, and other images or pictures. Putting things together, like jigsaw puzzles, or doing well on spatial relations tests, where understanding three-dimensional concepts is important, are skills that visual-spatial learners have. When faced with a mechanical problem, they may be able to look at an engine, and know which approach to take to fix it. Professions such as painting, engineering, geography, architecture, mechanics, and surgery appeal to these learners.

### Musical-Rhythmic

Some people are musical in many things that they do. They might hum, whistle, or turn phrases into brief musical songs. They appreciate rhythm, melody, and music. Often songs or music might go through their minds as they are daydreaming. When they work or study, they might like to have music in the background. If this style is very important for some individuals, they might go into musical fields such as music teaching, performing, conducting, and composing.

### Bodily-Kinesthetic

Some individuals learn best through hands-on experience. They are able to take physical objects and move them around, as mechanics do, or they like to move around themselves, as dancers do. When they talk, they often use their hands and other parts of their body to make a point. When talking, they might point to or touch objects or make shapes with their hands. Professors who have a bodily-kinesthetic learning style are likely to move around the classroom a lot, gesture with their hands, touch the blackboard, and use objects to illustrate points. Individuals who like to learn this way might choose occupations such as dancing, performing, carpentry, machine repair, or mechanics.

### Interpersonal

Talking to others, learning from study groups, and being involved in social activities are characteristics that are typical of interpersonal learners. They like to work in teams and learn best by relating to others and participating in groups that cooperate together. They often seek out others, rather than try to be alone. They can be quite good at taking responsibility for projects, leading others, and organizing activities or plans. Sometimes they can be manipulative, trying to urge their point of view on others. Often, however, they want to be cooperative, to share, and to help others. Careers such as teaching, counseling, community service, sales, and managing give individuals an opportunity to learn and to express themselves in an *interpersonal* way.

### Intrapersonal

In contrast with the interpersonal style, the intrapersonal style of learning is to work alone and to be thoughtful. Liking to think things through carefully and to evaluate carefully are typical of this style. Such individuals tend to be creative and independent thinkers, not easily convinced to change their opinions. Rather, they have strong opinions on controversial topics. Instead of working in groups, they often prefer projects where they can work alone. Some writers and philosophers fit this style very well.

Different courses and activities require people to use different styles of expression. Furthermore, some styles fit certain activities much more clearly than others do. For example, when you are playing a sport, your way of learning is probably going to be bodily-kinesthetic. If you are singing or in a band, your way of thinking might be more musical-rhythmic. Likewise, sometimes you like to be alone and to think, which fits more closely with the intrapersonal style. Some styles are more enjoyable for you, and you feel most comfortable with some styles than with others. These seven styles of learning provide a flexible way of viewing how individuals approach different topics. As you think about the chapters in this book, you might find that you learn about them differently, approaching some topics in an interpersonal way, some in an intrapersonal way, and yet others in a bodily-kinesthetic way.

## STUDYING

Although individuals use a number of learning styles, every student needs to do certain tasks. Most courses use one or more textbooks. Generally, the learning style that works best with these is the verbal-linguistic style, and often the logical-mathematical style, although other styles can be used too. The other major way of learning is through attending classes and lectures, a method that also fits best with the verbal-linguistic and the logical-mathematical learning styles. Another method for learning is the study

**Q 2.7** Which of these learning styles fits you best, and in what situations? Explain.

**Q 2.8** How do the seven learning styles relate to information about how students learn?

group; this combines the verbal-linguistic or logical-mathematical style with the interpersonal style. There are some proven approaches for each of these ways of learning.

### Learning from Textbooks

You probably have had the experience of reading a page and not having any idea what you just read. If you have not had this experience, you are fortunate, and you are probably being active when you read. When you are being passive, you are unlikely to concentrate on what you read and you might not remember the basic points being made. For example, you probably passed a house or apartment building that is seven buildings past your own between one hundred and several thousand times. Yet, I doubt very much that you would be able to describe it. If you were to deliberately set out to count the seventh house or building from your home in a particular direction, however, you could do so, and remember what it looks like. Studying requires attention, and those systems designed to help people study that work best are focused on helping people learn actively and attend to what they're reading. Highlighting is an example of a method that helps individuals learn. However, it must be done when individuals are paying attention to exactly what they will want to remember for later use, otherwise the page turns into lots of yellow marks.

**SQ3R** Survey, Question, Read, Recite, Review; a well known approach to studying that focuses on being able to understand material by answering questions about it.

Perhaps the best known and one of the earliest systems to help students retain what they are learning is Robinson's (1970) SQ3R method. Most other systems are modifications of this one. Basically the **SQ3R** study system has five steps: survey, question, read, recite, and review. The purpose of these steps is for a student to take a planful approach to a textbook and actively search out answers to questions. The system itself is rather straightforward, but using it and staying with it take effort and time. First, I'll explain the system and then give tips for overcoming problems when you use it.

- *Step 1: Survey*  When starting to read a chapter, review the topic headings. Generally, topic headings are at three levels. The main level, a subordinate level, and often a third level. You can spot them by the size of the type. The bigger the type, the higher the level is. A table of contents usually gives a summary of the first two levels of headings. For example, the first level of headings in this chapter is "Studying," the second level is "Learning from Textbooks." Going through a chapter just reading the first two levels of headings will give you a good overview of the chapter and what there is to be learned. You should then have an idea about why you are reading the chapter and the type of information that will be presented. Often, it can be

---

## Problems and Solutions

---

### What is a good study approach?

SQ3R

- Survey
- Question
- Read
- Recite
- Review

---

helpful to read the introduction and the conclusion of a chapter to find the important points that are to be discussed. Some textbooks also include chapter objectives, which can help you know what you are expected to learn from the chapter. This chapter lists headings on pages 22 and 23 and questions that will help you understand what topics will be discussed in the sections. These questions help you get an overview of the chapter.

- *Step 2: Question*   Take the major level headings and secondary headings as guides, then try to ask questions about the chapter. Sometimes the first sentence of the paragraph will help you do that. Sometimes as you read, you might find yourself rephrasing the question, which is fine because it shows that you're taking an active approach to learning the content. A question that you might ask for the "Studying" heading is "What methods are there for studying?" For the "Learning from Textbooks" heading, you might ask "What are recommended ways to study a textbook?" Generally, whether it is written material or the spoken word, people are more likely to learn and pay attention to an answer when they initiate the question than when material is just given to them.
- *Step 3: Read*   You can take a variety of approaches when you read to answer the questions that you have made from the headings. You might wish to underline the material that answers the question, or possibly write notes in the margins of the book. If there is something you don't understand, put a question mark by it, so that you can ask another student or the teacher. If you prefer, write notes in your notebook, so that you can compare these notes to lecture notes later on.

As you read, check to see if the questions that you are asking are answered in the text. If not, you might have to reread portions of the text and rephrase your question.

- *Step 4: Recite*  After you have read the answer, recite it to yourself. Use your own words for the answer so that the answer is understandable to you and relatively easy to remember. If possible, recite it out loud. When you cannot do that, recite it to yourself silently. If you can tell yourself what you have learned in a summary form, you are making progress. Repetition is an essential part of learning, so recite it to yourself more than once. For each section of the chapter, repeat the last three steps: Question, Read, and Recite.

- *Step 5: Review*  Once you have read the entire chapter, spend time reviewing the chapter. One way is to ask yourself the questions (look at the headings) and see if you can answer the questions without reading the material. If you need to read the material, go back and answer the question. Also, you can read the summary and add important points that are left out. Often you can write these in the margin or at the end of the summary. Although it is helpful to review right after you have completed the chapter, you can review at other times before you start to study for the exam. Reviewing the material just before you go to a class in which the material is going to be discussed can be very helpful. You might not read each chapter in one sitting because some chapters are quite long, so it will be helpful to review the whole chapter after you complete the last section of it.

The SQ3R method requires energy and concentration. Just reading a chapter without using this method is usually quicker and easier; however, you are likely to learn considerably less. Because the SQ3R method requires considerable attention, it is difficult to do when you are tired, or for long periods of time. Breaks of five to fifteen minutes between major headings can be very helpful.

Although the SQ3R method is relatively straightforward, it requires practice and effort. If you have not used it before, and try it for the first time, you are likely to feel somewhat frustrated, because it can take longer than reading the material through once. Also, this method can feel rough or jumpy, rather than smooth, such as when you read a novel or a magazine article. The best way to try it is to use this method on one full chapter and compare what you have learned using the SQ3R method with what you have learned using your own style.

Not all material lends itself to the SQ3R method. Textbooks that use headings (which is most of them) are the most appropriate for this method. You need to make adjustments when using this method for science and math courses, because some of them emphasize problems. With problem-oriented textbooks, it is helpful to read to try to solve the problems. Courses such as biology use diagrams frequently. Being able to label or reproduce a diagram can be a way of adapting the SQ3R method. Rather than turning a heading into a question, you can turn a diagram or chart into questions. With novels, essays, and articles, the appropriate questions to ask might not be readily apparent, so you might have to spend some time finding the major points or questions that you need to use to understand the material.

Sarah was a 36-year-old first semester freshman using the SQ3R method. At first she was annoyed by the method and found it cumbersome. When she sat down at her desk to learn, she wanted to learn, not have to ask questions, search for the answers, and restate them. She had worked as an assistant manager at a restaurant and was used to making requests and getting quick results. The week after I explained the method to her, she came back quite annoyed, and asked me if I didn't have any better ideas. She had used it for two sections of one chapter in general psychology. Rather than abandon doing it, I suggested that she try again, and be patient. She decided it would be best if she tried it in the afternoon rather than in the evening, and that she use it with psychology, and then follow this work with French using her own method. With French, she had been using flash cards, which she found helpful. Her method for studying verbs, nouns, and adjectives was working for her. Because she was comfortable using flash cards and going through them several times, it was relatively effortless for her compared with the SQ3R method.

The week after that, she came back, and described how she had been able to learn more in the psychology chapter by using the SQ3R method than from any of the previous psychology chapters. She still didn't like it, however, and was frustrated that it took such effort to study. Wanting something more efficient, she asked me again if I didn't have better ideas. I wished that I did, but I told her to persist with this method with psychology, and if it worked well, try it with her economics course. But for now, I told her not even to try to use it with French or math, unless she really felt there were sections that it would work with. At the end of the semester, Sarah reported that her final grade on the psychology exam was a B+, a considerable improvement from previous psychology exams. She said it took her about a month to get used to the SQ3R method. It required more attention than her previous methods. Once she got used to being more alert when studying, the SQ3R method seemed easier to use. She planned to use the SQ3R method with political science and sociology the next semester.

Changing study habits is difficult to do. The point of the SQ3R method is to keep active. Varying it—by asking fewer or more questions, by reciting more or less often—is fine. If a method helps you maintain interest in the subject matter and learn, that is the important point. For example, when studying about veins and arteries, it might be helpful to think about your own veins and observe them. If you want to use your own body as a way to remember important parts of human physiology, that's fine. Changing the SQ3R system to make it more creative and interesting can work for certain subjects. Thinking about how the material is being presented in lecture and how the material is explained in the book, can also be helpful.

## Learning from Lectures

Just as you should be active when learning from a textbook, you should also be active in learning in the classroom. Although you can control the pace at which you learn from a textbook, by going back to some sections or taking breaks, you can't control a professor's lecture. Being as prepared as possible helps you deal with a variety of styles of lectures or presentations from faculty.

You can do a few things before going to class. Perhaps the most important is doing the assigned reading before the professor talks about the material. This gives you an idea of how the material was presented in the text, and you will know something about what to expect from the professor. As the professor talks, you will recall certain material that you have read in the text. You might have questions about the readings that will be answered by the professor. Being able to hear the professor talk about broad concepts and then fit in smaller details will help you understand previously confusing material. By being active in trying to understand the professor and to look for details that correspond to major points, you will learn more than if you just try to copy everything a professor says. Other ways to be prepared are to go over notes from the previous class, or possibly look at the syllabus to see what might be talked about in future classes.

When in class, focus your attention on the action, which in most cases is the professor talking. Occasionally the action is a film, demonstration, or group discussion. If you find your mind wandering, or you start looking out the window, refocus your attention and to try to figure out where the professor is going with her lecture. Even if the professor is confusing or disorganized, take that as a challenge to try to understand what he or she is saying, rather than give up and cut class.

Sometimes when speaking, professors give cues about points that they think are important that can end up being on an exam. Such cues can be words such as "important," "fundamental," "extremely relevant," or, sometimes, "I think this is something that you should think about." At other times, professors will not be subtle: "This will be on the test." Even if a class seems boring, try to challenge yourself to learn pieces of the lecture that are going to help you do well on an exam.

Specific ideas for notes can help you stay organized. For example, date the notes for each lecture. Starting each lecture on a new page and a new

| Recall Column<br>Go over your notes<br>and write down key<br>information here | Lecture Notes<br>Write your lecture notes here |
|---|---|
| What is visual–<br>spatial learning? | Some people learn best by drawing or<br>building models.<br>They may use diagrams. |
|  |  |
|  | Visual-Spatial learning is good<br>for bio., chem. courses with<br>diagrams |
|  |  |
|  |  |

FIGURE **2.3  ORGANIZING YOUR NOTES**

topic on a new page will provide a better organized system for you to study from. Don't worry about wasting space; don't crowd your notes. Leave room to make additions or corrections later. Also, if you only use one side of a page, you may be able to organize your notes more easily as you review. Occasionally, you might want to remove notes from a pad and lay them out in front of you. If a lecturer speaks quickly or seems disorganized, then it is particularly important to leave room so that you can go over the notes with a friend or compare it with your readings and fill in and clarify notes. See Figure 2.3.

A number of students find it useful to use a "recall" column. If you leave about 2½ inches on the left hand side of a page for a "recall column," you can use this as a way of preparing for an exam. During the lecture, leave the recall column blank. After the lecture, preferably sometime the same day, write the main ideas for each major topic in the recall column. These can be select words or phrases that refer to the detail in the major part of your notes (the right hand column). The recall column can be used as a way of testing yourself. By putting your hand over the right hand side, you can recite to yourself the information that explains the major points in the recall column. This step is very similar to the fourth step of the SQ3R method in which you recite the important information back to yourself. Another purpose of the recall column is to prepare for the next class. When you are waiting for the professor to get started, take a look at the previous class's recall column and go over it. By using a recall column, you can repeat or go over information that is important when you prepare for an examination.

Peter's advisor suggested that he take economics as one of the courses needed for graduation. An incoming freshman, Peter thought he barely knew what economics was. When he went to class the first day, he was overwhelmed. The class was held in an auditorium that held about 400 students. The steps went down steeply so that the professor was on a small stage in what seemed to be the bottom of a pit. Behind the professor were huge white screens with dark green walls to the right and left. Peter's stomach became tight as a knot and he started to wonder not only if he were in the right course, but also why he was in school. Everyone around him seemed to know what was going on. He felt certain that he didn't. The professor went over the syllabus and the purpose of the course. Peter's focus went in and out, sometimes on the professor and how smart he seemed, and sometimes on how dumb Peter felt.

When he talked to his oldest brother, who had graduated from college two years earlier about what had happened, his brother told him what had worked for him. He stressed to Peter that it was very important to read the first chapter before he got to the next class. When Peter said, "Why bother, the professor will go over it anyway." His brother said, "So you don't flunk out of school. You don't know what's going on now and if you think that's bad wait till the first exam." Although Peter didn't like his brother's attitude, he took his advice. Peter recognized a lot of what his professor said, and at a few points could even anticipate what was going to happen next. When the class was over, Peter was exhausted. He was sweating, which wasn't typical for him. He felt like he did when he played center field and there were men on base, and the pitcher was pitching to a batter. He was tense and alert. Although not very sure of himself, he felt better because he had some sense about what was going on. Although he didn't like his brother's know-it-all attitude, at least his brother seemed to have a reasonably good idea of what Peter needed to do to prepare.

**Q 2.9** What do you do to learn from a class or a professor that is not interesting to you?

**Q 2.10** Using some of the information about learning in a classroom, describe what you could do differently in one course to help you learn more from the professor?

## Study Groups

Study groups have several advantages over studying alone. Most studying requires a verbal-linguistic or logical-mathematical style to some degree, so many people combine this with an interpersonal style of studying. When individuals work with others, they tend to be more active in their approach to studying and more responsible. If they don't contribute to the study group, they can feel that they are letting others down as well as themselves. Study groups can be of varying sizes. Sometimes the group can just be with

---

## Problems and Solutions

### How can other students help me learn?

Try study groups, then you can

- Clarify class notes
- Share views of course goals
- Go over definitions
- Enjoy repetitious learning
- Quiz each other
- Go over past tests

---

one other person, sometimes four or five others, or more. If possible, study groups should meet about a week before each exam to go over material. Sometimes they meet more frequently, until the night before an exam. For such groups to work well, each person should be prepared to go over material for the course.

Study groups have several advantages, and the form depends on the course and the members of the study group. For almost any course, study groups are an opportunity to clarify class notes and to share views of the instructor's approach to the class and goals. This is why it is important for each member of the study group to bring his or her lecture notes to the meeting. Also, group members can go over the vocabulary and definitions that are important in the course. When the group is able to agree on the main ideas from each lecture and how they fit with the readings, you get a sense of organization and continuity. One important part of a study group is that it makes repetitious learning more fun. Quizzing each other by using flash cards or notes is usually a more enjoyable way of practicing for the exam than is going over the material alone.

Some work in a study group can be very test focused. If past tests are available, go over the correct answers. You can also try to anticipate test questions and answers. Certain courses require different types of emphasis. In a language course, quizzing each other using English or the language that is studied can be helpful. In math and some science courses, you can gain a deeper understanding by working out problems together and helping each other solve problems. Study groups help many people improve their grades (Gardner & Jewler, 2000), understand material in greater depth, and enjoy the work more.

**Q 2.11** If you have participated in study groups, what has worked for you and what has not? If you have not worked in a study group, how do you think they might be able to help you, and how do you think they would not?

# TIME MANAGEMENT

Time is an unusual resource. Unlike food, money, or jewelry, it can't be stockpiled or accumulated (MacKenzie, 1997). To prevent wasting time, individuals should stick to their priorities, such as studying for an exam, rather than reading a short story for an English course. If you don't try to seek perfection, you have more flexibility in budgeting your time with several events rather than focusing on doing one project perfectly. Somewhat related to this is the idea of throwing things away. By getting rid of unimportant material, you can organize your notes, books, and so forth, and have less to look through when you try to find things. Saying "no" to others is also a way of choosing not to involve yourself in matters that interfere with goals. Of course, sometimes it can be best to help others, even if attaining goals is delayed.

To learn from texts, lectures, and study groups, it is important to schedule time during the day and plan for studying during a given week. Over the course of a semester, students have a variety of goals. Long-range goals involve planning for papers, exams, and final exams. Short-range goals involve learning a chapter for an exam or researching a part of a paper. Even when students try to be planful, many things cannot be anticipated. Using schedules and planners to organize time works for many students, but you might have to keep revising and changing your schedules and plans. However, putting things off—procrastination—makes it harder for you to stick to a schedule or personal planner.

## Personal Planners

Available in a variety of styles and shapes, personal planners help you keep track of many things that you need to get done. Office supply stores and bookstores often stock a variety of these. Some spread a week across two pages. Others spread a month's activity across two pages (Figure 2.4). Some people like to write in pencil so that they can change and edit their schedule. Others use magic markers. For example, term papers and exams might be in red, and personal appointments in black. Some people like to circle important dates or code their planners in different ways.

## Hourly Schedules

By planning what you will do during the day, you will have a better idea of how you can budget your time and how much time you have for studying. Using a weekly schedule, such as the example in Figure 2.5, can help you decide how much time to spend on studying and other activities. Rather

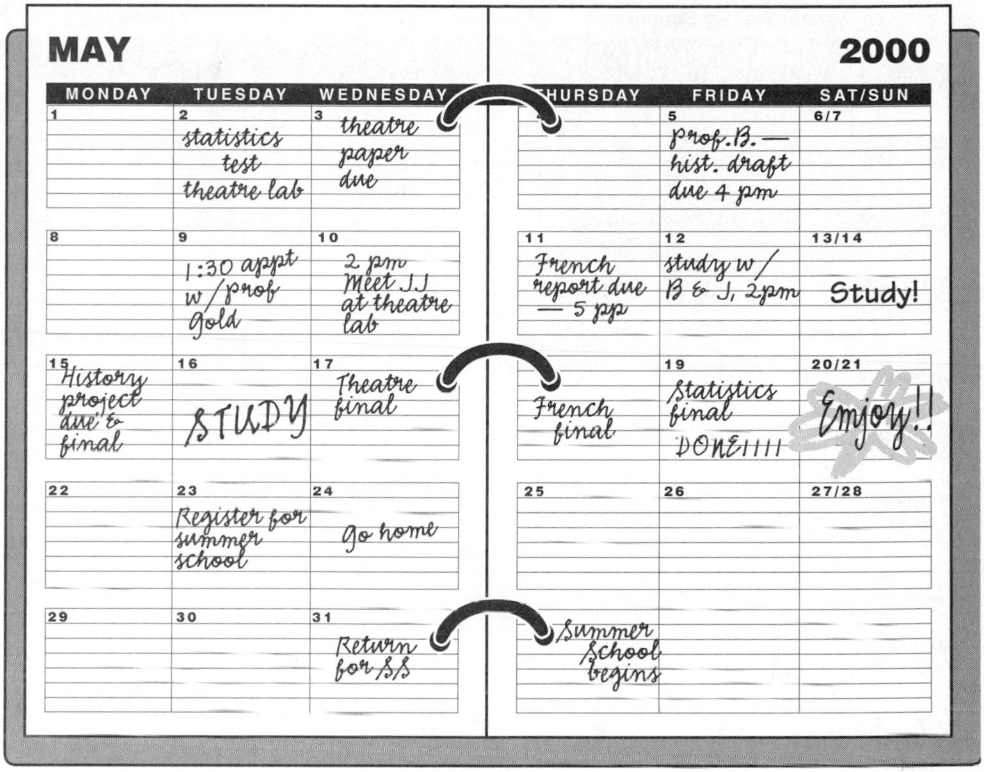

| MAY | | | | | 2000 |
|---|---|---|---|---|---|
| **MONDAY** | **TUESDAY** | **WEDNESDAY** | **THURSDAY** | **FRIDAY** | **SAT/SUN** |
| 1 | 2 *statistics test theatre lab* | 3 *theatre paper due* | | 5 *Prof. B. — hist. draft due 4 pm* | 6/7 |
| 8 | 9 *1:30 appt w/prof Gold* | 10 *2 pm Meet JJ at theatre lab* | 11 *French report due — 5 pp* | 12 *study w/ B & J, 2pm* | 13/14 **Study!** |
| 15 *History project due & final* | 16 *STUDY* | 17 *Theatre final* | 18 *French final* | 19 *statistics final DONE!!!!* | 20/21 *Enjoy!!* |
| 22 | 23 *Register for summer school* | 24 *Go home* | 25 | 26 | 27/28 |
| 29 | 30 | 31 *Return for SS* | *Summer School begins* | | |

FIGURE **2.4  AN EXAMPLE OF A PERSONAL PLANNER**

than just writing "study" in a schedule, try writing what you are going to study ("chap. 10, Bio.) or "re: WWI for H."—meaning research about reasons for World War I for history class. To see how their schedules are working, some students prefer to put what they plan to do in ink, then write in pencil what they actually do. This can give you a sense of how accurate you are in judging your time.

By planning a week's schedule, and revising it as necessary the evening before you start your activities, you can take advantage of the time you work best. For example, it is helpful to schedule some time before a course meets to review your notes. If you have material that you think is difficult to study, schedule it for when you are most alert. You might schedule courses that you find easiest as a type of "reward" to follow harder courses. However you do your scheduling, be realistic. In fact, it is better to schedule more leisure and less study time, rather than the reverse. For example, if you plan for two hours of study time and do three, you will have a greater

**Master Weekly Schedule**                                    **Name** _____

| | Sunday | Monday | Tuesday | Wednesday | Thursday | Friday | Saturday |
|---|---|---|---|---|---|---|---|
| **6:00** | | | | | | | |
| **7:00** | | | | | | | |
| **8:00** | | | | | | | |
| **9:00** | | | | | | | |
| **10:00** | | | | | | | |
| **11:00** | | | | | | | |
| **12:00** | | | | | | | |
| **1:00** | | | | | | | |
| **2:00** | | | | | | | |
| **3:00** | | | | | | | |
| **4:00** | | | | | | | |
| **5:00** | | | | | | | |
| **6:00** | | | | | | | |
| **7:00** | | | | | | | |
| **8:00** | | | | | | | |
| **9:00** | | | | | | | |
| **10:00** | | | | | | | |
| **11:00** | | | | | | | |

FIGURE **2.5  AN EXAMPLE OF A WEEKLY SCHEDULE**

(Corey, Corey & Corey, p. 55).

---

## Problems and Solutions

---

### *I often put things off. What can I do?*

Anti-procrastination tips

- Make projects small
- Choose where to study
- Choose when to take breaks
- Ask: How important is what I'm doing now?
- Use a schedule

---

sense of accomplishment than if you plan for four hours of study time and do three. A schedule is designed to help you organize your activity, not make you feel like you're a slave to your work.

## Procrastination

**procrastination** Putting off doing something until later. Delaying studying for another time is an example of procrastination.

The enemy of managing time is **procrastination.** In addition to affecting academic performance, procrastination can increase stress and negatively affect work, school performance, and health (Tice & Baumeister, 1997). Several strategies can help deal with putting off assignments. Taking a large project and making it smaller is probably one of the most effective methods. Rather than say, "I have so much math to do tonight," say to yourself, "Let me start with the first section in Chapter 3 and give myself about a half an hour to finish it." Another effective approach is to control what you do and where you do it. If you can't study in your room, go to a library, another room, or an empty classroom. When others want to do things with you and you are busy, it may be best to ask them if you can do it later or meet them at another time. When you do this, you're less likely to think about all the work that you have to do when you are trying to have fun with friends. Another approach is to ask yourself if you really want to get the particular work done at this time. If you don't, you might decide to take a break. You can also reschedule the work that you're doing and plan to do it at a time that you had scheduled to do a nonschool related activity.

For most students, scheduling problems tend to be value problems rather than not knowing how to keep a schedule. The problem is deciding how important studying is and being consistent in choosing to study rather than to spend time with friends or doing something else. Maureen's situation is not unusual, as she describes how she is trying to return to college after having been suspended.

> I really screwed things up last semester. I knew that I would have to study when I got to college. I didn't worry, as I figured that I could always do my work later. For the first two weeks, I went to most of my classes, but didn't bother to study much, because except for math, there wasn't much that was due. Then when I got my first "F," I decided I ought to study.
>
> I did try a schedule. I scheduled my classes, my work at the library, my studying. That lasted for about a week. My first schedule was very pretty, I had lots of colors for different activities. But after that, I got bored with schedules, and I wasn't keeping to them anyway.
>
> When my parents would ask me how I was doing, I'd say, "Fine, things are going well." So it was easy, sort of, when they asked me about my exams, and I was getting "D's" and "F's," I would tell them that I was getting "B's."
>
> The pressure really grew. They were mad as hell at me in December when they found out that I had been lying to them. My father told me that that was it, and that I was not going to go to school again, at least he wasn't going to pay for it. Well, I finally talked to him after he stopped glaring at me and got him to agree to let me take one course at a time. Now this spring, I'm going to take one course, that's all.
>
> I just registered for it and it starts in a week. This time the scheduling problem is different. I'm working 30 hours a week for a trucking firm, managing their office, and have one course at night. Now I've got to schedule some studying around my work rather than the reverse.

Q 2.12 Describe your reaction to using a schedule like the one in Figure 2.5.

When I have talked with students about their scheduling and studying concerns, they often have some ideas about how to schedule. The problem of keeping to the schedule is much more difficult. The temptations of parties, sports, video games, and just being with friends are real. But these activities can be scheduled too. Decisions about keeping to a schedule often have to be made deliberately and consciously, so that a person has control over his or her use of time. Because many professors give exams only 2 or 3 times during a four–month period, time management becomes a necessity for most students.

## EXAMS

Like studying, tests require organization. Knowing when tests are given is important. It is not unusual for some students to forget that they have a test in the next day or two, making preparation for the test rather difficult. Most instructors will describe the test so that you know the format. If they

---

## Problems and Solutions

---

***What questions should I ask about exams so that I can do better?***

- What type of items?
- Sample questions?
- What topics?
- Readings, notes, or both?
- Is speed being tested?

---

don't, you can ask. Because preparing for a multiple choice and an essay test are somewhat different, it's helpful to know what proportion of the test is going to be multiple choice, essay, and true-false. Being able to look at past copies of tests are helpful; if those are not available, sample questions are useful too. Knowing whether the test is based on lectures, readings, or some combination helps you decide what material to emphasize. Knowing the number of questions on a test can give you some idea about how you will have to pace yourself in an exam. The amount of time exams take to complete varies. In some courses, some professors put a premium on speed. How you use your time is important if a rather small percentage of students is expected to finish. In other exams, all students might have enough time to finish. The more information you have about the examination, the better you are able to decide what material you should concentrate on and how you should plan to learn it.

Objective tests are most typically multiple choice exams where you have to select from a list of four or five choices. Some objective tests include true false questions or two lists or columns that need to be matched. For these types of questions, it is important to read the directions carefully because often the answers hinge on one or two words. Qualifier words such as "always," "seldom," "never," "sometimes" are particularly important. Occasionally questions reveal answers to other questions. Only when you have new information about a question such as remembering information that you had forgotten previously, should you change it. Otherwise your first response is likely to be the best one.

When students lack confidence in their ability to take tests, they sometimes change answers because they think if they thought it was right, it must be wrong. Some students have a feeling that the answer that they selected just doesn't look right. This is not a reason to change an answer.

Trying to recall the information that you have studied works much more effectively than criticizing yourself for not having studied enough. Time pressure can cause students to stop thinking logically and start feeling anxious. For this reason, planning enough time to go back over the exam to review is quite helpful.

In multiple choice examinations, the information is already organized. In essay tests, you need to do the organizing. Because there are few questions, directions are critical, so if you're not sure what is meant by the question, ask the teacher. When only a few questions will be asked, decide how you are going to budget your time. Generally, it is best to answer the easiest questions first so that you will have more confidence and time for more difficult questions, but don't take so much time answering the easy questions that you don't have enough time for the harder questions. As you think about the question, jot some ideas down on a piece of scrap paper or a blank page in the examination book. Then you can organize your points by numbering them, or possibly rewriting them. Because organization is important in an essay exam, a brief introductory paragraph and a closing paragraph are helpful. Paragraphs should have connected thoughts that should be described in complete sentences. Legibility is important because teachers will be reading a lot of exams and are likely to lose patience with work that they can't read. If you leave space at the end of an essay, you'll have time to write in more information if you have more ideas later on.

When writing an answer to an essay question, think how you would answer the question if you were talking to someone in the class or in the study group. This might help you think of some of the important points and how you would describe particular situations, events, or objects. Some essay questions expect you to express your opinion, then back it up with facts. For such questions, think about the arguments that you would make when talking to another member of the class, such as a study group partner.

## SUMMARY

Learning is not a solitary activity. It is an interaction between you and someone else's ideas, as written in the text, thoughts and words as described by a professor, and discussions with the professor or other students. First, we examined how children learn because the curiosity and exploration that young children do helps to keep learning fun and enjoyable. When learning in college is fun, it can give you a sense of accomplishment rather than a sense of boredom. Learning works best when individuals approach it actively and are willing to practice what they are learning. Minimizing outside interferences and organizing information helps the learning process be less confusing and less frustrating.

Not everyone learns the same way. There are seven learning styles that fit different individuals. Some people learn through words and writing, others through logic and math, others are more musical, some quite visual, others like to touch and move when learning, others learn through social interactions, and others just by thinking. Individuals often use a combination of these.

The style and attitude with which individuals approach studying can affect what and how much they learn. For learning from textbooks, the SQ3R method (survey, question, read, recite, and review) is helpful. I also described some ways of learning from lectures and using study groups. Managing time to use the SQ3R method, learn from lectures, or other study related tasks requires patience. Although personal planners and hourly schedules can be helpful, sticking with them is challenging. When you manage your time well, however, and you have learned and understood the material, taking tests, such as essay and multiple choice exams becomes less of a problem and will provide a real sense of accomplishment.

# RECOMMENDED READINGS

*Your College Experience: Strategies for Success,* 4th ed.
J. N. Gardner and A. J. Jewler (Wadsworth, 2000)
> Gardner, Jewler, and a group of experts cover a wide range of topics that are aimed at helping individuals improve their success at college. The topics include studying techniques, taking examinations, and other areas of academic life such as time management. The authors address how students deal with social life and family life while being involved in college courses.

*Learning Skills for College and Career*
P. I. Hettich (Brooks/Cole, 1998)
> This is another excellent book on studying and learning while at college. Topics include study techniques, getting organized, time management, how to improve memory, and how to do well on tests. Suggestions for reading and note taking in class are also given. The exercises can help you analyze your current skills.

*Timelock: How Life Got So Hectic and What You Can Do About It*
R. Keyes (HarperCollins, 1991)
> This book deals with using and organizing time. Keyes discusses the social pressure of trying to do more and more with less time. One solution is to reevaluate what is important in one's life and to focus on that rather than on demands that might be relatively unimportant. Keyes also discusses new devices such as computers that are designed to save time, but might in fact require more time than they save.

*Emotional Intelligence: Why It Can Matter More Than IQ*
D. Goleman (Bantam, 1995)

> Goleman offers another view of different types of intelligence. Just as Gardner describes seven types of intelligence on pages 32 through 35, Goleman explains how emotional intelligence can be more important than a high IQ or cognitive intelligence. Emotional intelligence includes the ability to be aware and express, as well as control, one's own feelings or emotions. Also understanding and interpreting the emotions of others is a form of emotional intelligence. Goleman also discusses the importance of social skills and the motivation to succeed. Traits such as optimism and persistence also are covered by the term "emotional intelligence." This emphasis on skills in dealing with one's emotional life balances the focus on learning skills.

*CLASS: College Learning And Study Skills,* 5th ed.
D. G. Longman and R. H. Atkinson (Wadsworth, 1999)

*READ: Reading Enhancement And Development,* 6th ed.
R. H. Atkinson and D. G. Longman (Wadsworth, 1999)

*SMART: Study Methods And Reading Techniques,* 2nd ed.
D. G. Longman and R. H. Atkinson (Wadsworth, 1999)

> Atkinson and Longman take a practical approach to college preparation and study skills. All three books are filled with numerous exercises that help students learn and apply study skills by working with texts from other classes and actual textbook excerpts. *CLASS* emphasizes notetaking, time management techniques, stress-coping strategies, memory-maximizing techniques, critical thinking strategies, and library and research-paper essentials. In *READ*, students learn to apply the SQ3R method, use the context of what they're reading to identify parts of speech and understand figurative language, apply structural analysis to improve reader comprehension, and read graphs, maps, and tables effectively. *SMART* helps students apply reading skills and study techniques to college courses. Students can learn how to think critically, listen well, take good notes, and effectively synthesize and review course content to prepare for tests.

# RECOMMENDED WEB SITES

*Cal Ren Project Study Tips*
http://128.32.89.153/CalRENHP.html

> Designed for all students, but particularly for nontraditional age students, these tips are an excellent set of study resources. They were designed by staff at the University of California, Berkeley.

# CHOOSING CAREERS

Working is such an integral part of our lives that it can contribute greatly to the pleasures, frustrations, and annoyances that people experience throughout their lives. By choosing work that is interesting, that meets important personal values, and fits their personal style of doing things, individuals can feel a sense of exhilaration, or contribution to values that are important to them, and have an enduring sense of satisfaction. However, choosing work that is boring, that seems immoral, or that seems pointless, can give individuals the feeling that there is not much enjoyment in life. We will examine three steps in choosing a career based on a trait and factor approach to career development. We will also look at how to implement a choice. This includes some brief descriptions about job search strategies, writing a résumé, and having job interviews.

Before continuing, it is helpful to define some terms that are used in this chapter and the next so that they can be distinguished from each other: career, job, occupation, and work.

**career**  An individual's work and leisure that takes place over his or her life span.

**job**  Refers to the task that a worker is asked to perform by an employer.

**occupation**  Similar jobs that are found in many organizations.

**work**  An activity that produces something of value for other people

- **Career.** An individual's work and leisure that takes place over her or his life span. In this sense, career choice applies to decisions that individuals make at any point in their career about particular work or leisure activities that they choose to pursue at that time.
- **Job.** A position requiring similar skills within one organization. Basically, a job refers to specific tasks that a worker performs.
- **Occupations.** Similar jobs that are found in many organizations.
- **Work.** An activity that produces something of value for other people; a general term that relates to both paid and unpaid activity..

The focus in this chapter is on *career:* This term refers to the individual, and choices an individual can make, whereas, job, occupation, and work are positions that exist to be done or filled by someone.

Frequently, when individuals think of choosing a career, they think of choosing a major. Basically, a major is a concentration of similar courses that can affect an individual's career in a variety of ways. Some majors are specific training for a career, such as engineering, nursing, medical technology, teacher education, business, and plant science. For some occupations, training takes place during graduate school, and a wide variety of majors might be acceptable for careers in law, social work, psychology, and medicine. For other occupations, such as some sales, management, advertising, or administrative work, any major might be appropriate. When thinking about making career choices and choices about a major, it might be helpful to think of a major as training for a career. Thus, it is often helpful to ask first what career choices seem appropriate, and, second, what major or majors would fit those career choices. This usually works better than choosing a major first, then a career.

The pioneer of vocational guidance, or career counseling, was Frank Parsons who wrote *Choosing a Vocation* in 1909. His views, as expressed in

**trait** A characteristic of an individual that can be measured through testing or observation.

**factor** A characteristic required for successful job performance.

this book, became the foundation for what later evolved into trait and factor theory. The term **trait** refers to aspects, interests, values, and abilities of an individual that can be measured through testing. **Factor** refers to requirements needed for successful job performance. Thus, the terms *trait* and *factor* refer to the assessment of characteristics of a person and a job. Since 1909, researchers have developed a variety of tests and inventories to measure traits. In addition, researchers have developed theories that are based on trait and factor theory. One of these, John Holland's typology, is useful in helping individuals understand themselves and their career opportunities. In the next section, I will describe the first step of trait and factor theory that deals with understanding oneself—one's personality, interests, abilities, and values.

## GAINING SELF-UNDERSTANDING

To gain self-understanding, it is helpful to think of oneself in an unbiased way and to talk to someone who is unbiased. Talking to a counselor whose goal it is to help you figure out what you want can be helpful because the counselor does not have an investment in what you do. Others might. For example, a father might want his daughter to be a physician, but the daughter might want to be a dancer. To be helpful in discussing her career plans with his daughter, the father should be relatively unbiased. Likewise, when individuals think about what kind of occupation they might want later on, it is helpful to be able to assess themselves—personality, interests, abilities, and values—without saying to themselves, "I really should do this," or "I never could be a lawyer," or "Most engineers are smarter than I am." In Chapter 4, self-efficacy theory shows how a lack of confidence in your abilities can affect how you adjust to a job; it can also affect the type of career choice an individual makes. People who feel that they could never complete college (low self-efficacy) might be limiting their future career possibilities. In this section, you have an opportunity to examine your own personality, interests, abilities, and values. Although it is impossible to be totally objective, recognizing when you are being too self-demanding or self-critical is helpful when assessing yourself.

### *Personality*

**personality** Traits that describe an individual. These include thinking, feeling, and behaving.

Career choice and career adjustment represent an extension of a person's **personality.** This is a view that is held by John Holland (1997) who developed a theory of types that is useful in understanding personality as it relates to career choice. Holland believes that people express themselves, their interests, and their values through their work choices and experience.

---

## Problems and Solutions

*I don't know what I am going to do when I graduate. What if I can't get the career goal I want?*
*I think I know what I want, but are there some options I haven't thought about?*

- First: Assess your personality, interests, abilities, and values.
- Second: Find occupations that fit them.

---

**stereotypes (Holland)** Peoples' impressions and generalizations about occupations; Holland believes these generalizations are generally accurate.

**Holland type** Holland describes peoples' personalities using six categories: Realistic, Investigative, Artistic, Social, Enterprising, and Conventional; types of personalities are matched with working environments, which are Realistic, Investigative, Artistic, Social, Enterprising, and Conventional.

Holland assumes that people's impressions and generalizations about work, which he refers to as **stereotypes,** are generally accurate. By studying and refining these stereotypes, **Holland** identified six categories of people that fit with six types of occupations. When Holland refers to personality, he is not focusing on abnormal personality, such as depression, or schizophrenia but, rather, basically normal personality. Although some psychologists have focused on personality traits such as dominance, sociability, empathy, self-control, being suspicious, or being apprehensive, Holland has focused on how interests, values, and abilities and the work choices that follow from them are an indicator of a person's personality. The six personality types that are discussed here are Realistic, Investigative, Artistic, Social, Enterprising, and Conventional (pictured in Figure 3.1). Those that are most similar to each other are next to each other on the hexagon, and those that are least similar are across from each other.

*The Realistic Personality.*  Realistic people are likely to be practical, and want to give advice or receive advice to solve problems. They are likely to value money, power, and status, while placing a lesser value on human relationships. In general, they are likely to be very practical and have little tolerance for abstract and theoretical descriptions.

*The Investigative Personality.*  The challenge of an unanswered question is exciting for Investigative people. They often like to work on a difficult problem and will work hard to find a solution, regardless of the financial reward. They enjoy puzzles and challenges that require using their intelligence. They like the opportunity to use their ability to solve mathematical and scientific problems and enjoy the feeling that comes with solving the problem. Often, they prefer not to deal directly with

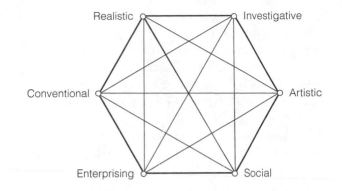

FIGURE **3.1** THE RELATIONSHIPS AMONG HOLLAND TYPES.

(Adapted from *Holland's Hoxagon, ACT Research Report No. 29,* by J. L. Holland, D. R. Whitney, N. S. Cole, and J. M. Richards Jr. Copyright (c)1969 The American College Testing Program). Used by permission.

personal problems but, rather, try to analyze them or search for solutions rather than talk directly with others. Although Investigative personalities can work as team players to solve problems, they might not like to supervise others.

***The Artistic Personality.*** Creativity characterizes the Artistic personality. Such individuals enjoy open personal expression, and an opportunity to express their views, whether in music, art, or in writing, creatively. Their ideas might be unconventional and new, and they might want to be relatively unstructured in keeping their appointments and in their approach to work. Unlike Investigative types, Artistic types are less interested in logical expression than they are in personal or emotional expression. They might enjoy discussing artistic products and commenting on or criticizing the products of others. Sometimes their expression is unclear; at other times, they use humor, which is a sign of their interest in creativity.

***The Social Personality.*** Being idealistic, kind, friendly, and generous are traits that describe the Social personality. These people emphasize human values and focus on being flexible with other people and understanding them. Social people enjoy helping people by teaching them or assisting them with personal problems. Rather than work with machines or give orders, Social personalities prefer to talk with others to resolve complex problems that might be ethical or idealistic in nature.

***The Enterprising Personality.*** Being with others and using verbal skills to sell, persuade, or lead others is enjoyable for Enterprising people. They are often assertive and popular and like to be in leadership positions. Furthermore, they like to be in powerful positions, to advance in their careers or to make money, and to manage and persuade others. Sometimes they seem more self-confident than they feel. Although they are verbal and enjoy talking with people, Enterprising people are more interested in convincing and persuading them than in helping them.

*The Conventional Personality.*  Planning and organizing best describes Conventional people. They value being dependable and following rules and orders. Because of this, they are often frustrated by vague or ambiguous requests and prefer regulations and guidelines. They enjoy earning money and dealing with financial situations. When solving problems, they like to use a clerical or numerical approach.

## Interests

In this section, I will describe Holland's six types and show how they can be used to describe interests in hobbies and occupations. **Interest** refers to things that you like or enjoy doing, even if you are not particularly good at them. Many researchers consider interests to be the most important trait that is used in occupational selection (Sharf, 1997). Interest inventories have been used to measure the likes and dislikes of successful and satisfied people in an occupation. Your interests then can be compared with the interests of those who like what they do and do it well. Often interest inventories provide scores comparing your interests to those of men and women in 50 to 100 occupations.

*Realistic Interests.*  Fixing machines, repairing electronic equipment, driving cars and trucks, hunting animals, are all examples of activities that Realistic people find interesting. They like to use tools or machines in their hobbies or work. They often like technical challenges such as plumbing, roofing, automotive repair, farming, and electronics. Other activities Realistic people enjoy are hunting, fishing, and fixing cars. They like to develop an expertise in using tools to fix cars, radios, or other machinery.

*Investigative Interests.*  Scientific questions that are found in math, physics, chemistry, biology, geology, and other physical or biological sciences are likely to appeal to Investigative people. They like to use complex and abstract thinking to solve such problems and to do research. The analytical challenges that face computer programmers, physicians, biologists, and science teachers are likely to appeal to them. In general, they like to use logic and precise thinking to solve problems.

**Q 3.1** Please list the Holland Type that describes you best. Then, if possible, list a second and third category.

**interest** Curiosity about or enjoyment in an activity.

**Q 3.2** List the Holland Type that describes your interests best. Then, if possible, list your second and third categories. In addition to seeing how similar your interests are to each of the six Holland categories, other questions about your activities also help assess interests.

**Q 3.3** What hobbies or leisure activities do you enjoy?

**Q 3.4** What courses or school subjects have you most enjoyed?

**Q 3.5** What activities or job duties have you enjoyed the most in the jobs that you have had?

**Q 3.6** If you could do anything that you wanted for a career, without regard to your ability level, financial support for schooling, or finding a job, what would it be?

**values** Concepts and attitudes that are important to individuals.

**work adjustment theory** A theory that focuses on the importance of values in predicting satisfaction with work. Values include achievement, comfort, status, altruism, safety, and autonomy.

*Artistic Interests.* Creating music, art, or writing are likely to be of interest to Artistic types. They like to use instruments, such as violins, sculpting tools, brushes, or word processors to create. They like to learn and improve their abilities in language, art, music, or writing. Paint-by-numbers kits and technical writing are too organized and would not allow them to express themselves creatively. Museums, concerts, and poetry readings are places where you might find Artistic types.

*Social Interests.* Individuals with Social interests like being with friends and helping them with their problems. They like to volunteer or work in settings like education, social service, and mental health where they can teach or help people with personal problems. Social people like being a part of a team and discussing problems to reach a decision, and they often enjoy working on problems of a religious or ethical nature.

*Enterprising Interests.* Managing and persuading others is fun for Enterprising people. They often like to deal with financial and economic issues, and sometimes take risks to make money: They might enjoy playing the stock market, lobbying people, or trying to get someone to buy insurance. Becoming more powerful and making money is characteristic of an Enterprising interest.

*Conventional Interests.* Organizing and counting are skills that Conventional people enjoy. They might be interested in financial and accounting analysis as well. Keeping records, copying materials, and organizing reports are fun for Conventional people. They are interested in activities where they can organize and be counted on to be dependable, such as keeping track of data and information.

## Values

There are two types of **values**: general values and work-related values. General values include political values such as being conservative or liberal, religious values that represent moral stands on various issues, and social values that represent attitudes toward helping people or being with people. General values could occur during time with family or friends and can be reflected in work-related values. In contrast, the work-related values on which I will focus here relate to on-the-job experiences. In this section, I will describe work-related values that are derived from **work adjustment theory** (Dawis & Lofquist, 1984; Lofquist & Dawis, 1991). These values (Achievement, Comfort, Status, Altruism, Safety, and Autonomy) are described again in Chapter 4, but as they relate to work adjustment rather than career choice.

*Achievement.*  Looking for a job where you could get a sense of accomplishment and use skills that you have is an expression of the value Achievement.

*Comfort.*  Finding a job that has aspects of work that would make life less stressful for you is an example of the value of Comfort. In such a job, you might value good working conditions, such as good lighting, a climate that is neither too hot nor too cold, and a clean office or work space. You might also want to be secure, knowing that you would not be likely to be laid off or fired. To be comfortable, you would want the job to pay well. Further, the job would keep you busy, provide variety, and be one where you could work independently when you wanted. You might want all these factors about a job if you value Comfort.

*Status.*  If you look for a job where you will be recognized for your contribution and have an opportunity to advance, then you would be looking for the value of Status. This might be a job where you could be an authority or supervise others and one where you would be respected in the community.

*Altruism.*  Wanting a job where you can help others is to want a job where you could be altruistic. It might be one where you could do things for other people by teaching, assisting with medical or personal problems, and so forth. Being in a job where you felt that the work was morally right is a part of the value of Altruism. For example, altruistic people would not like to work in a job selling something that they felt was an inferior product.

*Safety.*  Feeling safe or feeling that you are being treated fairly might be a particularly important value to you. You might want a job where you know that you and other workers would be trained well and that your boss would back you up. You want to feel that policies are administered fairly to you and your coworkers. Thus, the value of Safety refers to a feeling that you can trust the company that you work with to treat you fairly.

**Q 3.7** List the three values that are most important to you, in order of importance.

*Autonomy.*  Being able to develop your own ideas and make decisions on your own represents the value of Autonomy. You want to be free to be creative and take responsibility for your decisions, if Autonomy is an important value to you.

## Abilities

**achievement (abilities)**
Past performance; what the individual has done.

To understand what is meant by the term ability, compare it with two other terms that are easily confused with it. **Achievement** represents what you have done, **ability** represents what you are doing, and **aptitude**

**ability** Current perform-ance, what the individual is doing now.

**aptitude** Future perform-ance; what the individual will do in the future.

represents what you might do in the future. Often, there are tests of aptitude, ability, and achievement to assess skill level. Thus, an achieve-ment test is designed to show how much a person has learned. A test of ability measures a person's present ability to perform a task or his or her knowledge at the time. In contrast, an aptitude test shows how much a person is likely to learn in the future—what his or her future ability may be. Sometimes it is difficult to separate these three. For example, the assessment of past achievement can provide a measure of possible aptitude.

Tests or measures of achievement tend to refer to a broad range of events that people can do during their lifetimes. Three types of achieve-ments are related to career choice: The first is academic accomplish-ment, including grades at school, but also honors. The second type of achievement is accomplishments in work, such as how well you com-pleted certain tasks as measured by your supervisor. The third is tests of achievement for entry into an occupation, or being certified to enter an occupation. Achievement tests are used in a great number of different fields to make sure that individuals are competent. Examples are tests for accountants, cosmetologists, musicians, nurses, physicians, plumbers, psychologists, and life insurance agents. By passing such a test, an indi-vidual is certified or licensed to work in a particular area. These tests tend to be different from aptitude or ability tests, in that they are very specific to a given task or profession. Tests are not the only way to mea-sure achievement; the best assessment of musical achievement is a musi-cal audition.

Ability refers to what you know now or are able to do. Taking a test for a college course would be a test of your current ability. If you were an ice skater and could do a double axel, that would indicate what your current skating ability is. A driving test is an ability test because it measures your current ability to perform a task (driving).

Aptitude refers to trying to predict what a person will be able to do in the future. Common aptitude tests such as the College Board Scholastic Assessment Test (SAT) and the American College Testing Assessment Program: Academic Test (ACT) are used to predict how well individuals will do in college. Common aptitudes that are measured in such tests are verbal and quantitative (mathematical). Other academic skills such as abstract reasoning, clerical speed, spelling, and space per-ception can also be measured. Aptitudes do not need to be measured only by tests. For example, someone watching a gymnast might say, "I bet he would be a good ice skater." Or an English teacher might say about a student who writes a good paper, "I bet she has the aptitude to be a good journalist." In both cases, predictions are being made about the future.

**Q 3.8** List two or three achievements that you feel good about.

**Q 3.9** Describe two or three of your current abili-ties that might be related to selecting a career.

**Q 3.10** List two or three activities, tasks, or occu-pations that you believe you might have an apti-tude for.

## External Influences on Career Choice

Until now, we have been discussing individuals' traits that are involved in choosing a career—personality, interests, values, and abilities. Several factors that are not individual characteristics also influence career choice. For example, some people have parents who can help them finance their education, but others have much more limited financial resources. If you are responsible for supporting a child or a family, you might have responsibilities that make attending school more difficult than if you did not. This can make it more difficult, but not impossible, for you to attain certain occupational goals. Geography is yet another factor. If you live in a rural community, you are likely to have different opportunities for education and different exposure to music or art than you are if you live in a city. Parental values are important too. If parents value education, and if parents have worked in occupations that are prestigious, individuals are more likely to enter a prestigious occupation than they are if their parents are working in low prestige occupations (Sharf, 1997). Of course, there are many exceptions. Because scholarships are available to help individuals who need financial aid, and because people can work and go to college at the same time, individuals can overcome some constraints that can make it difficult to attain an occupational goal that requires two to eight years of full-time education beyond high school.

## The Process of Career Choice

Although I have described important characteristics (personality, interests, values, and ability) of individuals relative to career alternatives, I have not described the process of selecting a career. How individuals come to make career choices varies greatly. Young children often make choices based on fantasy. Seeing a detective, a dancer, or a basketball player on television can spark the excitement of five-year-olds, who then decide that is what they want to be. As children grow older, they may develop an increasingly accurate self-concept, a view of themselves. Usually, their ability to accurately assess their interests develops first, followed by being able to assess abilities, and finally values (Super, 1990). This process takes place over a long time, beginning around the age of six. Individuals who are more able to accurately assess their own interests, values, abilities, and personality than are others are said to possess more career maturity. Because the process of choosing a career is complex for most people, they often seek career counseling, or help from others. Counselors can not only point out occupational alternatives, but can also help people assess themselves.

To make the process of career choice seem less abstract, it will be helpful to discuss Katie's process of choosing among several career alternatives. I talked with Katie during the spring semester of her sophomore
year at college. She was very unsure about what she would major in and
what type of career she might pursue. For years, she had considered elementary education as a major, with the idea that she would teach third
graders. Her mother had been a teacher and now was an assistant principal in a large elementary school. Her father taught English in a high
school but had recently tired of teaching and was selling real estate in
Katie's hometown.

Katie had always enjoyed being around children and working with
children. She worked in a day camp during the summer teaching arts
and crafts to five- and six-year-old children. Although she had some
interest in painting and in clay sculpture, she really enjoyed her work
with the children. She liked the fact that they got so much enjoyment
out of the pictures and clay objects they made to show their parents.
Katie really looked forward to her summer work at the day camp, but
not her work during the school year at a fast-food restaurant. For the
last three years, Katie had worked at three different fast food chains.
Unfortunately, each seemed worse to her than the one before. She
found the work boring and unpleasant. When she had worked in the
kitchen, she disliked the hot stoves and the pressure to make sandwiches
so quickly during the rush times. When she was at the cash register,
waiting on customers seemed too superficial, and she found herself saying the same things over and over again.

In high school, Katie did well. She got As in English and history
courses. She received an A in biology, a B in physics, and a C in chemistry. She found that she liked her science courses even more than she
liked English and history. Chemistry started out being alright, but she
felt it was too difficult, and she questioned her ability to do chemistry in
college. Biology particularly appealed to her. She enjoyed learning about
the physiology of different animals and processes like osmosis. When she
got to college, she took a biology course freshman year and found it difficult but very interesting because it went into more depth than her high
school biology course had. Because biology was difficult, she decided
that she would major in history. What concerned her about history, however, was that it didn't seem to relate very much to what she might do.
Although it was fairly interesting, she did not think that she would want
to teach it in high school.

When Katie was a high school senior she had volunteered to work
in a hospital. Mainly, what she did was to wheel a cart full of magazines
around from room to room. What she enjoyed most about doing this
were the times she got to talk to the patients. She didn't have time to do
that type of volunteer work in college, but wished she did. What she also
missed from high school was field hockey. She had played field hockey
for three years in high school and really enjoyed it. Some of her closest

friends were girls that she had met when she first started to play field hockey. During her senior year, she also had the opportunity to do a little bit of coaching at a field hockey clinic, something that she liked a lot. When she was able to do something that felt like she was helping some-one feel better, then the activity became meaningful, even if it might seem boring to others. For example, pushing a cart of magazines might seem boring, but that really had little to do with what she liked about it. She enjoyed the patients and listening to them.

I found it helpful to use Holland's typology and Work Adjustment Theory to organize all the information that Katie gave me. From the perspective of Holland's theory, it seemed that several of Katie's interests and personality characteristics fit the Social description. She was inter-ested in helping other people, particularly children, and enjoyed being around others and talking to them about their lives. Also, she seemed to enjoy figuring out puzzles and trying to understand solutions to scientific problems. The Investigative category seemed to fit her interests rather well, and her personality somewhat because she seemed more Social than Investigative. Although we talked about several other interests and activities, it seemed that Social and Investigative categories fit her better than the others did. When I thought of her values in terms of Work Adjustment Theory, Altruism and Achievement seemed to be important. She really did want to do things for other people and seemed to value helping others with their problems. She also enjoyed the challenge of science and wanted to feel like she was accomplishing something, mak-ing use of her scientific ability. True, she was afraid of difficult challenges (chemistry), but she wanted to learn and apply her learning to something that would help others.

Although this information was useful, both Katie and I wanted to get more detailed information about her interests, values, and her view of her abilities. I assigned her the Strong Interest Inventory and SIGI PLUS. The Strong Interest Inventory compares the interests of the student with those of men and women in about 100 occupations who are successful and enjoying their work. SIGI PLUS is a computer pro-gram that matches students' values, interests, and preferred activities with more than 300 occupations. Using SIGI PLUS, Katie was able to rate her values, interests, and preferred activities so that she could find which jobs matched them. This gave her an opportunity to learn about some occupations that she had never even thought about. Some careers that she wanted to learn more about were rehabilitation coun-selor, employment counselor, preschool worker, recreation worker, social worker, psychologist, physician's assistant, nurse, optometrist, dietician, occupational therapist, physical therapist, speech pathologist, audiologist, and veterinarian. Although this might seem like a long list, Katie wanted to learn more about all these occupations and was excited about the prospect of finding some career alternatives that would appeal to her.

Although you do not have access to tests and interest inventory information here, you can review your answers to the questions that were asked after each of the previous four sections so that you can develop a list of occupations to explore. I've divided occupational information into thirteen categories that will be used in the next section about occupational information. Now, it would be helpful for you to choose two or three categories (more if you wish) that most closely fit your personality, interests, values, and abilities. You need to be interested in only a few aspects of a category to choose it, not all in aspects.

**Q 3.11** Write down the categories and occupations that you are interested in learning more about.

TABLE **3.1**   **OCCUPATIONAL CATEGORIES**

| Category | Characteristics | Types of occupations |
|---|---|---|
| 1. Science, Engineering, and Math | Analyzing, investigating, computing | Biologists, chemists, geologists, engineers, architects, drafters, computer operators and programmers, mathematicians and operations research managers. |
| 2. Health | Investigating and diagnosing health problems; helping people with physical problems. | Physicians, nurses, medical assistants, dentists, dental assistants, optometrists, lab technicians, dieticians, health service managers, pharmacists, and veterinarians. |
| 3. Social Service | Helping people with personal, recreational, or religious concerns or problems. | Counselors, preschool workers, psychiatrists, psychologists, recreation workers, social workers, and ministers. |
| 4. Education, Library, and Museum Work | Teaching others, providing or helping others use information, organizing information or valuable objects | Teachers, principals, college faculty, museum curators, and librarians. |
| 5. Communication and the Arts | Communicating with others through broadcasting, public relations, reporting, writing, designing, photographing, drawing, painting, acting, dancing, or singing. | Broadcast technicians, radio announcers, public relations specialists, reporters, writers, fashion designers, hair stylists, photojournalists, graphic artists, actors, dancers, musicians. |
| 6. Government and Protective Service | Making laws, advocating a point of view, learning laws, enforcing laws, planning cities, and studying large groups of people. | Legislators, lawyers, paralegals, judges, sociologists, urban planners, fire fighters, detectives, and guards. |
| 7. Agriculture and Forestry | Interest in nature, growing plants, or the outdoors. | Agricultural scientists, farm equipment mechanics, farm managers, gardeners, fishers, foresters, and loggers. |
| 8. Travel and Transportation | Flying or driving; operating bulldozers, trains, or ships; making travel plans or reservations for others. | Pilots, aircraft controllers, flight attendants, bus drivers, truck drivers, captains of a ship, locomotive engineers, and reservation and travel agents. |
| 9. Business | Interest in managing, selling, buying or persuading others; organizing or consulting on business problems, or working with personnel problems. | Accountants, budget analysts, industrial engineers, economists, financial managers, production managers, employment interviewers, consultants, manufacturer's representatives, retail sales workers, insurance agents, hotel managers, and real estate agents. |

*(continues)*

TABLE **3.1**    **OCCUPATIONAL CATEGORIES** *(CONTINUED)*

| Category | Characteristics | Types of occupations |
|---|---|---|
| **10. Clerical or Secretarial** | Collect, process, and file data, often using a computer; make appointments, take messages, contact clients. | Claim representatives, bank tellers, bookkeepers, cashiers, dispatchers, file clerks, postal clerks, receptionists, secretaries, stock clerks, and telephone operators. |
| **11. Construction** | Construct or build, use power tools, work outside (sometimes), do physically demanding work. | Construction managers and inspectors, bricklayers, carpenters, carpet installers, electricians, glaziers, painters, plumbers, roofers, and iron makers. |
| **12. Mechanics, Installation, and Repair** | Install or repair aircraft, cars, machines, communications equipment, elevators, air conditioning, musical instruments, or heavy equipment; can include heavy lifting and work in hot, cold, or dirty buildings. | Aircraft mechanics, auto mechanics, diesel mechanics, elevator installers, line installers, millwrights, telephone installers, and vending machine repairers. |
| **13. Manufacturing and Industrial Work** | Assembling, constructing, welding, and operating machines and equipment in industry. | Boilermakers, machinists, numerical control tool programmers, tool and die makers, welders, stationary engineers, and wastewater treatment plant operators. |

# OBTAINING KNOWLEDGE ABOUT THE WORLD OF WORK

The second step of the trait and factor model of choosing careers is to learn about occupations. Because occupational information can not be provided in this book, I will tell you where you can get more information and the kinds of information that might be helpful to you in learning about careers. Then, we will discuss the labor market, some growth trends for certain occupations, and other changes that are helpful to know about. Next, I will describe how Katie looked for information about some of the occupations that she thought she might be interested in.

Career information can be found in public and college libraries, career services offices, and in bookstores. Because the U.S. Department of Labor is continually researching and updating data about occupations, *Occupational Outlook Handbook* is an excellent source of occupational information. More information that specializes in career information is available in a number of pamphlets, books, and other resources published by commercial publishers and professional organizations.

You will find it helpful to know many characteristics of occupations. I will describe several of them here, then describe some places where you could look to find more occupational information (Sharf, 1993).

- **Description.** Most written occupational information describes how people typically do their work, where they work, and the tools or

---

## Problems and Solutions

---

### What is important information to learn about an occupation?

- Description
- Education
- Salary
- Working conditions
- Qualifications
- How to enter an occupation
- How to advance in an occupation
- Opportunities for underrepresented groups
- Job outlook

---

equipment they use. If new technologies are developing that affect the kind of work to be done, these trends are often described as well. Because those who are just starting out in an occupation are likely to be given less responsibility and less difficult tasks than more experienced workers are, changing job duties are explained. Work can also vary within the same occupation from company to company. In small organizations or businesses, individuals often have many responsibilities, whereas in large organizations, individuals might specialize and only do a few different tasks.

- **Education.** In some occupations, there are different ways to get necessary education or training. Some of the educational resources include home study courses, government training programs, the armed forces, formal training offered by employers, two-year community colleges, and four-year colleges and universities.
- **Salary.** Many salary listings include beginning, average, and top salaries earned in an occupation. Earnings are often difficult to summarize, as they differ from company to company, region to region, and responsibility to responsibility. Some workers are paid an annual salary, whereas others receive a commission based on a percentage of what they sell; still others are paid for an event or performance. Sometimes combinations of these are used to determine salary. Earnings tend to be higher in cities than rural areas. There are likely to be differences between regions based on the demand for workers in a particular occupation. Generally, the higher the salary, the greater

are the expectations regarding level of responsibility, amount of education, and experience.

Benefits can be considered a part of earnings. Included in benefits are vacations, health insurance, and retirement pensions. Sometimes there are benefits specific to an occupation, such as meal and housing allowances, reduced travel fares, use of a company car, or discounts on merchandise.

- **Working conditions.** Work conditions vary widely. Outdoor work, especially, can mean exposure to heat, cold, humidity, dirt, wind, rain, or other difficult conditions. Indoor work also varies considerably. Sometimes the work environment is clean and well lit; at other times, people must operate in cramped, cold, or hot conditions. Another important aspect of working conditions involves interaction with co-workers, customers, and supervisors. In some occupations, these relationships might be uncomfortable; in other occupations, these relationships might be a very positive part of the job. In some occupations, individuals tend to work alone, or they might work when others are not working. For example, dancers and actors often work in the evenings and on weekends, whereas many other people work a more traditional 40-hour week. In some services and industries, it is necessary to have 24-hour coverage, so some people work a day shift, an evening shift, or a late-night shift at various times of the year. A working condition that some employers now have introduced is periodic, required drug testing.

- **Qualifications.** In addition to a specified level of education, some occupations have other work requirements, such as weight or height requirements and minimum age requirements. Still other requirements involve physical abilities such as strength, endurance, good vision, hearing, or color perception. It is illegal to discriminate against individuals because or their age, sex, race, or unrelated disability. Therefore, employers must have a specific reason for having qualifications.

- **Entrance.** You can enter an occupation in a variety of ways. Sometimes individuals must take an examination; sometimes they must join a union. In some cases, they must have money to open their own businesses. How you apply to an employer can differ depending on the occupation.

- **Advancement.** Advancement varies greatly within occupations. Some occupations have specific career ladders with expected educational and salary levels; in other occupations the career ladder is less clear. Some occupations require specific certification or degrees before you can advance. In others, advancement is based on performance such as sales, quality of the work, or more subjective variables.

- **Opportunities for underrepresented groups.** Some occupations are noted for actively recruiting women or minorities.
- **Additional information.** Often, free or inexpensive sources of additional information are listed in brochures and books. Such sources can include unions, professional associations, and government agencies.
- **Job outlook.** The federal government, as well as other agencies, makes projections about growth and occupations based on assumptions about the growth of the labor force, the rate of employment, the rate of inflation, the amount of foreign trade, changes in defense spending, and other factors. Unanticipated political and world events can render these projections inaccurate. Estimates are made about the number of people who will leave an occupation to enter another one, advance, retire, or die. As some industries grow, certain occupations will be more in demand than others. Advances in technology can also mean changes in some occupations, obsolescence in others, or growth of new occupations. In the next section, I will describe some general features of the labor market and some recent changes.

## *The Labor Market*

**labor market** The process by which the needs of citizens of a state, nation, or world are met through employment.

A **labor market** fulfills the needs of citizens of a state, a nation, or the world. These needs can include food, shelter, clothing, health services, transportation, entertainment, fire and police protection, and so forth. When the demand for these services or products is high, there will be job availability in that area. When demand is low, there will be less job availability.

I will discuss some of the more significant changes that are occurring in the labor market. Particularly, I will focus on two related changes, the growth of the service sector and the development of technological advances. Other issues in the labor market are the growth in temporary jobs, the increase in the number of dual-career couples, and the "boundaryless" career.

*The Service Sector and Technology.* For many years, the greatest growth in the labor market has been in the service area. This area generally includes health, business, education, social services, engineering, and other services; it does not include goods-producing industries or agriculture. During the last 75 years, there has been a marked change in the United States, with a gradual movement from manufacturing, agricultural, and mining industries to an increased demand for workers in service industries. Much of this change is the result of technological efficiencies in goods-producing industries, which need many fewer workers than in the past. The automobile industry, with its use of robotic arms and computer technology, is an example of how technological change can slow employment growth in an industry.

## Problems and Solutions

*What important changes are taking place in the job market that I should be aware of when I look for a job?*

- More service jobs
- New jobs in technology
- New technological changes in most jobs
- More temporary workers
- More dual-earner couples
- Fewer boundaries in job descriptions

The availability of computers in the workplace has changed it greatly. Computers have been used to automate jobs in many areas of manufacturing. This includes the auto industry, printing, furniture making, iron and steel manufacturing, and a wide range of other industries. Computers have also made it easier for people to do their work. Word processors, spreadsheet programs, and the Internet allow people to automate many clerical functions and help people communicate more easily with each other. As computers perform more clerical tasks, those in secretarial positions who perform only clerical tasks risk having their jobs automated. With the easy access of e-mail and the Internet, individuals can work at many places: on an airplane, in a hotel room, or in their homes. Thus, technology is a double-edged sword, making it easier for some people to do their work, but threatening the work of others who perform tasks that can be automated or computerized. The trends in future growth in the United States are summarized in Figure 3.2, which shows the increase in professional specialties, technicians, and service.

Projecting growth in the United States economy to 2005, government projections (U.S. Department of Labor, 1997–1998) show that many of the growing occupations do not require a college education. As Figure 3.3 shows, eight of the ten occupations with the most projected growth require a high school education or less. Only registered nurses (second) and systems analysts (tenth) usually have a four-year bachelor's degree requirement. Occupations such as janitor, salesperson, and cashier often have a high turnover. Individuals leave them for a variety of reasons: to find a better paying job, to return to school, to care for children, and so forth. Thus growth reflects the need to replace these workers as well as to create new

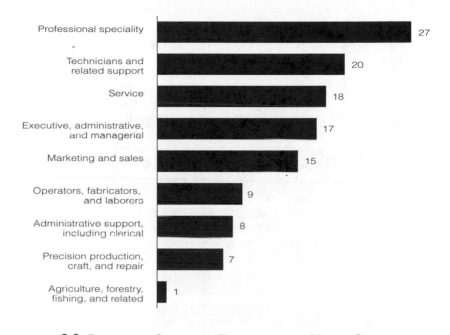

FIGURE **3.2** **PROJECTED CHANGE IN EMPLOYMENT BY MAJOR OCCUPATIONAL GROUP, 1996-2006, PERCENTS.**

(From *Occupational Outlook Quarterly*, U.S. Department of Labor Bureau of Labor Statistics, Washington, D.C., 1997–1998, p. 9.)

positions ("The American Workforce," 1993). The occupations listed in Figure 3.3 represent more than half of the projected total employment growth of occupations in the United States. The other 475 occupations surveyed by the Bureau of Labor Statistics represent the other half. Many of the jobs that are listed in Figure 3.3 also have low earnings, a factor related to having high replacement needs. Note that virtually all the occupations are service rather than manufacturing occupations.

***Temporary Employment.*** Many corporations are trying to restructure or economize so that they can become more globally competitive. As corporations eliminate large numbers of permanent jobs, they often replace them with temporary workers or with consulting contracts with temporary agencies or consulting firms. Because part-time workers usually do not receive benefits such as health insurance and pension plans, companies can save money. By having fewer employees, and more part-time workers or consultants, corporations can respond more quickly to changes in a worldwide market. Although professionals can make good incomes by doing consulting or part-time work, most temporary workers do not get high wages and

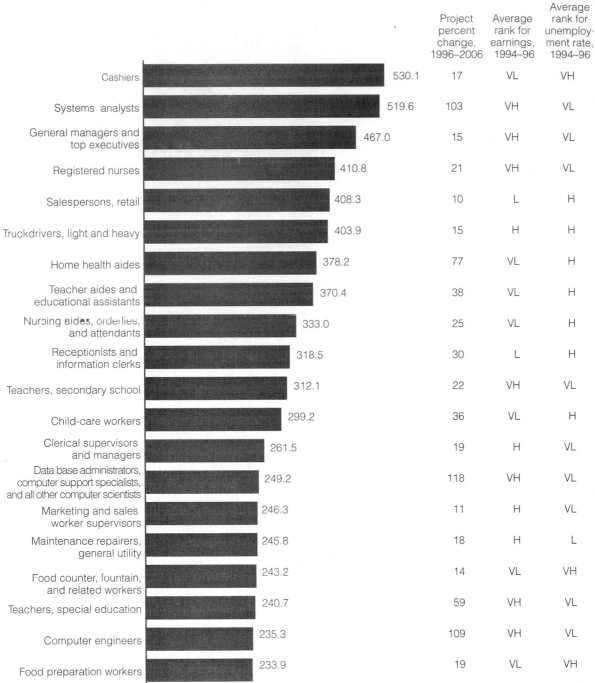

| | Project percent change, 1996–2006 | Average rank for earnings, 1994–96 | Average rank for unemployment rate, 1994–96 |
|---|---|---|---|
| Cashiers — 530.1 | 17 | VL | VH |
| Systems analysts — 519.6 | 103 | VH | VL |
| General managers and top executives — 467.0 | 15 | VH | VL |
| Registered nurses — 410.8 | 21 | VH | VL |
| Salespersons, retail — 408.3 | 10 | L | H |
| Truckdrivers, light and heavy — 403.9 | 15 | H | H |
| Home health aides — 378.2 | 77 | VL | H |
| Teacher aides and educational assistants — 370.4 | 38 | VL | H |
| Nursing aides, orderlies, and attendants — 333.0 | 25 | VL | H |
| Receptionists and information clerks — 318.5 | 30 | L | H |
| Teachers, secondary school — 312.1 | 22 | VH | VL |
| Child-care workers — 299.2 | 36 | VL | H |
| Clerical supervisors and managers — 261.5 | 19 | H | VL |
| Data base administrators, computer support specialists, and all other computer scientists — 249.2 | 118 | VH | VL |
| Marketing and sales worker supervisors — 246.3 | 11 | H | VL |
| Maintenance repairers, general utility — 245.8 | 18 | H | L |
| Food counter, fountain, and related workers — 243.2 | 14 | VL | VH |
| Teachers, special education — 240.7 | 59 | VH | VL |
| Computer engineers — 235.3 | 109 | VH | VL |
| Food preparation workers — 233.9 | 19 | VL | VH |

VH = very high; H = high; L = low; VL = very low

FIGURE **3.3** NUMERICAL GROWTH BY OCCUPATION (IN THOUSANDS), PROJECTED FOR **1996–2006.**

(From *Occupational Outlook Quarterly*, U.S. Department of Labor, Washington, DC, 1997–1998, p. 15.)

must have multiple jobs to make a satisfactory living. Benefits such as health and pension plans often are not available to part-time workers. Some experts believe that the number of temporary workers will increase to more than 50 percent of the workforce by the year 2000 (Morrow, 1993).

***Dual-Earner Couples.*** In 1975, 31 percent of women with children younger than 3 years old were employed outside the home, but in 1994, almost 60 percent of mothers with children younger than 3 years old were employed outside the home (U.S. Bureau of the Census, 1995). As more and more women enter the work force, this has implications for child raising and gender roles (discussed in Chapter 8).

**boundaryless career** A career that might have frequent job rotations, temporary assignments, and transfers from one part of a company to another.

***The "Boundaryless" Career.*** The **"boundaryless" career** is one in which there might be frequent job rotations, temporary assignments, and transfers from one part of a company to another, making the experience of transitions more frequent than in the past (Mirvis & Hall, 1994). Thus, individuals are less likely to feel a sense of security as they are transferred from one task to another. Because some people can work at home using the computer to stay in touch with the office, the physical boundaries will change, as some work is done at home and other work is done at the office. Although the home is becoming more like the office, in some companies, the office is becoming more like the home. One example is on-site day care being provided to attract dual-earner families.

To describe how some of this information can be used, let us return to Katie, who had a long list of occupations that she wanted to find more about.

First, if she wanted to, Katie could look at brief information on almost 300 occupations described in the SIGI PLUS computer program. Because she used the self-assessment section first, she only needed to look at about 25. Although she used SIGI PLUS, she could have used any number of other commercial computerized career counseling programs such as DISCOVER because they have similar information. As she read about occupations, Katie became increasingly interested in those in the health area. Although not interested in research positions, she was interested in occupations where she could help others, particularly occupational therapy, physical therapy, recreational therapy, speech pathology, and audiology. After she read information about these on SIGI PLUS, she followed up by reading pamphlets in a career library that described each of these occupations in detail.

When we talked about the occupations that she had learned about, it became clear that not only was she enthusiastic about some possibilities, but that she had a much greater knowledge of potential occupations than she had previously. Between our sessions, she continued to read a few books that described a variety of health-related occupations. Then, she talked to academic advisors who were familiar with physical therapy, occupational therapy, and speech pathology. In this way, she was prepared to make a well-informed choice about her preference for career options.

## INTEGRATING INFORMATION ABOUT ONESELF AND THE WORLD OF WORK

Putting it all together and making choices is the focus of the third step. Now that a person knows about his or her personality, interests, values, and ability and has used that information to learn about occupations that match those traits, choices can be made. The process of choosing is not done only once in a lifetime. Rather, this is an ongoing process. Once individuals have made choices about career alternatives, they often reconsider and reevaluate the choices as they advance in their occupation or change occupations. When individuals are still in college, they can choose some alternatives that will allow them to get more information later in their college careers before they make a decision. For example, an individual who is choosing between being a lawyer and a manufacturer's representative does not really need to make that choice until she graduates. Because many majors will prepare a person for being a manufacturer's representative and many majors are appropriate for applying to law school, that decision can be made later than can the choice to be a chemical engineer, which is usually made during the first, or possibly second year of college. Having alternatives, rather than one choice is often very helpful. There is not just one ideal job for most people. Often someone can be satisfied by a variety of occupations. Further, individuals can select an occupation that is close to what they want and then work toward getting their first choice. Thus, it is not necessary to narrow the focus so much that if you don't get what you want, you will accept no other alternative.

People differ in their decision-making strategies. Some are quite indecisive and delay or procrastinate in making a decision, sometimes because they are not sure of themselves and their ability to make a decision. Others are used to doing what they are told and might comply with another's wishes, usually a parent. For example, a person might decide that he will be an engineer because his father wants him to, rather than because his self-assessment points in that direction. Still others make an intuitive decision, one made on hunches. This approach works best when it is supplemented by an analysis of your own abilities and interests. Other people choose impulsively, not giving much thought to their future career decisions. Different styles of career decision making are not static. In other words, when people first start making career choices, they often use a more delaying style, but as they get older, their approaches might be more planful and they might take advantage of both their feelings (an intuitive approach) and knowledge of their own personality, interests, values, and abilities (Dinklage, 1968).

Making choices about the future is difficult. Making tentative choices that are just for practice are not quite so difficult. In the following exercise, try to match some information about yourself with some occupations that you are considering. It would be helpful to take some occupations from the previous exercise on page 65 (you can add others if you wish) and then note some of your characteristics, interests, values, or abilities that would seem to fit with those occupations.

Occupation                    Personality, Interests, Abilities, and Values

_____

_____

_____

_____

_____

_____

_____

In trying to decide about careers that she might pursue, Katie thought a lot about what she had learned about occupations. She was surprised about how the knowledge of physiology was required in occupations like occupational therapy and speech pathology. The idea of combining her interest in biology with working with children and helping them was very appealing. In performing the job duties for these three occupations, she would be able to do those things that she valued. She felt that she was a patient person, who could figure out answers that weren't easily forthcoming. Often, when children have medical problems, it is hard for them to describe what is wrong with them. During her spring vacation, Katie was able to go back to the hospital where she had volunteered and talk with people who were in the three occupations that seemed interesting to her. She was able to learn more about graduate schools, and more important, more about the kinds of work that these people did. In fact, two of them let her observe their work with certain patients.

After spring vacation, we talked about her experience observing an occupational therapist and a physical therapist. Katie was able to picture herself in both of these positions. She also learned a lot from her visit with a speech pathologist and could see herself doing that as well. In fact, she had arranged to sit in and observe the speech pathologist later. Observing others at work is sometimes referred to as "job shadowing," and some schools offer "day on the job" programs that allow students to watch a person at work during a day.

She had made excellent progress by greatly narrowing down the list of career alternatives that she still wished to know more about. The requirements for entering graduate school for each area are rather similar, so it was necessary that Katie only take certain biology and other science courses to be eligible for the graduate programs. Of course, she was aware that her grade point average needed to be high, especially for physical therapy. Although Katie was planning on returning to the day camp as an assistant director this summer, a new position that she was looking forward to, she felt that she would have time to volunteer in the hospital to assist in each of her areas of interest. She wanted an answer to her question about which of the three areas she thought she might wish to pursue, but she realized that this answer might have to wait. Although Katie had more decisions to make about her future career plans, she was excited that she had a good sense of where she was headed. The feelings of being lost and confused were now minimal.

When you are trying to make career decisions, a number of organizational resources are available to help you. One of these is the job fair, where employers set up booths to describe available jobs. Talking to representatives of companies can help you learn more about occupations, as well as about the company itself. Although company representatives vary in their knowledge about occupations, this is a very convenient source because often there are between 20 and 500 companies represented. Another resource is to talk to people about their work so that you can learn first hand what it's like to work in a particular occupation. This also has another advantage in that you can develop contacts for a future job search—networking. Volunteer and part-time work are excellent ways to learn more about job duties. With volunteer work, even though you aren't paid, you might have greater flexibility in your duties and more time to talk to full-time employees about their work than if you were doing paid work. Nevertheless, either volunteer or part-time work gives you an opportunity to observe and talk to people in a variety of jobs. Sometimes you can ask people about how work in one particular setting compares with work in another setting. These resources help you learn more about occupations and can give you time to think about the type of work that you are doing (or that others around you are doing) and how that fits with your own interests, values, and abilities.

Available on almost every college campus are resources for helping you decide about career directions. Often these resources, such as counseling centers and career services centers, provide career testing and occupational information, along with career counseling. In addition to helping you make choices about careers and majors, these offices can also help you when you're ready to find a summer job and a more permanent job after graduation.

# IMPLEMENTING A CHOICE

The process of getting a job is considered a job in itself. Depending on the field, many individuals will devote five or more hours per week for many weeks while they are at school or working, to find a new position. Because the process of finding a job often involves being turned down many times before you receive a job offer, the process can be discouraging. In health and engineering fields, where there are a relatively large number of opportunities, this is less likely to be true than in more competitive areas such as business and, especially, the arts (writing, reporting, acting, singing, and dancing). There are three significant aspects to finding a job: job search strategies, résumé writing, and job interviewing.

## *Job Search Strategies*

When you have chosen an occupation that you want, it is helpful to decide which employer you would like to work for. If you are going to be an engineer, you might think about the size of the company, the types of products they make, and other significant factors. If you are going to be a teacher, you might ask what type of school you would like to work for, and what educational philosophy appeals to you. Questions such as these are specific to the occupational specialty that you are in. Other questions, such as what part of the country you wish to work in, and where you want to live (rural or urban) are important questions for most job seekers.

Probably the first place to visit before starting a job search is a university or college career resource center or career placement office. Often, these centers have services that alumni can use, such as forwarding transcripts and letters of reference. These centers probably also have workshops on how to look for a job, write résumés, and conduct job interviews.

One approach to the job search on which virtually all experts agree is the importance of networking. By talking to friends, previous employers, friends of friends, friends of parents, teachers, associates of employers, and so forth and letting them know what you are interested in doing, you can get good job leads. By conducting an "informational interview—interviewing people who are already working in a job that is similar to one that you would like—you can find out more about the field. Usually, it is not appropriate to ask these sources for a job, rather your purpose should be to learn more about the job and the type of work that is being done in that area currently. Often this process is much more helpful than newspaper want ads are. Want ads tend to be more helpful for jobs that are in demand, such as for certain areas of computer programming or engineering. A good source for job search strategies is *What Color Is Your Parachute? A Practical Manual for*

---

## Problems and Solutions

---

### What are the essentials of finding a job?

- Develop appropriate job search strategies.
- Write a résumé.
- Learn how to interview for a job.

---

*Job-Hunters and Career-Changers* by Richard Bolles (1999). This book has been updated annually and is written in a humorous style with many helpful suggestions on job hunting that include on-line resources.

### The Résumé

The purpose of your résumé is not to get a job for you, but rather to get you a job interview. A good résumé should communicate your qualifications for a position. There are different styles of résumés for different fields. A relatively inexpensive investment is a résumé book that describes how to write a résumé and gives many samples of résumés. Often you can find a book that shows you how to write résumés in your own field.

Not all job-search experts believe that a résumé is useful in getting a job. Bolles (1999) questions the value of a résumé, whether it is made available on paper or on-line. He believes many employers ignore résumés and that networking is much more effective than is a résumé in finding a job. Most college students, however, develop a résumé as part of their job search process.

Some characteristics of résumés are almost universal. It is essential that there be no typographical errors. Therefore, it is helpful to have a few people check over your résumé—"spell check" is not sufficient. Most résumés are one or two pages long, especially for recent college graduates, who are likely to have relatively little experience. Résumés should only contain information that is relevant to a job. In fact, when individuals are applying for several different types of positions, they should consider having two or more résumés for different positions. For example, if a person wants a job as an administrator in a college and is applying for a Dean of Students position and an admissions office position, these two résumés need different emphasis. With the possible exception of advertising and commercial art careers, the résumé is not an opportunity to be creative; rather, it is an opportunity to present information about yourself as specifically as possible in a short amount of space. The amount of information you are conveying can help you decide what type size and style to use. Uniformity of style is important. Don't use too many different type sizes.

The cover letter that accompanies your résumé is an opportunity to explain why you are qualified for the position. Often the cover letter will suggest a follow-up interview so you can more fully present your background experiences. Generally in a cover letter, you first state why you are writing and the position you are applying for. Then you discuss why you are interested in working for the employer and your reasons for wanting to do this type of work. This is the place to mention your particular achievements or qualifications for the job. Making reference to your résumé is also appropriate. Then it is helpful to explain where you can be reached and your interest in having an interview.

## Interviewing for a Job

Developing effective interview techniques takes time. Some career centers have video cameras available that allow you to practice your interview approach and to get feedback from professionals. Being prepared for a job interview is essential. You should learn as much as possible about the company and the position beforehand. The interviewer will be evaluating not only your answer to his or her questions but also the kinds of questions that you ask about the company. Having answers to questions that employers are likely to ask can help you feel more prepared and less nervous. You are likely to want to appear confident, enthusiastic, and ambitious, so knowledge about the company and ideas about what you are likely to be asked will help you feel more relaxed.

The opportunity to interview with an employer gives you an opportunity to ask questions about the company. During the interview, you should be able to find out more about the type of work done and the amount of responsibility that you will have. Companies differ in the opportunities that they offer to help you develop your interests and to build on your education and experience. Some will be more permissive than others in allowing you to express your own creativity in developing ideas and methods. Whereas some employers offer a great variety of work assignments to new employees, others do not. Companies also vary in the amount of support they give to employees for participation in seminars and in making administrative decisions.

Finding out about how companies operate is helpful. Some employers are expanding into new types of production and services, whereas others are declining in production and sales. Some industries traditionally work with very large contracts; if a contract is not obtained or is canceled, layoffs can be substantial. Thus, some companies might be hiring for temporary rather than for permanent work. Related to the operation of a company are opportunities for advancement. Entry jobs might be different from other jobs that are further along on the career ladder.

In a job interview, salary is not likely to be discussed. This subject usually comes up after a job offer has been made. That is when it is appropriate to discuss salaries and how raises are made. Benefits should be considered a part of salary as well; examples are health benefits, dental benefits, pensions, employee investment programs, and other services.

To have an organized and planful approach to finding a job, it is important to be clear about what you want to do. In that way, the last phase of the career search process, implementing a choice, follows from the three steps of trait and factor theory.

## SUMMARY

With thousands of different occupations available in the United States, the process of choosing a career is complex and time consuming. In this chapter, I described the three steps of trait and factor theory that provide a good overview of the career choice process.

The first step is an assessment of your own personality, interests, values, and abilities. Holland's description of six types of personality and interests provide a start for assessing yourself (Realistic, Investigative, Artistic, Social, Enterprising, and Conventional). Lofquist and Dawis suggest a broad way of categorizing work values into six categories (Achievement, Comfort, Status, Altruism, Safety, and Autonomy). Ability, aptitude, and achievement are different concepts used in evaluating skills. However, factors external to the individual, such as where you live and how much money you have for educational costs, are important. Assessing your personality, interests, values, and abilities help you find occupations that can be divided into 13 different categories.

In the second step, this information is used to guide your search for occupational information. Occupational information is available from a variety of sources that includes pamphlets, books, counseling professionals, and those who are already working. Written information includes description, education, salary, working conditions, qualifications, how to enter an occupation, how to advance, the labor market, and job opportunities. When these two steps are completed, you can take the third step.

By integrating information about your personality, interests, values, and abilities with information about occupations, you can make decisions about career alternatives. Then, you will be in a good position to start the job search process by planning strategies to find job opportunities, by writing a résumé, and by having job interviews.

# RECOMMENDED READINGS

*What Color is Your Parachute? A practical manual for job-hunters and career-changers*
Bolles, R. N. (Ten Speed Press, 1999)

>This book has been updated yearly for more than 20 years and is probably the best-known book for job hunters and career changers. The first part of the book contains information about assessing yourself and looking for jobs. The second part of the book is directed toward those with unique interests, such as college students, women, minorities, and gays. Bolles also includes information about starting your own business and working overseas. Pictures and charts help to make this a lively, interesting book. Many of the topics deal with networking, finding jobs, and how to get hired.

*Occupational Outlook Handbook (OOH)*
U. S. Bureau of Labor Statistics (2000)

>Containing information about more than 250 occupations, this book is probably the best-known and most-respected single source of occupational information. Included are the job description, working conditions, educational requirements, future employment, salary, and where to find further information. This information is also available on the Web at http://stats.bls.gov/ocohome.htm.

# RECOMMENDED WEB SITES

*The Catapult on JOB WEB*
http://www.jobweb.org/catapult/catapult.htm

>The National Association of Colleges and Employers has assembled a comprehensive set of resources for both students and career guidance professionals. The site includes information about job searching, employment listings, educational updating, and college and university based resources.

*Careers.wsj.com*
http://careers.wsj.com/

>Compiled by an editorial team using Dow Jones information sources (including the *Wall Street Journal*), this site contains both daily updates of employment issues and more than 1,000 job-seeking and employment articles. Students can find an extraordinary wealth of tips and strategies on résumé and cover letter preparation, effective interviewing, and similar practical matters.

# ADJUSTING TO WORK

When people are working full-time, about half of each waking day is spent working. After a person has taken a job, several problems and concerns can arise about the job itself including boredom on the job, problems with coworkers or supervisors, difficult or vague assignments, and unpleasant working conditions. In addition, the types of activities and interests that individuals have can be very different than what is asked of them on the job. Sometimes unexpected developments occur: There is an accident at the work place, someone is fired, or someone experiences sexual harassment. These possibilities sound negative, but work is also an opportunity to experience a deep sense of fulfillment. Work allows for a sense of accomplishment, for being rewarded for efforts, for helping others in a variety of ways, and for the enjoyment of working with people that are respected, as well as making money. Because adjusting to work is such a large part of the life of so many people, we will discuss work adjustment from several different points of view.

In this chapter, we will look at work in a broad sense. Work can include full-time jobs but also part-time work, volunteer work, and summer, or temporary work. Most individuals have had work experience, so the issues that are discussed here can be related to your own experience. You should be able to get new insights into issues and problems at work by applying some of the points of view that are explained here.

## ADJUSTING TO A NEW JOB

Once a choice of an occupation or job has been made, the issue of adjusting to the choice arises. Tiedeman and O'Hara (1963) describe three phases of adjusting to a new job or work. The length of these three phases (induction, reformation, and integration) depends on the complexity of the job, the number and type of co-workers, and the variety of assignments. These phases of adjusting to a choice focus particularly on the interaction with other people, co-workers, superiors, and subordinates. In order to carry out job assignments, people need to talk to supervisors, colleagues, customers, sales people, or others. The phases of adjusting to a choice are described here, along with Tammy's adjustment to her new job.

### Induction

**induction** The beginning process of a new job or course.

Beginning something new is the basic concept of **induction.** In this phase, an individual starts something new such as a job, a second part-time job, or an adult education course that can lead to job advancement. During the beginning process of the new job or course, the individual will change depending on how much commitment she or he has made to the new activity. If you think of the first day that you spent on a job, you were probably getting acclimated to your responsibilities and the new

---

## Problems and Solutions

---

### *How do you know what to expect when you start a job?*

You can expect to go through three different stages of adjustment: Induction, reformation, and integration.

---

people you met. Although you might not have been particularly tense, you probably were alert and listening carefully to the new instructions that you were given.

> Just before the Christmas selling season began, Tammy decided that she needed to work to buy presents for her family. Also, she was not sure whether she wanted to return to her community college after she finished her first year at the school, transfer, or just get a job. Because she had mainly "Bs" in math and science and "As" in her other college courses, she wasn't sure what to do. Getting a job in a drug store that was part of a large national chain seemed like a good idea to her. She had heard from friends that you can get promoted to an assistant manager position.
>
> During her first day of work, Ralph, the 25-year-old assistant manager, told her about her responsibilities. She was to stock the cosmetic shelves and put merchandise that had been pulled out of the shelf back. Later she was told how to work with the food merchandise and how to put labels on the items that were to be put out to be sold. As she talked to Ralph, she felt her voice get higher and thinner. She was worried about all the new information that she was getting from him. Ralph seemed to talk very fast. He was a short, heavyset man who moved much more quickly than she would have thought. In fact, he went so fast at times as he told her what to do and how to price the merchandise and what happens if she priced it wrong that she found herself getting teary. When he was called away to another customer, Tammy was relieved and was able to compose herself and return to the reshelving. When Ralph came back, he said, "That's the idea." And went off again, not giving her a real sense of what was going to happen next.
>
> This was a difficult induction process for Tammy. She talked with very few co-workers the first day, and her main exposure was to Ralph. Tammy had started work on a Thursday evening and came in again on Saturday to work the whole day. Ralph was there again and told her how to handle sending out film for customers and how to use the cash

register. He would stay with her for a while, but then get called away. As the day ended, Tammy was more confident about what it was she was supposed to do, but found herself exhausted because she had been paying so much attention to getting things right.

For Tammy the induction process lasted about two weeks. She was working Tuesday and Thursday evenings and all day Saturday. By the time she got to work for her second Saturday at the drug store, she was more confident about what she was doing and had learned most of the major new tasks.

For Tammy, the induction phase lasted a few weeks; for others, it might last an hour, or, for those who do very complex work, it can last several months or even a year.

## *Reformation*

**reformation** The process that occurs with coworkers on a new job as individuals become more comfortable with them.

When individuals start a new job, they almost always work with coworkers, and a supervisor. Usually the people that new employees work with are new to them and new relationships need to be developed; this is **reformation.** Because of this, it is difficult to feel comfortable immediately about being a part of a group. Thus, many people are hesitant to join a group and to speak up with co-workers. This takes time.

Usually when Tammy was in the store in the evenings, there were three other workers. One was a manager or an assistant manager, one was usually a high school student, and a third was an older person, usually working a second job. Two additional people that she rarely saw worked in the pharmacy department. Generally, the same people tended to be there at the same times that she worked. However, because a number of students worked for the drug store, and they frequently changed their schedules, she was often with different people. In new situations, Tammy was often careful about speaking to others, and was rather quiet, although her friends who knew her well would not have described her that way.

Althea was a 37-year-old woman, divorced with three children. What Tammy soon learned was that Althea could be moody. When she was at the cash register and needed something, she was often sharp and quick. At other times, Althea could be fun. It took about three months for Tammy to feel comfortable with Althea and not to be afraid of her. Tammy found it easier with students her own age. Although they didn't have a lot of time to talk to each other because the assistant managers kept them busy, the students often would joke around when they had the opportunity. Because it was the holiday season, they usually had little time to talk to each other, especially on Saturdays when the store got really crowded.

For Tammy, the reformation period was fairly long and slow. Because she worked part-time rather than full-time, and often new people were working when she was, it took quite a while before she felt like a part of a group, rather than someone just working alone. Had she worked full-time with people who were there when she was, the reformation period might have taken a week or less. She might have felt more like she was part of a group than she did in the current situation. When the holiday season ended, it was a relief for Tammy, as she had less pressure on her to talk to customers, put things away, price material, and work the cash register. Then she got to know more of her coworkers and started to feel more comfortable in the job.

## *Integration*

**integration** The process of being comfortable with the work and coworkers, as one becomes familiar with a job.

When a job starts to become comfortable, the newness wears off, and **integration** into the group that individuals work with begins. Often there is less excitement about the job and fewer challenges. Coworkers start to know each other better and to accept each other. In relatively simple jobs, such as stocking jobs or sweeping floors, the integration process can start after a day or two. In large companies, where individuals work with people in many different groups or have long training periods, the integration process can take a much longer time.

> In January, the work at the drug store got slower and fewer people came in, especially on Saturdays. Whereas before Christmas, lots of people came in for stocking stuffers and inexpensive toys, now it was for the usual things—medicines, toothpaste, lipstick, and so forth. Work assignments that were new three months ago were now easy and accepted. Running the cash register, answering customer's questions, restocking shelves, putting merchandise away where it belonged, and pricing items were all tasks that seemed really easy to do. Now the job was starting to become repetitive and Tammy felt bored, particularly in the evenings. She had more time to chat with the high school students who worked there, and that was fun. This part of the job soon became the best part.

**Q 4.1** Describe a job that you have had using the phases of induction, reformation, and integration.

**Q 4.2** Compare the induction phase of two jobs, and explain how you reacted differently to them.

How a person responds to a job often depends on how long he or she has been working. Some enjoy a job for a few weeks, then lose interest quickly; others find that their job tasks differ greatly from month to month and that their work is stimulating, so they continue to enjoy their jobs. Others find the type of work they do to be exciting, and they look forward to it during their entire lifetimes. The value of Tiedeman and O'Hara's stage of adjusting to a choice is that it shows that changes can be expected when someone takes a new job. Although not everyone will experience induction, reformation, and integration, this model does provide a rather straightforward way to understand the process of adjusting to a new job.

# Self-Efficacy and Work Adjustment

**self-efficacy theory**
People's judgments about their own ability to complete tasks.

People differ in their views about their own potential effectiveness. **Self-efficacy theory,** developed by Albert Bandura (1986, 1997), is designed to make predictions about the way individuals make judgments that affect their lives. For example, a person who judges that she will do poorly on a math test or in a job interview might have a low sense of self-efficacy in that situation. A widely used theory, self-efficacy has been applied to career choice and adjustment by a number of researchers (Lent, Brown, & Hackett, 1994; Hackett & Betz, 1981). Bandura studied how people's judgments about their own skills to organize and carry out a task affected what they actually did. Lent, Hackett, and others were concerned that peoples' view of their own self-efficacy could prevent them from choosing some careers and advancing in their career choice. Lent, Hackett, and their colleagues were concerned that individuals who had a low sense of self-efficacy would not persist in a difficult task. Further, such individuals might have thoughts that they wouldn't be able to do the task well, would be overwhelmed or discouraged by the task, and not do it. Thus, they were concerned that women, who had often learned that math was not for women, or that women would have a difficult time with math, would not choose math courses or go into math or science careers.

Tammy had never done well in math or science. In eighth grade, she told herself that math and science weren't for her. Her father had his own plumbing business, and her mother was a secretary. Neither had gone to college, and neither had particularly valued a college education. Both felt that if you go through high school, you could get a good job. Rather than study, Tammy watched television. She liked the situation comedies the best and watched lots of them. She also had fun visiting with her friends, shopping, and, in the winter, skiing. Although not an excellent skier, Tammy was good, and she took advantage of the opportunity to do it. The main problem with working on Saturdays was that work interfered with her skiing.

She decided not to take calculus her senior year. She took an algebra class instead. Although she was barely aware of this in math class, because she didn't like the teacher, she often felt like she couldn't do it. She would become easily frustrated by the concepts that she studied during her senior year and felt a sense of relief when class was over. With the help of one of her friends, she managed to get a "B" in the course, but she disliked doing it and felt no matter how hard she tried, she'd never really master it.

In this way, Tammy's feeling that she was not effective was likely to affect her career choice and possibly her job satisfaction. Having been on the job for about four months, Tammy felt that she could do what was asked of her. The job did not seem very difficult or interesting; she was confident of her ability to work the cash register, help customers, and work with the merchandise; but her work satisfaction was relatively low. Believing that she was not very good in math contributed to her questioning what else she should do next year and reduced the strength of her self-efficacy beliefs. Tammy's questions about her current and future abilities relate to two important concepts that are a part of career self-efficacy theory: outcome expectations and goals.

## Outcome Expectations

**outcome expectations**
The estimate of a probability of an outcome.

Expectations about the outcome of a certain event are related to self-efficacy, one's view of one's ability to complete tasks. When individuals estimate the probability of an outcome, this is referred to as **outcome expectations.** Examples are "If I play basketball, what will happen?," "If I play well, what will happen?," "If I apply to a four-year college, what will happen?," and "If I ask Mrs. Sullivan for a reference, will she give me a good one?" In contrast, self-efficacy beliefs are concerned with "Can I do this activity?" Examples are "How well can I play basketball?," "Can I get into the University of Alabama?," "Will someone evaluate my job performance as being effective?," and "Will I write a good enough paper to get an 'A'?" Thus outcome expectations refer to what might happen, and self-efficacy is concerned with estimates of your ability to accomplish the goal.

Bandura (1986, 1997) has talked about several types of outcome expectations, including the anticipation of physical, social, and self-evaluative outcomes. An example of a physical outcome expectation is getting paid for working, a social outcome might be approval from your father for having done well at school, and a self-evaluative outcome might be being satisfied with your own performance in a class. Making judgments, individuals combine both outcome expectations ("If I do this activity, what can happen?") and self-efficacy ("Can I do this activity?"). Depending on the situation, either self-efficacy or outcome expectations can be the more important influence.

When Tammy considered her future, she had a number of questions. She wondered if she could get into a different college that she would like. She wondered if she could do the math that would be required. She also thought that she might want to major in business at college. Maybe she could be a manager of a store, maybe not a drug store, but possibly a clothing or department store. But she wondered if she was able to do that kind of work. "If I work in a store, will I be promoted? If I work as a manager, what work will I do?" Often her answer to these questions was negative. Tammy didn't bother to find out more about what different people, such as area managers, store managers and pharmacists, do within the store because she didn't think that she could do challenging jobs.

Tammy's outcome expectations were quite limited. Being involved in understanding the store and its operation might make Tammy's part-time job more appealing to her and change her outcome expectations. She uses her current view of her work satisfaction to guess (negatively) that work in several other areas will not be satisfying.

## Goals

**goal** An end that one tries to attain.

People do more than just respond to the events and the environment around them. They set **goals** for themselves to help them organize their actions, and to serve as guides for what they will do in the future. For example, a freshman in college who decides to be a lawyer must set some goals and choose behaviors that will help her reach the goal. The reinforcement of being a lawyer will not occur for another seven years. Goals are self-motivating and the satisfaction that comes with meeting goals, such as graduation, is highly significant.

At this point, Tammy's goals are quite limited. She wants to graduate from a community college, and her grades were certainly good enough to do that. Although she has no boyfriend, she thinks she would like to get married and have a family, but she's not really sure. She thinks she could get full-time work in the drug store, or if not this one, one near where she lives. Her supervisors have said nothing to her that has been negative. In fact, they have made some comments that indicate that her work is fine. She thinks that she would like to transfer to a four-year college, possibly work in retail management, but she is not sure. Because her self-efficacy and outcome expectations are relatively low, her goals are quite limited, and she is considering work that might be routine and not satisfying to her.

**Q 4.3** What are your outcome expectations and goals relative to your career choices?

**Q 4.4** In what work areas do you have a low sense of self-efficacy? In what areas do you have a strong positive sense of self-efficacy?

**Q 4.5** In what future work areas do you have a low sense of self-efficacy? In what areas do you have a strong positive sense of self-efficacy?

Goals, self-efficacy, and outcome expectations are related to each other and affect each other in a variety of ways. Tammy's questions about her academic ability, specifically her math ability, affect her outcome expectations and goals. If her math self-efficacy were stronger than it is, Tammy might feel that she could be successful in a four-year college. She might believe that if she gave more energy to her math work, and perhaps got more help from others, that she could accomplish the math that is necessary for a four-year business degree. Currently, she doesn't feel that she can be satisfied in working in similar positions to her current one, but she also doesn't feel she can do what is necessary to advance. Thus, a sense of self-efficacy is important for her to enjoy her work and to have a feeling that she is accomplishing important goals in her life.

Over the long-term, a lack of a sense of self-efficacy can lead people to feeling unfulfilled in their lives. Because people like this have minimal outcome expectations and goals, they might feel they cannot accomplish as much in their lives as they wish to. Many people have failed to get more education, to apply for new jobs, to make requests to their boss for new responsibilities because of their lack of self-efficacy. Consequently, they have found their present work boring, not challenging.

## WORK SATISFACTION

Once individuals have a job, many concerns can affect their satisfaction or adjustment to their work. Examples of these are problems with coworkers and superiors, boredom, inability to meet job demand, and retirement. Proponents of work adjustment theory have focused for more than 35 years on understanding employee satisfaction (Dawis & Lofquist, 1984; Lofquist & Dawis, 1991), finding that one of the best indicators of work performance was satisfaction. Individuals who are satisfied with a variety of aspects of work, such as the salary and type of work, will perform better on the job and be happier.

**satisfaction** Being satisfied with the work that you do; a feeling of accomplishment about completing an activity.

**satisfactoriness** An employer's assessment of the extent to which an individual adequately completes assigned work.

In their research, Dawis and Lofquist focused both on satisfaction and satisfactoriness. **Satisfaction** refers to being satisfied with the work that you do. In contrast, **satisfactoriness** refers to an employer's satisfaction with an employee's performance. Or, to rephrase, satisfaction refers to the extent to which a person's needs and requirements are fulfilled by the work that he or she does. Satisfactoriness concerns the appraisal of others, usually supervisors, of the extent to which an individual adequately completes the work that is assigned to him or her. These two concepts are clearly related. If you are satisfied and enjoy your work, your work is much more likely to be satisfactory. In this chapter, satisfaction is the focus, rather than satisfactoriness.

To be satisfied with your work, you should have work that is consistent with your values, abilities, and interests. Dawis and Lofquist have focused particularly on values as being important for employees to be satisfied. These researchers believe that employees have values that are important to them and that different jobs have a variety of values that are implied within them. In this section, we will examine six important values: achievement, comfort, status, altruism, safety, and autonomy. Workers vary in the degree to which they have needs that are represented by these broader value categories. Some jobs satisfy these values and their implied needs more than others do. In addition, employees should be interested in their work. This is likely if the work is consistent with most of the values of the individual. The individual employee must also be able to perform the job with sufficient ability to meet the employers' requirement for satisfactoriness.

---

## *Problems and Solutions*

---

### *What can you do when you are not satisfied at work?*

Assess the degree with which your values (achievement, comfort, status, altruism, safety, and autonomy), interests, and abilities are being met. Look for aspects of the job that could be changed to fit your values, interests, or abilities. Can you change your attitudes? If not satisfied with these strategies, look for work that will satisfy your values, interests, and abilities.

---

## *Values*

Work values represent a grouping of needs. Dawis and Lofquist have identified 20 needs that are important in describing work. These 20 needs can be categorized into 6 values. The 6 important values were described in Chapter 3 and are described here as they relate to work adjustment.

**achievement (value)**
Making use of one's abilities to have a sense of accomplishment.

*Achievement.* This value represents the need to make use of one's abilities and to do things that give a sense of accomplishment. For example, a carpenter who is proud of her abilities and the products she makes is likely to value **achievement.** She is able to use her carpentry skills in a variety of ways and feels good about the buildings and furniture that she can make.

**comfort** A variety of ways in which a job can be less stressful for an individual.

*Comfort.* This term refers to several needs that affect how a job can be less stressful for an individual. Individuals who have a job that is "comfortable" might find one where they are independent—so they can work alone on the job. They might want jobs where they can be active and busy all the time without having a lot of down time. Another need that contributes to a level of **comfort** on the job is one in which people can do a variety of work every day. Another aspect of a job that makes an individual comfortable is being well paid. Likewise, steady work, work that offers security contributes to the value of "comfort." In addition, a job that is comfortable has good working conditions: appropriately warm or cool, well lit, clean, and so forth. Although these are somewhat different needs, they all contribute to an individual feeling more comfortable on the job.

*Status.* Being recognized and valued for accomplishments is important to many people. This can be achieved in a variety of ways, such as being

**status** Being recognized and valued for accomplishments.

recognized by superiors for work that is done well, being in a position of authority, or being recognized through promotion and advancing your position. Wanting other people in the community to appreciate and recognize what you do is also important. For example, the job of physician carries a higher social status level than does "assembly line worker." The value of status is different than the value of achievement. **Status** emphasizes the importance of being recognized for your contribution, whereas achievement emphasizes the feeling of accomplishment and use of abilities.

**altruism** Wishing to help others by doing things for them or getting along with them.

*Altruism.* In general, **altruism** is the opposite of status because it is concerned not with how others perceive us, but with how we can help others. Those who value doing things for other people and getting along with their colleagues, and consider these to be important parts of their work, consider altruism to be a significant value. In addition, being able to do work that feels morally correct ties directly into this value. For example, people who are required to sell products that they feel are harmful or worthless might find that they have to quit their jobs because their moral values are being violated. Numerous categories of jobs can be considered altruistic. Clearly health professions, and social service do this; however, those in the sciences and engineering can have a sense that their work is helping others. Likewise, travel agents and bankers help others with personal and business needs.

**safety** Feeling safe or secure within a company and that one is being treated fairly.

*Safety.* The value **safety** refers to feeling safe within a company or being treated fairly. Included are the concerns that a company administers its policies fairly and backs up the workers when they need support. Also included is the belief that the company will train its employees well. Thus, there is a sense of knowing that the company will be consistent and can be relied upon. For example, an insurance adjuster who could not count on coworkers to do their jobs well and who felt that management would not back his decisions in making insurance adjustments for losses because of fire would feel that the company did not share his value of safety.

**autonomy** The opportunity to work independently or on one's own.

*Autonomy.* Some people are not concerned with how they are treated by their supervisors (safety) but want the opportunity to work on their own. This might include trying out some of their own ideas and being creative or making decisions on their own and taking responsibility for their actions. For example, an auto assembly worker who wants to try out new ideas to make her work easier or more efficient would be concerned with **autonomy** rather than with safety.

These values provide a way for understanding how satisfied you are with your work. One way to further understand this concept is to rate each of the six values from 1 to 4, with 4 being very important, 3 being important, 2 being somewhat important, and 1 being unimportant. Then think of a job that you have had recently and rate how well the company or job meets each of these six values using a similar rating scale.

| Values | Your rating from 1 to 4 | Your rating of your employer's emphasis |
|--------|-------------------------|-----------------------------------------|
| Achievement | _____ | _____ |
| Comfort | _____ | _____ |
| Status | _____ | _____ |
| Altruism | _____ | _____ |
| Safety | _____ | _____ |
| Autonomy | _____ | _____ |

(Try to vary your ratings—Don't rate all values the same).

**Q 4.6** Describe your own work values by relating them to achievement, comfort, status, altruism, safety, and autonomy. Which are most important to you and why?

If you rate values that were similar to those of the company that you work for or your job, then you should have been satisfied. If the company did not value what you were valuing, then you were probably dissatisfied. In addition to values, jobs need to be interesting to an individual, jobs must be able to be accomplished, and job requirements must be met (ability) for an employee to be satisfied.

## Interests

**interest** Curiosity about or enjoyment in an activity.

In addition to values, **interest** in the activity that you are doing would be a particularly important aspect of satisfaction. For example, if an individual likes to have a sense of accomplishment (achievement) and wants to help others with personal problems (altruism), he might find the work of a social worker or psychiatrist to be very satisfying. Other individuals might have interests in music, building things, or persuading others to buy a product. These interests do not have to be closely related to a particular value, but they are important. Being able to satisfy an interest, and have a job that meets your values, provides a sense of satisfaction.

## Abilities

**ability** Current performance, what the individual is doing now.

Meeting your values and satisfying your interests are not sufficient; you must also be **able** to do the work. Although I enjoy singing and being a professional singer would meet my values of autonomy and achievement, I would get no one to listen to me because my singing ability is terrible. In

**Q 4.7** To what extent does your current (or a recent) job provide work that is interesting? Describe your reaction to the interest level of the job.

the end, my job satisfaction as a singer would not be met because no one would come and see me perform or pay me for my singing. Thus, as much as I would want to have singing meet my needs for achievement and autonomy, they would not be met because I would not be able to have a sense of accomplishment or to be creative in a way that anyone could appreciate.

**Q 4.8** To what extent does your current (or a recent) job fit with your abilities? How does this contribute to your satisfaction with the job?

Some jobs, unlike being a singer or a scientist, are relatively easy to do. Although someone can accomplish these jobs, the jobs might not satisfy certain values. I can wash dishes; however, washing dishes would not satisfy my values of achievement and autonomy. This occupation might satisfy my value of safety, but not much more.

Being satisfied with what you do at work can affect not only your satisfaction about your career, but also your general satisfaction. When work is unpleasant, it is often difficult to stop this unpleasantness from generalizing to other activities. If you don't like your work, you might feel tense, irritable, and annoyed. This tension and irritation does not necessarily leave when you leave your work setting. Individuals whose work does not provide satisfaction often have to make efforts in their own lives to make other aspects important and meaningful. For example, an electrician or retail salesworker who doesn't like his or her work can invest more energy into areas such as family; community service groups; hobbies such as hunting, stamps, or needlework; or amusements such as television or reading fiction.

Sometimes you can find ways to make a job that is unsatisfying more satisfying. Counselors can help an individual find a solution so that more job satisfaction can be found. Sometimes this includes trying to change tasks or changing your attitude toward a task. Other times this means changing coworkers or changing attitudes toward coworkers. When these approaches fail, individuals often look for an opportunity to transfer within a company or to change jobs so that they can do similar work in a different company. Sometimes the problem is the nature of the work itself, however, and an individual might wish to change occupations. For example, an insurance salesperson or firefighter might wish to become a physical therapist.

Understanding work satisfaction by examining how well the work satisfies different values can be demonstrated by Brian's situation. Brian graduated with a "B+" average from a small business college in Indiana. For a few years, he had looked forward to a career in sales and marketing. When he graduated from college, he had difficulty finding the type of job that he wanted. Many of the sales jobs involved cold calling (calling people who had not expressed an interest in a product from a list of names and numbers). He had done telemarketing work during his summers and didn't want to continue this. Many of his friends had jobs and were working. Now, he was looking for a position. Finally, he was offered a job in the credit department of a large credit card company. After three weeks training, he was given his own cubicle and told to call people who had fallen behind in their credit card payments. His calls were monitored closely, at first, by a supervisor. After four months of this work, he was feeling very frustrated. He found himself irritable at the end of the day, and the first thing he did after work was go to the gym and lift weights. This seemed to help some as it made him feel less tied down. He expressed his concerns about his job this way:

*Brian:* When I was in college, I had this image of making a lot of money, being on my own, and working in a nice spacious office. Now look at me. I'm working in a cramped little cubicle, I'm not making a lot of money, and just about everything I say and do is monitored closely. This is really driving me nuts!

*RS (Richard Sharf):* It really is important to you to be independent in your work and to make money. (Brian values what Dawis and Lofquist refer to as Comfort, being independent, making money, and good working conditions.)

*Brian:* Yes. I guess I could be patient about the money, because I know I'm not going to come out of school and start making $50,000 right away. But working in that tiny office and being monitored so closely is difficult. I don't know how much longer I can take it.

*RS:* Sounds like you've really been looking around for other options. (It's a safe bet that if Brian is this dissatisfied with his work, he is thinking about what else he might be able to do within the company and without.)

*Brian:* I really hope that I could find something else in the company, get a promotion, something where I could be in charge, instead of being told what to do all the time. But it's really very difficult, because the work is monitored so closely, that there barely is an opportunity to talk with other workers here. I even think that my supervisors don't question what they're supposed to do. The company is so big, that's it's hard to get a sense of what other people do, and no one seems to tell you. I could manage with that, if I really believed that I was going somewhere and that I could be in a leadership position.

*RS:* It sounds like being in a position of leadership and advancing in your profession is really important. You could handle the lack of clarity of your supervisors if only the job seemed to go somewhere. (Although the company does not seem to be a "safe" place to work [using Dawis and Lofquist's definition], the value of Safety is less important to Brian than that of Status. He wants to be in an authoritative position and advance in his work.)

*Brian:* When I talk with the other people during lunch—that's about the only chance we get to talk—they either seem frustrated or brain-dead. It's not that they're stupid, but they just seem, some of them, to have given up, and just go through the motions. There are actually a few who don't mind it, who find the work okay. That's hard for me to understand. But it's okay for them.

*RS:* It's difficult sometimes, when your values and what's important to you seem so different from the people that you work with.

*Brian:* Yeah. Sometimes I feel alone there. I don't mean just because I work alone, but because I seem so different than the others. Some of them seem okay, and they seem to like their co-workers and don't mind doing what they're told. They don't mind the money; they don't mind working in something the size of a wastebasket.

*RS:* They seem to be able to satisfy their needs in the job, but it's pretty clear that you can't. (It's helpful for Brian to understand that some people's values are met by the company, and his are not. For some, the company offers sufficient "Comfort," "Status," and "Achievement," but not for Brian.)

*Brian:* As much as I am trying to find some way to get something that'll work for me in the company, I haven't been able to find a thing. I had such a hard time finding this job, I don't think that I really want to start all over again. I may talk to the Human Resources people, I guess I have nothing to lose. Maybe they'll have some ideas of other job options in the company.

*RS:* Sounds like a good idea. Because you don't seem to trust the people in the company, working there seems to be hurting you a lot.

Even though Brian doesn't find the company a "Safe" place to work, his satisfaction is so low that he's willing to look for other positions in the company, before he starts looking actively outside of the company. Brian's sense of self-efficacy also seems to have suffered from his four months of looking for a job and not being able to find one. He seems to have lost some of his confidence.

Brian's values were not being met by the work that he was doing. Because the work was so structured, it was not likely that he was going to be able to change any of the working conditions or job duties to make himself feel more comfortable. Finally, Brian stuck with the job for another six months and then returned to school to get a Masters of Business Administration degree. Brian thought if he had an MBA he could find a job where he could be on his own, supervise others, and make some money, at least more than he was making now. As we talked together, Brian became more clear about his values and his ability to meet them in the company he was working for. He felt a strong need to be independent, to make more money, and to be in a position where he could advance. His values of comfort and status could best be met by going to graduate school and searching for a management position.

**Q 4.9** If you were to get a new job, what two values would be most important for the job to offer you? Explain.

**Q 4.10** Explain the role that your values, interests, and abilities play in your being satisfied in work? In what way are each important?

## CAREER CRISES AND PROBLEMS

**career crisis** Event that can be traumatic and can have long-lasting effects.

**Career crises** can be traumatic and have long-term effects when they occur. Some crises are caused by accidents or unpredictable events

*Problems and Solutions*

---

*What do you do if you experience a career crisis or transition such as being laid off, leaving the job market, being discriminated against, or being sexually harassed?*

Understand how others experience these problems, so you do not feel alone. Read examples to learn how others coped with these problems and how they dealt with shock or despair.

---

whereas others are transitions that could be anticipated or unanticipated. Accidents include a variety of situations over which a person has no control: Workers falling while working or having a machine malfunction and hurt them; or a worker's carelessness causing an individual to be harmed. Sometimes natural causes such as floods or tornadoes can cause problems for an entire company and destroy a plant or building. For some companies, losing a large contract can mean having to lay off workers. In other cases, when companies are bought out, some workers will be terminated. Adjusting to such situations can be difficult, as there is usually no or little time to prepare adequately for them.

When a crisis happens, individuals can experience a sense of shock and despair (Hopson & Adams, 1977). Depending on the nature of the accident or crisis, they might try to minimize it or make it less important than it is. Sometimes there's an experience of self-questioning about whether one can recover from the crisis. Gradually, there is an attempt to recover from the crisis and find solutions to the problem.

Often less traumatic than crisis, **transitions** refer to the movement from one part of your career to another. Schlossberg (1984) has identified four transitions: anticipated, unanticipated, "chronic hassles," and events that don't happen (non-events). **Anticipated events** will happen in the lifespan of most individuals. Examples include graduating from high school, starting a job, and retiring. **Unanticipated transitions** are those that might be a surprise. Examples include being fired, transferred, or laid off. **Chronic hassles** are situations such as a long commute to work, an unreasonable supervisor, deadline pressures, or difficult physical working conditions. Experiencing work-related stress can involve physical, mental, and emotional exhaustion, commonly called burnout. In general, burnout is brought on by continuous job stress (Pines, 1993). Teachers and social

**transitions** The movement from one part of one's career to another.

**anticipated events** Events or occurrences that happen in the lifespan of most individuals.

**unanticipated transitions** Events that are surprises or unexpected.

**chronic hassles** Situations that interfere with the performance or satisfaction of a job.

**non-events** Something that an individual wants to happen but that never occurs.

**Q 4.11** Describe your own reaction (or that of some-one you know) to an un-anticipated career crisis such as an accident or losing a job. How did this affect other parts of your (or his or her) life?

**Q 4.12** List two or three chronic hassles that you have experienced when working.

**Q 4.13** Give an example of a "non-event" that you or someone you know has experienced.

workers, as well as those in health and social service occupations, are particularly subject to stress because of the nature of their relationships with clients (Maslach & Goldberg, 1998). A **non-event** is something that an individual wishes to happen but that never occurs. For some, this may be a promotion that does not happen or a transfer to a desired community that does not take place.

Although career crises and problems can affect anyone, some career crises are frequently faced by women and minorities. Women, more so than men, might need at several points during their lives to leave and reenter the workforce because of family responsibilities and child bearing. Furthermore, women, far more than men, experience sexual harassment at work, which can be very stressful and disruptive. In addition, women, African American men, Hispanic men, and other minority groups have experienced discrimination that can cause crises as well as long-term effects on their careers. Each will be discussed here.

## Reentering and Leaving the Labor Force

Women can follow numerous patterns as they go into and out of the labor force. For many women, leaving the work force is relatively easy. Some participate in maternity leave programs that allow them to reenter their position. Others wish to stay out for a longer period than their positions can be held. These women might have to go through the process of job hunting all over again. For some, a career that was satisfactory before leaving the work force might no longer be fulfilling.

Betz and Fitzgerald (1987) discuss the coping mechanisms that women develop to manage both marriage and career. Some of these include limiting social relationships, increasing organization and delegation of home and other activities, and developing flexible jobs that allow part-time work and time at home. Some women, especially those who have developed the ability to cope with a wide range of crises and events, experience relatively little difficulty. For some women, however, entry or reentry into the work force can be traumatic. Particularly if reentry is due to divorce or the death of a husband, a woman can find herself in an uncomfortable and unfamiliar position with sole responsibility for her income and survival, and possibly for her family. An example comparing Mary, who had a rather smooth transition, and Rachel, who did not, illustrates the wide range of reactions possible when women reenter the workforce.

Mary had been an elementary school teacher for seven years before having children, but then she decided to raise her family and stay at home with two young children for a six-year period. When her children were 4 and 6, she decided to return to the school system. In February, she contacted the principal of the school she had worked at. She interviewed for one of the two open positions and was offered a job for the following September. Excited about returning to work, she made plans for her children to go to school and attend an afternoon day-care program.

Rachel had worked as a teacher for six years before raising a family of four children. After 20 years of marriage, her husband died suddenly, leaving her with few financial resources and two children in high school and two in college. She had disliked teaching and had had no plans to return to the work force. Rachel had two crises to deal with: the death of her husband and the requirement that she return to work. Rachel was stunned by the sudden death of her husband, and for four weeks she could barely take care of herself and the two children who were in high school. Both helped her, by doing household chores, including cooking. Gradually she became more depressed, seeing no reason for living. Although her sister helped with the two children at home, this was difficult because her sister had three children of her own. Gradually, Rachel let go of some of her grief and started to help her children plan for the future. She made some attempts to get work and finally settled for a job as a grocery cashier. At this point, she had no energy to use her interests, abilities, or values. After a year as a cashier, she sought career counseling to help her decide what it was that she wished to do. Rachel's sense of her own self-efficacy was brought into question by her husband's death. After his death, she quickly lost confidence in herself. Rebuilding that confidence and a sense that she could be effective took her more than a year and a half.

**Q 4.14** How would it affect your career if you had to stop work for five years and then had to return? What kind of issues would you have to deal with when you reentered the labor market?

Because women are much more likely than men are to leave and reenter the workforce, women often have to do considerable planning. Difficult choices confront women who want to have a professional career and grow and advance in that career, while choosing to take time away from their career for duties such as child raising and caring for elderly parents. Some women try to be active in professional associations or do part-time work, mainly so that they will not lose ground when they reenter the labor force.

## Sexual Harassment

**sexual harassment**
Being subjected to unwelcome behavior that is sexual in nature.

For many years, **sexual harassment** has created difficulties and crises for women that can affect their career advancement and their psychological health. Although men can be victims of sexual harassment, women are much more often the victims. Thus, our discussion will be limited to the sexual harassment of women. Sexual harassment refers to being subjected to unwelcome behavior that is sexual in nature. Defining sexual behavior more specifically is rather difficult because individuals disagree about what constitutes harassment. Till's (1980) five levels of sexual harassment are helpful in defining the severity of types of sexual harassment that women experience.

- *Level 1: Gender Harassment.* This refers to verbal remarks or nontouching behaviors that are sexist in nature. Examples would include being told suggestive stories or being required to listen to rude, sexist remarks.
- *Level 2: Seductive Behavior.* This includes inappropriate sexual advances. An individual might attempt to discuss a woman's sex life or express sexual interest in the woman.
- *Level 3: Sexual Bribery.* This refers to the request for sexual activity in return for some kind of reward. Often offered by a superior, the bribe can be a higher grade in a course, a raise in pay, or a promotion.
- *Level 4: Sexual Coercion.* This is the opposite of sexual bribery in that an individual is coerced into sexual activity by threat or punishment. For example, if a woman is told that if she does not engage in sexual activity, she will fail a course, lose a job, or be demoted, she is being coerced. All are potentially threatening to a woman's career.
- *Level 5: Sexual Assault.* Such behavior includes forceful attempts to touch, grab, fondle, or kiss.

These definitions provide a useful way of viewing the different ways in which individuals perceive sexual harassment. Not surprisingly, males and females are likely to view sexual harassment quite differently (Fitzgerald & Ormerod, 1993). Men and supervisors, whether male or female, tended to blame the victim for sexual harassment more than do women coworkers or female victims. When sexual harassment is severe, however, both men and women are likely to agree that the behavior is harassment. When the behaviors are shown as being romantic or seductive, then both men and women can have difficulty determining if the activity is sexual harassment. Some research (Pryor, LaVite, & Stoller, 1993) has found that men who have tendencies toward sexual harassment are likely to link sexuality and being in charge or being an authority in their thinking. Given the problems in defining sexual harassment and different perceptions, it is difficult to know how common it is. Based on an extensive telephone study, Gutek (1985) suggests that about half of women report some levels of sexual harassment, with the most common being Level 1 and a relatively even spread across the other four categories.

The effects of sexual harassment can be quite powerful, affecting women's physical and psychological well-being. A number of women have been fired or had to quit because of fear of being harassed on the job or being frustrated by not being able to do anything about it.

Gutek and Koss (1993) describe four stages of reacting to sexual harassment that can occur over time.

- *Confusion and Self Blame.* Individuals can assume the responsibility for being harassed. They might be upset by their inability to stop the harassment, which might begin to worsen.

- *Fear and Anxiety.* Fear for her career or safety can cause a woman to be afraid to drive home or to answer the phone and can affect her work performance. Her attendance at work and her ability to concentrate on her work might suffer.
- *Depression and Anger.* When a woman recognizes that she is not responsible for the harassment, she might become less anxious and more angry. If charges are filed, the work situation can get worse, and the individual might feel despair over her progress on her job.
- *Disillusionment.* The process of bringing charges against a harasser can be long and arduous and does not always have a successful outcome. Many organizations do not support women who choose to follow through on harassment charges.

When harassed, women often feel powerless. Particularly when the harassment is by a supervisor or coworker, women might feel little support from other coworkers or superiors in their organization. Public examples of sexual harassment have had some effect on perceptions of harassment. In the fall of 1991, U.S. Supreme Court Justice Clarence Thomas's confirmation hearings were televised. A former coworker, Anita Hill had publicly accused him of sexual harassment. In 1995, Robert Packwood resigned his Senate seat because of multiple accusations of sexual harassment. In 1997, several military officers were tried not only for sexual harassment but also for rape and other sexually related charges. These and other public examples have made individuals more aware of methods to use to overcome and counter sexual harassment. However, women might still feel little support in dealing with sexual harassment. Following is an example showing how Roberta coped with sexual harassment.

Roberta is a 30-year-old lawyer working in a large New York City law firm. One of five children from a poor Puerto Rican family in New York, Roberta worked her way through college and law school with the help of scholarships that she has earned. Specializing in tax matters, Roberta has been pleased with her training and was looking forward to the opportunity to advance in her firm, which she joined six months ago. She worked for a smaller firm for three years after graduation but felt limited. She was offered a substantial pay raise to come to her new firm. One day, as she was bending over to pick up a pencil that fell off her desk, her immediate supervisor, the head of the tax law department patted her buttocks. She was shocked by what had happened and continued with her work, growing angrier and angrier throughout the day. When she was leaving at the end of the day, her supervisor said to her, "Let me help you on with your coat." Before she had a chance to respond, he helped her with her coat, brushing his hand against her breast. She said to him coldly, "Don't do that. Get your hands away from me." He responded, "Don't complain. I didn't mean anything." Shaking as she left work, she went home to her apartment, quickly calling a friend who was an affirmative action officer at the university that she attended as an undergraduate.

After talking with her friend for forty-five minutes, Roberta finally said, "I know I've got to do something about this." They talked about how to confront the supervisor, who else to talk to in the law firm, and how to proceed. By doing this, Roberta was letting go of her reaction to the situation so that she could deal with it. She decided who she could talk to in the law firm and discussed with her friend exactly what to say. Roberta was afraid not only of losing her job but also of facing a lengthy suit from her law firm. She was aware that if this incident were not handled carefully, her career as a lawyer could be affected. Her friend was worried about how Roberta's sense of self-esteem would be affected if her firm chose to deny allegations.

Sexual harassment concerns need to be handled carefully. Some firms have human resource personnel that are available to help. In other cases, communities and legal societies can also help.

### Hiring and Salary Patterns and Job Discrimination

**discrimination (job)**
Making employment or other decisions based on people's gender, race, cultural group, age, or other such characteristics.

**Discrimination** against women and minorities can take several forms in the labor market. It can be seen in studying unemployment rates where minorities often have much higher unemployment rates than men and in the types of occupations that women and minorities enter. Often, entry into high-paying and high-status occupations is blocked or difficult for women and minorities who are qualified applicants. Further, the salaries of women and minorities tend to be considerably lower than those for white males. When women are in a minority group, their earnings tend to be less favorable than that of men of their own ethnic minority. I will describe these issues in more detail and then discuss the more personal aspects of discrimination relative to the problems that individuals experience while on the job as well as when applying for a job.

When you examine unemployment data, look at the distribution of women in various occupations, and the salaries of women. As Table 4.1 shows, women tend to have unemployment rates that are similar to those of men. Note that U.S. Bureau of Labor Statistics employment rates include only those individuals who are actively looking for work and receiving unemployment benefits. These rates exclude individuals who are able to work but are not interested in doing so and individuals who would like to work but are discouraged because they believe they will not be able to find work. Unemployment rates appear to differ markedly more by race than by sex. One reason for women having a similar unemployment rate to men is that they move in and out of the labor force more frequently than men and might be

TABLE **4.1  UNEMPLOYMENT RATES IN PERCENTAGES BY DEMOGRAPHIC GROUP, 1998**

| Age | White Male | White Female | Black Male | Black Female | Hispanic Male | Hispanic Female | All |
|-----|-----------|-------------|-----------|-------------|--------------|----------------|-----|
| 16–17 | 17.1 | 12.4 | 33.9 | 33.2 | 29.0 | 26.4 | 17.2 |
| 18–19 | 12.1 | 9.8 | 27.9 | 20.9 | 16.4 | 20.2 | 12.8 |
| 20–24 | 6.7 | 6.3 | 18.0 | 15.7 | 8.9 | 10.1 | 7.9 |
| 25–54 | 2.9 | 3.2 | 6.2 | 7.1 | 4.7 | 6.6 | 3.5 |
| 55–64 | 2.8 | 2.2 | 4.5 | 3.4 | 5.3 | 5.4 | 2.6 |
| **Total** | **3.9** | **3.9** | **8.9** | **9.0** | **6.4** | **8.2** | **4.5** |

*Source:* Data from the U.S. Department of Labor, *Employment and Earnings* (January 1999), Table 3 (pp. 168–171).

TABLE **4.2  EMPLOYED PERSONS BY SELECTED OCCUPATION, SEX, RACE, AND HISPANIC ORIGIN, 1998**

| Occupation | Total Employed (in Thousands) | Percentage of Total | | |
|-----------|------------------------------|-------|-------|----------|
| | | Women | Black | Hispanic |
| Engineers | 2,052 | 11.1 | 4.1 | 3.8 |
| Physicians | 740 | 26.6 | 4.9 | 4.8 |
| Registered nurses | 2,032 | 92.5 | 9.3 | 3.2 |
| Managerial and professional | 38,957 | 49.0 | 7.6 | 5.0 |
| Teachers, college | 91p | 42.3 | 5.8 | 3.6 |
| Teachers, except college | 4,962 | 75.3 | 10.0 | 5.4 |
| Lawyers | 912 | 28.5 | 4.0 | 3.0 |
| Counseling, educational, and vocational | 230 | 68.8 | 13.2 | 5.5 |
| Sales occupations | 15,050 | 50.3 | 8.9 | 7.4 |
| Secretaries, stenographers, and typists | 3,599 | 92.6 | 9.6 | 7.0 |
| Food preparation workers | 6,071 | 56.5 | 11.8 | 17.0 |
| Nursing aides and orderlies | 1,913 | 89.0 | 34.0 | 9.8 |
| Janitors and cleaners | 2,233 | 34.8 | 21.7 | 19.6 |
| Maids and house cleaners | 653 | 82.8 | 26.7 | 25.0 |
| Mechanics and repairers | 4,527 | 4.0 | 8.0 | 10.5 |
| Truck drivers | 3,012 | 5.3 | 14.9 | 12.0 |
| Bus drivers | 471 | 50.4 | 20.3 | 11.7 |

*Source:* Data from the U.S. Department of Labor, *Employment and Earnings* (January 1999), Table 1 (pp. 68–78).

involved in family responsibilities that require them to temporarily drop out of the labor force. When they do look for work, they might accept work that men would not consider. Although women have similar unemployment rates as men, the types of occupations that they enter tend to pay less and to have less prestige than do those that are typically male dominated. As career self-efficacy theory would predict, women are less likely to enter prestigious occupations in the physical sciences or in math because they have less confidence in their math and science abilities. As Table 4.2 shows, women have

| | | |
|---|---|---|
| Hispanic Females | $17,760 | 52% |
| Hispanic Males | $22,859 | 67% |
| Black Females | $19,976 | 58% |
| Black Males | $24,041 | 70% |
| White Females | $22,198 | 65% |
| White Males | $34,300 | 100% |

FIGURE **4.1** EARNINGS AS A PERCENTAGE OF WHITE MALE EARNINGS, VARIOUS DEMOGRAPHIC GROUPS, FULL-TIME WORKERS OVER 18 YEARS OLD, 1990.

(From U.S. Bureau of the Census, *Money Income of Households, Families, and Persons in the United States, 1990.* Series P-60, No. 174. Washington, DC: U.S. Government Printing Office, 1991, Table 31.)

less than 30 percent of the high paying professional jobs, such as engineer, physician, and lawyer, and have more than 75 percent of lower-paying, professional jobs, such as registered nurse and elementary and high school teacher. In nonprofessional occupations, women represent 93 percent of secretaries and 83 percent of maids and house cleaners. Men dominate the higher-paying nonprofessional occupations, such as truck driver, mechanic, and repairer.

In general, the wages of women are between two-thirds and one-half of those of white men (see Figure 4.1). Analyzing gender-based earning inequalities, Anderson and Tomaskovic-Devey (1995) found that gender inequalities were lowest when specific rules were formulated about earnings and promotions. The researchers found that exclusion from traditionally male and highly skilled or authority jobs was part of the reason for unequal pay for women. Another issue was organizational culture, such as patriarchal views toward women, unequal promotion practices, and evaluating jobs by gender.

Just as women experience difficulty in the labor market, so do African Americans and Hispanics, as reflected by unemployment data, employment in specific occupations, and wage statistics. As Table 4.1 shows, the unemployment rate for African Americans in 1998 was more than double the rate for whites. For African American and Hispanic youth, ages 16 to 17, and 18 to 19, the rate was extremely high—about 20 to 35 percent were unemployed. In addition to higher unemployment, minorities work in different types of occupations. As Table 4.2 shows, Hispanics and African Americans tend to make up a relatively small proportion of the workers in high-skill jobs (at the top of Table 4.2) and a much larger proportion of the workers in semi-skilled and unskilled jobs (at the bottom of Table 4.2). Furthermore, the salaries of minorities tend to be about one-half to one-third less than that of white males in all jobs (Figure 4.1). Analyzing the effect of race on earnings in the United States, Ashraf (1995) notes differences within occupations and reports that African Americans earn about 54 percent less than whites in the South but earn about a third less than whites in the rest of the country. Explaining differences in unemployment and wages has been the task of many sociologists and economists.

A variety of factors prevent minorities from attaining high-status jobs, high wages, and lower unemployment rates (Sharf, 1997). Some evidence indicates that African American men are more likely than white men to be unemployed because of firings and layoffs. The lower average education of African American men also affects their unemployment rate, because there are fewer opportunities for less-educated workers. Another reason for higher unemployment of less-educated young African American men is that the labor market has shifted away from manufacturing, (a segment of the labor market that has traditionally employed less-educated young African Americans) toward the service sector. As African American poor have become isolated in large cities, especially in the midwestern and southwestern United States, they can find less access to some types of employment. In addition, adolescent African Americans tend to move in and out of the labor force more quickly and often than whites. Further, adolescent African Americans receive fewer job offers per time period than whites do. Evidence also indicates that African American youth have less information about jobs and the process of job application than white adolescents do.

Two studies (Culp & Dunson, 1986; Wallace, 1975) have found that when African American and white adolescents in the same community looked for jobs, the African American youth experienced more discrimination in the job application process. White employers chose white candidates even when black candidates were more qualified or equally qualified. More research has focused on African Americans than on Hispanics, but to some extent, we can generalize from the African American experience to that of Hispanics.

Statistical descriptions of discrimination do not convey the offensiveness and hurt of the psychological effects of discrimination as experienced by women and minorities. Being denied a job because you are African American, but are qualified, can be confusing and hurtful. Likewise, being denied promotion or attractive assignments while others receive them can be very discouraging. Not getting a raise because of your race can be devastating. Some individuals respond to these negative and hurtful experiences with anger, others with despair.

**double jeopardy**
Experiencing discrimination because of both gender and race or cultural identity.

For an example of discrimination as a crisis, let us return to Roberta who was discussed in the example on sexual harassment. By using Roberta as an example, I can illustrate the concept of "double jeopardy." Because Roberta is a member of a minority group (Puerto Rican), she might experience **double jeopardy,** discrimination because she is a member of a minority group as well as a woman.

> Roberta was able to handle the situation with her supervisor in a positive way. She discussed her experience with one of the law partners who had hired her. Three weeks after the incident, the supervisor left the firm. Roberta had heard rumors that similar incidents had happened to two other women in the firm. No forthright explanation was ever given of what had happened.
>
> Roberta continued to work for the firm, being given more and more responsible tasks and being put in charge of the tax portion of large corporate accounts and for wealthy clients. When a senior member of the tax department left to join another firm, his accounts were divided among the members of the department. Two weeks after being put in charge of the tax aspect of one of the firm's largest accounts, the Doe Corporation, Roberta was told that it would be given to someone else. When she asked her new superior why that was, he became embarrassed and talked about how another member of the department had expertise that she lacked. Roberta knew that the individual mentioned did not have more expertise than she had in that matter and that the Doe Corporation had a reputation of being discriminatory.
>
> Her immediate reaction was shock when she realized what was happening. Having experienced racism several times during her life because she was Puerto Rican, she was surprised that it would occur among people whom she believed to be philanthropic and intelligent. Unlike the previous situation of sexual harassment, Roberta did not experience shock or feel that her anger was out of control. She knew that some large corporations had an affirmative action policy that they did not always follow. Roberta was able to talk with her superior about different strategies for handling the situation. She talked with him about not making the switch and leaving the account in her hands.

**Q 4.15** Describe a job crisis or transition that you experienced. Explain what you did and how it affected you.

**Q 4.16** If you have experienced sexual harassment or discrimination when working or applying for a job, how did it affect you? If you have not, or do not wish to discuss it, describe your reaction to the discrimination or sexual harassment that someone else has experienced (preferably someone you know, or it can be a public figure).

He accepted her advice and returned to a representative of the Doe Corporation to discuss it. Roberta felt pleased that she was able to handle the situation assertively and quickly.

Dealing with discrimination when it occurs on a job can be quite complex and complicated. Often, it is difficult to be sure that discrimination is taking place. Sometimes it is helpful to talk to a trusted colleague in the company and discuss it. At other times, it might be helpful to talk to individuals in the Human Resource Department of a company. Sometimes, however, the nature of the situation is such that it would be helpful to discuss it outside of the company, as Roberta did when she talked with a friend who was an affirmative action officer elsewhere. Seeking advice from a friend who is knowledgeable about job discrimination can be helpful. Legal resources and community service agencies can also provide assistance. Discriminatory actions need not be tolerated; however, they may need to be examined and handled very carefully.

## Summary

Because half of a person's waking day is usually spent on the job, learning about issues related to work adjustment is important. First, we examined the process of starting a job and the growing familiarity with job duties and co-workers that can lead to a different reaction as you become more familiar with the work setting. To understand this process, Tiedeman's three stages of adjusting to a choice—induction, reformation, and integration—were described.

You can use the concept of career self-efficacy to understand work adjustment. Individuals who have low self-efficacy have little confidence in their academic or occupational abilities. This can prevent them from trying to make work more satisfying or looking for a more satisfying job. They might not believe that they can accomplish very much (outcome expectations), and they might set low goals for themselves. These individuals can easily accomplish these low goals, but the goals might not be satisfying.

Understanding your own work values and the work values that are implicit in a job can be helpful. Dawis and Lofquist's work adjustment theory explains six important values: Achievement, Comfort, Status, Altruism, Safety, and Autonomy. In addition, Dawis and Lofquist describe the importance of abilities and interests in experiencing job satisfaction. Some strategies were given for making changes so that individuals can feel more satisfied in their work.

Sometimes individuals experience crises or accidents in their work. Something very difficult to cope with might occur, such as hurting yourself in a machine. Additional problems include being laid off or being fired. Reentering and leaving the labor force, sexual harassment, and discrimination can affect women's work satisfaction. Further, minorities might have a more difficult time finding a job (higher unemployment rates) than white men do. When minorities do find a job, it might be lower paying and have lower status than jobs held by white men.

Being satisfied with your work is extremely important in general life satisfaction. Understanding work satisfaction and trying to make work as satisfying as possible has been the focus of this chapter.

# RECOMMENDED READINGS

*Technostress: Coping with Technology @ work @ home @ play*
Weil, M. M. & Rosen, L. D. (Wiley, 1997).

> Technology has both benefits and problems. This book discusses the stress that comes from the negative impact of technology on our thoughts, feelings, and actions. Although computers solve many problems, they also create other problems for people. This book describes the problems that technology causes and how to live with them.

*Sexual Harassment: What It Is and How to Stop It*
Petrocelli, W. & Repa, E. K. (Nolo Press, 1998)

> As described on page 99 of this text, sexual harassment can cause many difficulties for individuals. Increasingly, employees and employers need to recognize sexual harassment in the workplace. If you are harassed, this book suggests what to do and how to stop the harassment. Information is also provided for employers to institute programs that will reduce incidents of sexual harassment.

# RECOMMENDED WEB SITES

*U.S. Department of Labor*
http://www.dol.gov/

> The Labor Department has primary responsibility for many job- and work-related matters in the U.S. Government. This online site serves as a base you can use to explore topics such as unsafe working conditions, wages, worker productivity, and the legal rights of workers, including protection from sexual harassment.

*Stress and Workstress Directory*
http://web.inter.nl.net/hcc/P.Compernolle/strescat.htm
> Theo Compernolle offers a generous set of resource links relating to the impact of stress in general and especially in the work place.

*The Road to Burnout*
http://helping.apa.org/stress6.html
> Maintained by the American Psychological Association, this resource describes various stages and warning signs of burnout, which the APA defines as that "state of physical, emotional, and mental exhaustion caused by unrealistically high aspirations and illusory and impossible goals."

# RELATIONSHIPS

*Relationships with others are the most significant and meaningful activities in most people's lives. One view of the family is that it is our first exposure to society, and it is where we learn how to interact with others. Chapter 5 describes types of family relationships, both with parents and with brothers and sisters. Problems such as divorce and its effects on the family are also described. Chapter 6 covers developing friendships and loving relationships as well as difficulties that result in relationships. Loving relationships that are sexual in nature are often quite complex and lead to feelings ranging from extreme pleasure and happiness to desperate sadness and despair (Chapter 7). Relationships with those who are different from us can create misunderstanding or barriers, whether the difference is gender (Chapter 8) or cultural (Chapter 9). Chapter 10 describes approaches to understanding death and offers suggestions for helping those who are dying or grieving.*

# FAMILY RELATIONSHIPS

Our relationship with our families is our introduction to our world. We learn about loving and caring in our families and experience a full range of emotions—happiness, sadness, love, anger, compassion, hate, annoyance, frustration and many others. Unlike many relationships, most familial relationships extend to the end of a person's lifetime. Sometimes relationships with parents or brothers and sisters are stopped because of anger or lost as a result of other disruptions. Our relationships with parents and brothers and sisters affect our own development and our own relationships with other people. Perhaps no single factor creates more stress for so many families than divorce does. We will explore the effects of divorce on adolescent and adult children, as well as young single parents raising children. Issues of how children relate to each other and their parents and how they deal with divorce are the subjects of this chapter.

# ATTITUDES OF PARENTS TOWARD CHILD RAISING

Different styles of parenting can affect children in different ways. Parenting styles also provide a useful way of examining problems that can exist between children and parents. The relationship between parents and their children has been thoroughly studied by psychologists. In Chapter 6, we discuss the contribution of attachment theorists to understanding the development of friendships and romantic relationships. Other psychologists such as Roe (Roe & Lunneborg, 1990) and Baumrind (1971, 1978, 1989, 1991) have devoted more than 30 years of their professional careers to understanding parenting styles and their influence on children. In this chapter, I will focus on Diana Baumrind's work in understanding how parents' child-raising styles affects children's relationships in young adulthood.

## *Parenting Styles*

In her observations of parents and their children, Baumrind looked at two dimensions of child raising: accepting the child and controlling the child. From these two dimensions, she developed three parental styles that she studied for many years: authoritative, authoritarian, and permissive.

**authoritative parenting style** Parents having a high degree of acceptance of the child while having a high degree of control.

- The **authoritative** parenting style shows a high degree of acceptance of the child while maintaining a high degree of control. Authoritative parents discuss standards and expectations but also value obedience. Authoritative parents try to promote independence, however, while explaining the reasons for their decisions to the child.
- **Authoritarian** parents are likely to rank high in control of their children, yet low on acceptance. These parents are likely to have the attitude

**authoritarian parenting style**  Parents controlling what their children do, but being unlikely to accept their child's behavior.

"Do this because I told you to and don't ask questions." Their standards of behavior are clear, and often based on religious or political beliefs. Obedience is highly valued in an authoritarian home. Even as their children mature, parents continue to set rules for their children, usually without explanation. In their attitude toward their children, authoritarian parents can be somewhat distant emotionally and might reject the child when he or she doesn't follow the rules.

**permissive parenting style**  Parents having high acceptance of the child, but little control of what the child is allowed to do.

- **Permissive** parenting is the opposite of authoritarian parenting. Permissive parents are likely to rank high in acceptance of the child and low in control. These parents are likely to allow the child to express herself freely and to make her own decisions about what activities she participates in. Although permissive parents might try to reason with the child, they are less likely to set limits on appropriate behavior than are authoritarian or authoritative parents.

When parenting style studies report results, a question arises: Do both parents tend to have similar styles? In examining the expectations, attitudes toward discipline, and the degree of nurturance of both fathers and mothers who are parents of young children, one to four years of age, parents tended to be more alike than different in their parenting styles (Bentley & Fox, 1991). As a group, mothers tended to have stronger attitudes toward nurturance than do fathers, but mothers and fathers did not differ in their expectations or their attitudes toward disciplining their children. Certainly, there are instances of parents having different styles and of parents changing their styles as the child gets older, or as they have more children. Particularly interesting is the effect of the parenting style on the actual behavior of the children.

## The Effect of Parenting Style on Children's Behavior

In this section, the type of behaviors that children are likely to have as a result of parenting style, which stay with them into later life, will be described. Issues that arise between parents and their young adult children will be discussed using examples for each of the parenting styles: authoritative, authoritarian, and permissive.

***Characteristics of Children of Authoritative Parents.***  Children of authoritative parents often are friendly and self-confident. In interactions with other adults, these children tend to be cooperative and friendly. With their peers, they can be cheerful and energetic. They are curious about the world around them and explore it, but in a self-controlled manner. In their interactions with their parents, these children are likely to encounter standards that change as the child develops competencies and skills. The authoritative approach, which takes into consideration the growing abilities of the child, allows the child to have more experiences and to encounter success in those experiences. During adolescence, authoritative parents respond to their teenagers' questions and concerns about rules and regulations, such as staying out past midnight or dating issues.

In dealing with his parents, Barry has found them to be helpful and to support his goals. His father raises hogs in Iowa, and his mother is a secretary for the local elementary school. Although Barry has enjoyed helping his father with farm chores, he has never wanted to be a farmer. Rather he had decided that he would be a pediatrician when he grew up. Because finances are tight, Barry has decided to spend his freshman year at a local community college and live at home with his parents. This would allow him to work part time with his father in the spring and fall and full time during the summer. However, Barry's first semester at college did not fit his expectations for his own performance or for his view of the performance necessary to go to medical school. He received a "C" in math, chemistry, and biology and a "B" in English.

"I'm really disappointed in myself. I thought I could do better at college than I did at high school because I knew I would try harder. I did try and it didn't help me much. I'm not sure what I'm going to do. It was real hard for me to tell my parents because I knew that they would be disappointed. I've always wanted to be a doctor, and because of that, Mom and Dad have supported me in that, and now I feel like I'm failing myself. They seem to be okay with what I do, and what I may choose to do, but I'm not. I want to be a success and be financially successful and not worry about the weather all the time, the way my father does. He worries about the price of soybeans, of hogs, of every other thing. My parents didn't push me, didn't really ask me much about studying, because they saw me studying all the time. They really have been so nice and helpful to me, I feel real embarrassed about what has happened."

Although Barry sees his performance as a failure, his parents are unlikely to. Yet, Barry is feeling bad about himself. Despite Barry's parents having been open with him and not pushing their desires on him, he still has frustration about his academic situation.

**Q 5.1** Given Barry's parents' authoritative style, how do you think they will respond to his dilemma?

**Q 5.2** If you were in a situation like Barry's how do you think your parents would respond? How would you describe their parenting style?

### *Characteristics of Children with Authoritarian Parents.*   Children who are raised in an authoritarian style home are likely to feel a conflict between values they learn at home and values that they learn at school or with friends. Because these children are being told what to do for no apparent reason, they can be irritable and easily annoyed. Physical punishment often accompanies authoritarian parenting style, so these children can be fearful or apprehensive with their parents and with others. Because their parents are likely to set goals for them, they often have relatively few goals for themselves, or are unsure of their goals. When these children are

irritable or sulk, their parents sometimes respond by increasing the authority, thus increasing the child's sense of resentment or irritability. As children enter adolescence, a parental refusal to give some control to the child is likely to result in hostility, rebellion, or anxiety.

Valerie describes the control in her family as coming from her father. Her mother has always deferred to her father, who has a strong religious faith and a strong sense of what Valerie should do. When other girls were going out in high school, Valerie was permitted to be out only one evening a week, and then only until 11:00 P.M. Once as a freshman, Valerie snuck out the window of her second floor bedroom, onto the porch and onto an overhanging branch of a tree, and then shimmied down the trunk. About an hour later her father knocked on the door of her bedroom, saw that she was not there, and started immediately to call her friends. On the first call to Valerie's best friend, her father found out where she was. When she returned, he took off his belt and hit her several times. Valerie was furious, but more frightened than angry. She still has a vivid mental picture of the rage on his face and remembers the loudness of his voice. That incident, four years ago, changed her father's view toward her. He has been suspicious of her behavior when she's been at school or at work, wondering if she is coming straight home. When Valerie is home, there is silence and a sense of tension. Valerie feels it in her stomach. Sometimes, she feels knots when she is around her father.

"I met this guy at school about six months ago and we have been friends and then started dating. My father doesn't know anything about this. Carl is a great guy, he works steady, and he is real patient with me, and knows the rules that I have at home. I don't know what to do. I'm afraid to tell my mother because she'll tell my father. I'm afraid he'll throw me out of the house, and if he does, I don't know if that is good or bad. I worry about it so much, that sometimes when I'm with Carl, who makes me happy, I'm not happy. I find myself snapping at him when I don't want to and that just makes things worse."

**Q 5.3** How would you handle this situation if you were Valerie?

**Q 5.4** Have you had a disagreement with your parents that is so strong that it never seemed like anyone would give in? What did you do? Did your parents behave the way you expected them to do?

### *Characteristics of Children Raised in a Permissive Parenting Style.*
In her characterization of children whose parents have a permissive style, Baumrind (1978) emphasizes that such children are likely to be aggressive and rebellious. Because parents have exercised relatively little control over them, these children have learned little self-control. They sometimes act impulsively, on a whim, act angrily or physically, such as punching. Because they have not been controlled by parents or by themselves, they are likely to be domineering in relationships with others because they are not used to taking suggestions or direction from others. During their children's adolescence, permissive parents can be faced with very difficult problems with

adolescents who want to stay out all night or might be involved in illegal activity such as vandalism or drug use. Sometimes lack of direction can result in the adolescent feeling insecure and uncertain.

Mort is 25 and is a shipping clerk with United Parcel Service. He lives with his girlfriend, who is an assembly line worker at a manufacturing plant. When they are done working, they come back and smoke marijuana in their apartment. The apartment is full of CDs and posters. Mort has been working as a shipping clerk for six years and is really dissatisfied with it. He received Bs when he was in high school and thought that he might go to college. He still thinks about it but has done very little in that regard.

When he was growing up, his mother used cocaine. He can remember being at home with his younger brother, preparing his own meals, or taking care of his brother. He hated to take care of his brother and often pushed him around. His mother would get angry for a moment and yell at him. But he just learned to let her anger fly, because she was either leaving to go out or so high that she would just tune out any squabbles between Mort and his brother. Mort's father left the family when Mort was ten. Sometimes Mort's father would try to discipline Mort, but Mort's father got tired of the effort and was usually passive. He remarried and moved to another state, and Mort saw his father only in the summers after that. Mort felt angry at his father for leaving him alone with his brother and mother and angry at his mother for not helping him out. His mother never went to school plays or other activities, so Mort learned to do things on his own. However, most of his activities offered excitement, such as breaking windows, smoking, or using other drugs.

Now Mort is dissatisfied with his life, and his girlfriend has even less ambition than he does. He senses something is wrong, but finds it very difficult to stop smoking marijuana and find a job that isn't boring like the one he has.

**Q 5.5** What does Mort have to do to take control of his life?

**Q 5.6** Can you think of ways that Mort can deal with his father and mother that will help him in taking control of his own life?

**Q 5.7** How is your own relationship with your parents similar to or different from Mort's response to a permissive child-raising style?

**separation and individuation** Separating from parents to become responsible for one's life

## Coping with Parental Styles

Barry, Valerie, and Mort all have different situations that leave them frustrated and unhappy. All are trying to separate themselves from their parents in one way or another. They are trying to become their own persons. This process is called **separation and individuation**—taking responsibility for one's own life rather than looking for guidance from parents. Although it would be difficult to fault the parenting style of Barry's parents, Barry is concerned about his disappointment in himself and his fear of letting his parents down. Valerie is scared of her father and torn between doing what her father wants (not to see Carl) or doing what she wants (to see Carl). Mort has no sense of direction and feels himself behaving aimlessly. All are faced with taking care of themselves in one way or another.

**object relations theory** A point of view that examines the relationships between parents and children and how individuals develop to become independent.

**object** In object relations theory "object" refers to relationships with anyone or anything.

**Q 5.8** List ways in which you can be your own parent and take more responsibility for your own life.

**Q 5.9a** In your own relationship with your parents, do you find yourself more similar to Barry, Valerie, or Mort? Explain. Describe your own parents' style of parenting.

**Q 5.9b** If you are a parent, do you find your child or children more like Barry, Valerie, or Mort?

The challenges seem to be greatest for Mort, however, as he has limited more of his choices than Barry and Valerie have.

Some psychologists would believe that Barry, Valerie, and Mort must take responsibility for their own lives to compensate for parenting styles. Rather than blame their parents, **object relations theorists** suggests that adolescents should separate emotionally from their parents and be their own parents. Individuals (especially Mort) should provide themselves with the support and parenting they have not received. They can do this through their contacts with friends and romantic partners who support them in developing their own strengths and goals. Object relations theorists examine the parent-child relationship and how it develops as individuals become their own persons. The **object** in object relations refers to relationships with anyone or anything. Generally, the "objects" that object relations theorists are concerned with are parental objects. Theorists are interested in how the relationship with the parent affects the child, examining how the child separates from parents and grows into an adult. When they do psychotherapy, object relations therapists look for ways to help the individual separate from his or her parents and take full responsibility for his or her life.

## Parenting Tips

Given the many difficulties of raising children and adolescents, what are some basic guidelines that parents can follow? Authors of self-help books such as Haim Ginott (1972) and T. Berry Brazelton (1992) have many useful suggestions. We will explore some basic suggestions here:

- Set high expectations for children, but not so high that children cannot follow them. Permissive parents often do not set clear standards.
- Explain your expectations for children.
- Make requests clear and reasonable. Authoritarian parents often make requests but do not explain them.
- Be consistent in expectations and enforcement of them so that children know your standards. Permissive parents often are not clear or do not follow through on requests.
- Reward good behavior to increase the likelihood that children will meet your expectations. Praise is often a sufficient reward for children.
- Help children see others' point of view. Encourage children to think about what would happen or how they would feel if someone did that to them.

Self-help books for child raising offer more specific suggestions for children depending on their age and the nature of the situation or event.

*Problems and Solutions*

*When or if you are a parent, what are some strategies for helping your children behave?*

- Set reasonable, yet high expectations.
- Explain your expectations.
- Be consistent in your expectations.
- Reward good behavior.
- Help your children understand others' viewpoints.
- Be appropriately involved in your children's activities.

## SIBLING RELATIONSHIPS

Although psychologists have devoted much effort to the study of child-parent relationships, they have also studied sibling relationships. The variable that has been studied most frequently has been birth order, with researchers making predictions about achievement and personality based on whether one is the oldest or youngest child, or somewhere in between in the family. Alfred Adler, one of the first psychotherapists, believed that knowing the order of birth of individuals in a family could help therapists understand their clients. For example, he believed that first borns would attain higher levels of achievement, both academically and professionally, than their brothers or sisters would (Ansbacher & Ansbacher, 1970). Zajonc and Mullally (1997) and Maddi (1989) report that many studies support Adler's view. Adler also felt that last-born or only children were likely to be spoiled or pampered by parents or brothers and sisters. Some research supports this hypothesis (Longstreth, 1970). Although much research has been done on the effect of birth order on personality and intellectual achievement, much of the research is contradictory.

When helping individuals and families with their problems, Adler and Adlerian therapists often discuss early relationships that the client had with brothers or sisters in the family. Adlerian therapists are concerned not only with actual birth order but also with siblings' relationships with each other. For example, were brothers or sisters protective of each other, did they fight with each other, did they pick on each other? Did the oldest sister take care of her younger brothers and sisters, or did she rebel when parents asked her to take care of her younger siblings?

Relationships with siblings change dramatically as individuals mature. As small children, siblings often spend much time with each other before they go to school. When one sibling is in school and the other is not, the separation can be freeing to the older sibling and more frightening to the younger. When the older sibling enters adolescence, the younger sibling might be in awe of the sophistication of his older sister's friends or might feel put down by his older sister's friends. When the older sibling leaves to go to college or to work, the younger sibling is left alone. Of course, only children experience different changes in their relationships with peers, cousins, and their parents. In large families, with several brothers and sisters, the effect of changes in other siblings on individuals can become very complex. When the relationship between one sibling and another is strained, an individual is likely to experience more frustration than he or she would with a friend. Some friendships last only a short time, but relationships with siblings usually last a lifetime.

Juanita's patience with her younger sister Dolores was about up. Since her mother worked, Juanita always remembered her mother saying to her, "Now remember to take good care of your sister." From the time she was four, Juanita was well aware that her sister had medical problems, such as diabetes and frequent headaches. Later, Dolores was found to be dyslexic and hyperactive. For Juanita, that meant that not only was Dolores annoying at home but also that she annoyed others at school. Juanita remembers that when Dolores, two years younger than herself, was ten, Dolores took a head off of one of Juanita's Barbie dolls and used it as a ping pong ball. Juanita liked to dress her dolls, so she hated the way Dolores would tear the dresses off her Barbie dolls. When Juanita finally lost her temper and locked Dolores in a closet, Juanita's mother said, "You know you have to be more patient with Dolores. You're older, you should have more understanding." Juanita's mother was patient with Juanita because it was very unusual for Juanita to lose her temper. Now that Juanita is in her second year at community college and Dolores is a senior in high school, the same things seem to be happening. A difference is that instead of abusing Juanita's things, Dolores likes to taunt her sister and make fun of her. Dolores seems to know that Juanita is concerned about her appearance and her grades. This is the way Juanita sees the situation.

"I can't stand the way Dolores gets under my skin. I am getting As and Bs at college, she's getting Cs and Ds in high school and she calls me "Brain" or she'll call me "nerdy" or "geecky." I can't stand it. Whenever I tell her to shut up, she just gets angry or she'll cry and go whine to my mother, and then my mother says, "Now, Juanita, you know your sister has problems, you just have to be kinder toward her." I think those words will be engraved on my gravestone. What a pain! Dolores can't look at herself at all. She can't take any criticism. She just gets mad. Then she starts to call me fat. She knows I'm sensitive to this. I'm really

**Q 5.10** What can Juanita do to get along with Dolores?

**Q 5.11** What can Juanita do so that she is not hurt by Dolores's taunts and jibes?

**Q 5.12** If you have brothers and sisters, how would you characterize your relationship with each of them?

exercising and trying not to gain weight. When the Goodyear blimp comes on television, she'll just smile at me and point to it."

Although relationships with siblings can be very close and intimate, they can also be frustrating and annoying. Sometimes brothers and sisters help each other in dealing with their friends or their parents. Siblings who face a crisis, such as a serious illness of a parent, death of a parent, or divorce of parents, can be very helpful to each other. One of the more common events that siblings might face is that of parental divorce, which is the subject of the next section.

## PARENTAL DIVORCE

Dealing with parental divorce is an increasingly common experience for children of all ages. As Figure 5.1 shows, the divorce rate in the United States has been increasing slowly over the years. Recently, however, the rate has started to decline slightly. In 1940, annual divorces occurred at the rate of 2 per 1,000 people; in 1990, the rate was more than twice that number. Almost half of marriages in the United States end in divorce. This does not mean that the chances are 50-50 that a marriage will end in divorce, as included in the 50 percent rate are people who have been married two, three, or more times. Cherlin (1992) points out that there are several reasons for the increasing divorce rate. First, women have been growing in economic independence over the years, which makes it easier for them to support themselves financially. By working outside the home women might feel a sense of occupational as well as financial independence. Attitudes toward divorce have also changed—people are more accepting of divorce than they used to be. In this section, we will look at the effect of divorce on children, particularly those in late adolescence, and how they deal with divorce.

Divorce can affect children and adolescents in a negative way for a number of reasons (Amato, 1993). One reason is that the absence of a parent, usually a father, can force the remaining parent to fill some of the responsibilities of the absent parent as well as his or her own. Another factor is financial. In 1991, the average income of families in which a single mother was responsible was 60 percent of the income of a family in which the father was financially responsible, and the average income was 40 percent of families that had both parents present. A third reason is that parents in conflict (before, during, and after the divorce) are likely to produce much stress that is absorbed by children. These (and other) reasons usually represent many small events that take place over a period of years, eventually leading to a divorce (Morrison & Cherlin, 1995).

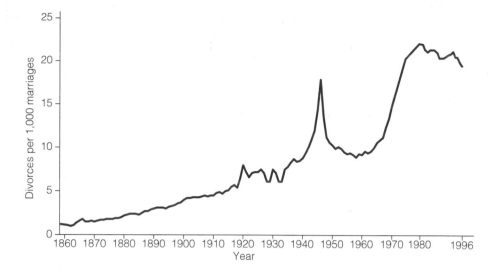

FIGURE **5.1  DIVORCE RATE**

(Number of Divorces Per 1,000 People from Stockard, J., *Sociology: Discovering Society,* Wadsworth, 1999, p. 255.)

When a divorce is finalized, certain factors can make the impact on children greater or lesser (Peterson, Leigh, & Day, 1984). Impact on children seems to be greatest when the noncustodial parent breaks all ties with his or her children, rather than continuing to see them. When the parents' break-up is relatively peaceful, there is less negative affect on the children. But, if the child perceives the marriage as happy right before the breakup, then the child is likely to suffer more negative consequences. Children who have been abused by one of the parents might not experience a high degree of stress and might even welcome the divorce. Or, put another way, when there is a close loving relationship between the parent and the child before the divorce, there can be a greater affect on the child.

There is some debate about what age group divorce most negatively affects. Some researchers say the issues are different at different ages, others such as Peterson, Leigh, and Day (1984), believe it is probably most severe between the ages of three and nine. Some researchers have suggested that as divorce becomes more common, the negative effects seem to be less. Studies of this type prompt the question: What can parents do to help their children when they have decided to get divorced?

When divorces do take place, parents can take certain actions to minimize the negative effects on the children (Hughes, 1996). Being sensitive to the losses that children are experiencing is helpful. Parents can assure children that there will always be a parent to take care of them.

Also, children sometimes believe the parents' divorce is their fault. Assuring children that this is not the case is important. As much as possible, it is helpful for children to continue doing the same things, participating in the same sports events, going to the same schools, playing with the same friends. Children are likely to be very sad, angry, and worried when a divorce is imminent. Encouraging children to talk about their feelings can be quite helpful.

Parents should also avoid some actions. When dealing with each other, parents should be aware of the impact that their frustration with each other can have on their children. Complaining to a child about the other parent can threaten the child's sense of security. Changing a positive image of the other parent to a more negative one can frighten a child. Likewise, violence or extreme anger or upset that is expressed by one parent toward the other in the presence of a child can frighten children. They can start to fear a parent, if emotional expression becomes too extreme. Parents need to continue to take the parental role and not put the child in the role of the parent.

These suggestions about actions to take and to avoid are appropriate for dealing with children under the age of twelve, but they also can be appropriately applied to older adolescents. Parental divorce at any age, including adolescence, can be traumatic because it signifies a major disruption in an individual's life. Divorce can affect children long after the actual divorce has taken place.

To understand how divorce can affect someone in their late teens or twenties, let us examine Ben's situation:

Ben is a senior in high school in Atlanta, Georgia. His sister is three years younger than Ben. When Ben was eight, his parents divorced. As Ben found out about seven years later, his father had had several affairs, and his mother felt that she could no longer tolerate his father's cheating. At the age of eight, Ben was not aware of the reason for the divorce. Because his father was a friendly, charming man, who liked to play with Ben and joke with him, Ben was quite angry at his mother. His father remarried when Ben was ten, and his mother remarried when Ben was thirteen. Ben saw his father one or two weekends a month. Sometimes his father would make a date with Ben, then not show up to take Ben out. Sometimes, Ben felt that that was because he was not doing very well at school and got into fights with his sister. He wondered if his father really wanted to see him.

When Ben's father remarried a few years later, Ben gave up all hope that they would ever get together, but he did hope that they would get along better. Unfortunately, this didn't happen. Ben's father sent smaller checks than he was supposed to and sometimes was several weeks or even months late. His mother was very angry at this because she needed to buy clothes, food, and pay the rent for her small family. When Ben

**Q 5.13** What should Ben do about his high school graduation, and his parents' attendance?

**Q 5.14** What can Ben do to manage his own feelings of anger, frustration, and sadness about the situation?

**Q 5.15** What would you do if you had a similar problem, in which no matter what you did, one of your parents (or another family member) would be angry?

would talk about his father, his mother would get angry. She wanted Ben to spend as little time as possible with his father and his father's family. Ben's mother was angry at Ben's father's parents, three brothers, and sister. She had cut off all ties with Ben's father's family. She told Ben that they were low lifes and the less he had to do with them the better. Whereas Ben's friends looked forward to holiday times, Ben knew that it was fighting time. It was time for his parents to argue about who he would visit and when. Christmas time was the worst, where would he open his presents, where would he have dinner, who would be at whose house when? Now as a senior in high school, his high school graduation is approaching.

"My mother says that if I invite my father to graduation, then she won't go. If I don't invite my father to graduation, he's gonna get really angry. If I just let the whole thing slide, then my father may show up with some of his brothers, and my mother will start shouting at my father. I've got this dark gray suit just for graduation and now I'm probably going to end up as a referee. This is supposed to be a good time for me. I've worked hard in high school, and what do I get at the end of it, a screaming match if I'm not careful."

As you can tell from the description and Ben's comments, Ben's parents did not do most of the things that experts say will help their children cope with divorce. They expressed their anger and hatred toward each other in front of Ben, they complained about each other to Ben, they didn't deal with Ben's feelings about the divorce, and they continued to disrupt Ben's life. Ben loves his parents and particularly appreciates the effort that his mother has made to provide for him when she was a single mother. Now she is asking him not to have his father attend his graduation.

Ben's options are limited. In this situation, Ben has to deal with two parents who dislike each other intensely. Attempts to get his parents to talk to each other have failed in the past and may do so again. Because his mother raised Ben, he is likely to choose to follow his mother's request. In managing his own feelings, Ben is trying to distance himself enough so that he won't be too upset by whatever reaction takes place. He is in a situation in which he has relatively little control. Recognizing this has helped him to cope with situations like this in the past. Ben is trying to develop his own identity as an individual and gradually separate himself from his parents (separation and individuation).

Sometimes individuals are raised by a single parent. Such a situation can raise different issues. Sometimes a child has no identified father, for example, a parent who left home when the child was young and was not seen again. The example of Merry is such a situation.

"Before I was born, my father just moved out on my mother. I grew up in Long Beach, right outside of Los Angeles. It was just three women, me,

---

## Problems and Solutions

---

### How can parents help children when the parents are going through a divorce?

- Don't be negative about the other parent in front of a child.
- Help the child deal with feelings about the divorce.
- Try to keep disruptions in a child's life to a minimum.
- Don't force the child to decide which parent he or she will spend time with or force the child to choose between parents in other ways.
- Don't use the child as a listener or counselor.

---

my mother, and her mother. I remember my childhood so fondly, my grandmother would take me to the beach a lot. I'd get to play in the sand, make these sand castles, carve them. When I'd go to the beach the next day I would always hope that they would be there, these little sand castles I made, but I knew that they wouldn't. My grandmother was always full of fun, she'd say, 'Well, let's go make another one,' and I would. She would make them with me sometimes, but as I got older I made them myself. After school, she was usually there when I got home. She took in sewing and had a big machine; that needle moved so fast! She was really good with me. When I would get close, she would never yell at me. She would just move me away gently, or point her finger at the silvery needle.

"Probably the best times were the weekends. We'd go to the gardens. My mother liked flowers, and we'd go to the arboretum. She really liked roses, reds, yellows, especially miniatures. My grandmother, my mother, myself, we'd all go and it was such fun. I remember them always being soft with me, rarely yelling, even when I was obnoxious, like when I would stick my tongue out at strangers.

"When I first started to date, my mother told me about guys, sex, all that. When I would stay out too late at night, my mother would explain to me why she wanted me in earlier. She never yelled.

"I am working right now repairing copy machines, computers, and other things to get myself through school. Part-time courses seem fine for me right now. When I was in high school, I didn't like it too much. I didn't like being told what to do by the teachers, to get my homework done in time. Things like that. My mother always told me to do my best but never pushed me when I didn't. My grandmother was great. Nothing I did was wrong.

"But now I find that I am getting frustrated with myself. With Jerry, my current boyfriend of about two months, which is long for me, I still get impatient. I liked it when he was so nice to me, brought me flowers that I could show to my mother. He seemed so interested in me, but now I'm not so sure."

On page 119, we noted that Alfred Adler observed that the youngest child is often pampered. Merry's situation might be similar in that her mother and grandmother paid a great deal of attention to her. Now she is having some difficulty when her boyfriends don't pay her that attention. She became disenchanted with school because her teachers, unlike her mother and grandmother were telling her what to do. She is trying to be more patient with others and to be less demanding of them. Certainly, not all only children raised by a mother and grandmother are going to have the same problems as Merry. This case study just points out that different types of parenting affect a child's personality development in different ways.

## *Raising a Child Alone*

We have examined issues that exist when a child is raised by a single parent. Now, let us look at the mother's point of view. What is it like for a young woman (or a young man) to raise a child alone, without the support of a partner?

Danielle was in her seventh month of pregnancy when she attended her high school graduation. Early in August, she gave birth to a baby boy, Bobby. She had not planned to marry Dave, and they finally broke up for the last time when Bobby was four months old. Now three years later, Danielle is trying to attend college while raising Bobby.

"I should have known that Dave was a bum then. But I didn't. I was stupid. He drank a lot and got caught twice stealing cars. Somehow I thought he would stop that. What a dope I was. Dumb. Dumb. Dumb. During my senior year of high school, I started to get the idea that he was a bum. But then I realized he was a real bum. Really bad. But he was cute, so I forgave him—jerk that I was. What really did it for me was when he came in to my apartment drunk, started yelling at me for not paying enough attention to him. Then he picked up Bobby and shook him in my face, I yelled at him to put him down, and then he threw him like he was a football. I had to take Bobby to the emergency room. They insisted that I report Dave for child abuse. After that I told Dave to stay out of my life. And he has.

"Now, Bobby is three, and life is really hard. I'm living with my sister, her husband, and her five- and six-year-old girls. I'm lucky because my sister doesn't work, and she can take care of Bobby along with her little girls. But, it's tough. My sister wants to get out sometimes too. So I have to go to school, work, feed Bobby, sometimes look after my sister's

**Q 5.16** Was Merry raised by a single parent or by two parents? Is her grandmother a parent? Explain.

**Q 5.17** If Merry had been raised by her mother and father, rather than by her mother and grandmother, what do you think might have been different?

**Q 5.18** What do you think it would be like to be raised in a single parent family (if you weren't raised that way) or with a mother and father (if you weren't raised that way)?

**Q 5.29** How has being responsible for Bobby changed Danielle's life?

**Q 5.30** How is Danielle's situation similar to or different from Merry's situation in the previous example?

kids, and try to have a life. I like my programming courses, I like learning C++, I like my networking courses, all that. But that takes work for me, and I'd like to have a social life. Sometimes I worry about guys who want to date a mother with a three-year-old. When do I have time to go out anyway? It's like I got old overnight. Now I'm a mother with Bobby, having to shop for clothes for him, go to the grocery store, take care of him when he's sick, stay up with him at night. I think I handle the responsibilities well, but this isn't the life I thought I'd have. Sometimes I want to be free of it all and be like so many of the other students at school and just study and have jobs and things like that. However, I have a child's future to consider, and I take that role seriously."

Although Danielle seems to constantly question herself and her judgment, she did decide to stop seeing Dave after he abused Bobby. Dave's treatment of Bobby brings up a question that has been of concern to many parents, teachers, and social agencies—that of child abuse, the focus of the next section.

## CHILD ABUSE

Child abuse has been a subject of much media coverage with television, magazines, and newspapers focusing on the most extreme forms of child abuse that can result in disfigurement or death. This section discusses the frequency of child abuse and the nature of it. We will also examine the characteristics of child abusers and why they abuse others. Discussion of how to prevent child abuse, and what to do about it when it occurs will provide some solutions to this very difficult problem. Then, we will look at Danielle and Dave's relationship in the context of child abuse.

**child abuse** Harm to children that includes physical, sexual, or emotional activity as well as neglect.

In the United States, **child abuse** continues to be a difficult problem, with estimates as high as three million children being physically abused every year (Emery & Lauman-Billings, 1998). When Americans were interviewed, one in seven reported being physically abused as a child, and one in eight reported that they had been assaulted by a parent (Moore, 1994). The assault might take the form of being punched, being kicked, being choked, or pushed against an object. Physical abuse can also take the form of neglect, failing to provide nourishment, shelter, or health care. Also emotional abuse can be harmful to children, and includes ridiculing children in front of others, isolating children, swearing and yelling at children, and severely criticizing them. In this section, however, we will focus primarily on physical abuse.

Several factors contribute to child abuse (Emery & Lauman-Billings, 1998). Although mothers are more likely than fathers are to physically

## Problems and Solutions

### How can child abuse be prevented?

- Teach parents nonphysical methods for disciplining children.
- Help parents control their anger.
- Educate parents about how children behave at different age levels.
- Counsel abusive parents to understand violence and other problems in their childhood.

abuse their children, fathers are more often reported to sexually abuse their children. Whereas boys are more likely to experience physical abuse, girls are more likely to experience sexual abuse. Infants who are abused have feeding problems, cry excessively, or become extremely irritable (Ammerman, 1990). For toddlers and older children, excessive crying, aggressiveness, and behavioral problems can cause parents to physically abuse their children, so it is difficult to know whether these types of behaviors are the consequence or the cause of abuse.

Who are the abusers of children, and why do they do this? Many researchers report that physically abusive parents are more likely to be from lower socioeconomic levels and have had less schooling than parents of children where child abuse is not reported. Having had limited schooling, abusive parents are also more likely to have less knowledge about how to raise children and how to develop alternatives to hitting or yelling at children. There is also evidence that those who physically abuse their children might have a history of alcohol or drug abuse (LeFranciois, 1996). Other factors that are related to child abuse are unemployment and growing up in an abusive home, although the relationship between abuse and being raised in an abusive home is greater for fathers than it is for mothers. Physical abuse can occur as a result of stress on the care giver, such as several children to take care of at once, financial concerns, or fighting with a partner. This, combined with misbehavior of a child, can result in physical abuse. What can be done about child abuse?

Approaches to dealing with child abuse tend to be in two areas: prevention and remediation. Prevention programs include educational programs developed by community agencies or school systems that teach parents how to discipline children without physical methods. They can also teach parents what to expect from children at different age levels. Sometimes, these programs deal with how to handle your own emotions and anger. When family, neighbors, or school administrators have reported individuals to the police, these individuals can be assigned to programs that try to educate in ways similar to prevention programs. However, remediation programs may focus more on self-awareness and a history of violence in the individual's own childhood. For programs to be effective, individuals must be motivated to make changes in their behavior.

> When Danielle witnessed Dave hurting Bobby, she knew that she could not tolerate the relationship anymore and refused to see Dave again. For Danielle, reporting the abuse to a social worker was helpful. He told her what to expect in terms of support from the legal system. She also sought out help through Legal Aid who advised her of legal choices she could make. However, the social worker's support helped her feel more confident about her decisions. He helped her not to blame herself for what Dave had done, but rather to decide how to help Bobby and stop seeing Dave.
>
> For Dave, several choices remained. First, he could learn why the relationship had finally ended and understand the severity of his actions. Knowing that Bobby had gone to the emergency room was enough to get him thinking about his own anger. Embarrassed as he was, he sought out his minister to talk about what had happened. The minister made several suggestions that included enrolling in a class on anger management, referral to a social worker or psychologist, and attendance at an Alcoholics Anonymous group. This last suggestion appealed to Dave the most as he was aware of his problem with drinking and felt that that might be a first step.

**family therapy** A form of counseling or psychotherapy designed to help family members improve relationships and solve problems.

**Q 5.21** What do you think will keep Dave from being an abusive parent again?

**Q 5.22** If you knew that a child was being physically abused by his mother or father, what would you do?

Another option for Danielle and Dave was family therapy. **Family therapy** helps members of a family improve relationships and solve problems within a family. Many family therapists focus on problems as they affect the whole family, rather than treating only the individual. Family therapists generally prefer to meet with the entire family together rather than separately with individuals. They often observe how family members interact with each other. Then they may suggest ways that alter relationships in the family. Sometimes they recommend new solutions to existing problems. Had Danielle decided to stay in the relationship with Dave, a family therapist might have focused on Dave's relationship with Bobby and ways for Dave to be more caring and responsible with Bobby. A family therapist might have observed the relationship between Danielle and Dave, then made suggestions about how to strengthen Danielle's approach to dealing with Dave's misbehavior.

## SUMMARY

This chapter has dealt with a variety of issues and concerns regarding relationships with family members. First, the impact of parental attitudes on later child, adolescent, and adult development was described. Three different styles were illustrated with examples: *authoritative,* where parents make rules and set expectations for their children but explain the rules and expectations; *authoritarian,* where rules and expectations are presented, but not explained and where violations might be punished severely; and *permissive,* where parents present little guidance for expected behavior to children.

After parental relationships were discussed, relationships with brothers and sisters and the role of birth order were explained. How to get along with brothers and sisters and some of the complications in such relationships were also described.

The effect of divorce on children of any age can be quite traumatic. Problems that arise in a divorce and how to cope with them were explained. Issues that arise when a child is raised by a single parent and being a single parent both present challenges that affect the development of independence for both parent and child.

Last, the damaging problem of child abuse was presented, including the frequency of the problem and the nature of those who abuse their children. Suggestions were given for ways to cope with this problem.

## RECOMMENDED READINGS

*The Hurried Child: Growing Up Too Fast Too Soon*
Elkind, D. (Addison-Wesley, 1988)
> Current family life in the United States is quite different than what it was in earlier generations. In earlier times, children were seen as needing adult protection and direction. Parents were more available to children than they are now. With more single-parent and dual-earner families, parents often spend less time with their children. Elkind discusses what happens when children are given more responsibility for taking care of themselves than they have had in the past. Elkind discusses the roles of various media such as television and movies on children. He believes that children are encouraged to be independent and to be less dependent on parents more quickly than in the past. Parents are given suggestions about how to reduce stress on children and to help them deal with societal pressures.

*Why Marriages Succeed or Fail ... And How You Can Make Yours Last*
Gottman, J. with Silber, M. (Simon & Schuster, 1994)
> Exercises, quizzes, and tips help to make this book interesting and useful for people wishing to examine their marriages. Gottman has done considerable research on predicting divorce. He describes marriages in which couples are able to work out problems

calmly and contrasts those with marriages in which couples do not confront their problems in an open manner. Also included is an explanation of marriages in which couples argue frequently and angrily. For all types of marriages, Gottman stresses the importance of positive rather than negative interactions. Suggestions are given for improving marital communication styles.

# RECOMMENDED WEB SITES

*Adolescence Directory Online*
http://education.indiana.edu/cas/adol/adol.html
> Resources about adolescents that cover many health, mental health, safety, personal, and parenting issues are provided. This site is sponsored by the University of Indiana Center for Adolescent Studies.

*National Parent Information Network (NPIN)*
http://npin.org/
> Parents are faced with all sorts of questions about development, and the NPIN site describes many guides to online and other resources to answer those questions.

*American Academy of Child and Adolescent Psychiatry (AACAP): Facts for Families*
http://www.aacap.org/web/aacap/factsFam/
> Parents may need help in coping with problems with their children. The brochures that are available online here cover a wide-range of psychological issues and psychiatric conditions. Material is also available in Spanish.

*The Whole Family Center*
http://www.wholefamily.com/
> Advice and links for issues that arise in families, such as raising children, and coping with family crises, can be found here. Two licensed psychologists (who are married to each other) serve as the experts at the Center.

*American Association of Marriage and Family Therapy (AAMFT)*
http://www.aamft.org/
> A well-designed site that is maintained by the American Association of Marriage and Family Therapy (AAMFT). This site provides individuals with an understanding of how professional therapy can help couples and families experiencing difficulty. The site also offers links to important family and marriage-related resources.

*Divorce Central*
http://www.divorcecentral.com/
> Divorce central is one of several excellent online sites that provide information and advice on legal, emotional, and financial issues for individuals who are considering getting a divorce. Links to other divorce-related sites are also available here.

# LOVE AND FRIENDSHIP

A distinguishing characteristic of human beings is their need for friendship and love. We see those who have no friends—hermits and loners— as unusual. This chapter raises questions and gives suggestions for dealing with friendship and love. First, we will examine love and friendship as a very basic human need, the need to be affiliated with or to attach oneself to others. Then we will see how love and friendship relate to other basic human needs. Shyness and how to cope with it, as well as how to initiate new relationships will be described. Questions dealing with the development of such relationships will be raised and discussed. This discussion provides a background for understanding why men and women choose certain people to develop relationships with. Finally, we will examine what makes relationships turn destructive and how to change such relationships so that they can be more constructive and positive.

## THE NEED FOR LOVE

What is love and why is it so important? First, I will describe how some psychologists explain love and its various aspects. Then we will examine the relationship that infants and children have with their parents. Maslow's hierarchy of human needs provides a way of viewing love and friendship as it relates to other needs that individuals have. Sometimes, problems develop when the need for love becomes desperate.

The need to love and to be loved can be a very positive and yet a very negative influence in individuals' lives. The experience of loving and caring can be intense and meaningful. In contrast, the hurt and rejection that comes with being spurned by a loved one can bring anger and depression. The need for love is described eloquently by Corey and Corey (1997, p. 238):

> To fully develop as a person and enjoy a rich existence we need to care about others and have them return this care to us. A loveless life is characterized by joyless isolation and alienation. Our need for love includes the need to know that, in at least one other person's world, our existence makes a difference. If we exclude ourselves from physical and emotional closeness with others, we pay the price in emotional and physical deprivation, which leads to isolation. (Corey & Corey, 1997, p. 238)

Because television, movies, and magazines tend to glamorize love, it is helpful to examine love and see how varied and different love can be. For example, love for a boyfriend or girlfriend, spouse, parent, grandparent, aunt, uncle, friend, brother or sister can all be quite different in the form that love takes. Romantic love is rarely constant: Sometimes it grows deeper; sometimes it deteriorates. When romantic love is very strong, people can have less time for their friends and families. Thus, intense romantic love can strain other relationships. For example, you might have had friends who, when they fell in love with someone, spent little time with you, thus changing your relationship and friendship.

Love is active. Fromm (1956), author of *The Art of Loving,* emphasizes the importance of being active, of giving to the other person, rather than receiving from them. We do things for other people to develop love. We detract from a loving relationship by ignoring loved ones or giving less time and emotional energy to the relationship. Loving relationships are not always smooth and harmonious. In romantic love or in familial love, being frustrated and angry is common. Actively trying to work on the anger or frustration often helps in the continuation and the development of the relationship (Corey & Corey, 1997).

## *Attachment*

**attachment** An emotional bond with another person that is usually powerful and long lasting; used most often to describe the relationship between infant and mother.

Besides understanding the complexities of love, it is helpful to understand how love develops. Many psychologists have studied the **attachments** that individuals develop from infancy to adulthood, particularly, Bowlby (1980, 1982) and Ainsworth (Ainsworth, Blehar, Waters, & Wall, 1978). These researchers devoted more than 30 years of research to understanding different patterns of attachment. Hazan and Shaver (1987, 1986) provide useful insights on the relationship between infant and adult attachment styles. These theorists believe that if children develop good relationships with parents when they are young, they will be able to build sound relationships in later life. Hazan and Shaver describe three styles of infant attachment to parents that are likely to be used by children as they become adults and develop friendships and relationships with others. These adult attachment styles are characterized as secure, avoidant, and anxious/ambivalent.

**secure attachment** An adult attachment style in which individuals trust others easily, are comfortable with others, and can be relied on in long-lasting relationships.

- **Secure.** Such individuals find it easy to trust others, become comfortable with others, and be relied on, as well as to rely on others. Such adults tend to have the longest lasting relationships, the fewest divorces, and fewer fears of being abandoned by their partner. As children, they might have enjoyed close contact with their parent(s) and with childhood friends. Trust and security might have developed.

**avoidant style** An adult attachment style in which individuals are likely to have difficulty developing close and trusting relationships, especially with romantic partners.

- **Avoidant.** These adults might have difficulty in getting close in a romantic relationship and in trusting their partners. They might experience a fear of getting close. As children they might have felt insecure with their mother or caregiver and might have avoided or ignored their mother or caregiver.

- **Anxious-ambivalent.** These adults were often worried about their relationships breaking up. They reported that their partners were not as close to them as they would have liked. Jealousy was characteristic

**anxious-ambivalent style**
An adult attachment style in which individuals might be anxious about relationships ending.

of these relationships. As children, they might have experienced inconsistent reactions from their caregivers, sometimes caring, sometimes not. When the caregiver withdrew for any period of time, they, as children, might have ignored or resisted the caring of their parent(s).

The attachment patterns that individuals experience as children tend to affect their development of love and friendship relationships throughout their lifetimes. Hazan and Shaver's research suggests that attachment experiences of individuals can affect the development of friendships, work relationships, interactions with relatives, and the development of romantic relationships.

## Maslow's Need Hierarchy

**need hierarchy** The hierarchy of needs developed by Abraham Maslow, in which the most basic needs, such as physiological and safety needs, must be satisfied before needs for love and belonging, self-esteem, and self actualization can be satisfied.

The need for love and friendship can be examined to see how it fits with other human needs. Abraham Maslow (1970) has grouped needs in a hierarchy from the lowest needs, those that must be satisfied first, to the highest needs (Figure 6.1). For our discussion, these needs are grouped into five categories, with love and belongingness needs listed third.

- **Physiological needs.** These needs are basic to survival and include the need to eat, drink, breathe, sleep, urinate, and so forth.
- **Safety and security needs.** These refer to the need to be safe from harm, to be safe from attack or danger.
- **Love and belongingness needs.** These are the needs discussed in this chapter—to share affection, to love, to affiliate with. All refer to interactions with other people.
- **Self-esteem needs.** This refers to having confidence in ourselves, feeling good about ourselves, and having a sense of being worthy.
- **Self-actualization needs.** This refers to the sense of fulfillment when we accomplish goals for ourselves. It includes the sense of being creative, feeling pleased at being able to express ourselves creatively, and feeling a sense of accomplishment. This is the highest of Maslow's needs and the one that people find the most difficult to achieve or meet (Hughes, 1996).

**self-esteem needs**
Having confidence in ourselves, feeling good about ourselves, and having a sense of being worthy.

**self-actualization needs**
A sense of fulfillment that comes from accomplishing goals for ourselves, being creative, and expressing ourselves creatively.

Next to basic needs (physiological and security needs), Maslow considered love and belongingness to be most essential to human beings. When these needs are not met, loneliness, sadness, and depression can result. Attachment theory provides a means of understanding how these needs develop and can be nurtured or thwarted. Thus, according to attachment theory, our relationships with parents and early caregivers provides us with a model for how we will interact in romantic relationships and in

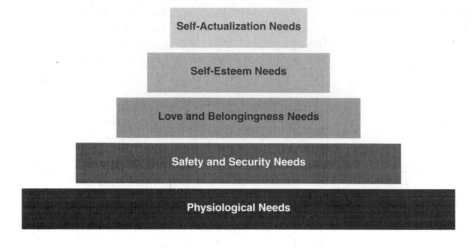

FIGURE **6.1** MASLOW'S HIERARCHY OF NEEDS.

(From Maslow, 1970.)

friendships in later life. Erica's situation with her ex-boyfriend illustrates the strength of belongingness and loving needs and the problems that exist when that need is frustrated.

> Erica is a 20-year-old junior at a small southern college. Her father is a manager in the postal system, and her mother is a third-grade teacher. Erica has an older brother and a younger sister who is still in high school. Erica met Ron at the beginning of her freshman year, when Ron was a sophomore at the school. They dated for about 18 months and broke up about a year ago. Although Erica had some friends in college, she spent most of her time with Ron. The friendships that she maintained were mainly with her high school friends whom she saw when she returned home on vacation.
>
> "I am always thinking about Ron. When I wake up in the morning, when I go to bed, it's terrible. I miss him so much. We did so many things together. We studied together; we would meet after class; we would go to lunch together. Now that I don't see him much, it's awful. And it's even worse when we do see each other.
>
> "When he started dating Bonnie, I was taken by total surprise. I remember I had gone over to his room in the first floor of Slazer, and that slime was sitting on his lap, had her dress up around her waist and I turned white and ran out. He tried to tell me he still loved me, but he was still seeing her, I knew it, I could smell that damn perfume of hers on him and then I would think of that little red skirt up around her

waist. The bad thing is I still want him back. I certainly don't want him with her. I want him back.

"I miss lots of times. I miss when we would study together, when he would help me with my biology course. He was real gentle and nice to me. Even though I had trouble, he would go over the problems with me and spend time with me. Then there was the time when he came home with me and I introduced him to my parents. I was worried what they would think, because my mom has always been so protective of me, never really wanted me to date in high school. But they liked him; he got along with my brother and sister, my parents. I really felt like maybe this was it, that I would be with him forever. But then it stopped.

"I'm not interested in anyone. I've gone out a few times with other people, but they seemed so boring. I can't get interested in them. I feel so alone at school, this is my third year, but I still don't have many friends. It's terrible. Sometimes it starts to get better when I get interested in some of my courses, but it doesn't last long."

Clearly, Erica's need for love and belongingness is high. Physiological or safety needs are not an issue for Erica now. There were times at the beginning of the breakup that she couldn't sleep, couldn't eat, and lost weight. Her attachment to Ron is so strong. We have a hint from what she says that her dependence on Ron might be similar to the dependence that she had on her mother. We might wonder if Erica relied too much on her mother for support and security.

A year and a half have passed since Erica described the situation. She still thinks of Ron some, feels a little anxious or tense when she does, but it is not as bad as it was before. She made an effort to develop her friendships with Dawn and Rita, whom she had known somewhat casually the first two years. These friendships continued even when Dawn had a boyfriend. It was really hard to not compare the depth of feeling that she had with Ron with someone else whom she was just beginning to know. When she first went out with Chuck, she didn't give him a chance. Two months later, he expressed interest in her again. She tried to keep herself from pushing him away immediately, but that was hard for her. He doesn't call her anymore.

Individuals often find that if they can shift their needs for belongingness from an ex-boyfriend or girlfriend to other friends, they can gradually get over a broken relationship. Learning to accept that nonromantic relationships offer value and help individuals feel a sense of belonging, usually in a more limited way, can be difficult. Developing new friendships and strengthening others often means making deliberate efforts that are not always comfortable at first. However, good friendships often meet belongingness and self-esteem needs for individuals dealing with the loss of a relationship.

---

**Q 6.1** How could Erica love Ron so desperately, even after he has left her?

---

**Q 6.2** What might help Erica get through the loneliness and move away from her sadness?

---

**Q 6.3** Have you been in a situation like Erica's? How did you handle it or would you handle it? What could you do?

---

## DEVELOPMENT OF RELATIONSHIPS

In Erica's case, it is clear that one relationship became very important to her in her life. In a sense, her life revolved around Ron. But how do relationships get started? How do they develop? Starting a relationship with individuals can be difficult, whether or not you are shy. However, shyness makes this process very difficult for some people. The next section discusses the difficulty some people have in feeling comfortable relating to others.

### *Shyness*

**shyness** Being uncomfortable or anxious in the presence of strangers or people with whom one is not familiar.

**state shyness** Being shy in only certain situations, such as meeting strangers or being in a large group.

**trait shyness** Being anxious or afraid in many interpersonal situations, such as being with small groups, strangers, or relatives; at work; or dating.

Researchers have identified two types of **shyness** (Asendorpf, 1989): Situationally specific shyness and trait shyness. Most shy people report that their shyness occurs in specific situations, such as in a dating situation or in a large group—**state shyness.** A small number identify themselves as being anxious or afraid in many situations—**trait shyness.** These situations might include being with large groups, small groups, strangers, relatives, friends, children, or parents; being evaluated; dating; and so forth. The shyness can be felt as anxiety, feeling flushed, feeling sweaty, not being able to talk, not knowing what to say, and finding it difficult to follow up in conversations.

Zimbardo (1977, 1990) describes several reasons why individuals develop the trait of shyness: They might be concerned about negative views that other people have of them. Sometimes they fear being rejected by potential friends or romantic partners. Frequently this is related to being afraid of being intimate or to lacking self confidence. Some might lack confidence in their ability to make conversation or to be perceived as interesting or attractive.

In his books, Zimbardo (1977, 1990) makes several suggestions that can help you understand shyness and do something about it if you are shy. Decreasing shyness should be approached gradually. Zimbardo suggests starting with relatively simple interactions with others that are relatively quick. Conversations with sales clerks, with people in a grocery line, or at sporting events might be relatively easy because these contacts tend to be rather impersonal and very brief. Watching someone of the same gender who can serve as a role model for developing relationships with others and listening actively can also be very helpful. When people talk about themselves, it is easier to talk about a subject that they are enthusiastic about, than to initiate a new topic. Because many people enjoy talking about themselves, encouraging them to do so will make it easier to develop a conversation than it will be if you try to find a topic you think they might be interested in. In a similar way, it is easier to talk about areas that you have

---

## Problems and Solutions

*What can you do in situations when you feel shy?*

- Start with relatively simple and brief interactions with others.
- Use others as role models.
- Listen actively to others.
- Talk about topics you know something about.

---

some knowledge about than areas with which you are less familiar. If you like movies, sports, or fiction, it is easier to talk about the stars and authors you know about than it is to discuss areas you're less familiar with.

### Initiating Relationships

Starting a conversation can be difficult for some people. Most people are able to do that with friends or relatives because they have much in common with them. However, starting conversations with strangers is more difficult. Often people discuss something they have in common with the new person. If it is at a sports event, perhaps "The Cowboys are really on a roll. What do you think?" If it is in a class, "What do you think about what the professor said about communism? How did you work out Problem 2?" Other general questions like "What did you think of the weather yesterday?" or "How do you like that new building over there?" are ways to begin a conversation. In general, it is more helpful to ask open-ended questions than it is closed-ended questions.

Closed-ended question: "Do you like this college?"
Open-ended question: "What has being at this college seemed like to you?"

Closed-ended question: "Did you do your homework?"
Open-ended question: "How did you handle that question about photo-
    synthesis?"

In general, closed questions receive very brief answers. Closed questions often require a follow-up question.

Closed-ended question: "Where are you from?"
Answer: "I'm from San Francisco."
Follow-up: "I hear that's an exciting city, what do you think?"

## Problems and Solutions

*How do you start a conversation with someone you have never met before?*

- Discuss something you have in common.
- Use open-ended rather than close-ended questions.
- Follow-up brief answers with open-ended questions.
- Look at but do not stare at the person.
- Use a body position that indicates that you are attending to the person.
- Face the person. If sitting, lean slightly toward him or her.

The follow-up question allows short closed-ended questions to lead into a longer discussion. For example, individuals can then talk about San Francisco and other cities that they have enjoyed visiting or living in. If the questioner talks about how she has liked living in Los Angeles, then she is disclosing some information about herself. This isn't very personal information, but it is enough to get the conversation going. Self-disclosures need to be limited and cautious at first. If a conversation concerns experiences of visiting or living in different cities, it might be inappropriate to ask about someone's family. Relationships develop slowly as people develop more confidence in each other.

**empathy** Understanding another's point of view and communicating that understanding to that person.

Expressing empathy for another person helps to establish an open rather than defensive atmosphere. **Empathy** refers to understanding another person's point of view and communicating that understanding to that person. For example, if a friend is concerned that he or she has developed a sexually transmitted disease, expressing support and concern for your friend would be empathic. Implicit in empathy is being nonjudgmental. Thus, you would not judge or chastise your friend for being immoral or careless. You approach your friend as an equal rather than as inferior. Rogers (1975) developed and relied on empathy as a major therapeutic attitude in his approach to psychotherapy.

So far we have been discussing the importance of attitudes toward others or questions or comments to use in conversations, but it is important to say something about nonverbal messages as well as about verbal ones. In conversations of any length, people normally use eye contact, looking at but not staring at each other frequently. When people are interested in each other, they usually face each other, leaning very slightly forward at times to show interest. Their arms are not likely to be folded across their chests, but more open, on their laps or by their sides, to indicate interest. People often vary the volume, pitch, or rate of speech when they are excited or interested. Showing genuine interest is a way of developing a conversation with people. Thus, the verbal and the nonverbal efforts that people make to learn about and talk with others starts to develop a relationship that can turn into a friendship or something more. An example of how Ralph made some strides in overcoming state shyness with a manager and a woman he liked shows some ways to initiate and develop relationships.

Ralph is in a two year community college program where he is studying computer technology. Although Ralph is 19, his parents are considerably older than most parents of 19-year-olds. Both are factory workers in a suburb of Chicago and are close to retirement. His two older brothers have moved to the West Coast and have married. Ralph lives at home, with only his dog and his parents. He has helped to support himself through school by working as an assistant manager at a fast food restaurant.

"When I am at work, I do not seem to have much of a problem with my shyness. We are always hiring and managing high school kids to be cooks, work the cash registers, and clean up. At work, things move quickly, and I find that I can give these kids instructions and answer their questions rather easily. It's like I don't even have time to be shy or be afraid. Since I started doing this job about three years ago, I've found that the types of situations that are difficult for me have narrowed. Interacting with customers, even my manager, has been easier. Two days ago, my manager said he wanted to meet with me to talk about some things in private. I really got nervous. When the meeting took place the next day, I found I was stammering; I felt flushed; my stomach was in a knot; I was a mess. It turned out all he wanted to talk to me about was some overall restructuring of scheduling of the employees, as summer time vacations were starting. I was really relieved after the meeting was over, but I could have kicked myself for making such a big deal about it at the beginning. Had he just talked about this while I was at the counter, I probably would not have gotten upset at all.

"But what really has me going is Veronica. We've known each other for a couple of years and have been real friendly, I think that she may like me but I'm not sure. I really want to ask her out, but I'm not sure what to do or how to do it. She seems real friendly, and I find her attractive—short, dark hair, nice smile."

*RS:* "How have you thought about approaching her?" (Ralph probably has some ideas, he may not be sure of them. He's thought about asking out Veronica for a long time.)

*Ralph:* "I've thought about asking her if we could go out for coffee after her shift. I've thought about lots of things, like taking her to the movies, going sailing, going out for a drive."

*RS:* "You seem to have a sense of what might be the best start for you." (Ralph's judgment about what might be most comfortable for him is probably quite good.)

*Ralph:* "Yeah. I think we can get some coffee at this nice place nearby, after she gets a chance to get out of uniform. I'll try that."

*RS:* "Sounds good!" (Encouraging Ralph and reinforcing his decision seems important here.)

For most people like Ralph, shyness is situationally specific. They feel comfortable with some people, such as friends and family, but feel anxious with others, such as a potential romantic interest or a boss. Often the skills that individuals have used with the people they're comfortable with also work in more anxious situations. In coming up with ideas about how to deal with Veronica, Ralph will be able to use ideas that work with his family. These include talking to Veronica about what she is interested in, listening to her as he does with the high school students that work for him, and looking at her directly as he does with his student employees and family.

## CHOICE AND RELATIONSHIPS

When we are able to develop relationships, how do we choose the people who become our friends or romantic partners? In some societies, choice of friends or romantic partners is more limited than in others. For example, parents commonly arrange the marriages of their children in a number of Asian societies. As Western attitudes have affected Asian and other cultures, arranged marriages are becoming less common. Many Americans place great emphasis on individual choice and freedom. This is particularly true in how Americans choose their friends and romantic partners. In this section, we will examine what conditions are necessary for relationships to develop, characteristics we look for in others, and characteristics that we see in ourselves. All these influence our choice of friends and partners. I will focus particularly on the choice of romantic partners and use this information to understand how Laura has continually made choices of romantic partners that have created great difficulty and dissatisfaction for her.

Three factors affect whether friendships or relationships get started. Hughes (1996) describes these as proximity, similarity, and reciprocity. **Proximity** refers to finding people who are nearby. We are more likely to become friendly with our neighbors at home or at school than with those who live far away. We can also become friendly with people whose paths

**Q 6.4** What other actions could Ralph take to overcome his shyness with Veronica?

**Q 6.5** List a few situations in your life in which you have felt shy.

**Q 6.6** What have you done (or could you have done) in these situations to overcome the feeling of shyness? List some specific actions.

**proximity** Finding people who are nearby.

**similarity** Seeking out people who are similar to ourselves.

**reciprocity** The tendency to like people who like us.

we cross (Berscheid & Reis, 1998). For example, in a residence hall, we are more likely to become friendly with those who live on the same floor as we do, whose doors are open, and who are frequently on their floor than we are with people who live on a different floor. Similarly, we are more likely to become friends with someone who sits next to us in class rather than someone three seats away from us. Furthermore, we are likely to seek out people who are similar to ourselves (**similarity**). They can be similar to ourselves in attractiveness (Cash & Derlega, 1978) or similar to ourselves in interests and personality. Although we certainly may have friends who are more or less outgoing than ourselves, or differ in other characteristics, we are likely to become friends with people who have similar interests and values, whether they be religious, social, or political. **Reciprocity,** another important factor, refers to liking people who like us. If individuals have a sense that someone doesn't like them, they are less likely to seek out that person as an acquaintance or as a friend. Proximity, similarity, and reciprocity influence whether or not friendships or romantic relationships are likely to be initiated.

In general, men place more emphasis on physical attractiveness than do women when they look for a romantic partner. By examining personal ads placed in newspapers, Gonzales and Meyers (1993) found that gay men emphasized physical characteristics more than heterosexual men did, and lesbians emphasized physical characteristics even less than heterosexual women did. A study by Buss (1989), Table 6.1 shows how individuals in 37 countries rated characteristics for their ideal mate. Notice that physical attractiveness is third for men and sixth for women. Because men particularly value physical attractiveness in women, it is not surprising that females then value physical attractiveness in themselves, more than males do (Feingold, 1990). Also, some research (Weiten & Lloyd, 2000) suggests that an attractive body is perceived by most people as being more important than an attractive face. This emphasis on physical attractiveness is discussed in more detail in Chapter 8, where body image in relationship to male and female roles is described.

Physical attractiveness is only one of several characteristics that are important in choosing a romantic partner. For example, Kenrick, Groth, Trost, and Sadalla (1993) report that American college students found characteristics such as being emotionally stable, easy going, friendly, exciting, and having a good sense of humor as being important in choosing a mate. Other important characteristics (Weiten & Lloyd, 2000) include intelligence and confidence. Not surprisingly, people seek out others who they believe are skilled, can make a good living, and can converse on a similar intellectual level. In the United States and many other cultures, it is not unusual for women to prefer to marry someone older than they are, and for men to seek out women somewhat younger. Seeking out people of higher

TABLE **6.1** CHARACTERISTICS COMMONLY SOUGHT IN A MATE

| Rank | Characteristics preferred by men | Characteristics preferred by women |
| --- | --- | --- |
| 1 | Kindness and understanding | Kindness and understanding |
| 2 | Intelligence | Intelligence |
| 3 | Physical attractiveness | Exciting personality |
| 4 | Exciting personality | Good health |
| 5 | Good health | Adaptability |
| 6 | Adaptability | Physical attractiveness |
| 7 | Creativity | Creativity |
| 8 | Desire for children | Good earning capacity |
| 9 | College graduate | College graduate |
| 10 | Good heredity | Desire for children |
| 11 | Good earning capacity | Good heredity |
| 12 | Good housekeeper | Good housekeeper |
| 13 | Religious orientation | Religious orientation |

From D. M. Buss, *Behavioral and Brain Sciences*, vol. 12 (1989, pp. 1–14). reprinted with permission of Cambridge University Press.

social status, or at least similar status, is not unusual. However, Feingold (1992) found that males "trade" occupational status for physical attractiveness in females. In other words, if a woman is seen as attractive, her occupational status will matter less. Similarly, some studies have shown that attractive women are more likely to look for high status in prospective mates than are less attractive women. In this way, characteristics such as attractiveness and social status tend to interact in complex ways in their influence on how men and women value characteristics in their prospective partners.

How we view the characteristics of others is important, but so is the way in which we view ourselves. Our self-esteem—that is our view of our worth as a person—significantly affects our choice of romantic partner. Some characteristics of people who have low self-esteem are awkwardness, self-consciousness, and shyness (Weiten & Lloyd, 2000). For example, such individuals might have a need for acceptance from others but are reluctant to seek it. Low self-esteem individuals are more likely to blame themselves for not being successful than they are to blame others. Not having confidence in their abilities, they are likely to feel anxious in social situations, such as meeting a partner, or in job situations, such as an interview. People with low self-esteem might seek out less attractive dates or people who share values that they don't like in themselves, such as not being competent or socially skilled. By doing this, they avoid being rejected by those they view as more attractive or competent, who they believe might reject them.

Choosing a prospective romantic partner who was very different from the way others perceived Laura, but not very different from the way Laura perceived herself created many problems for her.

A junior at Harvard University in Cambridge, Massachusetts, Laura was a highly competent student. She was an all "A" student throughout high school and has received "Bs" and "Cs" in college. Despite the fact that Laura's friends, parents, and teachers praised Laura's academic and other abilities, Laura never agreed with them. Laura's father was a surgeon who was very demanding of himself and of others. He was consumed by his work, coming home late at night and then retiring to his study. The strong demands that he placed on himself he also placed on Laura and her younger sister. "As" were expected and anything else seemed like a failure. Somewhat critical of her own self, Laura's mother was an accountant who worked in a large firm. Laura's impression was that Laura's father tolerated her mother's work, but did not really respect it, because it was not academically challenging. Laura said this about Doug:

"I met Doug when we were in the subway station. It was hot and very crowded, around rush hour, and people were pushing each other to get into the cars. The Massachusetts Transit station was always a mess and I hated it. I had just missed the train and started to laugh. Doug started a conversation with me. He was really funny, joking to me about how seriously people take themselves, the other people on the train, and how they ought to have competitions for being the best train chaser. I really liked his charm and relaxed style and so when he suggested that we go out to dinner after we got to my stop, I said fine. It seemed like one thing led easily to another, and after about a month, we were dating steadily.

"At first, I used to go to his little apartment in Chelsea a few times a week. He had a roommate who was hardly ever there. I didn't like it at first, as the furniture was old, there were no paintings or anything on the walls, and the rug was a grungy gray, with stains. When we would be at his place, we would have dinner, drinks, and sex. More and more, the drinking part became longer and longer. As we got used to each other, Doug was not so much fun. He was out of work and was complaining about the construction job that he had been on and how he was unfairly fired. He had thought about going to college, but barely graduated from high school and never thought that was something he would want to do.

"About two months ago, he said he would meet me at school and I waited for him in the library, and he never showed up. I got real mad at him for this and he swore at me. Then he laughed it off and said it would never happen again. The next week, I went to his place. He told me to get there at 7:00, I got there about 7:30, and he was real angry with me and slapped me across the face. I hit him back, and he hit me harder. Then he threw beer at me and got it all over me, and I left. He came running after me. Before I'd gotten far down the hallway, he apologized, and I came back. He really cares about me, and I really like him, I just wish he wouldn't hurt me. My friends at school all think I'm crazy. Why

**Q 6.7** Why do you think Laura is attracted to Doug?

**Q 6.8** What do you think would help Laura let go of this relationship?

**Q 6.9** Have you ever known people in relationships like this? Why do they keep trying to work things out?

**Q 6.10** What works to get out of such a relationship?

would I waste the time on somebody who treats me this way. But he really cares about me, and I really care about him. I really think that I can help him get through his problems."

We can speculate that Laura's proximity to Doug in the subway led to the start of the relationship. Her negative view of herself, very different from the way others see her, seems to have led to finding her someone who treats her badly. Sometimes relationships turn out very differently than is anticipated at the beginning. No one starts out looking for an abusive relationship; such relationships develop with familiarity and are the subject of the next section.

## ABUSIVE RELATIONSHIPS

When relationships develop problems, there is often a lack of listening and attending to the needs of the other person. Abuse tends to be an extreme form of this, with yelling, hitting (or threats of hitting), cheating, or destructive hurtful statements. This section will discuss the warning signs that occur before and during abusive situations. Then we will examine violent abuse, battering or hitting, especially the characteristics of individuals who batter and those who are battered. Ways to strengthen a relationship and ways of behaving in a relationship will then be described and illustrated, when we return to Laura's problems with Doug.

Even before abuse starts, some signs can indicate that a relationship is about to deteriorate or become more volatile. One of the first signs is the use of alcohol or drugs in a relationship. These alter behavior and make it much more difficult for an individual to attend to and be considerate of his or her partner. Alcohol and drug abuse are the leading contributors to divorce and marital discord. Another sign is when you start to feel bad about yourself when you are in a relationship. Sometimes individuals start to feel criticized or put down by their partner. Sometimes it's rather subtle, as individuals start to feel less attractive or less competent. They might feel ignored by the other person or not valued. Another warning that abuse might be coming is pressures from the partner to stay away from friends or family and be loyal only to the partner. Healthy relationships rarely threaten other healthy relationships.

Although yelling, negative statements, and cheating are very destructive to a relationship, hitting or battering affects a person's safety. Physical abuse is most commonly in the form of hitting, but it also includes kicking, burning, using a knife or gun, and forcing unwanted sexual contact—rape. Moore (1994) provides some data about the frequency and nature of abuse. About 90 percent of victims of domestic violence are women.

## Problems and Solutions

*How can you prevent relationships from becoming emotionally or physically abusive?*

- Don't blame the other person for your problems.
- Talk openly about problems.
- Don't let frustration build to anger.
- Show concern, verbally and nonverbally, for the person.
- Keep eye contact with the other person.
- Make specific rather than vague statements.
- Make positive statements rather than critical ones.
- Let the other person respond.
- Show you understand what the other person has said.

Husbands or boyfriends killed 28 percent of female murder victims, whereas wives or girlfriends killed only about 3 percent of male murder victims in 1994. Clearly, physical abuse is not a rare occurrence.

Who are the people who hit and batter? As shown, they are mainly men, who also share some general characteristics. They tend to have low self esteem and are often very jealous and possessive of their wives or girlfriends. Although they are likely to have been beaten as children or to have seen their mothers beaten, that does not mean that most abused men grow up to be batterers. About a third of them do (Weiten & Lloyd, 2000). As suggested earlier, alcohol and drugs affect individuals' judgment and male batterers tend to abuse alcohol and drugs. When confronted with their harmful physical behavior, male batterers commonly say that what they did was not really that serious or blame the woman or someone else for their behavior. Characteristics of battered women are less clear. Often they blame themselves for the man's behavior and, like the male, tend to minimize the battering. Sometimes they will deny the abuse and its severity and hope that things will get better (Walker, 1989). Not surprisingly, women who are abused and physically battered are likely to have low self-esteem because of continual negative treatment.

How can physical abuse be prevented? Are there ways that relationships can be conducted so that such extreme behavior does not occur? Often an abuser is not willing to do some of the things that lead to a good relationship and prevent a difficult or abusive one.

- A relationship requires effort from both partners to keep it alive and vibrant.
- Within a relationship, each person must work to make his or her own life happy and not blame the other for unhappiness. In an abusive relationship, the abuser commonly blames his partner for his own personal difficulties, such as drinking, job dissatisfaction, or problems with the children.
- When problems do occur, it is important to be able to talk openly with the other person about these difficulties. Letting frustrations develop and build can often lead to explosions of anger. When anger does occur, it is important to express it without sarcasm or hostility. Explaining why someone is angry and what they are angry about is helpful.
- Abuse is avoided by demonstrating concern for the person. This can be shown verbally or nonverbally, but an interest in the other person's well being and a desire to see that the other person is happy is important.

Although these suggestions might prevent abuse, they are not likely to be attractive to individuals who are abusers and want to give free vent to their anger. These suggestions might seem somewhat vague. Some suggestions for communicating more effectively with a partner are described here.

- Couples are in a position where they can make eye contact when they communicate, and one person speaks while the other listens. Talking while the other person turns away, or while the other person is talking, leads to ineffective communication.
- Specific statements are much more effective than vague ones. A specific statement is, "I get scared when you raise your voice and don't give me a chance to reply." Here, the speaker is clear in expressing herself, and the listener knows what she is referring to. This is preferable to "Sometimes you really frighten me." In this case, the listener does not know the situations that the speaker is referring to.
- Comments that are critical lead to arguments; positive statements are much more constructive. For example, it is better to say, "I really appreciate it when you take the time to listen to me," rather than to say, "You are so self-centered! You never listen to me." A listener can respond much more thoughtfully to the first statement than to the second.
- Statements that individuals make should fit with their facial and bodily expressions. For example to say, "I really care for you," while you are snarling can appear confusing, or even silly. Likewise, one's voice tone should be consistent with the statement. "I really care for you," said in a stilted manner, defeats the purpose of the statement.
- When making statements, the speaker needs to give the listener a chance to respond. Make one statement at a time, rather than several. It is difficult to respond to comments like this, "Why did you leave the

kitchen such a mess? You never take out the garbage. And when I went to use your car there was your stuff all over the front seat. Give me a break!" Responding to such a statement is quite difficult, and a listener faced with such a statement would do best to respond to one part of it rather than the entire statement. The listener can also acknowledge the speaker's anger and reply, "You really are upset with me. Let's talk about the kitchen."

- A helpful response is for the speaker to show that she understands what has just been said. For example, if someone has just said, "I resent all the time you spend at work with Jim," it can be useful to say, "I understand that you are worried about me spending as much of my time as I have spent with Jim," then go on to say, "This is because we have been working on a project for Betty that has to be completed by the fifteenth." The first statement shows that the speaker understood the concerns of the other person and the second statement responds to the concern of the listener.

There is a consistency in all these statements. The individual is patient in dealing with the other person by listening carefully and by exercising emotional control, not losing his temper. There is a respect for the other person as well that the other person has feelings, ideas, and concerns that are worthy of being heard. There is also an openness and directness. The individual is trying to be straightforward with her feelings and not be devious or manipulative. These ways of communicating foster a feeling of caring and love and prevent the building of a potentially abusive situation.

Using suggestions such as these just described is more difficult than it would appear. Other writers (Corey & Corey, 1997; Hughes, 1996) offer useful suggestions for communicating with another person. Would the description of a caring relationship and suggestions for improving communication with each other help Laura and Doug?

*RS:* Would you both be interested in working on your relationship to improve your ways of talking with each other? So that you don't get as angry and upset with each other?

*Laura:* I'd like to be able to talk with Doug without being angry and without having Doug be angry with me. (Laura takes responsibility for her anger and also expresses concern about Doug's.)

*Doug:* Sounds okay to me. Laura's always yelling at me and criticizing me for not working or something else like that. I'd like to get her to shut up about that. (Doug isn't getting the message. He's able to talk about changes he would like to see in Laura but expresses no willingness to make change on his own part.)

*RS:* Doug, you're real angry at Laura's criticism and that's what you want to focus on now. (I am trying to show my understanding of Doug.)

**Q 6.11** Can this relationship be saved? What are the strengths and weaknesses that Doug and Laura bring to their relationship?

**Q 6.12** Use this discussion of the caring relationship and the tips for communication to describe your relationship with one other person.

**Q 6.13** Have you ever been in a relationship like Doug and Laura's or witnessed one? How did you see communication skills improve or get worse?

*Doug:* You bet. She's always whining about me, I drink too much, I'm not ambitious. Whine. Whine. Whine.

*Laura:* Cut it out! You talk about me whining . . .

*RS:* Stop a minute Laura. Before you criticize Doug, take a moment to reflect on what he is saying. (I had better break in here fast, or they will be back to their typically destructive communication patterns.)

*Laura:* He says that I complain about his not working and his drinking.

*RS:* Good. That really helps to defuse the situation, and to get the two of you talking and listening again.

When working with couples in distress, marriage and family counselors try to help partners communicate more effectively with each other. Sometimes couples need outside help to improve their ability to relate to each other. Such help is often very effective in defusing potentially abusive situations. However, many couples knowingly or unknowingly use the communication skills that I have described here to help them have a more satisfying relationship.

## SUMMARY

In this chapter, I have asked you to consider friendship and love. First, we discussed how strong the need for love and affiliation can be in a person's life. We also looked at how difficult it can be when this need is not met, for example, when a relationship is over. Then we looked at how relationships develop. Shyness often interferes with individuals developing closer relationships with others. Situational (state) and pervasive (trait) shyness were discussed and suggestions for gradually becoming more comfortable with other people were given. Then we looked at how two people choose others to relate to and, particularly, how they choose romantic partners. Relationships do not always work out positively, so then we dealt with abusive relationships and how individuals can communicate more effectively and show their caring for one another.

## RECOMMENDED READINGS

*Just Friends: The Role of Friendship in our Lives.*
Rubin, L. (Harper & Rowe, 1985).
> This book deals with friendships and family relationships: The role of friendships and the development of men's and women's lifestyles; the relationship between marriage and friendship; different types of friendships, such as "best friends"; and differences

between females, lesbians, heterosexual men, and heterosexual women. This book is based on in-depth interviews with more than 300 men and women between the ages of 25 and 55.

*Shyness*
Zimbardo, P. G. (Addison Wesley, 1994)
> A well-known social psychologist, Zimbardo has been studying shyness for many years. In the first part of the book, Zimbardo describes causes of shyness, then gives examples of shyness and several suggestions about how to become less shy and less anxious in interpersonal situations. In the second part of the book, he gives exercises and practical suggestions for dealing with this problem.

## RECOMMENDED WEB SITES

*Philip R. Shaver's home page*
http://psychology.ucdavis.edu/Shaver/default.html
> A researcher on adult attachment and its relationship to romantic relationships, Shaver has done many studies on this topic. His home page describes his findings, provides online access to some of his more important papers, and introduces browsers to his Adult Attachment Lab.

*SUNY Buffalo Counseling Center: Relationship Page*
http://ub-counseling.buffalo.edu/RELATIONSHIPS/
> The Counseling Center at SUNY, Buffalo, has collected several excellent guides to interpersonal relationships and to methods to improving communication among college students. Online materials focus on questions and issues stemming from interpersonal and intimate relationships.

*The Shyness Home Page*
http://www.shyness.com/
> The Shyness Institute is co-directed by Philip Zimbardo and Lynne Henderson. This Web site offers "network resources seeking information and services for shyness."

# SEXUALITY AND INTIMACY

Talking openly about sexuality is difficult for most people. As a result, myths and misinformation about sexuality have developed. Even though more and more information is available about sex and sexual behavior, not all this information is accurate or useful in helping people make decisions about their own sexual behavior. For many people, the development of intimacy and the communication of sexual desires and concerns can be awkward or difficult. In this chapter, we will discuss a variety of concerns that include sexual behavior and intimacy as well as issues that can make sexual behavior problematic, such as contraception, sexually transmitted diseases, and rape. First, we will look at common misconceptions about sexuality.

## MYTHS

Because sex is considered to be very personal by many, and "dirty" by others, there are more myths and falsehoods about sexuality than about any other area of human life. Often, the major source for sexual information for children is other children, so it is not surprising that the information that they convey to each other is inaccurate. Some of the more common myths about sexuality relate to pregnancy and masturbation.

There is much misinformation about how women become pregnant. When people are totally uninformed, they can be unaware that sexual intercourse leads to pregnancy. A number of myths or "urban legends" have developed over time. Examples are the following: "The first time you have sex you won't get pregnant." "You can't get pregnant if you have sex standing up." "If the woman wears high heels, she won't get pregnant." "If the man does not ejaculate inside the woman, she won't get pregnant." "A woman can't get pregnant during her period." "You can't get pregnant if the man uses a condom." Learning accurate sexual information is important in making decisions both about relationships and about sex.

Because masturbation can start early, before the age of twelve in boys and somewhat later in girls, it is not surprising that there is much inaccurate information about masturbation. For example, boys might learn that if they masturbate "their penis will fall off," "they might go crazy," "they can become a sexual pervert," "they will lose their hair at an early age," "they will not develop intellectually," and "their adult sexual life will be limited because there are only a certain number of times that a man can ejaculate, and then he can't ever ejaculate again." Some of the myths for young girls about masturbation are that "they will become promiscuous," "that someone will be able to tell that they did this," "that they will become immoral," and "that masturbation leads to nymphomania." Some of these myths are quite damning and frightening. In fact, in the early 1900s, information about masturbation given by experts suggested that masturbation is not only sinful but also damages one's later health.

The myths that abound about sexuality are not limited to pregnancy and masturbation. Other examples are "women shouldn't be active in participating or seeking a sexual relationship"; "if women initiate sex, they won't be seen as being desirable"; "when individuals get older, they lose interest in sex"; "if I told my partner what I liked, he or she might be offended"; "sex should be spontaneous without a lot of talking"; "sexual satisfaction comes from understanding the mechanics of sex"; "AIDS only comes from gay men"; and "gay men are promiscuous." And there are many more common myths about sexuality.

Individuals have different views of sexuality and beliefs about what it means to them. The development of values about sexuality differs considerably for individuals. In the next sections, I will be describing some of the ways that people think about sexuality and some of the differences in attitudes and approaches to sexuality of men and women.

**Q 7.1** List a few myths or misinformation about sexuality that are not mentioned here.

## VIEWS OF SEXUALITY

Throughout the world, people from different cultures have different views of sexuality. Some cultures are quite open about the expression of sexual behaviors or feelings whereas others are quite closed and consider the expression of sexuality to be inappropriate or to be contrary to religious values. I will discuss some general views that people have about sexuality and some of the more specific reasons people seek sexual relationships.

Often called **sexual scripts,** sexual beliefs are expectations about how individuals should express themselves sexually (Nass, Libby, & Fisher, 1981; Gagnon & Simon, 1973; Simon & Gagnon, 1986). For some people, sex is appropriate mainly as a means of reproduction; pleasure is relatively incidental. This view agrees with those of some religions that believe the purpose of sexual behavior is to have children and that sexual behaviors, such as oral sex, are inappropriate. Perhaps one of the most common views of sex is that sex is an expression of love. Individuals who hold this point of view believe that sex is inappropriate if individuals are not in love. Others believe that sexual intercourse should occur only after marriage. Some people take a more liberal view, believing that it is not necessary to be in love, but people should be friends if they are going to have an intimate sexual relationship. In such a view, it is not necessary to limit sexuality to one partner. Others take an even more liberal view, looking at sex as recreation or enjoyment. In this view, sexuality is acceptable if both partners are interested. Previous knowledge of the partner or friendship is not important in this point of view. Thus, views of sexuality range across a wide spectrum in a country as diverse as the United States.

Reasons for choosing to have sex with another person are also varied (Nass, Libby, & Fisher, 1981). For some people, engaging in sex may be mainly to have a child; they might have a negative view of other reasons for sexuality. More common attitudes toward sex are as an expression of affection and an experience of physical intimacy or closeness. Others believe that reasons for being sexually involved include sexual arousal, wanting to touch and be touched, and wanting to act out, somewhat, sexual fantasies. Yet others become involved in sexual activity because they feel bound to do so. They might feel that others expect that a man or woman should act that way. Or they might feel that they must respond to their partner's sexual arousal so that their partner will not be angry or frustrated. Thus, how individuals believe people should make sexual decisions and how they act sexually themselves can be a subject of controversy because the opinions are so varied.

**sexual scripts**
Expectations about how individuals should express themselves sexually.

**Q 7.2** Which views of sexuality that are expressed in this section do you find inappropriate? Explain your rationale.

# INTIMACY

Talking about love, trying to define love and intimacy, have been concerns that are reflected in romantic literature over the ages. When people think of love, they often think of romantic love, but love for a parent or child, grandparent, or friend can also have intense bonds. Other forms of love might not be directed toward a person, yet be intense feelings of caring and devotion, such as love of God and love of country. In this section, we will focus on romantic love as it relates to sexual expression. Two types of love that have romantic implications are passionate love and companionate love (Walster & Walster, 1978; Crooks & Baur, 1999).

Sternberg (1986, 1988) has developed a triangular theory of love that provides a perspective we can use to view passionate love and companionate love. The theory includes both how individuals think about love and how they experience it in their own relationships (Aron & Westbay, 1996). Sternberg believes that consummate (full) love combines intimacy, passion, and commitment. Companionate love includes intimacy and commitment, but not passion (passionate love). For Sternberg, romantic love includes passion and intimacy. To focus our discussion, we will contrast passionate love and companionate love, as they represent two very different attitudes towards love and sexuality.

### *Passionate Love*

**passionate love** Strong feelings for someone else, being infatuated, being totally absorbed or smitten by another person.

Having a strong feeling for someone else, being infatuated, being totally absorbed by another person, are all examples of **passionate love.** Such broad feelings are often characterized by more specific feelings, such as a caring for, an excitement about being with, worry that the relationship might end, and feeling ecstatic or excited. A strong component of passionate love is sexual desire, a wish to touch, to be touched, to hold, and to be near. Usually these feelings are anything but stable; people are likely to experience changing emotions throughout the course of the infatuation period. When things go wrong in such a relationship, people are likely to feel very upset and even depressed. Such relationships, with strong emotional components, are often pictured in the movies or television and are the focus of novels and magazine stories.

Passionate love can be either a brief relationship or occur early in a longer relationship. Because passionate love is marked by excitement and strong feelings, logic and clear thinking might not be present. Sometimes partners realize that although there is great passion, they have little in common on which to build a longer-lasting relationship. In such a relationship, one or both partners can feel disillusioned as the passion fades. Perhaps this is one reason that in the United States, periods of engagement often last a year or longer. This allows a passionate relationship to build and to have a solid basis. Because the passionate relationship is so strong, it not only has powerful psychological effects but also physiological effects. Researchers who have studied neurological functioning have found several chemicals and chemical processes that occur when individuals experience strong passionate feelings (Walsh, 1991). Similarly, high levels of hormones such as androgen and testosterone are related to frequency of sexual activity and sexual motivation for men and women (Everitt & Bancroft, 1991; Knussmann, Christensen, & Couwenbergs, 1986; Sherwin, 1991). This strong sense of passion contrasts with a more quiet or subdued sense of friendship or attachment.

## Companionate Love

**companionate love**
Feelings of deep friendship and affection along with sexual feelings, thoughts, and concern for another person.

Unlike passionate love that is characterized by deep emotions and sexual feelings, **companionate love** represents feelings of deep friendship and affection. Intellect is a much stronger aspect of companionate love, with partners being thoughtful of each other's strengths and considerate of their weaknesses. Such relationships tend to be caring and considerate, taking place over a long period. In such relationships, individuals can feel a sense of being understood both emotionally and intellectually. They are likely to deeply care about the other person and to have a sense of being cared about. Such relationships are similar to deep and lasting friendships.

Like passionate relationships, companionate relationships have a sexual component; however, the sexuality is likely to be associated with feelings of intimacy or closeness and a sense of trust of the other person. This trust can encourage partners to try out different aspects of sexual behavior and to communicate openly about sexual desires, thus increasing passion. For many people, companionate sexual relationships can be more meaningful or more satisfying rather than highly exciting.

Because of the nature of passion, movies often show the development of exciting relationships. Sometimes these relationships end quickly in the movies, other times they can develop into longer-term relationships. Some people, however, experience friendships that can go on for a year or more before turning into a passionate loving relationship. Such relationships, although important, are seen infrequently in films and on television. Because they are such an important part of how many people learn about romantic relationships, films and television can influence the development of passionate or companionate relationships.

## The Building of an Intimate Sexual Relationship

Why are some people able to maintain a close caring relationship for a long period, while others can't? Why do some relationships seem to last, whereas others, despite efforts from both partners, seem to fizzle? Some components of relationships seem to contribute to developing feelings of intimacy (Crooks & Baur, 1999). Perhaps one of the most important elements in developing intimacy starts with oneself. Feeling effective and positive about oneself is a basic building block for the development of relationships with others. If individuals have a negative self-opinion, or especially, a dislike of themselves, it may be difficult for them to build a relationship with another person. If we dislike ourselves, it may be hard to understand why others would like us. If we then find someone who likes us, and we don't like ourselves, we might think that this person who likes us isn't very valuable either.

When relationships do start, they may go through phases, or at least have components, that lead to the development of strong feelings about one another. Relationships often start with reaching out to someone else, smiling, saying hello, or asking about a person. When one person makes a gesture to another, the other person must make a response that is somewhat similar. This could be a smile, a friendly answer to the question, a greeting, or some other response that encourages a continuing relationship. Some relationships seem to stop before they start. If a smile is greeted by a cold stare, that may be the last time the two people ever have contact with each other.

As sexual relationships develop, there are important components for their continuance. People want to feel that another person cares about them, likes them, or has some interest in them (Reis & Patrick, 1996). When there is some caring, trust can develop. Partners need to trust the other person, that what they say is valued, that the partners will not talk behind each other's back and so forth. With caring and trust, there can be a letting down of defenses. Partners can express their affection for each other, show the warmth and caring that they feel, and become physically close. Because they trust, they can be playful with each other and be less inhibited than they would with others. This expression of affection and playfulness, even if it is limited, makes it easier for a sexual relationship to develop.

**Q 7.3** In romantic relationships that you have observed (real, not TV) or experienced, what seems to start the relationship? How did caring, trust, and affection develop?

## Gender Differences in Intimacy

Men and women tend to view sex and love quite differently, because of both their physiology and their socialization. Physiologically, males often experience uncontrolled erections during puberty because of increased male hormones. Males are also likely to begin masturbating earlier than are girls and are more likely to masturbate during adolescence than are adolescent females (Weiten & Lloyd, 2000).

Perhaps because of these biological differences between men and women, societal expectations about how adolescent boys and girls should behave have developed over centuries. In general, boys might be taught that they should initiate sexual activities and that it is appropriate to experiment sexually. Among adolescent boys, being sexual is a way to be seen as a leader or as someone to be looked up to. For adolescent boys, sexuality is often seen as an accomplishment or something to do for fun. There is peer pressure to pretend that they are sexually active, even if they are not. Casual relationships are seen as appropriate and long-term sexual relationships might be desirable, but not necessary.

Adolescent girls, in contrast to adolescent boys, often learn that intimacy and love are important in a relationship, and without that, sex is not appropriate. Adolescents often learn that men should be socially active, but that women should be very careful in getting involved sexually. Sexually active girls run the risk of being gossiped about and developing a "bad reputation." Other reasons that discourage girls from becoming sexually active are fears of rape as well as fears of pregnancy or sexual intercourse. Girls learn that if they become pregnant and carry a child for nine months, their lives are likely to become very different than if they are not pregnant. On the other hand, sex is positively associated with closeness and love. Thus, adolescent girls tend to get two quite different messages about sexual behavior.

Given this view of sexuality, it is not surprising that men and women are likely to have different views of appropriate sexual behavior. Several studies (Crooks & Baur, 1999) have shown that women are less likely to have sexual intercourse without an emotional commitment than men are. Increasingly, however, the views of males and females are becoming more similar. Two studies of views of sexuality in *Parade* magazine showed that in the early 1980s, 59 percent of men reported that it was difficult to have sex without love, but in the early 1990s, 71 percent indicated that it was difficult to have sex without love. In both studies (Ubell, 1984, Clements, 1994) 86 percent of women felt that it was difficult to have sex without love. Adult views of love and sex might be changing more in society as men and women assume more equality with each other. Adolescent views of sexuality, however, still appear to be influenced by peer pressure.

Personal reactions to sexuality and discussions of sexuality can be quite varied. For many, pictures of beautiful male and female movie stars can be quite intimidating. Furthermore, there are implied pressures in peer groups about being sexually sophisticated or active. Individuals often wonder whether or not they will be attractive to someone that they find attractive.

For Brad, such pressures were intense. He fretted over whether or not girls would find him attractive. Because he had dated very little in high school, he felt less experienced than other men his age. He was sure that he was the only virgin on campus. He felt that women would not think that he was manly. In fact, he consciously walked in such a way as to try to look more masculine. Before he would initiate a conversation with a woman, he would tell himself that she wouldn't like him, that she would find him boring, that she would find him to be too fat. As a result, it was difficult for him to get past daydreaming about women. When he did start dating, he barely noticed that a relationship was developing. Barbara sat next to him in chemistry class and kept asking him questions. She would joke about the difficulties that she had in chemistry and then tease Brad about his neat handwriting. When she asked him to meet her in the library to study chemistry, he was surprised and anxious. It was probably her light, easy sense of humor that made it easy for him to start to enjoy being with her and not worry about what he thought she was thinking about him.

Janice, on the other hand, had no trouble getting attention from men. They often found her attractive, and would talk to her and try to get her to go to parties or other activities. Janice met just about every overture that a man made with suspicion. Her mother had cautioned her over and over again about what "men want." Particularly after Janice turned 21 and went into bars, she felt that she was some sort of trophy or prize. It seemed that men would try to win her over and show that they were sincere when they weren't. As a result, Janice became very cynical. Even her female friends noticed this. She found it harder and harder to trust people. Old childhood friends were still important, and she found that she was more comfortable being with these friends at home than she was when she was with people that she had met at college. As much as she wanted to have a relationship, her fears about being used for sex made it very difficult. Even in her church, where she felt comfortable, she still was not trusting. No matter what a man, who was her own age, said to her, she always thought he would initiate some kind of sexual behavior.

**Q 7.4** How typical do you think are the problems that Brad and Janice experience? Explain.

**Q 7.5** What factors affected your learning about the relationship between sex and intimacy?

## THE PHYSIOLOGY OF SEX

Just as there are similarities and differences in the way men and women experience intimacy and have values regarding sexual behavior, there are similarities and differences in actual sexual responding. How the body responds when engaged in sexual activity is the subject of this section. The sexual activity can be intercourse, masturbation, or some other sexual behavior. Probably the best-known research on sexuality and sexual responding is that of Masters and Johnson (1980) and Masters, Johnson, and Kolodny (1994). Acknowledging that people vary considerably in their sexual response patterns, Masters and Johnson describe four basic phases of the sexual response cycle: excitement, plateau, orgasm, and resolution.

- *Excitement Phase.* When individuals first start to feel sexually excited and aroused, several physiological processes take place. Breathing rate, heart rate, and blood pressure are likely to increase quickly, along with muscle tension. For men, blood vessels become engorged, which causes the penis to become erect and the testes or testicles to swell. In women, sexual excitement causes swelling of the clitoris and vaginal lips and vaginal lubrication. Most women also experience a swelling of the breasts and erection of the nipple.

- *Plateau Phase.* After initial sexual excitement, physiological arousal increases, but at a slower pace. This is not a true "plateau" in that excitement doesn't stop, it just increases more slowly than in the initial stage. In men, testicles can enlarge and the head of the penis continues to swell. Some semen might be released from the tip of the penis as sexual excitement increases. In women, the upper two-thirds of the vagina continues to open.

  If interrupted, this phase can be delayed or stopped. For example, feelings of guilt about sex, anger at one's partner, or worry about sexual performance can interfere with the continued development of the plateau phase. Physical distractions such as a phone ringing or a knock on the door can also cause physiological sexual changes to return to a non-arousal phase (Weiten & Lloyd, 2000).

- *Orgasm Phase.* When sexual intensity reaches its maximum strength, a discharge occurs in which there is a gradual decrease in heart rate, respiration rate, and blood pressure. For men, **orgasm** includes ejaculation of semen most, but not all, the time. Lasting slightly longer than male orgasms, female orgasms include the gradual closing and relaxing of the vagina; basically, muscles around the outer third of the vagina rhythmically contract.

- *Resolution Phase.* After orgasm, there is a gradual relaxation and subsiding of sexual tension. Men might not be able to experience another orgasm for some time after orgasm. Some women can experience several orgasms—occasionally as many as 50, if stimulation continues. If not, women's state of physiological arousal is likely to return to a relaxed state. The length of time of the resolution phase depends not only on the gender of the person but also on other individual differences.

**orgasm** The point at which sexual intensity reaches its maximum strength and a discharge occurs in which heart rate, respiration rate, and blood pressure gradually decrease.

## *Gender and Orgasm*

Two differences between orgasm as experienced by men and by women are described here: time to reach orgasm and the probability of reaching orgasm during intercourse. In general, the amount of stimulation time men need to reach orgasm is much briefer—it can range from 2 minutes to 10 minutes or longer. For women, the amount of time to reach orgasm with a partner can take 10 to 20 minutes. Masters and Johnson found that when women masturbated, however, the time needed was less than 5 minutes. Women are less likely than men to experience orgasm during intercourse. Women are more likely to experience orgasm when there is direct stimulation to the clitoris, usually a woman's most sensitive genital area, rather than from vaginal intercourse, where the stimulation is indirect. Many more men than women report "always" reaching an orgasm in their primary sexual relationships (Weiten & Lloyd, 2000).

## *Masturbation*

**masturbation** Producing sexual pleasure, often including orgasm, by stimulating one's own genitals.

The term **masturbation** refers to producing sexual pleasure, often including orgasm by stimulating one's own genitals. Mutual masturbation is the term used when two individuals stimulate each other. Masturbation practices in females and males differ considerably. A man usually masturbates by manipulating his penis with his hand. When a woman masturbates, she usually touches or rubs her clitoral area. On average, teenage males masturbate about five times per week, whereas teenage women typically masturbate much less frequently. By the end of adolescence, about three out of four females will have masturbated, and most males will have done so as well.

Historically, masturbation has been condemned as "self-abuse." Some religions feel that it is immoral because there is a "spilling of seed." Thus, masturbation prevents reproduction or procreation, which is seen as the main purpose of sexual behavior by some religions. Because of the negative view of masturbation, masturbation has been linked with sterility, insanity, loss of potency, blindness, immorality, and other negative behaviors.

There is no evidence that masturbation creates negative effects, nor is masturbation limited to adolescent behavior. In early studies of sexual behavior, Kinsey, Pomeroy, and Martin (1948) reported that 95 percent of men and 60 percent of women had masturbated. Masturbation continues after marriage, with about 70 percent of husbands and wives reporting that they have continued to masturbate after they were married (Hunt, 1974). As Hughes (1996) states, masturbation in marriage is not an indication of sexual dissatisfaction with a partner; it merely is another way of experiencing orgasm and is a way of obtaining sexual satisfaction. Masturbation can be a way of training or controlling sexual behavior. Often it is prescribed by sex therapists to both males and females. As a means of sexual expression, mutual masturbation is a safe form of sex because it can prevent people from contracting sexually transmitted diseases and can prevent pregnancy.

# HOMOSEXUALITY

So far, we have been discussing feelings, beliefs, and the physiology of sex. Most discussions of sexuality focus on heterosexuality—attraction to the other sex. However, not all individuals are attracted to people of the other

**homosexuality** Sexual desires and erotic behaviors directed toward one's own gender.

**bisexuality** Being attracted to members of one's own gender as well as to members of the other gender.

gender. Some individuals are attracted to members of their own gender (**homosexuality**), and some are attracted to both their own gender and the other gender (**bisexuality**). Experts on sexuality (Crooks & Baur, 1999) note that sexuality is a continuum, rather than a dichotomy. In other words, not all people are either exclusively homosexual or heterosexual; there are gradations in between, with some having a slight interest in members of their own sex but being predominately interested in the other sex. Other individuals have an equal amount of heterosexual and homosexual attraction. Sex researchers have sometimes used a 7-point scale developed by Alfred Kinsey to determine degree of heterosexuality and homosexuality.

Given this information, it is difficult to estimate the frequency of homosexuality or bisexuality in the United States. Early studies showed that the number of individuals who are predominately homosexual is about 10 percent. More recent studies conducted in Europe and the United States, however, have lower estimates, especially for women (Weiten & Lloyd, 2000). Estimates of those who are heterosexual indicate that about 80 percent of men and 90 percent of women could be classified as exclusively heterosexual. The other people surveyed report having had sexual experience, to varying degrees, with members of both genders.

Sometimes homosexuality has been referred to as a sexual preference. In actuality, this is an inaccurate term because it implies that people choose their sexual orientation. They do not. If individuals do not choose a sexual preference, how do they become homosexual? Sigmund Freud and some other early psychologists believed that having an interfering mother and a distant father was an explanation for why males became homosexual. However, no evidence supports this theory. Other theorists believed that early negative encounters with the other gender or poor relationships with same gender peers could cause homosexuality, but there is no evidence for this, either. There is also no evidence that parenting by homosexual parents is likely to bring about homosexual offspring. Thus, there has been little support for what has been called environmental explanations of homosexuality.

More evidence suggests that biological factors are involved. Researchers have investigated the role of genes and hereditary factors. There is some evidence for a biological role, but it is not clear yet. Although it seems that genetic factors are important, not all identical twins have the same sexual orientation (Gladue, 1994). Research on genetic factors and sexual orientation is extremely complicated. Both biological and environmental factors seem to play a part.

Some individuals have associated personality traits or maladjustment with homosexuality. In fact, before 1973, homosexuality was considered a psychological disorder. Since then psychologists and psychiatrists have considered it to be another form of sexual orientation. Studies of psychological adjustment have shown little difference between men or women who are homosexual and those who are not. There is also no evidence to suggest that children from homosexual families have poorer adjustment than those raised in heterosexual families (Crooks & Baur, 1999).

## SEXUAL CONCERNS

Sexual responding is not just a physiological process. As the section on intimacy shows, many psychological feelings (love, caring, anxiety, and anger) can influence sexual behavior. Furthermore, sexual concerns and problems can affect all people, regardless of their sexual orientation. Although treatment for sexual problems can become quite technical and complex, sex therapists have some suggestions for dealing with mild sexual concerns. I will describe some concerns about sexual desire that both men and women might have. In addition, we will examine some specific problems that men and women can experience in sexual relations. Explanations for how couples cope with these problems will show a variety of ways of dealing with sexual dysfunctions.

### Problems of Sexual Desire

Both men and women can lack sexual desire for a variety of reasons. This lack of sexual desire can include lack of sexual fantasies and lack of interest in sexual activity. Sometimes, medication or drugs can suppress sexual desire. Often, lack of desire reflects problems with a romantic partner. When couples are arguing, fighting, or silently harboring hostility toward each other, lack of sexual interest can develop. Disinterest in sex can also develop from early childhood training that can result in individuals feeling that sex is dirty or wrong. Other people develop fears as a result of childhood sexual abuse, negative sexual experiences as an adolescent, or negative views of their sexuality or appearance.

**sensate focus** A way for treating sexual concerns that teaches partners how to please each other sensuously without reaching orgasm.

Couple or individual counseling is often helpful for these problems. Because sexuality is a very private matter, and public discussion of one's own sexuality is discouraged, counseling must take place in an atmosphere of trust. Some couples counselors are sex therapists, but not all are. Sex therapists help individuals with a variety of sexual concerns, such as achieving orgasm or being aroused. With arousal problems, sex therapists might examine attitudes toward masturbation and suggest ways of gently exploring one's own sexuality. Another treatment called **sensate focus** suggests ways that couples can explore each other's bodies without achieving orgasm. This takes the pressure off couples who may be concerned about orgasm as a goal. Emphasis is put on pleasurable touching instead.

---

## Problems and Solutions

---

### What if I have worries or problems about my sexual relationship?

- Consider counseling or sex therapy. Problems might be the result of childhood training or negative sexual experiences. Sex therapy includes sensate focus or other exercises to overcome sexual problems.
- Men with erectile problems should have a medical exam to explore physical problems.
- Both men and women should explore problems within the relationship.

---

## Male Sexual Concerns

Some men experience problems having an erection or maintaining one. Because "impotence" is a rather negative term, therapists use the phrase "erectile difficulties" instead. Often difficulties in having or maintaining an erection are due to anxiety or depression. A man might be concerned about his manliness or ability to please his partner or have moral questions. Sometimes erectile difficulties are caused by drug or alcohol use. Diseases such as diabetes cause about half of erectile dysfunctions (Buvat, Buvat-Herbaut, Lemaire, & Marcolin, 1990).

A physical examination is one of the first approaches to erectile difficulties. In that way, a man's physical condition can be checked and medications changed or initiated. When the problem appears to be psychologically based, many sex therapists suggest sensate focus. In this treatment, partners touch each other but avoid touching each other's genitals. Gradually, after the man has had successful erections, the therapist suggests that the partners touch each other's genitals. Even at this point, sexual intercourse is not permitted. Only when the man's confidence returns, and he has had repeated arousals, do couples begin to attempt intercourse.

With premature ejaculation, when a man reaches orgasm too quickly, a different approach is often used. Reaching orgasm too quickly is a subjective opinion. When either of the two partners feels that the man is ejaculating too quickly, then there is a problem. Often slowing the tempo of intercourse helps to delay ejaculation. Sometimes it is helpful for a man to ejaculate once, so that he might be able to delay or slow the next ejaculation. Depending on the nature of the problem, and the quickness of the ejaculation, sex therapists might suggest several other techniques including sensate focus.

### Female Sexual Concerns

**vaginismus** Involuntary contractions of the vagina before intercourse.

Some women report difficulties in having an orgasm, others experience genital pain, and some report both. **Vaginismus,** for example, makes attempts at penetration painful and difficult. Difficulty in experiencing orgasm in women is often due to attitudes toward sexuality and sometimes attitudes toward the partner. On occasion, orgasmic difficulties arise in relationships as problems develop in the relationship. Other problems of achieving orgasm can be caused by concern about becoming pregnant or fear of contracting sexually transmitted diseases (STDs).

In dealing with sexual problems with women, couples counselors and sex therapists often explore the relationship between the partners. Working on communication problems between partners is a common approach to sexual problems that affect women. Furthermore, dealing with women's attitudes toward sex because of inappropriate previous sexual behavior (such as child sexual abuse) can help women's sexual functioning. Often sensate focus is used as a way of focusing on the pleasures of being touched and of touching, so that the focus is not on orgasm or sexual performance.

In this section, I have only briefly described some of the approaches to treating sexual concerns. Knowledgeable sex therapists and couples counselors are trained to work sensitively with couples who express such concerns. Sometimes these concerns require dealing with attitudes about sex, communication difficulties between partners, or lack of information about sexuality. Furthermore, concerns about becoming pregnant and concerns about developing sexually transmitted diseases, which are described next, can be issues for both men and women that can affect experiencing pleasure in the sexual relationship.

## CONTRACEPTION

Sexual attraction leads to expression of sexual behavior and, in heterosexual couples, sexual intercourse. Being sexually attracted to another person is rarely based on the desire to have a child. To enjoy sexuality, but not have a child, individuals practice a number of contraceptive methods: Condoms, birth control pills, and, more recently, chemical devices. These replace less reliable methods, such as withdrawal of the penis before ejaculation, which

---

## *Problems and Solutions*

---

### *How can I avoid pregnancy or sexually transmitted diseases?*

New technological advances in birth control and STD prevention provide many alternatives (see pages 168, 169, 171, 172).

---

## *Problems and Solutions*

---

### *How can I ask my partner to use a condom (or other birth control method)?*

- Be firm in your response, but also show understanding of your partner.
- Explain your answer.
- Talk about how you can continue to enjoy yourselves sexually.

---

does not normally provide effective birth control because semen can leak out before ejaculation. Douching is not likely to prevent conception because water pressure tends to push sperm deeper into a woman's reproductive organs, rather than wash away the sperm.

Next, we will examine some common methods of contraception, explaining disadvantages and advantages of each, while presenting some evidence about their effectiveness (see Table 7.1). Much of this information is derived from Hatcher et al. (1994) whose book, *Contraceptive Technology*, thoroughly describes many features of a variety of contraceptive measures. Because asking a partner to use contraceptive measures, particularly condoms, can be difficult, I will describe some common beliefs of partners who do not wish to use contraceptives and ways to reply to them.

Of all of these methods, only condoms and abstinence are effective methods of stopping sexually transmitted diseases (STDs). The male condom is used frequently because it can be applied with very little preparation. Because unprotected sex can lead to possible pregnancy or STDs, it is important for individuals who are sexually involved to be able to make decisions that will protect themselves from possible pregnancy or STDs.

**TABLE 7.1 METHODS OF BIRTH CONTROL**

Note that the numbers in parentheses represent the approximate effectiveness rates that are based on one year of using the particular method. When two numbers are presented, the lower percentage represents the typical effectiveness while the higher number represents the possible effectiveness if that method is used consistently and accurately.

- *Combined Pill.* Referred to as "the pill," this is really a series of four pills that are taken for three weeks of four. The pills contain synthetic hormones that are similar to those normally produced by a woman. The pill stops the ovulation process, so that a woman cannot become pregnant. These pills are highly effective and allow sexual spontaneity. They can also improve some medical conditions, such as acne. However, they can produce some side effects such as nausea, headaches, decreased sex drive, and possibly weight gain. Available for more than 35 years, the pill has a long record of being safe. (95–99%)

- *Mini-Pill.* More recently developed than "the pill," this pill contains only progesterone, whereas "the pill" contains progesterone and estrogen. The mini-pill must be taken daily. Because it does not have estrogen, women who cannot normally take estrogen can use it. (95–99.5%)

- *Intrauterine Device (IUD).* The IUD is a small device that is inserted into the uterus by a medical practitioner. This device immobilizes the sperm. Depending on the health of the woman and the type of IUD, it can be left in for one to eight years. It tends to be less expensive over the long term than other methods; however, complications such as menstrual problems and pelvic inflammatory disease can

result. Generally, it is not recommended for women who have never been pregnant. (98–99%)

- *Diaphragm and Cervical Cap.* Both of these are flexible rubber barriers that are used with spermicidal cream or jelly. The woman inserts the diaphragm or the cap in her vagina to cover the cervix before intercourse. The cap can be left in place longer than the diaphragm can and additional cream or jelly is not necessary for repeated intercourse during a particular time. These products are considered to be medically safe and can be inserted ahead of time to allow for sexual spontaneity. Effectiveness of the diaphragm tends to vary depending on the fit of the diaphragm. Cervical caps are prescribed less frequently, and not all practitioners are trained in fitting them. Both must be fitted by medical practitioners to determine the correct size. (diaphragm 80–94%, cervical cap 80–91%)

- *Contraceptive Sponge.* A small sponge that contains spermicide, the "sponge" is easy to obtain in drug stores and to use. It is effective for 24 hours after insertion, but it must be left in for six to eight hours after intercourse. It is difficult to remove and can be less effective for women who have had a child. (80–91%)

- *Spermicides.* These are foams, creams, or jellies that, when inserted into the vagina, kill sperm. Often, they are used with other methods such as the diaphragm, cervical cap, and condoms. Spermicides must be inserted before every act of intercourse and can cause genital irritations. Their effectiveness is lower than most other methods. (74–94%)

## Communicating about Contraception

Typically, but not always, it is the male who does not wish to use condoms or other birth control methods. Being able to respond to a partner who does not want to use a condom or other birth control method is important. In the following section, I describe some common statements that show resistance to using a condom, and some ways to respond to them (Breitman, Knutson, & Reed, 1987).

- *Statement:* Using a condom doesn't feel good. I miss the skin-to-skin contact and can't feel really intimate with you.
- *Reply:* It may feel different at first, but can we try it a few times? I would feel safer and more comfortable. The difference in sensations might not seem so much after we get used to them.

- *Statement:* We don't need to use a condom, AIDS is a gay disease.
- *Reply:* That's not true. Anyone can get AIDS, whether they're straight or gay.

**TABLE 7.1 METHODS OF BIRTH CONTROL (CONTINUED)**

• *Norplant.* This implant includes six matchstick-sized silicone rubber capsules that are inserted into a woman's arm. They continually release a very low dose of progesterone. This method is highly effective and safe and works for as long as five years. There can be some medical side effects, however, such as weight gain or breast tenderness, and the implants can be very difficult to remove. Both insertion and removal are very expensive, so costs have prevented this from being more widely used. (99.5%)

• *Abstinence.* This is the only foolproof way to avoid pregnancy. Abstinence refers to not having sexual intercourse. To avoid sexually transmitted diseases (STD), abstinence must include avoiding all oral and genital sex. The disadvantage, of course, is that it limits sexual behavior and sexual communication between partners. (100%)

• *Sterilization.* Surgical procedures are available for those who do not want to have children in the future. Although sterilization procedures are usually reversible, they should be considered permanent because surgery to reverse sterilization can be complex and results are not guaranteed. For women, tubal ligation involves stopping the flow of semen to eggs by cutting the fallopian tubes. For men, a vasectomy removes a section from the *vas deferens,* a tube that carries sperm. (almost 100%)

• *Natural Family Planning.* Called the "rhythm method," this plan requires predicting ovulation and abstaining from sex during the time that a woman is ovulating. Advantages include the fact that no devices or chemicals are used and that the method is acceptable to the

Catholic Church and some other religious groups. For this plan to work, couples must have a good understanding of reproductive physiology and agree to abstain during ovulation. Because reproductive physiology is complex, however, it is difficult to predict ovulation. This method tends to be less effective than many others because individuals often are not consistent in applying the method. (75–99%)

• *Female Condom.* This is a polyurethane sheath that lines the vagina completely and acts as a barrier against sperm. A ring is visible outside the vagina, and another ring inside the vagina holds it in place. This condom can be inserted as long as eight hours before intercourse. Compared with other methods, it is relatively expensive, and it can be difficult or cumbersome for women to insert. The female condom tends to have lower effectiveness rates than other methods. To date, it has not been widely used. (80–95%)

• *Male Condoms.* This covering is usually made of latex, but can be made of animal membranes or other materials. The condom fits over the penis and keeps semen from entering the vagina. The most widely used contraceptive, it is easily available and inexpensive. Partners sometimes complain because of reduced sensitivity and possible interference with having or maintaining an erection and completing intercourse. There is some risk of breakage, but very little since these are tested in the factories. Breakage tends to be caused by misuse. Condoms are often used in conjunction with spermicides. (86–97%)

• *Statement:* I've never been exposed to AIDS or any other STDs. Don't you believe me?
• *Reply:* I do trust you, but it's hard to know for sure. Either of us might be infected, but not know. I'd feel so much better for both of us if we used condoms.

• *Statement:* Condoms are like wearing shoes to bed. They are uncomfortable.
• *Reply:* Once we start using condoms and get used to them, it'll be second nature. Besides there are lots of fun things we can do besides actual intercourse. After a while, using condoms will be fine, it's so crucial to use them.

There is a common thread in all the responses to the statements: The replies are firm, but they are also caring and understanding. The partner insists on protecting himself or herself from pregnancy or STDs, but at the same time gives a brief explanatory answer and usually an explanation of how the partners can continue to enjoy each other sexually. Being able to choose when you and your partner want to have a child is of the utmost importance. Being able to plan your life, your marriage, your education, your job, your leisure time, and your family are significant considerations for most people. Some find it hard to believe that sexual intercourse that can be so pleasurable can influence one's life a year, 10 years, and even 30 years from now. Just as an unchosen pregnancy can create significant problems that affect people's lives, so can STDs.

## SEXUALLY TRANSMITTED DISEASES (STDs)

**sexually transmitted diseases (STDs)** A disease contracted through sexual contact with another person, usually involving exchange of bodily fluids.

Despite public education about **sexually transmitted diseases,** the availability of condoms, and renewed emphasis on abstinence as a method of avoiding STDs, the numbers of individuals who are diagnosed with STDs continues to be very high. Knowing how STDs are contracted and knowing symptoms of STDs can help you avoid them. STDs vary in the symptoms that arise. Although all STDs are treatable, not all can be cured. Seeking medical attention as soon as possible is the only solution. Most STDs that go untreated get worse and sometimes can no longer be able to be treated as effectively. Some STDs, such as pubic lice, are nuisances, but most are much more serious than that. Although there are more than 20 STDs, we will only discuss the most common: pubic lice, chlamydia, gonorrhea, syphilis, herpes, genital warts, Hepatitis B, and HIV/AIDS. I will provide some brief information on each and then discuss ways of avoiding contracting STDs. Some of the problems that arise when individuals have contracted an STD and then are involved in a new intimate relationship will also be explored. See Table 7.2.

### Avoiding STDs

Sexually transmitted diseases, as is clear from the previous discussion, are serious and frightening. Furthermore, they are widespread among young people. Because of possible negative consequences about sexual behavior, choices about sex can be difficult. In addition, some people try to seduce or persuade others to be sexual when they might not want to. Alcohol and other drugs also affect the sexual decision-making process. This does not mean that there are no good choices, only that decisions about sexual behavior should be considered carefully and not be impulsive.

One of the first choices about dealing with sexuality is abstinence. Abstinence does not mean no holding hands, no kissing, and no petting. From a scientific or technical point of view, abstinence refers to no exchange of bodily fluids. This means no oral, vaginal, or anal intercourse.

**TABLE 7.2 EXAMPLES OF SEXUALLY TRANSMITTED DISEASES**

- *Pubic Lice.* Sometimes called "crabs," pubic lice are tiny lice that are visible and often are found in pubic hair or other body hair. The main symptom is persistent itching. Pubic lice are spread easily through body contact or through shared clothing or sheets. Pubic lice reproduce quickly, new eggs often hatch after seven to nine days. Although pubic lice can be treated by preparations such as Kwell, it is best to consult a physician.

- *Chlamydia.* Particularly dangerous to women, chlamydia is reported in more than 4 million new cases each year. The most common STD in the United States, it can be quite insidious because not all women who are infected show initial symptoms. Some symptoms are disrupted menstrual periods, elevated temperature, nausea, headaches, and stomach pain.

  For men, symptoms usually include pain or burning with urination. Sometimes there is a discharge from the penis, and on occasion, symptoms will be too mild to notice. Especially women, but also men, can become infertile if chlamydia is not treated.

  When detected, chlamydia is treated with antibiotics. Because symptoms are not readily apparent, however, individuals infected with chlamydia can transmit the disease to their partners without knowing it.

- *Gonorrhea.* A bacterial infection, gonorrhea can be treated with antibiotics; however, recent strains of gonorrhea have been more resistant to traditional treatment. Symptoms in men of gonorrhea, often called "the clap," are burning during urination and a cloudy discharge from the penis. When the disease is untreated, men can experience inflammation of the skin of the scrotum and swelling in the testicles. In women, gonorrhea is often undetected, but some women have some green or yellowish discharge. If gonorrhea is undetected in women, pelvic inflammatory disease can develop, which can result in infertility.

- *Syphilis.* Syphilis is transmitted from open sores during genital, oral, or anal sex and, if not treated, can result in death. The disease has four stages: First, a painless sore appears at the site where syphilis bacteria have entered the body. Second, the sore disappears and a skin rash develops. Third is a latent stage in which no symptoms might be seen. Finally, severe symptoms such as heart failure, blindness, and mental disturbance can result, followed by death.

- *Herpes.* Researchers estimate that more than 45 million people have contracted genital herpes. About 300,000 new cases are diagnosed each year in the United States. The symptoms of herpes are small red bumps that can be quite painful and can appear in the genitals or mouth. These bumps can become blisters that rupture to form open sores. Usually, the first outbreak is the worst. Of those who are infected, about 50 percent will never have a reoccurrence. Of the remaining 50 percent, many are likely to have several outbreaks during a year. Symptoms seem to be worse when individuals are under stress.

These symptoms can appear on the genitals or mouth and can be a result of different strains of the herpes virus.

Physicians often prescribe drugs such as Zovirax, which usually reduces the length and the strength of the herpes outbreak. As with other viruses, there is a method of treatment but no cure. When sores and lesions erupt, those with the herpes virus should abstain from sex because herpes can be passed from one partner to another by kissing or other sexual contact. Because herpes exists in people's bodies throughout their lives, it is possible that herpes can be transmitted even when individuals with herpes do not experience the symptoms.

- *Genital Warts.* Referred to also as venereal warts and technically known as human papilloma virus (HPV), genital warts have been increasing dramatically among young people as a significant STD. HPV causes genital warts, which can be identified in both men and women as hard and yellow-gray warts on dry skin. On moist areas, they are soft, pinkish and red, and somewhat cauliflower-like. They grow on the outer genitals or in the rectum and possibly even in a man's urethra or a woman's vagina. As a rule, these warts are not painful; however, they can have long-term health effects in women. Some strains of HPV can invade the cervix, which can bring about a precancerous condition that can eventually lead to cervical cancer. Pap smears are used to detect HPV. Genital warts in the cervix can be treated. When warts are visible, they are often removed by burning, freezing, or, occasionally, surgery. Often wart removal takes several treatments that can be painful. Because HPV is a virus, recurrences can occur because the virus remains in the body for an indefinite period.

- *Viral Hepatitis.* Far more infectious than HIV, Hepatitis B is transmitted through blood, semen, vaginal secretions, and saliva. It seems to be particularly associated with anal sex, whether penile, oral, or manual.

  The symptoms of Hepatitis B are quite varied. Sometimes there are no symptoms; other individuals experience flu-like symptoms. Sometimes there is a yellowing of the skin and eyes. Occasionally, individuals become so sick that they will be disabled for weeks or months. Most people recover totally, but many become carriers for life and transmit the virus to others.

  A vaccine that costs more than $100 for three shots prevents but does not cure Hepatitis B. The typical treatment for Hepatitis B is rest and a healthy diet.

- *HIV/AIDS.* Discussing HIV/AIDS, its effects, and its treatment is quite complex, so I will cover only the major points here. The human immunodeficiency virus (HIV) attacks then weakens the body's natural immune system. The last stage of this disease is called *acquired immunodeficiency syndrome* (AIDS). When the immune system is attacked, individuals can easily get infections and cancers that their bodies cannot fight. Thus, flus and other diseases that would not normally pose health risks do pose severe health risks for people with HIV/AIDS.

*(continues)*

**TABLE 7.2 EXAMPLES OF SEXUALLY TRANSMITTED DISEASES (CONTINUED)**

Researchers at the National Institute for Health note that, in the United States, 645,000 cases of AIDS had been reported by January 1998 (NIH, 1999). Not all individuals who are infected with HIV develop AIDS. Almost everyone with HIV becomes ill, to some extent, within five to ten years after infection; about half will develop AIDS. Although researchers know how AIDS is transmitted, they do not know how to destroy the virus.

HIV is transmitted through bodily fluids: blood, semen, vaginal fluids, and breast milk. Thus, unprotected sexual intercourse, vaginal or anal, can transmit HIV from one person to another. Blood transfusions or intravenous drug use can also bring infected blood from one person to another. Careful testing of donated blood for HIV antibodies has helped eliminate blood transfusions as a significant cause of HIV in the United States. The virus enters the body through contact with an outside source—the vagina, penis, rectum, mouth, or infected needles used for bringing drugs into the body. Infants can get HIV from their mothers through breast milk and contact with other bodily fluids. Although not frequent, HIV has been found in saliva, urine, and tears. However, HIV cannot be caught through sharing a drinking glass or eating utensils. Breathing the same air does not transmit HIV, nor do casual kissing, handshakes, and mosquito bites.

Although HIV can be contracted by anyone, it is most likely found among those who engage in high-risk behaviors. Thus, bisexual and gay men who engage in unprotected sex (don't use a condom) are more likely to develop AIDS than are those who do not. Furthermore, intravenous drug users who share needles are more likely to develop AIDS than others are. The World Health Organization reports that at the end of 1998, 33 million adults and children had developed HIV/AIDS worldwide (NIH, 1999).

Because HIV can reside in the body for years before symptoms are found, it is not unusual for individuals to have no symptoms of HIV for some years. Some may never develop symptoms. Others, however, might become very tired, have night sweats or fever, lose weight, or have diarrhea and swollen lymph glands in the neck. To test for HIV, an HIV antibody (a substance in the body that counteracts disease) test is used to detect antibodies, rather than the virus itself. It can take six months from the time a person contracts the HIV virus to when it shows up in a test. Positive results on the test do not mean that an individual will get AIDS—some people who test positive remain symptom-free—but it can tell that the individual might develop symptoms caused by HIV or develop AIDS. Although there is no cure for HIV/AIDS, new treatments being developed can treat HIV so that individuals can live longer and have minimal symptoms. Important in treatment of HIV/AIDS is early intervention. Individuals who suspect that they have been exposed to HIV should get tested and, if the test is positive, seek medical attention soon.

---

Sexual intimacy can still be experienced through touching, holding, mutual masturbation, or other sexual behavior. Different religions have a variety of definitions as to what abstinence means. If individuals have had intercourse in the past, it does not mean that they cannot return to abstinence. Many do.

**Monogamy** Maintaining a sexual relationship with only one person.

Another way of preventing or reducing the risk of STDs is having sex with only one partner who is unaffected, **monogamy.** The difficulties in doing this are that often individuals have a problem finding the right person or date several people during college. Determining who you wish to be monogamous with is difficult, which is one reason that waiting to have sexual intercourse until marriage is often urged. Unless both people who have sex in a monogamous relationship are virgins, it is difficult to be certain that the sexual partners will be free of STDs. Monogamy reduces the risk of developing a sexually transmitted disease.

If individuals decide to be sexually active, the best way to prevent STDs and to provide good protection against pregnancy is the condom. Condoms can be used for anal, vaginal, and oral intercourse. Condoms that are made of latex are much more effective against STDs than are those made of "nat-

---

## Problems and Solutions

---

### How can I reduce the risk of contracting an STD?

- Abstain from sexual activity that involves the exchange of bodily fluids.
- Be in a monogamous relationship.
- Use condoms.

---

ural membrane" because latex does not have pores that lambskin or other animal fibers do. For more protection, many people use spermicides along with condoms, which has the added effect of killing many viruses. When a spermicide is used, it is used in the tip of the condom and on the outside of the condom. When using a condom with a lubricant, it is helpful to use one that is water-based rather than petroleum-based because petroleum-based solutions can weaken the condom and can cause it to break.

Many men object to using a condom because they feel that it is a less spontaneous method of sex and that it diminishes pleasurable sensations. If you were going to have sex in a nonmonogamous situation, however, the condom is the best, if not only, protection. In the previous section on preventing pregnancy, I described some arguments that people use when faced with resistance to using a condom on the part of a romantic partner. In the next section, we explore some problems for people confronting their own feelings and dealing with a partner after they have contracted an STD.

## Dealing with STDs

When individuals think that they have an STD, the first step is to seek medical treatment. Although it might be embarrassing to do so, STDs, when left untreated, can develop into very serious illnesses and can become fatal. Viruses such as herpes, HPV, Hepatitis B, and HIV can be treated but not cured. Treatment might have to be done on several occasions, possibly many. Treatment for HIV is extremely expensive and requires following a carefully prescribed regimen of pills and diet.

STDs affect people physically and psychologically. Some individuals feel dirty, tainted, or unhealthy, which affects the way they feel about themselves and their relationships with other people. Sometimes individuals blame themselves for having made a mistake; others blame a partner for lying about STDs or feel that they want to be alone or away from others.

Jeff was a six-foot-seven-inch sophomore who was in his second year at a community college. He was looking forward to getting a bachelor's degree in business administration. Jeff felt very awkward and embarrassed about his height. During high school, he usually avoided girls and felt very shy when around them. He met Crystal at a party at a friend's house one weekend. Although Jeff was shy, Crystal, who had been interested in Jeff for a while, was comfortable and had a good sense of humor. They dated for about three months. When Crystal said that she was interested in seeing other guys, Jeff was really hurt because he had grown quite fond of her. He had looked forward to going to Crystal's house, watching television, and generally feeling relaxed with a girl, in a way that he never had before.

After the third time they went out, Jeff initiated sexual intercourse with Crystal. For him, this was the first time, and he felt awkward asking about birth control. Crystal assured him that she had taken care of it, and he didn't have to worry.

Right after Crystal broke up with him, Jeff developed blisters near his genitals. Not knowing what they were, he went to a doctor and found out that he had the herpes virus. When he confronted Crystal about this, she said, "Oh, I didn't think my herpes was active then." When Jeff asked Crystal why she hadn't told him, she said, "I figured that I had the situation under control."

Worrying constantly, Jeff thought that the herpes virus might lead to AIDS. (It can't). He wondered what to do if he met another woman. The knowledge that he had herpes brought with it a feeling that he was different than he had ever been before: like there were two phases of his life, pre-herpes and herpes. Innocence was gone. What if herpes showed around his mouth? What if he wanted to be sexual with a woman? He grew quieter and didn't go out very much with his friends. Playing sports in the afternoon was okay, but that was about it.

Finally, he talked to Christine, who had been a friend from childhood. She was probably his best friend. They had never dated, nor did they plan to. Talking to her about what had happened was extremely helpful. She was able to reassure him that he was okay, he was still Jeff, and that he wasn't tainted. She was able to talk to him about ways that he could talk to another woman about herpes and feel that he was being responsible. Worrying about transmitting herpes to other people had been very much on his mind. When Jeff had a follow-up visit with his doctor, he came in with a list of questions. The doctor was patient with him and gave him information about herpes and how it was different than other STDs.

Having an STD brings with it health questions, psychological issues, and questions about moral responsibility. Questions such as those Jeff dealt

**Q 7.6** If people have a sexually transmitted disease, what is their moral responsibility to tell a prospective partner?

**Q 7.7** How would you advise a friend about whether or not to abstain from sexual intercourse before marriage? What issues do you feel are most important?

**Q 7.8** Why do you think some people ignore information about birth control and STDs and engage in casual sex?

with are both complex and intimate. Talking with a friend, clergy, or counselor can help you examine the issues.

## SEXUAL ASSAULT AND RAPE

**rape** Unwanted, forced sexual oral, anal, or vaginal intercourse with another person.

Experts (Browne & Williams, 1993) see **rape** as an expression of hostility and aggression, rather than one of sexuality. About 95 percent of rape survivors are women. Male-male rape, which is most likely to occur in prison settings, is relatively rare, and examples of women raping men are extremely rare. Because rape is an act of violence, the trauma that individuals who have been raped experience is severe and long lasting. Next, we examine ways in which individuals might avoid rape, what to do if you have been raped, the consequences of being raped, and how to help someone who has experienced this trauma. First, however, I will describe three categories of rape that occur under different circumstances and vary in the frequency that they occur.

- *Stranger Rape.* When most people think about rape, they think about being raped by a stranger, but stranger rapes account for only about 20 percent of reported rapes that are reported. (Estimates are that perhaps only one of ten rapes is reported.) For college students, stranger rape is likely to be even less frequent than that for women in general, perhaps 10 percent (Koss, Gidycz, & Wisniewski, 1987; Koss, 1993).

**acquaintance rape** Rape that occurs when someone is raped by someone she or he knows from a nonromantic situation.

- *Acquaintance Rape.* When women are raped by acquaintances with whom they are familiar from nonromantic situations, this is referred to as **acquaintance rape.** Such individuals could be coworkers, neighbors, friends, or relatives. Of college women, about 25 to 30 percent have experienced acquaintance rape (Koss et al., 1987).

**date rape** Rape that occurs in the context of a dating, romantic relationship.

- *Date Rape.* Occurring in the context of a dating or romantic relationship, **date rape** is more restricted in its meaning than is acquaintance rape. Rape refers to unwanted sexual intercourse or penetration. In the context of date rape, a woman might allow some sexual behavior, but not others. When a woman refuses to agree to have sex, and the man forces her to have sexual relations with him, that is rape. Being persuaded to and agreeing to having sex is not rape. Some men believe that under certain circumstances it is alright to have sex with a woman without her consent. It is not. Typically, verbal coercion, such as threats, is a more commonly used tactic than are physical restraint and physical aggression (Rapaport & Burkhart, 1984).

Why do men rape, and what social factors contribute to rape? In many societies, the male role is associated with power and aggressiveness.

Researchers (Sanday, 1981) who have studied rape in many different societies have found that some societies are more "rape-prone" than others are. Societies with a relatively high incidence of rape have attitudes that tolerate or value violence in boys and young men. Such societies tend to give men greater economic, political, and family power than do those where rape occurs more rarely. The United States is an example of a "rape-prone" society, where male aggressiveness and competitiveness is accepted, and female passivity and acceptance is likely to be expected. In addition, sexually explicit magazines or films, especially violent pornography, have been shown to be related to attitudes and behavior of men with regard to rape (Crooks & Baur, 1999). In acquaintance and date rape, the use of alcohol and drugs plays a significant role, as does a man's view of women as sexual objects.

What type of men rape? Researchers such as Abel and Rouleau (1990) suggest that men who rape are likely to view the male role as one of dominance. Further, rapists might have been involved in a variety of sexual assaults or victimization such as exhibitionism, voyeurism, sadism, and sexual abuse of children. They have likely fantasized about rape and violence before they started to rape. Fantasies of rape while masturbating are common among men who eventually rape. There is no single reason for rape, but many motivations are related to power and domination issues, such as strong feelings of hatred and resentment, desire to exert control over another person, a desire to torture or abuse, as well as sexual gratification (Crooks & Baur, 1999). Rape is a reality, and, as stated earlier, acquaintance and date rape are more common than stranger rape is. How then can rape be avoided?

## Avoiding Rape

Experts (Crooks & Baur, 1999; Fischhoff, 1992) make a variety of suggestions for avoiding both stranger rape and acquaintance or date rape, most of which are related to personal security. For example, installing and using secure locks on doors and windows is helpful. Not opening doors to strangers and making repairmen and public officials identify themselves is appropriate. Avoiding dark and deserted areas, having house and car keys in hand, and carrying a device for making a loud noise (such as a whistle) are helpful when walking alone, especially at night. Demonstrating self-confidence through body language (walking with your head looking forward rather than down) can communicate to a potential rapist that a woman cannot be intimidated. Although these suggestions are helpful, they are not guaranteed to prevent a stranger rape.

Sexual assaults vary, and each potential rapist is different; however, some suggestions might be helpful in a situation where a woman is approached by a man who intends to rape her (Fischhoff, 1992). If you cannot run away from a situation, it might be appropriate to shout, cause a scene, fight back, or otherwise try to deter the rapist. Sometimes talking can be another strategy ("What has made you so angry?" "It's really tough to be fired and not have a job"). Looking for ways to escape from the situation while talking is a good idea. Some women have found that self-defense classes give them more confidence and methods for physically resisting an attacker. Because each situation is different, not all of these suggestions will work. There are many situations where women are unable to escape from an attacker. When an attacker has a weapon, the woman might have few or no ways of resisting. An unfortunate myth has developed that some women are "looking to be raped" and are responsible in some way for the rape. The responsibility for the rape lies with the rapist, not the victim.

In situations of date rape, the blame for the rape is sometimes confusing. Again, responsibility for rape is with the sexual coercer, not the victim. "She asked for it" is not an acceptable defense against rape.

To reduce the risk of acquaintance or date rape, women should not meet men that they don't know well in public places. Using alcohol can make a potential perpetrator more likely to act inappropriately and can diminish a woman's ability to escape from an assault and to resist it. When a man does not listen to a woman's request to stop unwanted sexual behavior, forcefulness is helpful. Saying "If you don't stop, I'm calling 911" might be appropriate. Shouting or physical force such as pushing and kicking might also work. Rape, whether stranger, acquaintance, or date rape, is a crime that is punishable by years in prison, depending on the offense and the laws of the state in which the incident occurs.

## What If You Have Been Raped?

When a woman has been raped, she must decide whether to report the attack to the police. By providing information about a rape or an unsuccessful rape, women can help other women from being victims of the rapist or potential rapist. When you report a rape, the more information you can provide about the attack and the attacker the better. This includes information about what the attacker looks like, what he was wearing, his smell, or anything else that would help the police identify him. By reporting the rape as soon as possible, and going to a hospital where semen, hair, and other evidence can be gathered, a woman can help in the identification of the rapist. One of the most important things that women can do is not to blame themselves for the rape. Being raped is not a crime, raping is. Calling a rape crisis center or sexual assault hotline can be very helpful in deciding what to do and how to handle the situation.

After being raped, women are likely to experience the trauma in two phases, an immediate reaction, and a longer-term reaction lasting months

---

## Problems and Solutions

---

### How can I help a friend who has been raped?

- Recommend and support the use of counseling.
- Encourage or permit your friend to keep talking about the rape.
- Support her judgment in handling the situation, when possible.
- Support her making her own decisions about how to handle the situation.

---

or years (Crooks & Baur, 1999). Immediately after an attack, a woman might be visibly upset, crying or appearing fearful. On the other hand, many women will try to control the feelings that they have inside—such as shame, anger, guilt, self-blame, or a sense of powerlessness—by trying to be matter-of-fact and appearing calm. Some women experience physical symptoms because of the assault itself as well as headaches, problems sleeping, and nightmares.

After the immediate reaction, which can take place over a few days or weeks, women are likely to continue to feel fearful or unsafe. Many women report difficulties in their sexual desire and arousal as well as in their participation in sexual behavior. For some women, the experience of being raped interferes more with the psychological aspects of sex than the physiological aspects. Sex that previously had been associated with love and intimacy might now be associated with fear and trauma. Counseling can often help ease the trauma that women experience after a rape. Seeking counseling soon after the rape can be very helpful in dealing with the fear, anger, and other strong emotions. Talking about the rape can help individuals deal with their pain and help them begin to heal the psychological wounds.

## Helping Someone Who Has Been Raped

When a woman confides in you that she has been raped, you can do a number of things, but you do not have to take on the burden of dealing with such a traumatic event. Encouraging a woman to seek counseling can be one of the most helpful things that you can do. Other helpful actions include listening. It is helpful for a person who has experienced a traumatic event to talk about this repeatedly. Don't discourage a person from talking about a rape again and again. When a person talks about a rape, don't question her

**Q 7.9** If a female friend of yours told you that she has been raped, how would you react and what would you want to say?

**Q 7.10** What could you say that might change the behavior of a male friend who boasted about coercing women to have sex?

judgment. Saying "Why did you talk to him at all?," "Why didn't you run away?" are not helpful because these comments encourage a woman to blame herself for the rape. After the rape has occurred, allow a woman to make decisions for herself, rather than telling her what she should do after the rape. Gaining a sense of control over one's life after a rape is important, so helping a person to do this is useful. Concern about a rape can go on for weeks, months, or years. Supporting a woman by allowing her to talk about the rape whenever she feels the need to is a way of providing important assistance. The acceptance and support offered by romantic partners or close friends can be very helpful when women are trying to deal with this severe psychological trauma.

## SUMMARY

Because sexual behavior is such a personal and intimate matter, individuals are often reluctant to discuss it. As a result, myths about sexuality have developed, often quite inaccurately, that can inhibit or scare individuals. Some of these myths were discussed along with views that different individuals have of sexuality. Religion, parental views, and relationships with others often influence sexual values. Not all sexuality is directed toward the other gender. Issues regarding homosexual behavior and negativity surrounding values about homosexual behavior were also discussed here.

Regardless of sexual orientation, to be understood, sexuality needs to be discussed in relationship to intimacy. Both passionate and companionate love were explained, as were the phases of relationships and how a casual relationship can develop into a loving relationship. How men and women view intimate and sexual relationships differently was also a topic of this section. Understanding the beliefs and values that men and women have about sex provides a context for understanding the human sexual response. Typical patterns of sexual responding and the phases of sexual excitement were explained as they apply to both men and women. Despite information about sexuality and because of societal inhibitions about sex, both men and women might have problems of sexual responding. Some suggestions for how people can cope with these were made.

Sexual behavior carries with it responsibilities and concerns, as irresponsible sexual behavior can lead to unwanted pregnancy or to a sexually transmitted disease. Because medical technology has considerably advanced, new methods of contraception have been developed and were explained. Contraceptive methods include abstinence, birth control pills, condoms, spermicides, diaphragms, the rhythm method, as well as other methods. Of all the methods of contraception, however, abstinence and condoms are most effective in preventing sexually transmitted diseases.

Throughout most of the chapter, sex is described in the context of a mutually consenting relationship; however, sexual assault and rape are significant problems in the United States and other countries. Dealing with stranger, acquaintance, or date rape can be very traumatic for women. Discussed were how to avoid rape, what to do if you have been raped, and how to help someone who has experienced a traumatic sexual situation. A variety of sexual behaviors, values, and concerns make sexuality a particularly complex issue.

## RECOMMENDED READINGS

*Our Sexuality*
Crooks, R. and Baur, K. (Brooks/Cole, 1999)
> Sexuality is discussed in thorough detail in this comprehensive textbook used widely in courses on sexuality. The text is accurate and clear. First-person accounts are a part of most of the chapters. Attitudes, values, and the physiology of sexuality are discussed. Coverage includes homosexuality, transsexuality, aging, and unwanted sexuality.

*Love and Sex: Cross-Cultural Perspectives*
Hatfield, E. and Rapson, R. L. (Allyn & Bacon, 1996)
> Romantic relationships and sexuality are viewed from different cultural perspectives. Concepts such as passionate and companionate love (pages 156 and 157 of this text) are described fully. Sexual values and attitudes of different cultural groups are discussed. Exercises and tests help readers assess their own values and attitudes. This book provides a broad view of love and sex and the role that culture plays in romantic relationships.

*Loving Someone Gay*
Clark, D. (Celestial Arts, 1997)
> This book is designed both for those who are gay and for those who know someone who is gay. Written by a clinical psychologist who is gay, this book uses real examples to illustrate important issues. The first section of the book deals with issues concerning those who are gay, such as being invisible and the hostility that gay individuals encounter. Issues such as emotional and sexual aspects of relationships as well as coming out are also discussed. Another section contains advice for people who know someone who is gay, such as children, friends, or neighbors. Suggestions are also given to professionals, such as physicians, clergy, and teachers, who interact with gay people.

*Recovering from Rape*
Ledray, L. E. (Holt, 1994)
> Written for rape survivors and their friends and family, this book provides both emotional support and practical advice in dealing with the trauma of rape. Each chapter of the book contains sections for the survivor and for the significant other of the survivor. Initial psychological reactions toward rape and toward recovery are discussed. Ways for dealing with police, medical personnel, and friends and others are discussed. Specific chapters are devoted to issues such as childhood sexual assault and the motives of rapists.

# RECOMMENDED WEB SITES

*Love Page*
http://www.tc.umn.edu/nlhome/g296/parkx032/LBindex.html
> James Park, an existentialist philosopher and advocate of freedom and authenticity in relationships offers a distinctive challenge to more traditional notions of romantic love at this site. He provides bibliographies on a host of topics, such as jealousy, sexual scripts, and the decision to have children.

*SIECUS (Sexuality Information and Education Council of the United States)*
http://www.siecus.org/
> Produced by one of the oldest organizations in the United States devoted to educating the public about matters of sexuality, this contains links to many different topics related to sexuality.

*Office of Population Research*
http://opr.princeton.edu/
> The Office of Population Research at Princeton University has studied population issues from many different perspectives. This online resource includes extensive links and guides to the topics of pregnancy prevention and reproductive choice.

*Sexual Health Network*
http://www.sexualhealth.com/
> This site provides a comprehensive set of information and resources related to all aspects of human sexual health. Especially notable here are materials discussing sexual functioning for persons with physical injuries or disabilities.

*Queer Resources Directory (QRD)*
http://www.qrd.org/QRD/
> The Queer Resource Directory is an electronic research library dedicated to sexual minorities —"groups which have traditionally been labeled as 'queer' and systematically discriminated against." This directory provides a rich array of resources.

*AIDS HIV AEGIS*
http://www.aegis.com/
> This is the largest and one of the most important Internet resources dealing with the human immunodeficiency virus (HIV) and acquired immune deficiency syndrome (AIDS). This site provides an extensive collection of information sources, both printed and online.

*Sexual Assault Information Page*
http://www.cs.utk.edu/bartley/sainfoPage.html
> Chris Bartley has offered a very valuable group of resources related to sexual assault, including date and acquaintance rape. This site offers detailed discussions of factors that contribute to sexual assault such as defective communication.

*Sex Education Resources on the World-Wide-Web: Recommended Sites*
http://www.jagunet.com/~dgotlib/meanstreets.htm
> Compiled by David A. Gotlib and Peter Fagan of John Hopkins University, this site contains a survey of some of the best online resources about sexuality.

# GENDER ROLES

## GENDER DEVELOPMENT

## VIEWS OF GENDER

---

**gender** Refers to whether one is male or female.

**gender roles** Expectations about appropriate behavior for males and females.

**gender stereotypes** Beliefs about the skills, personalities, and behaviors that are expected of males and females.

**sex** Used to refer to sexual behavior, such as kissing or sexual intercourse.

**sexual orientation** A preference for individuals of one gender or the other gender or both.

The following question illustrates the importance we put on gender roles in our society: What would you think about someone in your class who came to class dressed in clothes that are worn by the other gender? The shock and other feelings that people feel highlights the strong gender-role expectations individuals have. Gender roles are often taken for granted in most societies as children are indoctrinated into them without being aware of the lessons they are learning. In this chapter, we examine gender role differences and different ways of understanding them. Before discussing sex, gender, and gender role, it will be helpful to identify terms that we will use throughout this chapter (Weiten & Lloyd, 2000).

- **Gender.** This term refers to whether one is male or female. Male and female differences can be learned or inherited.
- **Gender roles.** Societies have expectations about appropriate behavior for males and females. The roles that males and females are expected to play vary somewhat depending on cultural background.
- **Gender stereotypes.** In many cultures, there are beliefs about the skills, personalities, and behaviors that are expected of males and females. An example of a gender stereotype is to say that women should be nurses and men should be doctors.
- **Sex.** In this book, we will use sex to refer to sexual behavior. Kissing, sexual intercourse, and rape are sexual behaviors.
- **Sexual orientation.** Many cultures assume that individuals will have a heterosexual sexual orientation, a preference for individuals of the other gender. Some individuals, however, have a sexual orientation toward people of their same gender (homosexual) or toward both genders (bisexual).

**normative** Common guidelines for social actions.

In recent years, gender role has been the subject of thousands of articles and hundreds of books. Feminism has developed as an academic discipline, and feminist therapy has developed as a way of helping individuals with problems. Many colleges and universities have courses in women's studies, and many have departments of women's studies. Perhaps the best explanation for this is that for many years the male was viewed as **normative.** In other words, when one thought of history, science, or other fields, the focus was often on the male. For example, throughout history, women have most frequently achieved recognition as being the "wife of" or "mother of" the general, king, scientist, or world leader. From this vantage point, women follow the "norms"; they do not set them. Until the late 1960s, terms such as *mankind* and *man* were often used to refer to people in general. The pronoun *he* used to be used that way, but now authors use terms such as "he or she" or "they" to avoid this focus on the male as the norm. When the male is the norm, women become a subset of the norm (Hyde, 1996).

An early study by Broverman, Broverman, Clarkson, Rosenkrantz, and Vogel (1970) documented how therapists viewed men as the norm. Using a sample of psychiatrists, clinical psychologists, and social workers, Broverman and colleagues asked one-third of the sample to evaluate mature and healthy males, one-third to evaluate mature and healthy females, and one-third to evaluate mature and healthy adults. When they compared the ratings on 122 adjectives, the researchers found that mental health standards for males and adults were similar, but that there were differences between standards for females and for adults (an example of men as the "normative" group). Traits for males included being objective, independent, aggressive, direct, and unemotional, whereas female traits included being submissive, sensitive, and emotionally expressive (Broverman et al., 1970). Although other studies have shown evidence of gender-role stereotyping, increased knowledge of gender-role issues, and changes in the attitudes of therapists explain why repeating this study probably would not get similar results 30 years later. By questioning the view of the male as the norm for all people, useful information can be provided about how men and women differ and how they relate to each other.

How men and women view themselves and each other profoundly affects their own development. There are differences in each individual's view of gender roles, as well as wider cultural differences. Although studying the development of gender is important, it is essential not to attribute common stereotypes to all individuals. There are so many different factors in individual development that each person's reaction to cultural gender role forces is different.

# GENDER DEVELOPMENT

Research on gender-related characteristics is extensive, especially for children, and includes research on many biological, psychological, sociological, and environmental factors. In such research, there are two related problems (Hare-Mustin & Marecek, 1988). One is the problem of separating women and men into two categories, then treating them as separate and unequal, furthering male-female stereotypes. The opposite problem is ignoring real differences between the lives of women and the lives of men and treating them as identical. In this section, I focus on differences in the development of men and women, thus running the risk of overgeneralizing about differences. First, I will examine the development of gender role in children, then adolescence, and then adults. Because cultural and gender roles affect each other, I will discuss this issue as well.

## *Childhood*

Even before birth, parents have gender preferences for their children. Especially men, but also women have a clear preference for a son rather than a daughter in many cultures (Unger & Crawford, 1996). This is particularly true in Asia, where selective abortion of female children occurs. If one or both parents have a strong preference for a male child and a daughter is born, it is possible that these preferences can affect parental child-raising attitudes.

Compared with adolescent and adult development, there is generally more similarity among young children than there are differences in gender role behavior (Hyde, 1996). In general, the behavior of male and female infants is similar. Their treatment by adults creates gender role behavior. For example, adults select clothing and toys for young children, often based on gender role expectations. For example, the traditional pink for girls and blue for boys is a small illustration of gender role beliefs. By the way that children are dressed, play, and learn about life through stories and television, children begin to adopt different gender-role expectations.

In early relationships with parents and peers, children learn behavior that is considered appropriate for their gender. Usually, children start to separate into same-gender groups between the ages of four and six. Between the ages four and six, the amount of time that children spent playing with playmates of the same gender versus those of the other gender increased from 3:1 to 11:1 (Maccoby, 1990). The play of boys is also different from that of girls: Boys tend to roam farther away from home and play in larger groups, whereas girls are more likely to stay near the house

(Feiring & Lewis, 1987). Another difference between boys and girls is that girls are more likely to express suggestions, whereas boys more often make demands or requests (Maltz & Borker, 1983). Because boys have fewer male role models available to them than do girls, who have mothers and female teachers as role models, researchers suggest that peers play a more important role for boys than for girls (Weiten & Lloyd, 2000). Boys might get more information about the male role from their peers than girls do about the female role from their peers.

Within the elementary school, gender segregation is common. During these years, there is pressure to unlearn behaviors associated with the other gender. In other words, girls might be taunted or teased for being a "tomboy" and boys might be called "sissy." Partly because of the devaluing of opposite-gender stereotypic characteristics, friendships between boys and girls that were common earlier become increasingly uncommon. The nature of the interactions between parents, teachers, and other adults can be such that it encourages independence and efficacy in boys and nurturing and helplessness in girls (Unger & Crawford, 1996). Even when some parents choose consciously not to impart gender-role expectations to their children, children might communicate their own gender role views through their preferences for play, toys, and stereotyped expectations based on gender, which can come from television, movies, and peers.

## *Adolescence*

**menstruation** The periodic flow, occurring about monthly, of blood from the uterus.

Because of physical changes and peer pressure, gender-role pressures tend to be greater in adolescence than in any other time of life. In general, puberty provides more conflicts for girls than for boys because of the ways that society views the female body and the role of female sexuality (Unger & Crawford, 1996). For girls, **menstruation** starts between the ages of 11 and 13. Sometimes girls and their parents respond negatively to this. Similarly, because others can easily observe breast development, it can be the subject of embarrassment for girls and teasing by boys. Girls often become well aware of the need to be thin and to be seen as physically attractive. Although different peer groups (friends at church or synagogue, female athletes, or close friends) might have different expectations, exposure of expectations of women's appearance through magazines and television can have profound effects. For some girls, dating can become an important factor for the development of self-esteem, with girls being valued for their appearance whereas boys are valued for achievements as well as appearance. Girls compete against other girls for the attention of boys, whereas boys are focused more broadly on academic and athletic accomplishments. Girls, not boys, must learn to regulate sexual activity to prevent becoming pregnant. The use of contraception and the consequences of teenage pregnancy are usually a much greater problem for the adolescent girl than for the boy. Gender role stereotypes affect parental expectations and, with growing independence, conflicts between parents and teenage adolescents arise. These are often different for mother-daughter, mother-son, father-daughter, and father-son pairs (Unger & Crawford, 1996). Although adolescent-parent relationships are important, the emphasis on the need to develop relationships (particularly with men) and thus to be valued for their appearance carries over into women's experience in adulthood. Relationships are important for men, but relationships tend to be a particular focus for women (Jordan, 1997).

## Adulthood

Because there are such a variety of ways that men and women deal with educational, occupational, social, and family issues in their lives, it is difficult to clearly describe women's or men's adult development. However, some important issues have a particular impact on both men and women, and I will discuss them here: child raising, work, mid-life issues, and violence.

Although childbearing is something only a woman can do, child raising can be shared in a variety of ways by men and women. For women, physiological changes occur during pregnancy that affect work, marital relationships, and physical self-image. How women react to childbearing depends on a variety of factors, such as the number of previous children; a woman's social class, race, sexual orientation; and relationships with the child and husband or partner. Research (Aneshensel, 1986) has shown that women with strained marriages experienced the most depression, an intermediate amount occurred with unmarried women, and the least depression was experienced by happily married women. More so than men, married women who decide not to have children feel considerable social pressure to have children. Controlling the decision to have children requires dealing with sexual issues such as contraception and possibly abortion. Women, more than men, are given the responsibility for raising children in American society and are likely to receive blame if children are not raised properly (Unger & Crawford, 1996).

Married women often have a different experience and approach to work than do married men. Although some men share in housework, women usually do most of it (Ferree, 1987). In fact, many married women see housework as a significant aspect of their role within the family (Robinson & Milkie, 1998). Other related tasks include taking care of a husband, children, and possibly aged parents. In their paid work, women are six times more likely to do clerical work than men are, and men are six times more likely to be involved in trades such as plumbing (Ciancanelli & Birch, 1987). Furthermore, women are likely to earn considerably less than men. Although traditional women's professions such as teaching, social work, and health occupations have status because they require skill and dedication, their pay is lower than many high-status occupations (lawyer, physician, business executive) that are traditionally held by men. Furthermore, in applying for a job and in the actual work itself, women are more likely than men to experience discrimination and sexual harassment (Sharf, 1997). Relatively recent changes in laws have made it more difficult to discriminate against women. Before the 1970s, however, women received active discouragement when they tried to enter nontraditional fields such as business, science, or high level positions within traditional fields. It was acceptable for women to become nurses, but not to be doctors. Although laws prevent active discrimination, behaviors tend to change more slowly.

**menopause** The permanent ending of menstruation. Generally, this occurs when women reach their 50s.

Women and men age differently. For example, women are perceived as losing their sexual attractiveness at an earlier age than are men. A part of aging for women is **menopause,** which is often seen as being a time in which women change negatively in physical and psychological ways. Some women feel devalued as their children leave home or their role in child care decreases significantly. To the extent that much of society values women in a relational or caring role, this change can be difficult. For some women, however, it is an opportunity to achieve and be active. Regarding finances, older women are almost twice as likely to have incomes at or below the poverty level than are men of the same age (Grambs, 1989). For those who have been widowed or divorced, insufficient income can be a particularly difficult problem. In summary, aging women are likely to be seen more negatively than men and to experience more financial hardship than men. This is more commonly found in the United States than in other cultures. The ability of aging women to develop friendships because of their involvement in nurturing activities, however, is likely to help them deal effectively with children leaving home, the death of husbands, and other losses. Men can have more difficulty in dealing with close losses because they might not have the same skills to develop relationships as women.

The issue of violence is different for men than for women. Although women more commonly experience violence than men do, there are some exceptions. Chapter 10 describes the problem of homicides of African American men by African American men. Still, violence to women is much more common than is violence to men, occurring at all age levels. For children, child abuse and incest can have terrible consequences for later psychological development. In adolescence and adulthood, women can be victims of date rape, stranger rape, or wife battering. Although statistics are kept on such crimes, acts of violence are likely to be underreported because victims fear further attacks through physical intimidation or being blamed for provoking an incident. As Hyde (1996) points out, women can be viewed as strong for surviving and returning to a productive life rather than as weak for being victimized.

I have tried to highlight the major developmental issues that men and women confront at different times during their lives. In such a summary, many of these comments are generalizations, applying to some men or women, but not to others. Another factor that greatly affects gender roles and how they develop is the culture in which people are raised.

## Cultural Differences

Is the assignment of gender roles unique to the United States and modern industrial nations? Sociologists (Stockard, 1997) have found that all societies have gender role divisions. In fact, there are no societies where women control the lives of men in the political or economic world. Societies differ in which functions men and women perform. In some societies, women may be given a substantial amount of freedom or authority in one area, but not in another. In pre-industrial societies, women take care of small animals like chickens, but in others, men do so. Likewise women herd cows in one society, whereas in another, men do this. In hunting and war, however, men carry out the hunt or war, whereas women can be involved in planning the activities. In almost every society, men are assigned more prestigious and worthwhile tasks than women are. For example, in some parts of New Guinea, men grow yams that are eaten at feasts and considered a prestigious food. Women grow sweet potatoes, which are everyday food. Also in New Guinea, in another tribe, men and women fish, but the women's fishing is considered to be a part of their work, whereas for men it is seen as an exciting expedition (Weiner, 1976). Thus, the issues of men and women having different roles in society, and women having roles that are less valued than those of men, are not limited to the United States. How men and women experience gender role expectations varies widely.

## VIEWS OF GENDER

In the previous section, we examined some general ways in which men and women grow up differently. In this section, I will describe some specific gender role issues that research psychologists have identified as being helpful in understanding the impact of gender roles on men and women. First, we will explore Sandra Bem's (1981, 1987) concept of androgyny—possessing both masculine and feminine psychological traits. This is followed by a discussion of "gender schema theory," which concerns the

**Q 8.1** Give two examples of how you experienced gender limitations or expectations before you were 12 years old.

**Q 8.2** Give an example of when you considered or tried to cross gender lines (do something that was not expected of your gender).

**Q 8.3** Give an example of someone you knew who suffered because of gender role expectations.

importance that individuals attribute to gender in their view of their world. Another way of viewing gender roles is to look at how men and women use different judgments when they make moral decisions. This provides some insight into differences in values that men and women have. Yet another way of viewing gender is that of relational theory or how men and women relate differently to others. Perhaps the area where sex role expectations are strongest is that of perceptions about homosexuality. As we explore each of these areas, you should be able to see male-female relationships in a different way.

## *Androgyny*

**androgyny** The idea that each person has both masculine and feminine personality traits.

Developed by Sandra Bem (1981, 1987), the concept of **androgyny** refers to the idea that each person has both masculine and feminine personality traits. Thus, an androgynous person would score above average on masculinity and femininity scales on a test of androgyny. Males who score high only on a scale of masculinity would be assumed to be traditionally male, and women who score high only on femininity would be assumed to be traditionally feminine. Bem believed that traditionally masculine men and feminine women would follow gender roles more closely, and would be more limited in their behavior, than would those who were androgynous. Some research evidence (Weiten & Lloyd, 2000) shows that androgynous individuals are more flexible than are gender-type males or females. Traditional males seemed to be less nurturant than androgynous males, and traditional females were less independent than androgynous females. Androgynous individuals or those scoring high on the feminine scale reported higher satisfaction in their relationships than did those who were undifferentiated or scored high on the masculine scale.

Some problems with the concept of androgyny have bothered gender role researchers and others. These deal with idealizing or stereotyping "masculinity" and "femininity" rather than focusing on other characteristics. Another criticism is that individuals can feel the need to have both masculine and feminine traits. Instead, it can be argued that emphasizing gender traits can be a mistake: Rather than label traits as "masculine" or "feminine," it is better to look at the traits within individuals.

## *Gender Schema Theory*

**schema** A way of making associations that helps individuals interpret what they see.

Instead of emphasizing masculine and feminine traits, gender schema theory asks how important are gender roles in an individual's thinking. Individuals use a **schema** to make associations that help them interpret what they see. For example, individuals viewing 4- to 5-year-olds playing in the mud might use different schemas to describe the situation. One person

**gender schema theory**
Looking at how much individuals evaluate others from the perspective of gender.

might think, "Here are four kids having a great time." A second might think, "The smallest of the children is directing the play of the others." A third might think, "The two girls are getting mud all over their dresses. What will their mother think?" The first example might be called a "play schema." The second a "leadership schema." And the third a "gender schema." **Gender schema theory** looks at individuals relative to how how much they focus on gender. Some individuals are more likely to view situations from a gender point of view than are others. Some situations can be presented to fit into a gender schema. Hyde (1996) gives the following brain teaser. See if you can solve it.

> A father and a son were involved in a car accident in which the father was killed and the son was seriously injured. The father was pronounced dead at the scene of the accident and his body was taken to a local mortuary. The son was taken by ambulance to a hospital and was immediately wheeled into an operating room. A surgeon was called. Upon seeing the patient, the attending surgeon exclaimed, "Oh, my God, it's my son!"
>
> Can you explain this? (Keep in mind that the father that was killed in the accident was not a stepfather, nor is the attending physician the boy's stepfather. p. 55)

For most of us, our gender schemas make it difficult to realize that the surgeon is the boy's *mother.*

Gender schema theory can be applied to all levels of development. As Bem (1981) has observed, children not only learn society's views of gender but also learn to apply it to themselves. For example, they learn that girls wear dresses, boys do not; girls wear lipstick and nail polish, boys do not; and boys are called *handsome,* and girls are called *pretty.* Adolescents, in particular, are likely to be highly gender focused as they become concerned about the physical attractiveness of the other gender and of themselves. Adults who are gender focused are much more likely to view behaviors of associates as "unmanly" or "unfeminine" than are those who use other schemas in attributing characteristics to associates. Bem believes that gender schema theory is one of the strongest schemas, or ways of looking at society. She feels that a strong gender schema is a very limiting way to view oneself and others. Differentiating between the necessity for children to learn about physiological sex differences and gender typing of gender role behaviors, Bem suggests that parents help their children learn other schemas. An "individual differences" schema emphasizes the variability of individuals within a group. For example, when the young child says, "Harry is a sissy because he likes to paint," a parent might point out that both boys and girls paint and enjoy it. The parent might suggest then that not everyone thinks the same way and that people in different groups or cultures can have different beliefs. Fairy tales, which often contain

**Q 8.4** Describe yourself using Bem's concept of androgyny (how androgynous are you?) and her concept of gender schema (how important are gender schemas to you?).

many gender-role stereotypes, can be explained as beliefs that reflect a culture that is different than our own culture (if the child is old enough to understand this concept). Gender schema theory has applications for child raising, and for how we view ourselves. We can examine our own gender schemas and ask ourselves how important gender is to us in making judgments about others.

## Morality and Gender

Gender role affects how both men and women make moral choices. Lawrence Kohlberg (1981) conceived a stage model of moral development based on justice (Table 8.1). He showed how moral decisions evolved from following rules so that one wouldn't be punished, but would be rewarded for conforming to the rules of others. Another step in moral development is that of understanding the need for rules and making judgments based on a sense of justice. Carol Gilligan (1982), a colleague of Kohlberg's, saw his model as one that was oriented toward rules and more in keeping with a male point of view. Just as Kohlberg had studied the moral decision making of children and adolescents, so did Gilligan, however, she focused on the moral development of girls and young women, whereas Kohlberg had focused on men. Her view of women's approach to morality is that they emphasize care and responsibility. Her levels of morality (Table 8.1) start with being concerned with oneself and gradually developing a concern for the responsibilities of self and others and seeing how one person and others need to interact with each other for mutual benefit.

An example will help to explain the difference between Kohlberg's morality of justice and Gilligan's morality of care and responsibility. This difference can be seen by comparing the comments of two 8-year-old children, Jeffrey and Karen, who are both asked to describe a situation when they were not sure what the correct approach should be. Where Jeffrey uses an ordering system to resolve a conflict between desire and duty, Karen uses a relational system that includes her friends. Jeffrey thinks about what to do first, Karen is concerned about who is left out (Gilligan, 1982, pp. 32–33; Sharf, 2000, p. 463).

*Jeffrey:* When I really want to go to my friends and my mother is cleaning the cellar, I think about my friends, and then I think about my mother, and then I think about the right thing to do. (But how do you know if it's the right thing to do?) Because some things go before other things.

*Karen:* I have a lot of friends and I can't always play with all of them, so everybody's going to have to take a turn, because they're all my friends. Like if someone's all alone, I'll play with them. (What kind of things do you think about when you are trying to make that decision?) Um, someone all alone, loneliness.

TABLE **8.1** KOHLBERG'S AND GILLIGAN'S LEVELS OF MORAL DEVELOPMENT

| Kohlberg's Morality of Justice | Gilligan's Morality of Care |
|---|---|
| **Preconventional Morality** | |
| 1. Do what you are told to avoid punishment. | 1. Take care of yourself and your needs. |
| 2. Do what you are told to get your needs met. | |
| **Conventional Morality** | |
| 3. Seek approval by conforming to the rules of others; obey rules to avoid their disapproval. | 2. Use social norms to guide you in meeting the needs of others. |
| 4. Follow society's rules and don't question them. | |
| **Postconventional Morality** | |
| 5. Know the importance of societal rules, but question them when they seem to no longer benefit society. | 3. Focus on caring in human relationships, both for yourself and others. |

**Q 8.5** Describe a situation such as Heinz's dilemma. It should be a situation in which there are moral choices. Identify a morality of justice solution and a morality of care solution.

**Q 8.6** Does your gender and your moral decision making style fit with Kohlberg's (male) morality of justice or Gilligan's (female) morality of care? Are Kohlberg's and Gilligan's systems too narrow or do they fit you well? Explain.

Gilligan (1982) was critical of Kohlberg for using hypothetical examples that portrayed males rather than females and for using, in his first study, a sample of 84 males. In Kohlberg's studies, women generally reached stage 3, whereas men reached stage 4. Rather than interpret this as a deficiency in women, Gilligan saw it as a deficiency in Kohlberg's theory. A typical hypothetical example that people were asked to respond to was the case of Heinz, who was faced with a moral dilemma when his wife was near death from cancer and only one drug might save her. Although the druggist paid only $200 dollars for the drug, he wanted to charge Heinz $2,000 for a small dose of the drug. The druggist would not let Heinz pay later, so Heinz broke into the store and stole the drug. Participants were asked if they thought Heinz should have stolen the drug, whether his action was right or wrong, and why (Kohlberg, 1981). To this example, and similar ones, women tended to give answers that reflected the morality of care and responsibility, whereas men tended to give answers that reflected morality of justice (reflecting Kohlberg's six stages). For example in the situation with Heinz, women might be more concerned about caring for Heinz's wife, whereas men may be concerned about violating laws and breaking into a store.

In summarizing the differences between the approach of males and females to morality, Gilligan emphasized that women took on a responsibility to examine a situation in which someone was in trouble and looked for ways to help the situation. Men, on the other hand, tended to be concerned with respecting the rights of others and protecting those rights from being interfered with. Gilligan also saw women first being rather self-critical rather than self-protective in assessing a situation, whereas men initially assessed a situation in terms of not interfering with the rights of others. When discussing male's and female's view of morality, many researchers point out that not all women and all men view situations in similar ways. Some men will use a morality of care and responsibility in assessing some situations and some women will use a sense of justice in evaluating situations. Depending on the situation, both men and women might emphasize morality of justice or morality of care, but clearly, gender role can affect how individuals examine and make choices about moral dilemmas.

## Relational Views

**relational theory**
Psychological theory that studies the importance of relationships for women in finding a sense of identity.

Just as Gilligan emphasizes the importance of caring and responsibility in her model of women's moral decision-making, **relational theorists** have examined the importance of relationships for women in finding a sense of identity. Whereas men often have a sense of self based on their accomplishments and physical or intellectual skills, women's sense of self is based on their ability to develop and maintain relationships (Miller, 1991). Miller believes that women develop skills in relating because they were subordinate to men historically and had to develop ways to assist men. Because of being in a subordinate position, women can feel less important than men and strive to improve their relationships with both men and women by attending to the emotional and physical needs of others and by helping them develop their strength and improve their well-being (mothering or nursing). Miller and Surrey and their colleagues at the Stone Center for Developmental Services at Wellesly College see the relationship skills of women as a strength that should be valued and appreciated. Further, they do not criticize men's focus on achievement and performance.

An example of how women may relate differently than men because of their emphasis on responding to emotions and relationships rather than deciding or taking charge helps illustrate relational theory.

*Eileen:* When I was walking home, two men came up next to me and started to tease me, making sexual remarks.

*Joan:* Oh, you must have been scared, not knowing what they'd do.

*Eileen:* I was frightened. I didn't know whether they would touch me or what they would do. I just kept walking.

*Joan:* I'd be so frightened too. It can feel like there's nothing you can do.

Joan pays attention to Eileen's emotions, her fear of being attacked. Joan expresses concern about Eileen and there is a sense that they have or are building a relationship. If Eileen were to talk to a man, however, he might respond the way Joan does, but it is more likely that he would focus on taking action or doing something about the situation. Contrast this brief conversation with the previous one.

> *Eileen:* When I was walking home, two men came up next to me and started to tease me, making sexual remarks.
>
> *Dick:* What did you do? Did you look at them?
>
> *Eileen:* No. I just walked faster and looked straight ahead.
>
> *Dick:* Good, because if you looked at them, you probably would've given them the attention they were looking for.
>
> *Eileen:* I just tried to get out of that situation as fast as I could.
>
> *Dick:* Did they stay with you long, or did they leave you alone?

Notice that Dick is trying to be helpful by giving Eileen suggestions about what to do and is trying to solve the problem that has scared Eileen. He asks problem-solving questions while Joan empathizes with Eileen. Although both men and women are likely to respond the way that both Joan and Dick did at different times, Miller (1991) and Surrey (1991) believe that women are more likely to respond the way Joan does and men are more likely to respond the way Dick does.

Women are more likely to focus on relationships and the emotional and physical needs of others, whereas men are more likely to focus on accomplishments and skills, so the topics of conversations when men talk to men and women talk to women are likely to be quite different from each other. Women are more likely to talk to women about relationships with others such as with their friends, their boyfriend, spouse, or partner, or to talk about problems that they had with other people such as parents or acquaintances. Men, on the other hand, are more likely to talk about things that they enjoy or have done. Common examples would be discussions of sports or attractive cars. Men might talk about their work and focus on projects and tasks. Often when they talk about relationships at work, men might focus on how their boss or coworker helped or hindered them in performing tasks. Women might discuss relationships at work in terms of their associates' families and health. Again, it is important not to overgeneralize about these distinctions. Both men and women could talk about any of these topics.

## Gender View of Homosexuality

Perhaps one of the strongest views in the United States and many other countries regarding gender role is that sexual relationships should be between members of the opposite gender. This view is supported not only by common social and cultural assumptions but also by religious writings

**Q 8.7** Think of a conversation between two men and one between two women. What did they talk about? Does the content of what they talked about fit with the predictions of relational theory?

**Q 8.8** When you talk to casual acquaintances who are men or women, do you find that the conversations with women tend to be more relationship focused and the ones with men focus more on content or achievement? Explain.

and in some cases, laws. Individuals who make public their attraction and involvement in sexual relations with their own gender run the risk of job discrimination, ridicule, and being social outcasts. In recent years, the acceptability of homosexuality has been widely debated and continues to be. Because of this controversy, it will be helpful to define a few words that make explicit some of the issues.

**heterosexuality** Sexual desires and erotic behaviors directed toward the other gender.

**heterosexism** The position that being heterosexual is inherently better than being homosexual.

**homophobia** The fear or hatred of homosexual people.

**homosexuality** Sexual desires and erotic behaviors directed toward one's own gender.

- **Heterosexuality.** Sexual desires and erotic behaviors directed toward the other gender
- **Heterosexism.** The view that being heterosexual is inherently better than being homosexual
- **Homophobia.** The dislike, fear, or hatred of homosexual people
- **Homosexuality.** Sexual desires and erotic behaviors that are directed toward one's own gender

During adolescence, individuals continue to learn gender roles, and they learn about sexual behavior and begin to initiate it. In adolescence, variations from generally accepted views of behavior, particularly sexual behavior can meet with scorn and ridicule. When terms such as "fag," "sissy," or "butch" are used in junior high school or high school, it is often with a more negative tone than at any other period of life. Individuals who are attracted to their same gender are likely to have a feeling that they are different in a negative way and that they carry a secret that should not be revealed. Commonly accepted gender roles are so strong that homosexual teenagers soon learn not to share this secret or, if they do, to share it only with those who they trust implicitly. The process of telling others about one's homosexual feelings or behavior is referred to as "coming out." Because homosexual individuals are often afraid of negative consequences of telling people about their sexuality, they often are reluctant to come out to bosses or parents for fear of losing their job or damaging important relationships.

Because of the negative views that many people have (homophobia) of homosexuals, homosexual individuals might be slow not only in "coming out" but also in being aware of their own homosexuality (Garnets & Kimmel, 1991). Negative views of homosexuality, employment and housing discrimination, and hate crimes against homosexuals contribute to the perception that homosexual individuals have that they will not be accepted in society, in general (Herek, Gillis, Cogan, & Glunt, 1997). When individuals first start to become aware of emotional and sexual attraction to members of their own gender, they often feel different and alone. Gradually, they might, in their own view, transform a negative societal stereotype of being "gay" or "lesbian" into a more positive one that applies to themselves. Then, they might start to explore gay and lesbian subcultures that exist in most cities. They may take advantage of toll-free information services and read newspapers and magazines about the homosexual subculture in their area. During or after that time they go through the process of disclosing their own sexual orientation to others. Because homosexual individuals can feel that they might be discriminated against, physically attacked, or disliked because of their homosexuality, they are often careful in revealing this information to others.

The pain and difficulty of feeling different than and ostracized by other individuals is often difficult to express. Mark's experience in junior high school was a painful one that has stayed with him throughout his life. Even at the age of 25, when he now is much more comfortable with his sexuality, he winces when he remembers the loneliness and hurt he experienced in the ninth grade.

> When I think of junior high school, I remember those gray green lockers we had where everyone kept their books, lunch, all that stuff. I even remember the little silver tag with the black number "576." This was my locker and whenever I went to it, it seemed like it was the only tiny little refuge that I had, that was mine in the entire school. The floors were polished daily so that the brown linoleum shone in the morning sun like it was there to welcome everybody but me. Somehow, I felt safe when I stared into my locker, but not other times. It didn't take me long in school to get teased. I think people thought I had girlish mannerisms and features. I did everything not to show that. I hated the whisperings of "fag" or "queer." I even went out for football just so I could try to be the opposite of what I felt. I never liked sports, I never felt athletic. But I tried to do anything to fit in. I just thought maybe I could hide myself in a football uniform. It didn't work. I tried track and I did stick with that in high school; that seemed to help. At least in track we could talk about track meets, joke around, and there seemed to be less emphasis on who I was. I went to dances, I did everything I could just to try to fit in.
>
> I never came out to anyone until my freshman year of college. I worked so hard to be what I wasn't. I hated it, but I did it. It was tough in ninth grade. When I first met Arnie, I liked him a lot. He seemed different because everybody considered him a brain and geeky. We both liked to talk about politics and religion, strange topics in ninth grade and so it was fun. Although he wasn't handsome, I found myself becoming more and more attracted to him. This was so hard because I didn't want to scare him away. I was sure he was "straight." In fact, I think at that time I thought everybody else but me was. We stayed friends through high school and it was really helpful. We had good times together, but there was always this strain that I felt, this taboo that I could not break. I couldn't tell him how I felt.

**Q 8.9** If a boy or girl had come out about their sexuality in your ninth grade class, what do you think would have been the consequences for them?

Gender role expectations in adolescence are often extremely rigid and difficult. When individuals feel that they don't fit them, the obsession with fitting in can be overwhelming.

In most societies, views of gender are extremely important to the way individuals view themselves and others. We have discussed androgyny, the notion that men and women possess varying degrees of masculinity and femininity, and that being "too" masculine or "too" feminine limit people's experiences and views of others. Gender schema theory explains how viewing other people's actions (and one's own) from a perspective of appropriate gender role can be very limiting. Another way of viewing gender role is to examine how individuals make moral decisions. Carol Gilligan and Lawrence Kohlberg provide ways of viewing moral decision making from a gender perspective. Relational theorists discuss how women are brought up to value relationships, caring, and responsibility, in contrast to men's emphasis on achievement and success. Last, we examined the strong gender roles that individuals in many societies attribute to homosexuality. In the next section, we will explore ways of dealing with gender stereotyping.

## RESPONDING TO GENDER STEREOTYPING

Individuals can encounter challenges to their chosen activities or preferences based on the gender role stereotypes of other people. When individuals challenge others based on their own gender role beliefs, they are expressing their own value system and implying that another person should follow it. Often gender role statements imply more than a person's belief about what is best for another. Another component within such statements is that of *power.* If I tell you what to do, I am talking from a position of power.

As I have pointed out elsewhere in this chapter, being male is a norm in most societies. Traditionally, men have made political, religious, and military decisions (although there are a few notable exceptions). Even in families, it has been traditional for the male to be head of the household. As I will show in the next section, this power is often implied in the way men and women communicate to each other. Dealing with power and gender role issues can be divided into two parts: recognizing a statement as being influenced by someone else's gender-role views and then responding appropriately. To respond appropriately, it is helpful to recognize that there is often a question of who is more powerful than the other when a gender role statement is made. For example, "Women shouldn't be roofers, they are too delicate." In this statement, the speaker expresses his (or her) gender-role view, and does so strongly. Implied in the statement is that if you wanted to be a roofer, and you were a female, you shouldn't be one.

An individual can respond to this statement in a number of ways. One is to ignore it because it does not need a response. You don't have to accept another person's view. Another way of responding is, "That's your view. I

---

## Problems and Solutions

---

### How can I deal with an inappropriate gender-role or sexist comment?

- You can ignore it.
- You can explain that the comment reflects the speaker's opinions, not yours.
- You can make an assertive rather than a passive or an aggressive comment.

---

**assertiveness** A way of expressing oneself such that likes are expressed clearly; distinguished from passive and aggressive behavior.

**aggressive behavior** Insisting on one's own rights while violating other's rights.

**passive behavior** Known also as non-assertive behavior; doing what others want even when you do not wish to do so.

think some women have the skills and abilities to be roofers." In responding this way, I am saying this is my view, you have your view, our views are equally acceptable, and we are equal in the level of power that we have. Other ways of responding might also be appropriate. A useful concept in responding to inappropriate statements or requests is that of assertiveness.

**Assertiveness** is a way of expressing yourself in such a way that your rights are expressed clearly. To understand assertiveness, it is helpful to distinguish between assertive behavior and passive or aggressive behavior (Jakubowski, 1977). Assertiveness refers to standing up for one's rights without violating the rights of others. Assertive behavior is a clear or direct statement or request without humor or sarcasm. **Aggressive behavior** refers to insisting on one's own rights while violating the rights of others. Making fun of, dominating, belittling, or yelling at another person is aggressive behavior. **Passive** or nonassertive **behavior** means giving up one's rights and doing what others want. Here are some examples:

*Statement:* I borrowed a mirror from your desk drawer. I hope you don't mind.

*Assertive:* Please don't take things from my desk drawer. If you want to borrow something, I'll probably be able to help you out. Just ask.

*Aggressive:* Don't go through my drawers. Leave my things alone!

*Passive:* I don't mind.

In the previous situation, the assertive statement is clear and to the point. It is relatively brief, without sarcasm or digressions. Furthermore, it is helpful and friendly in the sense that the assertive remark offers another solution. In this situation, the person asserts his or her preference and makes it easy for the listener to be cooperative. On the other hand, the aggressive statement is likely to anger the listener and escalate into an argument. In the passive statement, the individual is essentially saying, "I don't mind. (But I really do mind, I wish I could tell you that I don't want you to go through my desk)." Gender role development is such that women are more likely to make passive comments than aggressive ones, and men more likely to make aggressive comments than passive ones. Here is a different situation:

*John:* When we get married, I don't want you to work. I don't think that it's right for women to work, it is the role of the man.

*Assertive:* I plan to work. I don't tell you what you should do about work, and I would like it if you would not do the same to me.

*Aggressive:* Where do you get off telling me what to do! Go stuff it!

*Passive:* Well, I guess I won't work then.

John's statement would be an unusual one to hear now, but before the 1970s, it was not uncommon. John's statement has far greater implications than the statement in the previous example. Telling someone what they can and can't do after they get married is far more significant than borrowing a mirror from a desk drawer. When making the assertive statement, the individual also has an opportunity to decide if John's behavior is acceptable. Many women would choose not to marry someone who held John's view, unless they held it themselves. Both the aggressive and passive remarks make it difficult to have a meaningful discussion about John's statement.

In both of the examples, the assertive statement was immediate and to the point. An assertive statement works best when it is made directly in response to a request or statement that a person feels is inappropriate. When possible, as in the first example, it is helpful to be pleasant, so that the individual will respond favorably to a request. In both assertive examples, the remarks are clear: There is no hedging and no apologizing.

There are many different ways of acting assertively, and situations vary considerably. For example, being assertive with a parent is often quite different than other situations because of the history that we have with our parents. Our parents have been our teachers, often telling us what to do and enforcing rules. Because they are usually in a position of authority, parents might interpret assertiveness statements differently than they would if the statements were given to an equal. For example, being assertive with a boss is very different than being assertive with an employee. It is the boss's role to make requests. Clearly, employees can refuse them if they feel that the request is inappropriate, but doing so is difficult and can mean being disciplined or losing a job. When being assertive, think through a statement clearly. Sometimes, you will have opportunities to practice a statement with a friend or say it aloud. Because situations in which individuals can be

**Q 8.10** Describe a situation in which you responded passively or aggressively. Write down what you said. Then write an assertive response. In what ways do you think the situation might have turned out differently?

assertive can be so different, careful thought about what to say and how to say it is often necessary. With individuals who have a style of responding that is either frequently aggressive or frequently passive, you might find it very difficult to change their styles without thinking through appropriate responses. In any case, assertive statements are often helpful ways to respond to inappropriate gender role expectations or statements from others. Of course, assertiveness statements can be applied to a much broader range of requests and statements than gender role comments.

## COMMUNICATION STYLES

Deborah Tannen (1990) has written a national best seller called *You Just Don't Understand: Women and Men in Conversation.* Tannen comments on styles and approaches that men and women use in communicating with each other. Many of her observations are based on studying actual conversations as well as knowledge about how men and women relate to each other. My previous discussion about how gender roles develop and the importance of relational styles is reflected in Tannen's observations about communicating. In her work, she takes examples of conversations between men and women and illustrates how different styles of responding operate. She believes frustrations and problems that men and women have, particularly in close relationships, result from the different ways men and women have been taught to respond.

To use a small example, if a man holds a woman's coat so that she can get into it before she leaves a building, a woman can have a view of this situation that is totally unintended by the man. The man is intending to be helpful and courteous but the man can also be seen as acting from a position of power or control: He chooses to take her coat and hold it for her. He doesn't ask. In this way, she has been treated as subordinate to the man. Some women would interpret the man's holding the coat as being polite, whereas others may feel that they are in a subordinate position. Being able to see men's and women's behavior from different points of view gives us an opportunity to respond flexibly rather than to make assumptions about situations.

Tannen and others have talked about instrumental and expressive styles of communication. These are similar to the differences that Gilligan and relational theorists have talked about when describing men's behavior and women's behavior. In using an **instrumental style**, people are trying to achieve solutions or reach goals. In contrast, an **expressive style** concerns expressing emotions and being sensitive to the feelings of others. The instrumental style is not the exclusive style of responding for a man,

**instrumental style** A style of behavior designed to achieve solutions or reach goals.

**expressive style** A style of behavior that includes expressing emotions and being sensitive to the feelings of others.

---

## Problems and Solutions for Men

*How can I understand and get along better with women?*

- Make requests not demands.
- Don't interrupt.
- Ask about ideas.
- Talk about feelings, interests, and relationships.
- Give details in answers rather than brief replies.

---

nor is the expressive style the exclusive responding style of women—most use both styles in a variety of situations.

Because women are more likely to use an expressive style of communication, they are likely to use it more frequently in both positive and negative ways than are men (Weiten & Lloyd, 2000). In the dialogue between Eileen and Joan and Eileen and Dick on pages 194 and 195, we have seen how Joan tends to use an expressive style, whereas Dick uses an instrumental style. When Joan responds to Eileen, she consoles Eileen, whereas Dick does not. In general, women have been found to be better at consoling individuals in emotional distress than are men. However, women sometimes use their expressive skills in negative ways by expressing strong emotions, or using coercive tactics such as inducing guilt or verbally attacking someone. Just as women are able to reconcile relationships, they can also use that ability to refuse to reconcile relationships. Because women are generally more concerned about emotional relationships than are men, they are more likely to have a wider range of tactics in dealing with emotions than men. Again, these are generalizations, and they do not apply to all, or even most, situations, for men or women.

Tannen presents some interesting ways that men and women relate differently to each other. We will examine four of these and some suggestions that Tannen gives to men for dealing with women, and to women for dealing with men.

### People versus Things

In general, men tend to talk more about events and situations in their lives, and women are more likely to talk about people. Men may talk about politics, sports, or current events. Women on the other hand are more likely to

---

## Problems and Solutions for Women

*How can I understand and get along better with men?*

- Be assertive when appropriate.
- Talk about possible solutions and goals.
- Talk about events and situations.
- Don't use tag questions.

---

talk about people in their lives such as friends, children, and parents. Men are likely to feel a need to know what is happening in the world and to be aware of public events such as the Super Bowl or elections. Women are more likely to be concerned with what is happening in their friends' or children's lives. Whereas men are discussing public information, women share private information that can include secrets or issues that are emotional, such as a friend's divorce.

Men and women would communicate better if each were to try adopting some of the communication attributes of the other. For example, when communicating with women, men should talk more about personal and private events, whereas when communicating with men, women should discuss public events more than they usually do. Tannen suggests that some women are more comfortable talking about events and some men are more comfortable talking more about people. This tends to make communication between some men and some women flow more easily.

### Rapport and Report

**report** Talking about what one knows and how one does things; used most frequently by men.

**rapport** Establishing relationships with others through sharing similar experiences and empathizing with others; used more often by women.

Just as men tend to prefer talking about things and women about people, men tend to **report,** whereas women are more concerned with establishing **rapport.** Women might prefer to talk about how their experiences are similar to each other's and to empathize with friends or families. Men, on the other hand, are more likely to talk about what they know and how they do things. Thus a man is more likely to talk about activities, his work, and his hobbies, whereas a woman is more likely to talk about personal details, such as an argument with a friend or a conversation with an acquaintance that she has not talked to in ten years.

Tannen suggests that it is helpful for men to be concerned about establishing rapport with others and for women to talk about their activities and accomplishments. Sometimes women's contributions are undervalued because they talk about who they know rather than what they know. Likewise, men can be seen as not caring about others because they are talking about what they know rather than who they know and how well they know them. It is helpful for men to learn that expressing emotions, especially negative ones, can be positive, rather than causing problems. For women, it is useful to learn that men are interested in what they do.

## Talking to versus Talking at

In general, men are more likely to try to prove a point to someone, whereas women are concerned about people's opinion of them. This is particularly true in educational and work settings where men are concerned about being respected for their achievements and accomplishments. Women are more likely to be concerned about what their teachers, fellow students, or coworkers think of them as individuals. Men might be more likely to challenge authority and be concerned with their position in the company, whereas women might be concerned with being criticized for what they say. In general, women take a more defensive approach in presenting materials, and men take a more assertive one.

In school and work settings, women should make special efforts to make their points and to get the attention of others, especially men, when they are speaking. Men, who are used to being in control in situations, should make efforts to allow women to contribute and to complete what they are saying.

## Male Communication as Norm

**double bind** Giving contradictory messages or conflicting demands that can induce stress.

As mentioned at the beginning of the chapter (p. 184), men have been the normative group throughout history. Thus, their style of communicating tends to be the predominant one and the one that is considered "correct." Because the male style of communicating is the norm against which women's style is compared, women's communication patterns are devalued, and their style might be defensive. Women can find themselves in a **double bind.** If they do not express themselves, they can be seen as timid or unassertive. If they do express themselves, they may be labeled as "pushy," "tough," or "interfering." Women can find themselves apologizing for what they say or being tentative in their remarks. Because the male communication style is the norm, men are likely to be more assertive and confident in what they say.

**tag question** Questions added to the end of a sentence; style associated with use by women.

Being aware of male communication styles as being the norm can be useful to women in several ways. Sometimes women are tentative in arguing or use **tag questions.** These questions are tagged onto the end of a sentence, for example, "That movie was great, *wasn't it?*" Words such as

**hedges** An expression of opinion or view that is tentative or unsure.

"sort of" and "kind of" are **hedges** that show that a person is tentative or unsure. Women tend to use hedges and tag questions more than men do. Knowing that, women should try to change their styles to present their ideas more assertively.

## Changing Communication Styles

**communication style** A general way of communicating to another person.

To communicate with each other more effectively, both men and women can find it helpful to try to change or broaden their **communication styles.** When men communicate in one style, and women in another, what results can be a mismatch or frustration because both might feel that the other is not listening and doesn't understand. For example, if a woman is upset about something, the man might feel that he should give advice or find a solution, but that is not what the woman might want. She might prefer to be shown understanding and given support. By understanding and incorporating both male and female communication styles, men and women can not only understand each other more easily, but are more likely to feel understood. Tannen gives some suggestions for both men and women.

*Men.* Because men tend to represent the norm, it is helpful for them to be aware of this. When talking to women, it is helpful to make requests rather than demands and not interrupt. "Would you look for that report?" works better than "Find that report for me." Because men have often been in positions of authority, they have often been in a position of ordering women around. For example, men have been executives and doctors whereas women have been secretaries and nurses. To ask women about their ideas and to listen carefully can be very helpful. Because women tend to discuss their feelings, interests, and relationships, it can be helpful for men to do some of this as well, and to express interest when women are talking about their personal issues. Because women often give details when talking with each other, men may find it helpful to give some details rather than just "yes" or "no" answers.

*Women.* Because women's relationships with men are sometimes tentative or defensive, it is helpful for women to be more assertive. This can be done in small nonverbal ways by looking men directly in the eye or by lowering the pitch of the voice so that women will get more attention. Verbally, it can be useful to talk about accomplishments and events and share knowledge. Finishing sentences when interrupted and avoiding tag questions can also be helpful.

In discussions of communication style, I want to be very careful not to overemphasize differences between men's style and women's style. Many men and women use communicating patterns that have been attributed

**Q 8.11** Use Tannen's communicating styles to characterize the way that you talk with people of the other gender. Explain your pattern. How closely do you fit the styles described by Tannen?

both to men and women. However, Tannen's observations of some typical ways of responding for men and for women can be useful in examining how men and women talk when speaking to the other gender. In romantic relationships, communication styles tend to be intensified because the relationships are intimate and deep. Difficulties in understanding the other gender can present significant problems. Marriage counselors often point out to their clients some observations about communicating styles that I have described here.

These communication styles reflect broader issues that men and women have to face because of others' expectations about their gender roles. For example, men are often expected to be successful in many different ways: educationally, financially, and occupationally. They are often expected to be competitive and to win. Rather than express their emotions, they are often encouraged to hide them so that they don't appear weak. This can create stress and pressure for men, and fear of failure if they do not meet these expectations.

In contrast, women have very different pressures. Although there have been recent efforts to encourage women to achieve, for many years, they were expected to have limited educational and career aspirations. Until the 1950s, women were strongly encouraged to consider nurturing or assisting occupations such as teaching, nursing, and secretarial careers. Often they were strongly discouraged from positions of responsibility, business, or trade careers. At the same time, they were encouraged to have many roles, whereas men were encouraged primarily to be wage earners. Often, women are expected to take care of the house and take care of children and work. These expectations put pressure on women to do many things, but not to have these accomplishments valued. Thus, women feel the pressures of not being expected to do much of value, yet wanting to accomplish much for themselves.

In comparison, men feel the pressures of having to show others that they can succeed. They might feel pressured because their own expectations don't match that of others. For example, in our society male secretaries are not well accepted, and it is difficult for males to aspire to such a position, without questioning themselves or feeling criticized by others. Besides being concerned about how to communicate to the other gender, men and women are often concerned about how they will be seen by the other gender.

## APPEARANCE AND BODY IMAGE

In many cultures, especially in the United States, physical appearance and attractiveness are extremely important to most individuals. In childhood,

*Problems and Solutions*

---

***What can I do to help a friend who has an eating disorder?***

- Talk to them about it.
- Ask what you can do to help.
- Don't nag or pester them about food.
- Listen to their concerns and fears.

children who are overweight or have physical defects, such as scars or a clubfoot, are often picked on or teased. In adolescence, a premium is placed on how you look, and individuals who are not perceived as attractive might not be valued. Being attractive is so important that a term exists for this—"what-is-beautiful-is-good" stereotype (Dion, Berscheid, & Walster, 1972). Thus, if a person is considered to be attractive, other characteristics can be associated with him or her, such as being better adjusted, being smarter, being more socially skilled, and so forth. Research (Weiten & Lloyd, 2000) suggests that these assumptions are not accurate. However, research does suggest that attractive people tend to be more comfortable in social interactions with the other gender. This emphasis on appearance affects most aspects of our culture and can have such effects that it contributes to psychological disorders such as anorexia and bulimia.

Pressures to look attractive are particularly felt by women. If males are the normative or dominant group then naturally women would dress or present themselves in an attractive way so men will appreciate them. In general, advertising of clothing and food products tends to be aimed more at women than at men. Magazine covers, television programming, movies, and newspapers often present attractive women. There seems to be more freedom for men. For example, there are more roles on television for men who are not traditionally handsome than for women who are not beautiful. In addition, there is an emphasis on thinness for women that is not as strong as for men. Advertisements on television for food products that are low in calories and fat and weight loss plans are aimed much more at women than at men. In department stores, much more space is devoted toward clothing and accessories for women than for men. People of all ages are constantly exposed to media images of attractiveness on a daily basis.

The emphasis on attractiveness can also be seen in women's performance and sports. Championship figure skating and gymnastics emphasize thinness and weight loss. Both events require difficult movements, so having as little extra weight as possible is important. For men in these events, there is a greater emphasis on strength and agility, and less on thinness. Traditionally, female ballet dancers have been urged to lose weight and be thin. More recently, instructors of ballet, gymnastics, and figure skating have been aware of the relationship between eating disorders in young women and participation in these events. Many instructors are careful not to ask children and adolescents in these events to lose weight because it can cause women to stop eating (anorexia) or purge or vomit their food (bulimia) in an attempt to lose weight.

## Anorexia

**anorexia** A life-threatening disorder in which individuals refuse to eat enough to maintain minimal weight.

**Anorexia** is a life-threatening disorder in which individuals starve themselves to maintain minimal weight. They starve themselves because of an intense fear of becoming obese. One feature of anorexia is a distorted body image. Even when individuals with anorexia have protruding ribs and hip bones and have skull-like faces, they are likely to see themselves as fat. Anorexia occurs about 20 times more often in women than in men (Barlow & Durand, 1999). Individuals who have anorexia think about food very frequently. In fact, they might be interested in dietetics, nutrition, cooking, planning menus, and other food related activities. Some may admit to feeling hungry, whereas others do not.

Anorexia is treated in two phases. The first is to help the person with anorexia gain weight, and the second is to help an individual maintain a normal body weight and deal with issues related to self-image. People with anorexia whose weight falls below 25 percent of their recommended weight might require hospitalization. Sometimes intravenous feeding is necessary. In any case, close medical supervision of eating is a part of treatment so that the patient will not die. After this initial phase, individuals with anorexia might continue to have psychotherapy to help them deal with their self-esteem and body image. A frequent approach to treatment includes family therapy. In this way, the person's interactions with the family can be evaluated, and family members can change behaviors that make it difficult for the person with anorexia to develop self-esteem and an appropriate self-image. Sometimes family therapists meet during meal time with the family so that they can help the person with anorexia change her role in the family as it relates to both food and relationship issues (Rosman, Minuchin, & Liebman, 1975).

How do you deal with a friend who has anorexia? Because individuals who have anorexia are relatively easily identified, as opposed to those who are bulimic, it is helpful to be aware of her family and support system. If you are concerned about a person who you think might have anorexia, it is probably best to talk with her about this or with her spouse or family. Urging people with anorexia to eat is not helpful. Usually, this urging is interpreted by a person with anorexia as additional external pressure from someone who might not understand. Maintaining a caring friendship with an individual who has anorexia is helpful, but nagging is not. Suggesting and encouraging treatment can be useful.

## Bulimia

**bulimia** A means of trying to maintain weight control by inducing vomiting or using laxatives to rid the body of food.

In contrast to anorexia, individuals with bulimia usually are of average weight. People with **bulimia** usually go through a binge-purge cycle in which they eat great amounts of food followed by induced vomiting or occasionally overdoses of laxatives to rid the body of the food. Often individuals with bulimia choose food that can be eaten rapidly and vomited easily. Consuming a half-gallon of ice cream and a bag of cookies is not unusual. During this binge, individuals with bulimia are likely to feel disgusted with themselves, feel helpless, and have a sense of panic. Often purging brings a sense of relief. As individuals go through this cycle many times, their ability to vomit without pain or discomfort increases. Bulimia is far more prevalent among women than among men (about 20 to 1) (Barlow & Durand, 1999). The frequency of binge-purge cycles ranges from once a month to more than once a day. Some individuals purge but do not binge. People with bulimia often feel depressed and anxious because of their inability to control their bingeing or purging.

Bulimia brings with it a number of physical complications that can eventually lead to death. As a result of vomiting, sore throats can develop, tooth enamel can be destroyed, and intestinal damage can develop. Because the food is expelled, the person with bulimia can have a number of nutritional problems, and dehydration can result. Similar to anorexia, decreased levels of potassium and electrolyte difficulties can lead to serious health problems. Some individuals with anorexia and bulimia have died from heart failure because of strain on the cardiovascular system.

Negative thoughts about how individuals look are very common throughout American culture. For women, these thoughts are quite strong, and relatively few women are not critical of their appearance. For individuals with anorexia and bulimia, self-criticism about their body is pervasive and frequent. Thoughts like these are common:

- There's nothing attractive about me.
- I'm too fat.
- Everyone is more attractive than I am.
- If I only lose 15 pounds, then my life will change.
- My stomach is too big—my hips are too big.

For individuals with bulimia, constant preoccupation with appearance and valuing appearance present an obstacle to returning to nonbinge—purge eating. Along with negative thoughts about one's body, individuals with eating disorders are constantly thinking about food. Individuals with bulimia know in advance which foods will start them on a binge-purge cycle. Because women with bulimia are concerned with body image and food, therapy requires patience by both patient and therapist. Shonda's preoccupation with food is typical of this.

"I can't believe that Rhoda can eat anything she wants and stays so thin. She'll have two slices of lemon meringue pie and nothing happens. I look at the pie and I turn into fat. I eat pie and I can see it on me, I can feel it.

"When I go back to my room after classes, I try to study and concentrate but I'm thinking of cookies. After four years now, it's become so easy. I get the cookies at the convenience store and then they go in and I just toss them out easily. When Anne sees me going to the grocery store, I've caught her rolling her eyes. She know what's gonna happen. I hate it. I want it to stop, but it is so hard for me to control anything. I just hate that full feeling. I don't have to eat much and I feel that full feeling. It just seems so disgusting. I can't stand it."

Shonda, in her junior year at college, is five foot six inches tall and is an attractive young woman. She is concerned about her weight, and feels that if she lost ten pounds her problems would be over. However, she knows from experience that if she loses ten pounds, she will still be concerned about her weight. Friends have assured her that she looks fine. This doesn't seem to have any impact on her.

Shonda and I worked together on her eating problems and her bulimia for more than a year. During this time, Shonda was doing clinical work for her nursing courses in a hospital. Focusing on other people and their problems seemed to help somewhat in taking the pressure off Shonda's preoccupation about her appearance. What was most difficult for Shonda was her mother's concern about her own weight. When Shonda's mother learned about Shonda's bulimia, she was shocked. Her mother had been able to maintain her own weight for many years by careful dieting. She had criticized Shonda when Shonda gained weight or would eat a lot. By not letting her mother's comments about Shonda's weight disturb her, Shonda was able to focus on activities other than eating. In fact, Shonda found that her annoyance and anger at her mother for focusing on food helped Shonda change her view of food, enough to decrease her bulimic episodes from twice a week to once a month. Shonda was a bright, caring, friendly person who did not value these qualities about herself. As she was able to appreciate her qualities, she could start to evaluate herself in positive ways and not just evaluate herself based on her appearance.

Unlike other psychological disorders, bulimia presents certain problems for friends and family who are close to the individual with bulimia.

For individuals who don't have bulimia, vomiting is so unpleasant that it is hard to understand why anyone would do it. I have tried to show in this chapter that the pressures on being attractive are so strong that some women vomit their food so that they can be thin.

**Q 8.12** What societal factors have influenced your own view of how you look?

**Q 8.13** How would you respond to a slender friend who said "When I lose 15 more pounds, then I can feel good about myself."?

**Q 8.14** Why do you think being attractive is such an important goal for so many young women?

Friends often want to know what they can do to help a person who purges. Nagging and criticizing don't help. Confronting a person with an eating disorder, and asking her how you can help is more useful. Sometimes individuals with eating disorders can get their friends to help, by asking them to avoid certain situations for them. Ordering pizza at ten o'clock in the evening presents a difficult problem for many individuals with bulimia. Sometimes friends of individuals with bulimia will talk to the individuals with bulimia about the best way to act around issues having to do with food. Checking up on an individual with bulimia and asking her about what she did in the bathroom can only be helpful if the individual with bulimia wants that kind of help. Letting someone with bulimia explain why they do what they do and talk about their fears and concerns can often be helpful for those who are close friends with an individual with an eating disorder.

## SUMMARY

How we view our own gender roles greatly affects how we view ourselves and others. Historical reasons include the fact that males traditionally have had much more powerful positions in society than women have. This and other social and biological factors affect gender development in childhood, adolescence, and adulthood.

We can view gender in a number of ways that helps us understand ourselves. Androgyny is a concept that examines the male and female personality characteristics within each individual. Gender schema theory focuses on how important being male or female is in how we view events and situations around us. Carol Gilligan and Lawrence Kohlberg have shown that males and females make moral decisions in different ways based on their perceptions of gender roles. Relational theorists describe how males and females learn different ways of relating to their family and others, thus affecting their own gender roles. Traditional negative perceptions of homosexuality are a reflection of how individuals view their own gender role and those of others.

Understanding your own views of gender is important. These views become a basis for making changes in how we relate to the other gender. Understanding gender-role motives and the role of power in people's communication with each other is helpful. Assertiveness techniques help us effectively make requests and talk to others, especially if we have been reluctant to do so previously. Deborah Tannen's discussion of communications styles can help us understand different ways that men and women communicate with each other. Some of these have been discussed in this chapter.

Body image and appearance are a significant aspect of gender role. In this chapter, I discussed some cultural factors that make attractiveness such an important goal for individuals, especially women. Concern about appearance and weight is an important aspect of eating disorders such as anorexia and bulimia. Symptoms of these disorders and how to deal with friends who might have these disorders were described.

# RECOMMENDED READINGS

*In a Different Voice*
C. Gilligan (Harvard University Press, 1982)

> Some consider this book a classic. It deals with different views of morality that men and women are likely to hold. Comparisons are made with Lawrence Kohlberg's views of moral development.

*The Mismeasure of Woman*
C. Tavris (New York: Simon & Schuster, 1992)

> Tavris is a social psychologist who has written many books for nonprofessionals. She has an excellent sense of humor that helps her discussion of the fallacy of using male norms for deciding what is correct for both men and women. She uses research to explain why myths about men and women lead to misunderstanding and confusion. She shows how "gender schemas" lead to stereotyping about men and women. Suggestions are given for ways that men and women can improve relationships.

*You Just Don't Understand: Women and Men in Conversation,*
D. Tannen (Ballantine, 1990)

> A sociolinguist, Deborah Tannen has appeared on numerous television shows to discuss communication styles of men and women. This book describes in a clear manner her view of different styles that men and women learn in childhood as they communicate with members of the other gender and their own gender. This book has been the source of the Communication Styles Section described on pages 201 through 206. Tannen gives numerous examples of communication styles and translates conversations between men and women. She helps readers see the difference between what individuals believe they are saying and how members of the other gender can interpret their messages.

# RECOMMENDED WEB SITES

*Women's Studies Database*
http://www.inform.umd.edu/EdRes/Topic/WomensStudies/
    Developed at the University of Maryland, this database can be used to find information about issues related to women and gender studies.

*SPSSMM (Society for the Psychological Study of Men and Masculinity)*
http://web.indstate.edu:80/spsmm/
    A division of the American Psychological Association, SPSSMM offers a site that introduces contemporary psychological approaches to masculinity. Information focuses on men and their identity.

*Partners Task Force for Gay and Lesbian Couples*
http://www.buddybuddy.com/toc.html
    Reflecting the belief that "same sex couples deserve the same treatment as all other couples," this site's resources address a wide range of issues including relationships, parenting, domestic partnership, ceremonial marriage, and legal and civil rights matters.

*Deborah Tannen's Home Page*
http://www.georgetown.edu/tannen/
    A professor at Georgetown University, Deborah Tannen has created a home page that has a complete bibliography of professional and general interest publications that explain her sociolinguistic theories, which were discussed on pages 201 through 206.

# CULTURAL DIVERSITY

**WHITE PRIVILEGE**. . . . . . . . . . . . . . . . . . . . . *In the United States, do whites have privileges that others do not?*

**RACIAL IDENTITY MODELS** . . . . . . . . . . . . . . . . *How do people become different as their racial attitudes change?*

---

Racism, bigotry, and discrimination cause many problems that exist between people throughout the world. In this chapter, we will look at cultural diversity from a variety of perspectives. By taking these perspectives, we can look at our beliefs and behaviors in the past as they effect present and future beliefs and behaviors. In this chapter more than any other, your belief systems may be challenged. Consider the information about cultural diversity and how it fits with your own view of different cultures. First, let me define three words or phrases that occur frequently in this chapter: culture, race, and ethnic group.

**culture** A set of attitudes, values, beliefs, and behaviors that are shared by a group of people.

- **Culture.** A set of attitudes, values, beliefs, and behaviors that are shared by a group of people, although culture can be experienced differently by each individual. These attitudes, values, beliefs, and behaviors, are communicated, intentionally or not, from one generation to the next. Note that this definition focuses on psychological aspects of sharing, rather than physical attributes.

**race** A physiological concept, race is related to our biological and genetic heritage.

- **Race.** A physiological concept, race is related to our biological and genetic heritage. Experts (Zuckerman, 1990) disagree about the number of races that exist (two, three, four, or five?). Common racial groups are based on skin color, Caucasian (white), African and African-American (black), Asian and Asian-American (yellow), and Native American (red). As you read this, you might argue accurately that there are greater differences in cultures within racial groups than there are similarities. Individuals from racial groups might or might not share the same culture. For example, the cultures of Vietnamese, Japanese, and Chinese peoples vary greatly from each other. Within each country, there may be great cultural variations as well.

**ethnic group** In general, national origin defines ethnic group or ethnicity.

- **Ethnic group.** In general, national origin defines ethnic group or ethnicity. For example, Portuguese and Brazilian people may share the same language, Portuguese, but have distinctive cultural patterns. Native Americans may share some cultural patterns, but differ widely from each other depending on their tribal affiliation.

As you can see, the definitions of culture, race, and ethnic group or ethnicity are quite different. This chapter will focus on different aspects of an individual's culture and how they affect individual happiness and interactions with others. Another focus is on learning about how a lack of understanding about culture, race, and ethnicity can lead to the development of stereotypes, prejudice, and the experience of discrimination.

## VIEWS OF CULTURE

Culture can be seen from a variety of points of views. Three common ways of viewing culture are looking at how personality or psychological adjustment relates to culture, the structure of social systems as they relate to culture, and the variety of diverse cultural systems that developed from specific geographical locations. These ways of viewing culture provide a background for understanding views of culture such as centering one's values around one's own culture (ethnocentrism), cultural relativity, cultural universals, and cultural markers (Axelson, 1999).

### *Personality and Culture*

The type of person that I am is based not only on how I think, feel, speak and act, but also on how each of these is affected by the specific culture that I grew up in. You have learned specific ways to behave that are appropriate and inappropriate, and know what happens if you behave inappropriately. You have learned values that tell you what are appropriate ways to speak and act. In these ways, culture has affected the kind of person that you are. Your attitude toward learning, toward many of the subjects covered in this book, are influenced by what you learn from peers, family members, and teachers.

So far I have been referring to cultural group as if we are members of only one group. However, we are all members of several cultural groups. These can include religious, gender, and generational groups (children, parents, and grandparents). We come in contact with people in a variety of social-cultural groups, such as ministers (religion), teachers (education), politicians and police officers (law), and others.

Our personality develops from the way we interact with these cultural forces. Often our reactions are spontaneous rather than thought out or planned. How we react to teachers and parents often is a means of adjusting and coping with pressures. We develop support systems and meet needs based on those aspects of social and cultural groups that feel comfortable for us or that we choose to join. When we encounter cultural groups (ethnic or other) that are different than our own, we might find their teachings or methods to be uncomfortable or inappropriate.

**Q 9.1** Describe a situation where you were or might be in a group in which you were the only member of your cultural group. If you were uncomfortable, what did you do to become more comfortable in the group?

## Social Structure and Culture

Social systems vary in how they are organized and in how their systems interact within themselves and with people from outside their system. For example, different cultures have different beliefs and attitudes about education, religion, and childraising practices. Often, different cultures have political and economic systems based on past practices. Changes made in a social structure can affect members in radical ways. For example, inhabitants of China lived for thousands of years under a political system that was directed by emperors and their governors. When communism replaced this system, inhabitants of China needed to learn new ways of relating to each other and to their government. Such changes can affect the family unit, how elders are treated, child-raising practices, and relationships with extended family.

Another factor affecting the interaction of the social structure and culture is that of wealth and prestige. When individuals acquire wealth or political power, their relationships with others are likely to change. However, social and economic status do not necessarily bring power and prestige to individuals. For example, in the United States, African Americans who have acquired wealth or social status after becoming doctors or lawyers might find that they are not accepted by members of other cultural groups (Sharf, 1997). Social structures are complex combinations of societal values, attitudes, and behaviors. The ability of individuals to act within a social structure is determined not only by their own personal variables (values, attitudes, and behaviors), but also by those of the variety of groups that they encounter.

## Ethnic Diversity

Civilization developed many thousands of years ago as members of tribes developed their own religions, languages, and customs. Physically, these tribes were of the same race and from a small geographical area. Climate and agricultural conditions affected the way individuals hunted or grew crops. In times of famine, groups sometimes moved to another location. Some groups became wealthy by conquering others and forcing people into slavery. Thus, both voluntary and involuntary migration developed. The culture in power generally dominated the less powerful cultures and sometimes might have penalized or punished members of less powerful cultures for their religious or occupational practices. Many examples of religious discrimination can be found in both Europe and the United States.

Historically, there have been many examples of people moving from one part of the world to a very distant part. In many cases, this has been

TABLE **9.1** **ETHNOCULTURAL GROUPS IN THE UNITED STATES (1999)**[a]

| White | Black | Hispanic Origin[b] | Asian | Native American | Total |
|---|---|---|---|---|---|
| *1980* | | | | | |
| 180.9m | 26.1m | 14.6m | 3.5m | 1.3m | 226.5m |
| 80.9% | 11.5% | 6.4% | 1.5% | 0.6% | 100% |
| *1990* | | | | | |
| 188.3m | 29.2m | 22.3m | 6.9m | 1.7m | 248.7m |
| 75.7% | 11.8% | 9.0% | 2.8% | 0.7% | 100% |
| *1995* | | | | | |
| 193.5m | 31.5m | 26.9m | 8.7m | 1.9m | 262.7m |
| 73.7% | 12.0% | 10.3% | 3.3% | 0.7% | 100% |

*Subgroups:*

| *Anglo-Saxons* | African Americans | Mexicans | Chinese | American Indians[c] |
|---|---|---|---|---|
| English | West Indians | Puerto Ricans | Filipinos | Eskimos |
| Celtics | Haitians | Cubans | Japanese | Aleuts |
|   Welsh | | Other Central & | Koreans | |
|   Scots | |   South Americans | | |
|   N. Ireland Irish | | Spaniards | *Indochinese* | |
| Swedes | | | Vietnamese | |
| Norwegians | | | Cambodians | |
| Danes | | | Lao | |
| Finns | | | | |
| Germans | | | *Pacific Islanders* | |
| Dutch | | | Native Hawaiians | |
| Appalachians | | | Guamanians | |
| | | | Samoans | |
| | | | Fijians | |
| *White Ethnics* | | | | |
| S. &E. Ireland Irish | | | *Asia/Middle East* | |
| Italians | | | Indians | |
| Sicilians | | | Arabs | |
| Poles | | | Ethiopians | |
| Austrians | | | Iranians | |
| Hungarians | | | Egyptians | |
| Czechs | | | Turks | |
| Greeks | | | Pakistani | |
| Portuguese | | | | |
| Russians | | | | |
| Yugoslavs | | | | |

*Socioreligious  Ethnics*

*Source:* Axelson, 1999, pp. 30, 31. Data from Tables No. 19 and 51. Statistical Abstract of the United States: 1996 (116th edition) by U.S. Bureau of the Census. Numbers for the five ethnocultural groups are rounded and thus do not add up exactly to the total population for each census year. The totals are the population figures as reported by the U.S. Census Bureau.

*Notes:* [a] Approximate numerical or percentage increase, 1990, 1995. Factors accounting for population increases, besides biological, are immigration (accounts for almost 40% of the increase, largely from Asia, Latin America, and the Caribbean), census definitions, and personal changes in racial/ethnic self-identification.

[b] Persons who identified their origin or ancestry as "Spanish/Hispanic" also reported their "race" category (that is, White, Black or Negro, Asian or Pacific Islander, American Indian or Eskimo or Aleut, or other).

[c] 550 federally recognized tribal entities, including about 226 village groups in Alaska; largest tribes are Cherokee and Navajo, followed by the Sioux and Chippewa; about 22% of All Native Americans, including Eskimos and Aleuts, lived on 287 reservations and trust lands in 1990.

voluntary, such as the migration of Irish tenant farmers to the United States because of the potato famine in the 1800s. In other cases, this migration has been involuntary, such as Europeans' capture of Africans during the 1700s, who forced Africans to relocate to the United States. How individuals deal with cultural forces depends on whether migration is voluntary or involuntary (Ogbu, 1993) as well as many other factors, such as the age at which they arrived in a new country, the amount of wealth that they have, their acceptance into the new culture by previous migrants from their culture and the values of the majority culture.

The United States is known as a country with a wide variety of ethnic groups (see Table 9.1). The original inhabitants, Native Americans, constitute less than 1 percent of the entire population. About 74 percent of the population is white. It is beyond the scope of this book to describe the great variety of cultures that are listed here. Rather, we will examine different views of culture that affect how individuals live their lives in the United States. These include a focus on one's own culture, cultural relativity (judging behavior by how it relates to your own culture), elements of life that are universal to all cultures, and cultural markers (types of experiences that individuals encounter depending on their age).

## Ethnocentrism (Own-Culture Centered)

**ethnocentrism** Believing that the values and attitudes of one's own group is the standard by which other groups should be evaluated.

When individuals believe that the values and attitudes of their group are the standard by which other groups should be evaluated, this is called **ethnocentrism.** Ethnocentric individuals not only measure other people by their own cultural values, but also believe that their own values are the best and correct ways of behaving. This concept can be applied to religious, racial, and socioeconomic groups. Furthermore, ethnocentrism can also be applied by older members of a group to younger members. For example, when older members say, "We didn't do that when we were your age," they are saying that their older values are more appropriate than the newer ones are. When ethnocentrism is applied from a religious point of view, individuals might say, "Our way of worshiping God is the correct way, and you need to learn how to worship God our way." From a racial ethnocentric point of view, the values of the majority group become the correct way of doing things, and these values become superior to the values of minority groups. Until the 1950s, it was common in the southern United States to have bathrooms for white and bathrooms for "colored," because white individuals living in the South believed that their group was superior and that African Americans should use separate facilities. Wealthier people might assume that poorer people are dumb or lazy and assume that their own group is better. Not surprisingly, individuals who value their own culture above others are likely to be regarded with distrust or animosity by

**Q 9.2** Give an example of problems you have seen when individuals are *ethnocentric,* that is believe that their own culture is superior to that of another.

people whose cultures are different and who view their own culture as equal or superior.

## Cultural Relativity

Perhaps the opposite of being centered in one's own culture is the concept of **cultural relativity.** From this perspective, behavior of individuals should first be understood relative to a culture, and then later for its meaning for individuals. By doing this, the evaluator of a behavior first examines the meaning of the behavior relative to the background of individuals and the norms of their culture.

An example of the application of cultural relativity would be a situation in which two men in their early 20s are seen kissing each other on the cheek. Knowing that in some countries in Europe, men greet each other in this way helps interpret the meaning of this behavior. Someone not familiar with European culture could interpret this action from the point of view of his and her own culture (for example the United States) as a display of homosexual behavior. Understanding people from the perspective of their own situations and cultures, even though different from ours, helps us to understand why individuals react in ways that they do.

## Cultural Universals

Although many different customs and behaviors separate cultures from each other, virtually all people are likely to experience some universal situations and events, **cultural universals.** For example, the family unit is a basic unit in all cultures, even though a husband or wife may have more than one marriage partner at a time in some cultures. In all cultures, parenting takes place, though not always by the father or mother—rather, sometimes by grandparents, aunts or uncles, or others. All cultures have some method of educating children, whether it be through schools or some other means. Because illness is experienced by all cultures, medicine and the development of medicines can be found universally. All individuals have basic physiological needs such as eating and drinking. As a result, individuals need to work to meet physiological needs, and work whether paid or not, is a universal activity regardless of culture. Not only do individuals have physiological needs, but they also have psychological and spiritual needs. All cultures have developed religions to answer difficult questions and explain actions and events.

People's attitudes toward cultural universals vary. Those who focus on the uniqueness of their own culture are likely to see the differences in the way people express themselves. For example, they might emphasize different parenting styles, depending on a person's culture, and believe that their culture's parenting style is the best. Those individuals who view culture as relative are likely to see common themes that are expressed in cultural universals. For example, they might comment on some similar ways that people from different cultures raise their children rather than on the different ways people raise their children.

## Cultural Markers

**cultural markers**
Sometimes called rites of passage; signify the transition from one role to another.

Although growth and development from childhood, adolescence, adulthood, and old age are cultural universal experiences, how individuals make the transitions through their development varies considerably from culture to culture. Sometimes called rites of passage, **cultural markers** are events that signify the transition from one role to another. For example, graduation from middle school, high school, and college are ceremonies that mark a significant milestone in individuals' lives (Kail & Cavanaugh, 1996). In the United States, these ceremonies may include speeches, processions, and hats and gowns that are reserved only for this event. Perhaps the most well-known and often elaborate marker event in the United States is the wedding. Elaborate efforts and much money can go into making this single event a success. Food, flowers, music, invitations, and other aspects of weddings are often considered and planned carefully to denote the significant event. Cultures within the United States may celebrate weddings differently, however, and not all individuals within a culture will have the same type of wedding. Furthermore, not all individuals get married, nor do all individuals get married as young adults. Ceremonies marking these events vary depending on the age of the individuals getting married, whether it is a first, second, or later marriage, whether parents approve of the marriage, and other factors. Although marriage is a cultural marker, it is only broadly related to age. Many first marriages take place between the ages of 18 and 30, but others marry much later, either again or for the first time. On the other hand, graduation from high school is generally associated with the ages of 17, 18, and 19. A few individuals may be younger or older when they graduate from high school. Understanding the value of cultural markers and the events used to celebrate them can help individuals appreciate cultural differences.

Gender roles provide another way of viewing cultural markers because significant events mark the coming into adulthood for boys and girls (Gilmore, 1990). For example, in many non-Western cultures, menarche is the primary marker for girls to become women. For boys, it is quite different. They must show that they can provide for family, protect others, and impregnate. This is particularly true in nonliterate cultures where boys must show that they can do these things before they can be considered men. Different cultures have different markers and ceremonies that represent the transition from being a child to becoming an adult. For example in

**Q 9.3** Describe a culturally related event (such as the cheek kissing example given earlier) and give an ethnocentric explanation for it and an explanation derived from the principle of cultural relativity.

**Q 9.4** Describe a culturally universal event or behavior and two different ways that cultures deal with the universal. (Examples might be different ways of parenting or educating children.)

**Q 9.5** Describe a cultural marker, other than graduation and marriage, and how two different cultures use ceremonies to mark these events.

**Q 9.6** Describe Warren's situation from the perspective of cultural relativity.

**Q 9.7** What could be done to help a student like Warren become more comfortable in a situation such as that described?

Jewish culture, the *bar mitzvah* for boys and the *bat mitzvah* for girls at the age of 12 is a ceremony marking the transition from childhood to adulthood. Learning about a variety of cultural markers and the events used to celebrate them is a way of understanding how different cultures view both men and women.

A 19-year-old African American, Warren has grown up in inner-city Philadelphia. Now he takes the bus across town to a community college that is primarily white. Having been to a high school that is predominately African American, Warren is aware of differences between the behavior of students at his high school and those at his college. Students at this new school are much less friendly. Only a few talk to him about school or what he is doing. Warren feels differently than he did last year at school. In the new community college, where students come from different sections of the city, Warren feels tension. He is finding it hard to make friends because few of the students that he went to school with are taking courses at the same time that he is. The white students seem more reserved, even afraid of him, when they are outside of class. In class, because some of the teachers have an easy manner, the classes are fun, and the students seem more relaxed and friendly.

## DIFFERENCES BETWEEN CULTURES

**individualistic culture** A culture in which the needs of an individual are more important than those of friends, family members, or neighbors.

**collectivist culture** A culture in which individuals learn to attend to the needs and values of others and place them above their own needs and values.

Researchers have been trying to understand meaningful variables for differentiating one cultural group from another (Matsumoto, 1996). The dimension of cultural variability that is best known is probably that of *individualism-collectivism.* In **individualistic cultures,** the needs of an individual are more important than are those of friends, family members, or neighbors. In contrast, in a **collectivist culture,** individuals learn to attend to the needs and values of others and place them above their own. For example, in collectivist cultures, the choice of going to college might be seen as a way to help a family socially and economically, whereas in an individualistic culture, going to college might be seen as a way one person can obtain more prestige and income. Researchers have given questionnaires to individuals in 50 different countries and have been able to rank each country by how much their citizens valued individualism versus collectivism (Hofstede, 1984). The countries whose citizens most valued individualism were the United States, Australia, and Great Britain. The countries whose citizens most valued collectivism were Pakistan, Columbia, and Venezuela. Such studies are helpful in pointing out that values such as individualism, are less valued by other cultures. Knowing that we make judgments about ourselves and others based on such values can help us in seeing ourselves more objectively. Of course, individuals who live in a culture that ranks high

**Q 9.8** How would you rate yourself on the variable of individualism versus collectivism?

**Q 9.9** List three ways that you think the United States, as a culture, values individualism over collectivism (or three reasons you disagree).

**achievement motivation**
Refers to the striving for excellence.

on individualistic values can be collectivist in their views, and the reverse is true as well. Knowing how you compare with members of your own culture and that of others on traits such as individualism-collectivism can help you view yourself and your culture in a new way.

Researchers have also used other ways of viewing cultural variables to understand culture (Matsumoto, 1996). Achievement motivation is another variable that has been studied for many years across cultures (Atkinson, 1964). At first, **achievement motivation,** which refers to the striving for excellence, was defined from an individualist perspective. Thus, if Kay could be said to show achievement motivation then she would have been said to push herself to do well academically or at work to be individually successful. Later, Yang (1982) showed that one could have achievement motivation for oneself or for others. For example, if you want to get good grades for yourself so that you can advance in your job and get paid more, then this is an individualistic perspective. However, if you wish to do well so that you can improve your family's social standing, meet their needs for success, or satisfy a sense of obligation to your family, then this is achievement motivation from a collectivistic perspective. Many Western cultures have an individualistic view of achievement motivation whereas many Asian cultures take a more collectivistic view of achievement motivation.

Cultures also differ in how individuals are taught to view themselves. For example, in the United States, individuals are often taught to see themselves as better than others, whereas in Japan individuals do not share the same value, and people raised in that culture see others as better than themselves (Matsumoto, 1996). Thus, Japanese students might rate other people as being more intelligent or attractive than themselves more than would American students. In contrast, American students are more likely to see themselves as better than others. Again, this is very general information, and certainly there are many exceptions to these generalizations in each culture. Thus, there are Americans who would be more self effacing than they are self-enhancing. This line of research shows, however, that the way people view themselves varies from culture to culture.

A 19-year-old freshman who has just come to the United States from Korea, Soomi has been looking forward to studying psychology at the University of Maryland. She had heard about how American universities were different from those in Korea, but has found America different than she expected. She misses her family and the support that they provided for her. Although she studied English in Korea, she has difficulty dealing with the speed with which American students talk. She is also self-conscious about her own speaking. Living in a dormitory, she has observed how quickly American students seem to make friendships but feels lost at times because she has not been able to do so.

Q 9.10 If you were to start college in another country using a language that you had learned in high school (such as Spanish or French), how do you think you would feel? Explain.

Her roommate, an 18-year-old white woman from the suburbs of Washington, D.C., has been friendly, but spends much of her time with friends she knew from high school. Soomi very much misses the girls that she knew in school in Korea.

In class, she has difficulty following the professors' English and their, sometimes, abstract language. Because math uses symbols that she has seen before, she finds that class easier. She wonders very much about how well she will do on her first round of examinations and is very worried about failing and returning home without completing school. She wants to make her parents proud of her.

# PREJUDICE AND RACISM

**stereotypes** Beliefs, either positive or negative, that are held by an individual about a group of people.

**prejudice** A judgment, feeling, or attitude about a cultural or other type of group.

**discrimination** Actual behavior toward a person or persons based on belief, usually prejudice.

**racism** Beliefs that one's own race is biologically superior to that of someone from a different race.

I've described some ways that sociologists and psychologists view culture and measure differences across cultures based on several characteristics. However, individuals develop their own views of people of different cultures that are based on information that they learn from others around them. In this section, I will describe *stereotypes, prejudice, discrimination,* and *racism*. **Stereotypes** are beliefs (positive or negative) held by an individual about a group of people. Following from these beliefs, **prejudice** can develop, a judgment, feeling, or attitude about a cultural or other type of group. Whereas stereotypes are beliefs and prejudice represents attitudes or feelings, **discrimination** is actual behavior toward a person or persons based on belief. **Racism** refers to beliefs that one's own race is biologically superior to that of someone from a different race. These concepts play a role in the lives of people throughout the world, whether they are perpetuators or recipients of cultural views and actions. I describe each of these concepts in more detail here.

## *Stereotypes*

If you or I stereotype, we are applying our own theory of personality to an individual or group. We have a set of beliefs about an individual or group that can vary in accuracy. My beliefs or stereotypes might be similar to yours or very different (Jones, 1997). We can have beliefs about different racial groups, different occupational groups, people of different sexual orientation, religious groups, or nationalities. These beliefs can arise from a variety of sources.

Being aware of the many sources of beliefs that we have about individuals and groups can help us in understanding our own stereotypes. Often stereotypes develop from ethnocentrism: Individuals make judgments based on rules or values that we learn from our own culture (Matsumoto, 1996). Beliefs are commonly passed down from one generation to another. For example, some parents have the belief that African Americans are less industrious than whites are. This belief or value can be passed to their children. Radio, television, newspapers, and magazines can also foster important stereotypes. For example, if you were to base your belief of what Caucasian, 20-year-old women look like using only magazine photos and advertisements rather than images of friends and classmates, how would that be different from a more broadly based belief?

Our own direct observation is an important source of stereotypes (Matsumoto, 1996). We can identify a characteristic of one person and generalize that to many people in that group. For example, if we feel that we have been manipulated by a car salesman, we can generalize that to believing that all car salesmen are manipulative in all situations. Statements such as "lawyers are _____," "Jews are _____," and "Chinese are _____," are examples of statements that are followed by stereotypes.

A characteristic of stereotypes is that they are often inflexible. Individuals usually resist changing their stereotypes and will make observations to maintain the stereotype rather than change it. If for example, a person has a stereotype that "lawyers are sleazy" then has a good and helpful interaction with a lawyer, then the individual might say "Well, she is an exception to my rule." Because stereotypes are inflexible, we tend to see what we want to see. This is also known as "selective perception." If we are watching television and we see a young African American arrested for possession of drugs, then we can further maintain our stereotype by saying to ourselves, "See, there's another example of an African American getting in trouble, proving what I already knew." We might not pay attention to a story about a young African American getting an award for scholarship or to information about the number of whites arrested for drug possession. In this way we focus on evidence that supports our stereotype and tend to dismiss evidence that contradicts our stereotype.

Stereotypes often limit our understanding of our world and can prejudice our views. So what can be done to change the way we stereotype others? Sometimes our observations are not accurate, or they are based on few facts (Matsumoto, 1996). If we try to learn more about a culture, we are less likely to stereotype. For example, if we see two Japanese men bowing to each other, we could consider this formal or silly. If we understand more about the Japanese culture and do not make judgments from our own culture, then we have a new perspective on our stereotyping beliefs. Sometimes we have stereotyped beliefs without knowing why. Knowing how we learned about our own stereotypes helps us to identify them. For example, if we know that hearing crude jokes about lawyers has influenced our stereotype about lawyers, we can try to view each lawyer as an individual rather than as a member of a group with many similarities. It is also helpful to emphasize the similarities that we share with others rather than the differences. Thus, we might share with a lawyer the desire to achieve professionally, to help someone in distress, and the need to make money.

Finding exceptions to our stereotypes can also help us broaden the way we view people (Jones, 1997). To use a simple example, we can view all professional basketball players as being tall. However, a professional basketball player, Mugsy Bogues at 5'3" tall, does not fit the stereotype. Focusing on the exceptions to our "rule" that professional basketball players must be tall helps us focus on the real qualities of basketball players'— that they be able to run, pass, and shoot well. By questioning our stereotypes or beliefs about individuals we can alter attitudes that are prejudiced.

## Prejudice

When we hold attitudes, make judgments about individuals, or have feelings about a person that are based on our beliefs about a group, then we are *prejudiced.* The prejudices can be positive or negative (most often negative), and they are usually without sufficient knowledge to form an appropriate judgment or opinion (Axelson, 1999; Jones, 1997). Prejudiced attitudes, judgments, or feelings can be beliefs that we are or are not aware of. Prejudiced beliefs differ from stereotypes in that stereotypes are beliefs whereas prejudice conveys attitudes or feelings about these beliefs. Thus, we can have a stereotype that members of a certain ethnic group are manipulative. Very likely, we will have a negative attitude or feeling about this group because of the way we feel about manipulativeness. At this point, we are said to be prejudiced against this group.

The most common groups toward which individuals have prejudice are those that can be categorized into nationalities, races, religious beliefs, or occupations. Stereotypes or beliefs about people in these categories can easily turn into negative attitudes. Common in the United States are prejudices against African Americans, Latin Americans, and Asians referred to as racism. Also, there is evidence of prejudice against people for being of a different socioeconomic class than we are—lower class or higher class—examples of classism. Attitudes that are negative (and occasionally positive) about males or females as a group are referred to as sexism. Negative feelings about older people or younger people are referred to as ageism. These "isms" often include not just one attitude in regard to an individual but a whole set of negative attitudes or feelings. These are sometimes so well formed that these "isms" constitute a "doctrine" or well-formed set of prejudices.

## *Discrimination*

When negative attitudes, thoughts, or feelings (prejudices) are acted on, these behaviors are referred to as discrimination. Laws and rules can be developed to regulate and punish discrimination, but stereotypes and prejudices are ideas, thoughts, feelings, and attitudes that cannot be regulated by governments. It is illegal to discriminate against people based on their race, religious preference, gender, age, sexual orientation, or other such characteristics in hiring, promoting, and in giving raises. Acceptance into colleges and universities are similarly regulated, as are the selling of homes, and providing business services such as renting cars. The extent to which laws are enforced and respected depends on the stereotypes and prejudices of those who violate the laws and those who regulate them.

In a country as large as the United States, it is not uncommon for groups of individuals in one area of the country to have stereotypes and prejudices that are not held to the same degree by individuals in another part of the country. For example, there was evidence before the 1960s that white juries would acquit white men who were accused of murdering black men when evidence of guilt was clear. Had African Americans been on the jury or had the trial been held in the northern parts of the United States, a different verdict might have followed.

Laws against discrimination in the United States are relatively recent, many taking place after the civil rights movement in the 1960s. Before that, there were many examples of laws that were discriminatory against different groups. For example, segregation in the southern parts of the United States before the 1960s required that African Americans ride in the back of the bus, have separate rest rooms from whites, eat in separate restaurants, go to separate schools, and stay in separate hotels. Thus laws provided a way of socially controlling African Americans to isolate them from Caucasians. Although discrimination that isolated African Americans was more blatant in the South, it was also common in the North. For example, African Americans participated in their own professional sports leagues such as the well-known Negro leagues in baseball. Blacks were also discriminated against when they tried to find jobs or go to schools in many Northern areas.

The United States has a history of discrimination against Asians. In 1882, the Chinese Exclusion Act was passed, suspending the immigration of Chinese workers (Axelson, 1999). Those born in China were made ineligible for citizenship. This policy lasted for another 60 years, reflecting negative attitudes of the United States Government toward Chinese people. Another immigration act in 1924 denied admission to the United States to Japanese, Korean, and other Asians. During World War II, more than 100,000 people of Japanese ancestry were removed from their homes and placed in relocation camps for the duration of the war. Many lost their homes and suffered great financial losses.

A relatively recent and brutal form of "legal" discrimination was that of the Nazi government in Germany in the late 1930s and early 1940s. Jews, gypsies, homosexuals, and others were considered to be inferior and to threaten the pollution of the Aryan race. Governmental regulations and institutions (death camps) were established to kill those who were not Aryan, as defined by Nazi law. This murder of millions of people was based on stereotyped beliefs, prejudiced attitudes, and feelings that resulted in severe discriminatory behaviors.

## Racism

Racism can best be described as a specific type of prejudice for which there are negative attitudes or feelings about others (Jones, 1997). This form of prejudice is based on the biological concept of race. In such a view, the persons, institutions, or cultures believe that they are superior to an individual or individuals of a particular race. For example, over a period of years, some people in the United States have developed a set of beliefs that whites are superior in some ways to African Americans and Native Americans, Asian Americans, and others. When people, whether as individuals or as a part of institutions, emphasize their perceptions of negative attributes of people of another race, they tend to contrast these with their own perceived positive attributes. In this way individuals emphasize what they perceive as their strengths at the expense of others. In this section we will examine three types of racism: individual, institutional, and cultural (Jones, 1997).

**individual racism**
Thoughts, feelings, and attitudes based on beliefs that one individual is superior to a person or people of another race.

*Individual Racism.*  When individuals have thoughts, feelings, and attitudes that are based on beliefs that they are superior to a person or people of another race, they are demonstrating **individual racism.** Such individuals are likely to look for evidence to support their own views that they are superior to people of another race and to discount evidence that people of another race are equal to or superior to them. Perhaps the most obvious example of racism in the United States is that of "white supremacists" who believe that they are superior in many ways to all other races and are able to cite examples of how individuals of other races are inferior to them.

Individual racism can be seen in a variety of thoughts, feelings, and attitudes that are expressed by people in their interaction with people of other races. Just a few examples will be given here. Some white people believe that they are superior genetically to African Americans and to Native Americans. They may also believe that African Americans are dirty and ignorant and that Native Americans are primitive and that most are alcoholic. Often individuals who have racist beliefs act in a discriminatory way with regard to others. They sometimes use slang with racial language labels such as "dago," "wop," "redskin," "kike," "nigger," and "pollack." For each of many cultures represented in the world there are several very derogatory words or phrases to describe them. Telling and laughing at racist jokes are other examples of individual racism. More blatant examples are damage to physical property, writing racial messages on walls, burning crosses on lawns, and yelling racist words at people. Such views and behaviors expressed by individuals who are part of a dominant culture are often met by a variety of defenses by members of minority groups that are under attack. For example, minority groups might develop positive personal expectations, such as "Black is beautiful" and work together in church groups or community action groups to protect and represent themselves. Thus, they counteract racism experienced from institutions, as well as individuals.

**institutional racism**
Governmental or organizational policies that have discriminated against people of different races.

*Institutional Racism.*   Institutions, such as schools, employers, the military, churches, and others, can also act in negative ways and hold negative attitudes about people of other cultures—this is **institutional racism.** Often governmental policies have discriminated against people of different races. For many years, in the United States, African Americans were forbidden to vote. Even when they had voting rights, laws, particularly in the southern United States, were developed to make the voting requirements very difficult for African Americans. Thus, state and local institutions found ways to act in a racially discriminatory manner. Governments often found more subtle ways of discriminating against people of different racial groups by gerrymandering legislative voting districts. For example, states might structure voting districts in such a way that white Americans would constitute a majority in each.

Racially discriminatory actions have been found in other institutions as well as in governments. For years, admission to many colleges was denied to African Americans. Even now, the issue of whether admissions tests are culturally biased continues. In the past, schools for African Americans were often funded poorly based on the belief that African Americans had little educational potential. In employment, some African Americans, Latinos, and other members of minorities have been excluded from unions and professional organizations. In other situations, they might not be hired or they might be denied promotions. Also, services such as police protection and trash pick-up have often been less adequate in minority-group neighborhoods. These are just some examples of ways in which institutions act in racially discriminatory ways.

**cultural racism** When one cultural group is able to use its cultural values to define the value system for a country, then other cultural values tend to be ignored and to be considered inferior.

*Cultural Racism.*   When one cultural group is able to use its cultural values to define the value system for a country, other cultural values tend to be ignored and to be considered inferior—**cultural racism.** In the United States, the values of European Americans have been the predominant value system, and other values (African Americans, Asian Americans and Native Americans, to name a few) have been discriminated against. In many countries, the majority culture suppresses the culture of other groups or races. The majority culture, in cultural racism, often feels superior to other groups and considers other groups inferior. When a majority culture's approach to racism is to be "color blind" and to ignore culture differences, problems are likely to develop because real cultural differences are ignored. Some argue that ignoring differences is a passive rather than active form of racism. Others argue that it is not a form of racism at all.

Cultural racism can be found in a wide variety of aspects of culture in the United States. The American educational system is often, but not always, considered to be better than all others. Many Americans consider their science and practice of medicine to be the superior way for dealing with health problems and conducting research. American laws, the Constitution, and the political system are considered by some to be superior to all others. Furthermore, morality in the United States, an outgrowth of Christianity, is often considered to be better than the moral systems found in other countries. Prejudiced views can also be found in the beliefs about what is the best art, music, films, and architecture. All these important aspects of society are a reflection of the major value system of the majority culture. This is not to say that the minority cultures do not have an influence on various aspects of these areas of living, however, the majority view usually prevails. Having cultural values does not constitute cultural racism, putting down or devaluing the values of others does contribute to cultural racism.

Although I have focused on the United States, many of the same observations could be applied to other countries. In China, rather than European values prevailing, a variety of value systems developed over centuries by a variety of Chinese cultures prevail. The political value system of communism is also an important component of the majority culture in China. In most countries, the majority culture sets the standard for a basic value system that others should follow.; however, there are exceptions: in South Africa, Dutch and English Caucasians value systems prevailed over native South African systems. In this case, the wealth, military force, and power of the minority population was stronger than the majority population. Being aware of cultural racism by understanding how a set of values of one group can reject or subjugate the values of another can be helpful in understanding a wide variety of cultures.

A discussion of individual, institutional, and cultural racism often makes the hurt of prejudice and discrimination seem abstract. Individuals who are stereotyped by another are seen not for what they are, but for what the person wants them to be. When individuals experience prejudice, attitudes, or feelings that people have about one another based on attitudes about their group, they are likely to be hurt, angry, alienated, or upset in other ways. When the prejudice results in action that discriminates against another person and keeps them from participating in educational, health, political, employment, or other aspects of work, negative views are likely to be developed. In the United States, this has been particularly true in racial relations. Focusing on individual racism helps illustrate the destructiveness that one person can experience in a situation where prejudice and discrimination exist.

> Having started his freshman year of college four months ago, Dominic is unsure about returning to school next semester. Dominic had lived all of his life in a predominately African American section of Brooklyn, New York. Both of his parents are bus drivers for the New York Transit Authority. His parents urged his two older sisters, Dominic, and his younger brother to go to college. Their religious values have been passed onto their children, and Dominic is no exception. Attending church, youth activities, and the choir have been a part of his life since he was in middle school.
>
> More than a year ago he was recruited by several universities to attend their schools. An outstanding defensive cornerback on his high school football team, Dominic impressed a number of college football scouts. Large, well-known universities were not interested in him because he was only about five feet nine inches tall, and, although he had very good speed, he did not have the tackling ability that they were interested in. Often he would hear remarks from acquaintances that he didn't look like a football player. When he had an offer from a small, predominantly white, well-respected college in Pennsylvania, he decided to take it. When he visited the school less than three hours away, it seemed like a thousand miles away. The school was attractive and well-landscaped, and the coaches, football players, and other students seemed quite friendly.
>
> When he arrived on campus in September, the school and his classes seemed so different than what he was used to. He was very aware of some classes in which he was the only African American student. Although his white roommate and the other men on the hall were friendly to him, the friendliness seemed superficial and the feeling was very different than he had had with his friends at home. Going to a meeting of the African American Student Union during freshman week helped. He met other African American students, but was surprised that not many upper classmen were at the event. Only 45 of the 1200 freshman at school were African American. When he was on campus, it often felt as if he were the only one.

Football practice seemed more comfortable. Because football practice is so structured, and he was used to drills and scrimmages, it was like being back at high school. Meeting other African American football players also helped. In fact, those were the times he felt he most belonged.

In his second week of school after he was just beginning to get used to the lecture and group discussion format that his professors used, he returned to his room in the early afternoon. On the message board that he and his roommate had put on their door was scrawled the message in black magic marker ink "Nigger Go Home." Dominic was startled. This was not something that he had expected, but, he was not totally surprised. Furious and hurt, he told his roommate and hall director. Both expressed concern but neither brought the subject up again.

After a month had gone by, he found that he had difficulty getting that incident off his mind. He continued to go to practice and go to classes, but he seemed to feel more distance between himself and the white students on campus. He felt a sense of loneliness.

When his parents visited on parents' weekend, they told him how proud they were of him and of his accomplishments. He didn't want to disappoint them and tell them about how he was feeling, hoping that it would go away and he would feel better later on. When his parents left late Sunday afternoon, he realized how much he enjoyed the visit and how much he missed them. When he walked back to his dormitory from the visitor's parking lot, he realized how alone he felt. He remembered the excited anticipation he had had during the summer about coming to the school and how different he felt now.

When preparing for finals, he was not sure that he would return. The courses had been difficult for him, although he was maintaining Bs and Cs. Sometimes the school just seemed like another planet to him and the hateful message that he had received earlier in the semester would come back into his mind when he would consider whether or not he wanted to return to school in the spring semester.

When prejudice and racism are a significant part of a society's history, it is hard for them to disappear. Racism that is a legacy of educational institutions, businesses, and political systems is referred to as institutional racism. When racism permeates a culture, cultural racism is identified. Sometimes the past effects of prejudice cannot be easily seen in the majority of individuals in a culture, as it is an integral part of the culture. The next section describes this sometimes subtle aspect of cultural racism in more detail.

**Q 9.11** If you were Dominic, how would you feel if you had received the same message on your bulletin board?

**Q 9.12** Evidence of individual racism is clear in this case example. Is there evidence of institutional racism? Explain.

# White Privilege

**white privilege** Privileges that those in the majority (in Western Cultures) tend to have without being aware of them.

We have seen that individuals who are members of minority groups often are at a disadvantage compared with those in the white majority because of stereotypes, prejudice, and discrimination. Conversely, those in the majority can be seen as having privileges or advantages that members of minority groups do not have. McIntosh (1989) describes 26 privileges that come with being white in the United States. We might disagree with some of these or be able to add more; however, these privileges or advantages help illustrate the cultural racism that exists in the United States.

Does this mean that all white people are racist? No. Does it mean that white people consciously take advantage of these privileges? No. Individual racism is a reflection of negative attitudes and feelings toward people of another culture, and white people might not have a negative feeling or attitude. Cultural racism presents a climate of attitudes and beliefs that are pervasive and go beyond the control of one individual. Often people are not aware that they get things that others don't.

In the following section, I will list half of the privileges of being white that McIntosh (1989) lists. Many of these, by themselves, are small events that occur daily, weekly, or monthly.

- I can if I wish arrange to be in the company of people of my race most of the time.
- If I should need to move, I can be pretty sure of renting or purchasing housing in an area that I can afford in an area in which I would want to live.
- I can go shopping alone most of the time, pretty well assured that I will not be followed or harassed. I can turn on the television or open to the front page of the paper and see people of my race widely represented.
- When I am told about our national heritage or about "civilization," I am shown that people of my color made it what it is.
- Whether I use checks, credit cards, or cash, I can count on my skin color not to work against the appearance of financial reliability.
- I can swear, or dress in second hand clothes or not answer letters, without having people attribute these choices to the bad morals, the poverty, or the illiteracy of my race.
- I can do well in a challenging situation without being called a credit to my race.
- I am never asked to speak for all the people of my racial group.
- If a traffic cop pulls me over or if the I.R.S. audits my tax return, I can be sure I haven't been singled out because of my race.
- I can easily buy posters, postcards, picture books, greeting cards, dolls, toys, and children's magazines featuring people of my race.
- I can be sure that if I need legal or medical help my race will not work against me.

**Q 9.13** Do you think that this list represents some privileges that whites have in our society that other members of minority groups do not? Explain.

**Q 9.14** Would you eliminate some of the these privileges from the list because you don't think that they are accurate? Are there others that you would add? Please describe.

**racial identity models**
Explanations that show common stages that individuals go through in understanding their own experience and that of others as it relates to culture.

- I can choose blemish cover or bandages in "flesh" color and have them more or less match my skin. (Peggy McIntosh, 1989, "White Privilege: Unpacking the Invisible Knapsack, *Peace and Freedom,* July/August, pp. 10–11.)

Until now, I have discussed different views of culture and definitions of stereotypes, prejudice, discrimination, and racism. I have tried to show how these concepts affect relationships between the white majority and minority groups in the United States. The next section deals with how individuals of minority and majority groups view themselves as racial beings and how these views can change.

# RACIAL IDENTITY MODELS

Individuals do not automatically acquire a view of their own and others' racial identity. Researchers have developed a variety of models to show common stages that individuals go through in understanding their own experience and that of others. In this section, we will focus on Helms's (1995) model of how racial identity can influence and affect human interaction in relationships with people of other races. **Racial identity models** tend to be rather similar to each other and I will draw from Helms's 1995 description of a minority identity developmental model and a white racial consciousness model. Other models have been developed for African Americans and Latinos.

At first it might seem surprising that there would be a model of white racial consciousness. Most whites do not identify themselves as a single racial group but, rather, as specific cultural groups. For example, white people often think of their ancestral heritage and label themselves as Italian, Jewish, Polish, Irish, German, English, Hungarian, and so forth. As members of these groups, they also can experience prejudice and discrimination. In the United States, however, a significant amount of prejudice and discrimination exists between people of different races. Therefore, psychologists have found it helpful to focus on racial identity theory as a way of understanding racism. Furthermore, as I have shown in the previous section on white privilege, there are ways that whites behave as a racially identifiable group, even though they do not think of themselves as being one.

In the following table I will describe five stages for both the minority identity development model and the white racial consciousness model. Each stage is described briefly. These are not static. In other words, individuals can go back and forth between stages and for some situations they might be in one stage but in another stage for other situations. The stage approach can help us understand how individuals' perceptions about themselves and others, with regard to race, can change through time.

TABLE **9.2** FIVE STAGES OF DEVELOPMENT IN TWO MODELS

| Stage One | Stage Two | Stage Three | Stage Four | Stage Five |
|---|---|---|---|---|
| **Minority Identity Development Model** | | | | |
| *Conformity*<br><br>In this early stage, individuals tend to accept and believe stereotypes that majority groups have about their own racial group. In fact, they may have negative attitudes about themselves and other members of their own ethnic group. There is a lack of awareness of one's own ethnic perspective and cultural values. | *Dissonance*<br><br>Confusion exists about the conflict between one's own values and beliefs and those of the dominant culture. Issues about racism and oppression seem to evolve. There is more interest in the history and culture of one's own ethnic group. | *Immersion-Emersion*<br><br>At this point a forceful rejection and distrust of the majority culture can begin. There is clear identification with one's own cultural group rather than with the dominant one. Involvement in ethnic history and traditions of the culture such as learning stories, eating foods, and speaking the language develop. Individuals may separate themselves from the dominant culture and actively combat racism and oppression. | *Internalization*<br><br>The conflict between loyalty to one's own cultural group and the values of the dominant culture start to emerge. An individual might question his or her rejection of dominant culture and values as he or she struggles for greater self-awareness. | *Integrative Awareness*<br><br>Individuals start not only to appreciate their own cultural group but also the values of other groups and the dominant cultural values. There is a sense of fulfillment regarding one's own cultural identity. Specific values of any culture are accepted or rejected based on prior experience. There is an awareness of the oppression of others and efforts to eradicate them. |
| **White Racial Consciousness Model** | | | | |
| *Contact*<br><br>Although individuals at this stage are aware of minority groups, they tend to have stereotyped knowledge about minorities. Differences between themselves and other cultural groups are often considered unimportant, and they might view all people as just people. They might not see themselves as being white or as a racial person. They are becoming aware of pressures that they feel as they interact with people of other cultures. | *Disintegration*<br><br>Individuals might become aware of racism and start to feel guilty and depressed about it. There is conflict between standards of what seems right for others and what their own specific cultural expectations are. Some over-identify with minority groups, others become paternalistic by doing things for rather than interacting with, and others retreat back into their own culture. | *Reintegration*<br><br>Individuals consciously acknowledge that they are white. They might behave in ways that conform to stereotypes of people of color. They might seek out people from minority cultures who share their negative views of these cultures. | *Pseudo-independence*<br><br>The development of positive white identity begins. Individuals deal with distortions that perpetuate racism and become more curious about people of all cultures including their own. Thus there is significant interest in the similarities and differences between racial groups. | *Autonomy*<br><br>There is an appreciation of racial differences and similarities and a respect for different minority groups. Differences are not seen as deficits, but as positive values. Individuals seek out relationships with people from other cultural groups. |

Melissa, a Caucasian 18-year old woman was born and raised in Greenville, Maine, a small town in the northern woods in a part of the state known for its forest and lumber. Her interaction with African Americans was very limited. In the summer, Greenville was a tourist attraction, known for its very large and beautiful lake, Moosehead Lake. Although she had seen African Americans, she had only very superficial contact with them in her job as a drug store clerk during the summers of her junior and senior year of high school.

When she went to the University of Connecticut for her freshman year, she became aware of a number of African American, Asian, and Hispanic students. Her major interactions with them were in classes and later in study groups (Stage One, Contact).

Her view of African Americans was based mainly on what she had seen on television in comedies and action dramas. Large cities such as New Haven and New York frightened her. When she went to Hartford, Connecticut, she was surprised by the poverty in some sections of the city and started to think about what she could do to help those who were less advantaged than she (Stage Two, Disintegration).

When she started to become friendly with Candace, a young African American woman in her French class, she learned about Candace's family. Her questions started to become annoying to Candace and Candace started to think of Melissa like the white people who came to her church to give Christmas presents to the poor children. Finally, Candace snapped at Melissa and told her to leave her alone. Very hurt, Melissa avoided Candace and started to see African Americans as people who weren't as caring or sensitive as she (Stage Three, Reintegration). In her sophomore year, Melissa met other African American and Asian students. When they talked about how their parents treated them, parental attitudes toward dating and wedding ceremonies, Melissa started to be less defensive and more interested in how these other young women were similar to and different from her (Stage Four, Pseudo-independence). Melissa saw herself as coming from a culture that was protective and not open to people of other cultures. Taking a Black Studies course helped her understand the history of African Americans that was so different from her own Scandinavian culture.

Currently a junior at the University of Connecticut, Melissa developed friendships with some Asian women on her floor. She is still somewhat hurt by her earlier interaction with Candace, and, although she would like to be more comfortable with African American women that she knows, she finds herself somewhat shy with them. Melissa has not yet achieved Stage Five, Autonomy.

This description is not typical of how individuals develop white racial consciousness. In reality, relationships with individuals are more complex and move back and forth between stages, as individuals interact with a variety of people from different cultures and experience different events. Often individuals do not move beyond the contact stage (Stage One).

**Q 9.41** How well do racial identity models describe you? Explain.

**Q 9.42** Try to identify a stage that best describes you.

**Q 9.43** What factors seem to be important to determining a stage that you are in currently?

One problem with identity models is that individuals are likely to feel self-critical if they see themselves in an early stage of a model. The purpose of the model is to show that individuals grow and change over time. Accepting oneself as being in a particular stage at a particular time can be helpful rather than a cause for shame. By being aware of models of racial identity, students can have a broader view of prejudice, discrimination, and racism.

# SUMMARY

As individuals of different cultures increasingly interact through travel, education, and business, understanding cultural diversity becomes more and more important. In this chapter, we have defined culture, race, and ethnicity. A person's personality interacts with his or her culture and vice versa. These are not separate entities. Both affect how people in different societies interact with each other.

Different views of culture help to provide ways of understanding one's own culture and the culture of others. The concept of cultural relativity allows people to understand the behavior of others in relationship to their culture as well as understanding the behavior from one's own cultural experience. Some behaviors such as parenting and educating are cultural universals. Furthermore, there are cultural markers, ways people develop at different ages. For example, in some cultures, individuals tend to marry later than in others. Having a system for viewing a number of different cultural behaviors and values can help individuals develop a respect for a wide variety of cultures.

Psychologists and sociologists have studied how cultures differ from each other on a variety of variables. For example, some cultures value individualism more than others do, whereas other cultures value collectivism (working as a group) more than they value individualism. Somewhat similarly, cultures vary in their view of people's ability to achieve on their own (independence) versus achieving as a part of a group (interdependence). In some cultures, presenting oneself as being competent and able is seen as appropriate; in others it is seen as bragging and inappropriate. Being able to understand that different nations emphasize different values and behaviors helps us see our culture not as the right one but, rather, as one of several approaches to appropriate values, morality, and behavior.

This broad view of culture suggests caution in stereotyping your beliefs about other people's behaviors. It can also help in preventing prejudice, a negative attitude or feeling about a group of people. When individuals act on their prejudiced beliefs, they discriminate against others and cause harm and pain. Racism, which has individual, institutional, and cultural aspects is a type of prejudice. Understanding the concept of white privilege and models of racial identity can help individuals to understand their relationships and interactions with people from different cultures in a new light.

## RECOMMENDED READINGS

*Understanding Diversity: A Learning-As-Practice-Primer*
Okun, B. F., Fried, J., & Okun, M. L. (Brooks/Cole, 1999)
> This book is designed to promote both self-awareness and awareness of others. Discussions of gender, class, religion, and race and ethnicity provide a context for viewing people with different cultural backgrounds. Numerous exercises help readers become more aware of their own cultural values and the cultural values of others.

*Culture and Psychology*
Matsumoto, D. (Brooks/Cole, 1996)
> This brief book provides an excellent overview of the role of culture in the lives of individuals. Psychological research on cultural issues such as achievement and ethno-centricity are described. References are made to psychological research.

*Prejudice and Racism*
Jones, J. M. (McGraw-Hill, 1997)
> This is a second edition of a thorough book on prejudice and racism. The emphasis is more thorough and scholarly than the two books previously listed. Jones describes the development of prejudice and racism and methods for coping with them.

## RECOMMENDED WEB SITES

*Gender and Race in Media*
http://www.uiowa.edu/~comnstud/resources/GenderMedia/index.html
> The University of Iowa's communications studies program offers a focused guide to the ways in which gender and racial differences are expressed in various media.

*The Web of Culture*
http://www.webofculture.com/home/home.html
> This business-oriented site suggests a wide range of issues and approaches to increase cross-cultural understanding. The focus is on communicating across cultures on a world-wide basis with sensitivity and knowledge.

# DYING AND LIVING

The loss of a friend, parent, spouse, brother, sister, or relative can be the most traumatic event in a person's life. Our grief and sorrow over losing someone who has been close to us can be measured by our caring and love for that person. The depth of our love and caring creates the individual and varied reaction that people have to death and loss. In a study of the most stressful events of 43 life events, the death of a spouse was listed first, followed by divorce, and death of a close family member (Holmes & Rahe, 1967). In the United States, the stressfulness of dealing with death might be particularly great because we often avoid the subject. Discussing the possibility of one's own death, and the death of others, is a very difficult topic of conversation, and one that is rarely addressed. When an individual is dying, others are often uncomfortable talking to the person about that person's dying. Because death is such a difficult topic for many people to deal with, and because it can signify the end of a close relationship, I have included it in this book. Before continuing, I will define four terms that are used throughout this chapter: loss, bereavement, grief, and mourning (Corr, Nabe, & Corr, 2000).

**loss** Broadly used to refer to being separated from or deprived from a person, object, status, or relationship.

- **Loss.** Loss is used broadly to refer to being separated from or deprived from a person, object, status, or relationship. This can include break-up with a romantic partner, being fired from a job, leaving home to go to college, or losing a wallet. The effect of these losses varies considerably depending on the strength of the attachment, however, this chapter will examine loss as it relates to the death of a loved one.

**bereavement** Usually associated with the loss or death of a loved one, associated with loneliness, missing someone, and grief.

- **Bereavement.** When we experience a loss, we are deprived or bereaved of something. Although we could say that when we lose our wallet or a job, we are bereaved of the wallet or the job, bereavement is usually associated with death.

**grief** The effect of loss on an individual; can be internal or external, such as crying.

- **Grief.** The effect of loss on an individual brings about grief. Sometimes a person grieves internally and sometimes externally, going to a gravesite, crying, or talking to someone about the loss. Grief can be experienced in a variety of ways (Worden, 1991):

  Feelings of sadness, anger or guilt
  Physical sensations, such as lack of energy, hollowness in the stomach, or shortness of breath
  Cognitions, such as disbelief, confusion, unusual thoughts about the dead person
  Behaviors, such as disturbances in sleeping or eating, crying, loss of interest in activities, and dreams of the deceased

**mourning** Coping or dealing with loss and grief in one's own way.

- **Mourning.** When individuals experience loss and grief, they cope or deal with it in different ways. This process is referred to as mourning, the way in which we try to live with the loss we've experienced and

TABLE **10.1** MORTALITY RATES IN THE TWENTIETH CENTURY

| 12 Months Ending November, 1997 | | | |
|---|---|---|---|
| | **Both Sexes** | **Males** | **Females** |
| All ages | 8.6 | 8.8 | 8.4 |
| Under 1 | 7.3 | 8.1 | 6.3 |
| 1–4 | 0.3 | 0.4 | 0.3 |
| 5–14 | 0.2 | 0.2 | 0.2 |
| 15–24 | 0.9 | 1.3 | 0.5 |
| 25–34 | 1.2 | 1.6 | 0.7 |
| 35–44 | 2.0 | 2.7 | 1.4 |
| 45–54 | 4.3 | 5.5 | 3.1 |
| 55–64 | 10.6 | 13.4 | 8.1 |
| 65–74 | 24.9 | 31.7 | 19.4 |
| 75–84 | 57.1 | 70.5 | 48.3 |
| 85+ | 153.0 | 175.3 | 144.2 |

*Source:* National Center for Health Statistics, 1998.

our bereavement and grief. We can mourn both such that others cannot see us mourn (internal) and more publicly, at a funeral, or crying with friends (external).

In addition to these psychological responses to grief, individuals respond in other ways, social and spiritual. They can experience difficulties with other people in *social* situations. Individuals might also challenge their religious beliefs, experience anger toward God, or find a renewed faith in God. Thus they change their *spiritual* or religious life as a result of grief.

The frequency of death at certain ages has changed dramatically since the turn of the century. In 1997, mortality rates of all people were much lower than they were in 1900. This is especially true of infant mortality rates, which have dropped dramatically, as can be seen from Table 10.1. For individuals who died in 1996, the ten leading causes of death are listed in Table 10.2. Notice that two of these are caused by humans, (No. 5) accidents and adverse effects and (No. 9) suicide. In the rest of this chapter, we will focus on reactions to the dying process, the death of a friend or loved one, and death by homicide or suicide.

Besides providing more information about the dying and the mourning process, I try to help you feel more comfortable in dealing with dying

TABLE **10.2** MOST COMMON CAUSES OF DEATH, **1996**

|  | Deaths per 100,000 Population | Percent of All Deaths |
|---|---|---|
| All causes | 875.4 | 100.0 |
| 1  Diseases of the heart | 276.6 | 31.6 |
| 2  Malignant neoplasma | 205.2 | 23.4 |
| 3  Cerebrovascular diseases | 60.5 | 6.9 |
| 4  Chronic obstructive pulmonary diseases and allied conditions | 40.0 | 4.6 |
| 5  Accidents and adverse affects | 35.4 | 4.0 |
| 6  Pneumonia and influenza | 31.1 | 3.6 |
| 7  Diabetes mellitus | 23.2 | 2.7 |
| 8  Human immunodeficiency virus infection | 12 | 1.4 |
| 9  Suicide | 11.6 | 1.3 |
| 10  Chronic liver disease and cirrhosis | 9.5 | 1.1 |

Source: Ventura et al, 1997.

people or with people who have suffered the loss of a loved one. By becoming more aware of your own feelings about grief and loss, you can develop new perspectives on life and living.

# THE DYING PROCESS

Because the process of dying is so complex and varies so widely from person to person, researchers have tried to provide ways to explain the process more clearly. The pioneer in this work was Elisabeth Kübler-Ross who described five stages of the dying process. Others such as Corr (1992) have developed a task approach to understanding dying. These stages and tasks will be discussed in some detail here, as will support groups and hospices that exist to help individuals who are dying or need help to deal with dying family or friends. People often feel awkward when faced with helping those who are dying. Some suggestions for being helpful will be given here. But first, we will look at some of the issues that make the dying process so different for so many people.

There are probably three important variables in understanding and dealing with dying: certainty, length of the dying process, and awareness of one's own death (Corr, Nabe, & Corr, 2000). The ability to predict another person's death and the length of the dying process varies considerably. Often it is difficult to predict the effects of medications and the progress of disease. With complex medical conditions, misdiagnosis can occur, or some physical conditions might be undiscovered during initial diagnosis. The length of the dying process can vary from moments to years. Sometimes individuals might get better for a while, get worse, get better again, and so forth, or a person might deteriorate rapidly. A third factor is being aware of one's own death. Sometimes, individuals are not aware that they are dying, and neither are their family members. In other cases, individuals are not aware that they are dying, but family members try to keep that knowledge from them. In such cases, individuals might suspect that they are dying, but be frustrated because they are not getting sufficient information about their condition. Sometimes family members believe the dying person suspects, yet none of them talk to each other about their suspicions. This contrasts with the situation in which there is no pretense, and the dying person, as well as the family is aware that the individual is dying. These three factors: certainty, length of the dying process, and awareness of one's own dying make it very difficult to find a model for understanding the process of dying that will be applicable to a great many people. Despite these difficulties, however, models have been developed to try to explain stages of dying.

## *Stages*

Elisabeth Kübler-Ross's stages of dying that include denial, anger, bargaining, depression, and acceptance are well known, but it is helpful to explain them. To illustrate Kübler-Ross's approach, let us follow the case of Nadine, a 26-year-old medical technologist who was diagnosed with cancer.

> Nadine was engaged to be married, and was living at home with her parents. Her wedding was planned to take place in a year and a half. Shortly after her engagement, she was diagnosed with cancer that was not treatable by surgery, or radiation treatments. Chemotherapy was offered to her, although doctors told her that few people with cancer as severe as hers recovered even with its application.

**denial** A common initial reaction to loss; Kübler-Ross's first stage reaction to hearing that an individual has been diagnosed with a terminal illness.

- **Denial.** Kübler-Ross often felt that the first reaction to hearing that no medical treatment is available and that one only has a certain amount of time to live is shock. The shock often results in thoughts such as "this can't be happening to me," "maybe the test results were switched," "I know that I will get better and I will be the one to beat the odds."

Nadine did not believe that this could happen to her. After all, she was only 26, and too young to die from cancer. When she told her fiancé, he also agreed, saying that there must be some mistake. Thus not only was Nadine denying the possibility of death from cancer, but so was her boyfriend.

- **Anger.** When people start to accept that they might be dying and they can no longer deny the severity and eventuality of their illness, they are likely to experience anger. The anger can be at the illness, people around them, or themselves. However, frequently the anger is with fate or with God—anger that I have to be the one to die.

When Nadine finally accepted that there was no cure for her cancer, something that occurred gradually in a two-month period after she had been informed of the diagnosis, she started to experience bouts of rage. For a brief time, she was angry at the messengers, the physicians that told her of her condition. She felt that they were cold and unfeeling and were only interested in the money that they would get from her Health Maintenance Organization. Her fiancé was not angry, but was still denying her cancer because in the beginning stages, she did not appear to be any different to him. Surprisingly Nadine's father was the most helpful. Nadine had never been that close to him. He had been a salesman, often away from home for days at a time. She was able to talk to him about her anger and to tell him about how angry she was at God and at her religion for failing her. Rather than ask her to have more faith, and not to question her religion, her father just listened, sometimes hugging her, sometimes sitting quietly across from her in a chair across from her bed where she sat. By expressing her rage to her father, Nadine started to move toward accepting her approaching death.

**bargaining** Asking God for more time, asking for special dispensation, or asking to be spared from death; Kübler-Ross's third stage of dying.

- **Bargaining.** When individuals start to accept their impending death, they might bargain, ask for more time, ask for special dispensation, or ask to be spared. Often this phase deals with bargaining with God for more time. Thus, "If I do certain things, God, please give me my life or more time."

When Nadine started to accept her death, she wanted very much to marry Roger. They had known each other for five years, and Nadine had looked forward to being married and raising a family. She very much wanted to have a child with Roger. When she prayed to God, she promised to be helpful to others, to help others who had cancer, to be more considerate to others, if only she could get married, if only she could have a family. In part, she was hopeful that the chemotherapy treatments might help. They were very uncomfortable, as they made her nauseous, and weak. Perhaps this would serve as punishment, and she then could pay her "dues," be forgiven, and have time to start a family.

- **Depression.** When there seems to be no hope, and bargaining fails, depression can take over. There seems to be no other possibility, but death. There is now a sense of loss, of losing family members, friends, everyone.

When Nadine no longer felt that treatment was helping, she started to experience a profound sense of sadness and depression. She was feeling physically weaker and losing weight. When she would look at herself in the mirror, she hated the wig that she used to replace her lost hair. She felt unattractive, contaminated, and alone. As much as her fiancé tried to comfort her, it seemed to be of little help. She and Roger could no longer do the things that they used to do together. She had to leave her job and was living at home. Roger's visits felt like sickroom visits, not like the close times they had shared together. There was much sadness when she was around her mother, who was now working part-time so that she could be at home with Nadine more frequently. During this time, Nadine became aware of her sadness and started to feel less desperate and more tranquil.

- **Acceptance.** When individuals have enough time to work through the previous stages, they might reach a final stage of acceptance. They are no longer fighting what is happening, no longer deeply sad and depressed about their death, but accepting of it. This does not mean that such a person might feel happy, but rather there is a sense of the inevitability of death.

  Nadine became quite weak, unable to get out of bed without help. She was appreciative of the efforts her mother had made to comfort her, to make her feel less pain. Her struggles with religion had changed. She was no longer bitter and angry at God, but accepted her death as a part of a greater plan. When Nadine was close to death, she felt a sense of peace, rather than a sense of desperateness and fright.

Kübler-Ross acknowledged that not everyone reaches the stage of acceptance. Furthermore, some people do not experience all stages or they experience a stage, revert to an earlier one, and then continue. Her work was particularly important because she was able to focus on the experience of dying and its meaning for the individual.

Kübler-Ross's stage theory has been widely criticized, however. Further, studies that tried to document these stages by interviewing dying patients and their family found little confirmation (Corr, Nabe, & Corr, 2000). Furthermore, other individuals who dealt with the dying felt that their experience with dying patients did not fit with Kübler-Ross's observations, and they found that her stage theory was sometimes inadequate or misleading. Some found the stages to be very vague, and somewhat prescriptive. In other words, these were stages that people were supposed to go through, and if they didn't, perhaps something was wrong with them. Some nurses and others that dealt with the dying sometimes would be upset with patients if they did not go through the stages of bargaining and depression to reach the stage of acceptance. Many thought the stages seemed superficial. To say that one has "reached acceptance" does not explain much about the experience of dying. Some individuals, however, go through the stages described by Kübler-Ross, and some families might have a better understanding of their loved ones by knowing about Kübler-Ross's theory. Many professionals who deal with dying patients find a task-based approach to be more useful, in understanding their patients.

## Tasks of Dying

Another approach to the process of dying looks at the tasks that individuals cope with as they deal with their own deaths. Each of these tasks has many different ways to fulfill it; and some tasks will require more attention than others. These tasks are broad and will be handled differently during the dying process. They include physical, psychological, social, and spiritual tasks. To contrast them with the stage approach, I will use Nadine's illness as an example.

**physical tasks** The physical tasks that individuals perform as they're dying, including nutritional and fluid needs.

- **Physical tasks.** In our lives, we all have physical tasks eating, breathing, and sleeping, for example. The dying person has many more physical tasks to attend to, because he or she might feel extreme pain or distress. Physical tasks that the well person takes for granted, such as drinking and eating, become conscious tasks for the dying person as he or she attends to nutritional and fluid needs. Also, where the well person can take care of his or her physical needs, the dying person might rely on others, family members, hospital staff, and so forth.

  When Nadine first learned of her cancer, her physical tasks changed very little. As her condition deteriorated, however, she paid more attention to physical sensations in her body. She dealt with nausea that resulted from chemotherapy. She was very aware of her hair loss that resulted from her cancer treatment. This made her attend even more to her facial appearance than she had ever done before.

**psychological tasks** Changes caused by the dying process, including a different sense of security, less control over oneself, and a different experience of what it means to be alive.

- **Psychological tasks.** Some of the psychological tasks that individuals deal with include having a changed sense of security, a different level of autonomy (control over oneself), and a different experience of what it means to be alive. When individuals become sicker, they often need to rely more on others and can have less of a sense of security. They might ask if others can really help them, will they be well taken care of in a particular hospital, and so forth. As other people take more care of them, it is necessary for the dying person to take more care of himself or herself, and thus retain a sense of autonomy. Individuals need to make some important decisions about their medical treatment, finances, and how they interact with families and friends. When doing so, they want to retain a sense of living, to be involved in political conversations, if that has always been important to them.

By having a sense of security, making decisions about one's life, and having as full a life as possible, the individual can retain a sense of dignity (Corr, Nabe, & Corr, 2000).

After Nadine was first diagnosed with cancer, she talked with three different doctors. Although they agreed on their advice, she found that she was particularly comfortable with the second doctor that she consulted, Dr. Scott. Dr. Scott explained the meaning of the analyses of blood samples and x-rays to Nadine in a way that Nadine understood. This gave Nadine a sense of security and confidence in someone who was helping her. Dr. Scott also provided Nadine with a number of choices about her treatment, such as when to have treatments, and helped Nadine make choices about what other activities she would be involved in around those times. Thus, Nadine regained a sense of autonomy about her life. She was also able to choose with whom she spent time. She found that her preference was to spend time with her parents and Roger, and less time with other friends and colleagues at work. It was not that she turned against her friends, but rather that she felt more comfortable with those who were very close to her. One of Nadine's hobbies before she became ill was gardening, raising plants and flowers. This became even more important to her as she enjoyed having small flowering plants, like miniature roses, in her bedroom. Although some would find this insignificant, for Nadine this was special and the colors and the shapes of the flowers gave her a sense of enjoyment while she was managing difficult medical problems.

**social tasks** Referring to the dying process, these tasks deal with the importance of interpersonal relationships and dealing with social systems such as hospitals.

- **Social tasks.**   There are two basic types of social tasks, one that deals with the importance of interpersonal relationships when a person is dying and one that relates to social systems, such as hospitals and ambulances (Corr, Nabe, & Corr, 2000). Interpersonal attachments are particularly important when an individual is coping with dying. For some individuals, interests change in that the focus might be on relationships with loved ones, more so than with leisure activities, work, or national events. Social tasks may focus on the concerns of family members as they assist the dying person. Being able to choose with whom one spends time is important in being able to retain a sense of autonomy. The second set of tasks has to do with those that relate to managing one's health: Issues such as hospital bills, doctors fees, and those dealing with nurses and other medical staff. As an individual's illness becomes more serious, the person is likely to focus more and more on dealing with others in regard to his or her own dying.

As Nadine's illness progressed, she found that she had to make more and more decisions about her own care. She often talked with her parents about doctors' visits and trips to the hospital for chemotherapy and radiation therapy. She relied on her mother for transportation to the hospital.

As much as Nadine was concerned about visits and treatments, she was also worried about her mother. She tried to get friends and Roger to take her to the hospital sometimes, not so much because she wanted to be with them, but because she recognized the stress that her mother was experiencing and wanted to give her mother a break. Because she and her mother shared interests about flowers, Nadine often turned the conversation to that topic because it seemed to provide some stress reduction for both of them. It was particularly important to Nadine to have some time that she could share with her mother, father, and Roger that did not focus on medical management. Trips to the hospital, doctor's office, and dealing with her Health Maintenance Organization were stressful for her, and she enjoyed having other activities that she could temporarily plunge into and lose herself.

**spiritual tasks**
Questioning the meaning of one's life, the nature of one's values, and one's religious and spiritual beliefs as part of the dying process.

- **Spiritual tasks.** Coping with dying raises questions about the meaning of one's life, the nature of one's values, and one's religious or spiritual beliefs. When individuals think about the fact that they might be dying, they might have a new view of their life. Many individuals review their lives and evaluate their accomplishments or lack of accomplishments. This provides a way to understand what one's life means. Individuals have a variety of hopes and wishes that go beyond their immediate lives. For example, they might hope that they will have less discomfort in their dying, or that their children will have happy lives. Hopes are often expressed as religious concerns, such as hoping to be accepted into Heaven. Because dying gives a new way of viewing living, dying people sometimes become more philosophical or religious than they have been during most of their lifetimes. Material concerns matter less, and values such as helpfulness, caring, and love can matter much more.

Nadine's mother was Catholic and went to church every Sunday morning. As a child, Nadine would go with her mother because she had to. During her junior and senior years of high school, Nadine stopped going, but recently, when she was able, she would attend with her mother. At first, when Nadine went to church or thought about religion, it was to do battle with God or to question Him. During the beginning of her illness, when she would go to church, she felt odd, like she didn't belong, because she could not understand why God was doing this to her. Later she came to accept God and to find comfort in His being. Her priest was solicitous and patient in discussing Nadine's religious doubts. He visited her several times in the hospital and at home, and was there to administer the last rites of the Catholic church. Nadine had enjoyed her talks with the priest and this helped her to accept her own death, and to appreciate the life that she had led.

Kübler-Ross's stage model and Corr's (1992) task model provide two different views of the dying process. The stage model applied to Nadine focused on changes as she dealt with the fact of her dying. In contrast, the task model focused on different aspects that take place throughout the dying process. Because virtually anyone who is dying is going to deal with the four tasks discussed, this approach seems to be almost universal. In contrast, many people do not go through the stages of dying that Kübler-Ross hypothesizes. Although Kübler-Ross's stages provide an interesting way of viewing changes as one copes with one's own death, it is difficult to know which individuals would find it applicable to their situation. By examining the dying process through the use of stages or tasks, it is easier to understand how people react to dying and easier to give support to those who are dying. Many individuals find themselves, during a part of their lives, giving support to a dying loved one. Others find that working with the dying and supporting them is a part of their work.

## Support Services for the Dying

**hospice** Programs or facilities that are designed to take care of dying people and their families and friends.

Caring for the dying has received much more attention in the last 30 years than it had previously (Marrone, 1997). One of the biggest changes has been the development of the **hospice,** which is a program that provides for the terminally ill. A variety of hospice programs exist, and I will describe several here. A number of individuals such as doctors, nurses, and grief counselors also provide support to the dying and the families of the dying as a part of their work. How these individuals perform their work and deal with the stresses of their jobs will be discussed briefly here, as well.

**palliative unit** Facilities set up to care for dying patients; usually a separate ward of a hospital.

In the United States, more than 2,100 hospice programs are either being planned or in operation. Several hospice program models exist. In some cases, a hospice is a house where dying people and their families and friends go for visits and counseling. Other hospices are separate wards of hospitals, which are called **palliative units** in hospitals. Palliative units are facilities that are set up to care for dying patients. Perhaps the most common model in the United States is home service provided so that patients can remain in their homes as long as possible. Several models are a combination of these three: they include counseling at a hospice, hospital care, and home care.

In general, hospice programs have several goals, all related to dealing with the dying patient, and his or her family. These include providing care from doctors, nurses, counselors, or other health care professionals. This service can be at a hospital or in the home. Controlling pain and alleviating symptoms is a common function of hospice programs. They also provide bereavement services, providing help for the families of the patient who has died.

A number of individuals are connected with hospice programs or provide care to dying patients. Nurses are often responsible for coordinating hospice programs and other professionals working in the programs. Such individuals recognize that medical care is just a part of working with dying patients and families. The hospice nurse usually serves as the liaison between the family and other health professionals. Home health aides often provide light housekeeping duties and some personal care for the dying person and his or her family. Because the role is informal, the home health aide might develop closer relationships with the family than many of the other professionals do. Grief counselors, often trained as psychologists or social workers, help families work through difficult issues relating to the dying patient. Counselors can also help with financial, legal, or insurance issues. A part of most hospice programs are volunteers, who provide housework, grocery shopping, baby sitting, and other family support. Usually they have 20 to 40 hours of training before starting to work in the hospice or in homes. Hospice physicians often work as liaisons between hospitals and the hospice and are involved in symptom and pain management. Other individuals who play important roles in hospice programs are clergy, nutritionists, physical therapists, speech therapists, and massage therapists. Often, art and music therapists can be helpful as well. Other individuals might provide informal support. Suggestions for how people who are not involved in hospice work can be helpful to dying patients and their families are the subject of the next section.

## How to Help Dying Patients and Their Families

Many individuals who visit dying friends or relatives are often uncomfortable and not sure about what to do. Rinpoche (1992) writing from the perspective of the Tibetan culture, which is very involved with the process of dying and life after death makes several useful suggestions. One first step is to try to make the atmosphere somewhat relaxed. If you don't expect a lot to come from the conversation, relaxation will be easier, which can allow the dying person to express his or her thoughts, feelings, or emotions about death, dying, or other things, and make it easier for you to accept the situation in which the dying person does not respond to you very much. Give people your full attention so that they will feel that they can express themselves to you. Just because a person is dying does not mean that humor has no place. Often joking and humor are helpful. This is not the time to give advice or preach to dying people, unless they ask specifically for this. Depending on your relationship with the person, touching can be helpful. In general, the more that you are able to deal with the reality of your own eventual death, the more comfortable you are likely to be when talking with a dying person.

These comments have addressed primarily psychological needs—what to do when talking with a dying person. However, it is often helpful to respond to social needs as well. Dying people are usually concerned with

---

## *Problems and Solutions*

---

### *How can I help someone who is terminally ill talk about his or her illness or about dying?*

- Don't expect a lot from the conversation.
- Try to make the atmosphere relaxed.
- Let the person express himself or herself about spiritual or other issues.
- Don't preach.
- Offer to help with social needs.

---

**Q 10.1** Compare the usefulness of Kübler-Ross's stage theory of dying and Corr's task model. How would they be helpful, or not helpful if you were dying?

**Q 10.2** What has it been like for you to sit with a dying person? If you have not done so, what do you think it would be like?

**Q 10.3** How do you feel when you think about the inevitability that your life will end sometime?

**Q 10.4** How do you feel when reading about Nadine's attempts to cope with her death?

what will happen in various aspects of their life. For example, they might be concerned about how their families will survive. They might have distress about the cost of health care and the effect of this on their family. Some individuals will be concerned about their work. Will their job tasks be completed, what will happen to their customers, employees, students, or parishioners. They might ask what will happen to their grandchildren or children. Other questions might be more concrete, such as what will happen to their house or car? To the extent that individuals can help answer these questions and support the dying person by carrying out wishes related to such questions, concrete help can be quite useful (Corr, Nabe, & Corr, 2000).

As mentioned previously, spiritual issues can become particularly important in the dying process. Being able to talk about issues such as "Why is there so much pain now?" "Has God left me?" can be very helpful. These questions are an opportunity for the dying person to express his or her point of view. Encouraging the person to express his or her beliefs is useful. It is not helpful to say "I know exactly how you feel" or "I know exactly how you believe." We can't know exactly what other people feel or believe. Also, it is rarely helpful to give long answers about what your spiritual beliefs are. If it is necessary to discuss them, do so rather briefly so that the dying person can express beliefs and concerns.

As Nadine lay in bed in her room with a few plants on the dresser and a chair by her bedside, she found it helpful to talk with her father. Although her priest was comforting in talking with her and answering questions about Catholic theology, she found her father's support especially meaningful. Sometimes they would talk about her father's business and his sales visits. Other times he would just let Nadine talk about her life and her concerns about the family. Often he sat close to her leaning toward her, with a hand gently resting on her shoulder. He was very much in tune to her facial expression, and if this seemed to be uncomfortable, he would remove his hand. Twice Nadine got angry at him for not doing enough for her mother. Rather than argue with her, he listened to her and showed that he understood her point of view. Occasionally she would talk about Roger and be very sad about not being able to be with him and to raise a family with him. Again, her father listened, and showed that he understood Nadine's concern. He wanted to be there for her and with her as much as possible.

# THE DEATH OF LOVED ONES

Words expressing the depth of loss and bereavement that come with the death of someone who is close to us always seem to be lacking in strength. The death of a loved one is so powerful and extreme that verbal expression seems inadequate. I will discuss some issues that are special to dealing with the death of a child, the death of a spouse or friend, and the death of a parent or grandparent. Adolescents and adults deal with death differently. But there are some commonalities. Examining the stages and tasks of mourning helps to understand what we or those close to us might go through when we lose someone we love. The process of working through grief is long and difficult in many cases. What to say, and not to say, to those who are mourning can be helpful, as we deal with the grief of others.

## Grief and Relationships

Loss of someone close is extremely difficult. Some issues affect particular types of loss. When parents lose a child, especially when the child is still in childhood or adolescence, certain issues can be particularly difficult, such as guilt. When the loss is that of a romantic partner or close friend, intimacy and sharing stop and a vacuum exists where the closeness was. Somewhat similar occurrences take place with the death of a parent or grandparent.

When parents lose children in childhood or adolescence, the loss is often sudden. Maybe the young person died in an auto accident, through homicide or suicide, or sometimes through illness. With the loss of a child's life comes the loss of a part of the parent a loss of hopes and dreams for the child (Corr, Nabe, & Corr, 2000). Adding to the death can be experiences of anger, blame, or guilt. Blaming oneself and feeling guilty is a common reaction. Miles and Demi (1986) believe that guilt that parents feel often results from feeling helpless or responsible for the loss. When the loss is due to illness, parents can feel that they did not do enough for the child to stop the illness or in some way might have contributed to the death of the child or failed to protect the child from death. In other cases, not necessarily related to illness, parents can feel that they failed to live up to their own views of what a good parent should be. Parents might also feel that it is not right that they should outlive their child, or they might feel that the death of the child was punishment for an immoral act of their own. Compounding the guilt further, parents can feel upset about the way they acted at the time of the child's death or shortly thereafter.

Parents deal with the death of a child in a great variety of ways. For example, men are often taught to contain their grief and not talk about it, whereas women are expected to show grief more readily. Other issues depend on whether the parents are married, unmarried, or divorced. Grief of stepparents can be different than that of the mother or father. Single parents are likely to have a different reaction than married parents. Grief reactions can often affect the relationship of the parents with each other, and they might have difficulty understanding each other's reaction.

Loss of a romantic partner can be extremely upsetting and disorienting. Both partners played such important roles in each other lives that it can be difficult to envision life without the other. When one partner dies, the other loses not only the other person, but also a relationship. The person who was available for comfort when the grieving partner was left alone is no longer there to help with the deep sadness. Depending on the closeness of friends, the loss of a friend can bring about similar reactions.

When individuals lose their parents or grandparents, a lifelong relationship has ended. There is no longer a continuation of the shared experiences, either enjoyable or sad. With the death of parents, the role of adult children changes because they now are the oldest generation, and responsibilities can change as well. Furthermore, there is a renewed sense of mortality, as one becomes more aware of the possibility of one's own death.

When adolescents experience the death of a close friend or parent, they can experience some reactions that are similar to those of adults. Fleming and Balmer (1996) report that adolescents are often resilient when facing the loss of someone close to them. Older adolescents are more likely to talk with friends about their loss, whereas younger adolescents might experience more physiological distress. Adolescents who experience loss, might have changes in sleeping and eating, exhaustion, or loneliness. When adolescents do not talk about this loss with others, they might feel that no one has ever lost as deeply, or loved as deeply, as they have. Being able to talk about the loss with friends, parents, or professionals can be very helpful, as can involvement in school and leisure activities.

Because losses are experienced so differently and by people at different developmental levels, it is difficult to make generalizations about loss. One example of the depth of loss, expressed eloquently in a eulogy is that by Noa Ben-Artzi Pelossof, at the funeral of her grandfather, Yitzhak Rabin, the Prime Minister of Israel. When Yitzhak Rabin was assassinated by one of his own countrymen, many politicians were concerned about the effect of his loss on peace in the Mid-East. In contrast, the reaction of his eighteen-year-old granddaughter expresses the loss of her grandfather, in a very personal way. At the funeral, she read this message to her grandfather:

Please excuse me for not wanting to talk about the peace. I want to talk about my grandfather.

You always awake from a nightmare, but since yesterday I was continually awakening to a nightmare. It is not possible to get used to the nightmare of life without you. The television never ceases to broadcast pictures of you, and you are so alive that I can almost touch you—but only almost, and I won't be able to anymore.

Grandfather, you were the pillar of fire in front of the camp and now we are left in the camp alone, in the dark; and we are so cold and so sad.

I know that people talk in terms of a national tragedy, and of comforting an entire nation, but we feel the huge void that remains in your absence when grandmother doesn't stop crying.

Few people really knew you. Now they will talk about you for quite some time, but I feel that they really don't know how great the pain is, how great the tragedy is; something has been destroyed.

Grandfather, you were and still are our hero. I wanted you to know that every time I did anything, I saw you in front of me.

Your appreciation and your love accompanied us every step down the road, and our lives were always shaped after your values. You, who never abandoned anything, are now abandoned. And here you are, my ever-present hero, cold, alone, and I cannot do anything to save you. You are missed so much.

Others greater than I have already eulogized you, but none of them have ever had the pleasure I had to feel the caresses of your warm, soft, hands, to merit your warm embrace that was reserved only for us, to see your half-smile that always told me so much, that same smile that is no longer, frozen in the grave with you.

I have no feelings of revenge because my pain and feelings of loss are so large, too large. The ground has been swept out from below us, and we are groping now, trying to wander about in this empty void, without any success so far.

I am not able to finish this; left with no alternative. I say goodbye to you, hero, and ask you to rest in peace, and think about us, and miss us as down here we love you so very much. I imagine angels are accompanying you now and I ask them to take care of you, because you deserve their protection.

*Source:* "From Goodbye to Grandfather," by M. Ben-Artzi Pelossof, *New York Times,* November 7, 1995, p. A9. Copyright (c)1995 by The New York Times. Reprinted by permission.

## Awareness of Feelings

This young woman had to be aware of her own feelings to express herself so eloquently. Furthermore, she needed to find words to express these feelings. For some people this can be a difficult process. They might not allow themselves to feel sadness, and when they experience the sadness, they might not be able to cry or express their pain. Before you can feel such pain you have to have a sense of closeness to another person and the ability to experience it. People are often likely to express their upset in ways that they have learned. For some, this might be in a very articulate way, and for others it might be sounds of sadness and grief, with little verbal expression. Whether or not they have clear awareness of their feelings, individuals are likely to experience the process of mourning in a variety of ways.

## Stages of Mourning

By examining the phases or stages of mourning, individuals can understand the grief process as many experience it. Parkes (1987) has presented a model that is helpful because it talks about four general phases: shock and numbness, yearning and searching, disorganization and despair, and reorganization.

- **Shock and numbness.** When impact of the loss is especially sudden, individuals can feel detached or numb. Often this response is only for a few hours or days, but the full impact of the death is not yet absorbed.

  Three years ago when Terry was nineteen, he had dated Angela for a year and a half. They had grown very close, and Terry and Angela had discussed marriage. However, Angela started to grow more distant as she became interested in Peter. When Angela told Terry that she was no longer interested in seeing him, he was devastated. At first, he thought she was joking, then the enormity of what happened sunk in.

  When Terry learned that Angela and Peter had been killed in an auto accident in which their car had been struck by a train, he was devastated. Although not aware of it at the time, he experienced a sudden sense of disbelief. Was it really Angela, maybe it was somebody else with Peter, no it couldn't be true. This wasn't a desperate feeling, but rather a dazed one; he was able to feel the loss the next day.

- **Yearning and searching.** With the loss comes a searching for what was good and meaningful. There is a desire to return to the past.

  Although Terry had dated a little bit after he and Angela broke up, he had never developed a relationship with another woman that was close to what he felt for Angela. His feelings for Angela would strengthen when he heard some songs that they would sing together. Now with her death, he experienced an even stronger sense of yearning, vivid recollections of times when they had been to the amusement parks, to the beach, and in each other's homes.

- **Disorganization and despair.** After a searching for what was, there is often confusion. The individual might be bewildered about what to do or where to turn. Life has changed, and responsibilities can feel trivial and unimportant.

Terry was unable to concentrate on his job as a credit analyst. He would talk to people, but lose track of the conversations. Several times, he was reprimanded by his boss, who usually listened to a few of his conversations with the customers. The day's business that Terry was involved in seemed so unimportant to him. He asked himself why he was so upset if they weren't dating anymore, and he found himself being angry at Peter and blaming Peter for the accident, although there was no reason to do so. He found himself loving Angela very much and missing her deeply, and these thoughts took him away from his work.

- **Reorganization.** Gradually individuals start to reorganize their life, so that they can find a way to continue. Often the loss is very large, and reorganizing one's life so that new relationships can be built and older ones developed takes time and energy.

Terry attended Angela's funeral. He tried to explain what was happening to his boss, but his boss was unforgiving and continued to follow his work carefully and to write up his errors. Because Terry had only been on the job six months, he desperately didn't want to lose it. He couldn't stand the prospect of another loss. He used all the energy he could to concentrate on his job. Sometimes he would try to imagine what the people looked like who he was talking to on the phone. At other times he would grip the phone tightly, just to remind himself that he was in a conversation. This added effort worked for him, and the boss finally stopped following his work so closely and made some minimal comments about his improved performance. However, this took a great effort by Terry. He was exhausted at the end of the day and often would go home, have dinner, and go to sleep. On the weekends, he spent time with some friends. Terry had two important friendships with old high school friends. These, more than anything else, helped Terry deal with Angela's death.

Parkes's model is not an elaborate one, but it helps to understand how an individual can cope with a deep loss. Others have discussed different stages or phases, but Parkes's model is clear enough to provide one way of dealing with the loss of a relationship. It helps explain Terry's initial shock and bewilderment and his confusion that affected so many aspects of his life. Support from friends was helpful to him in continuing on with his life.

Examining stages of mourning provides one perspective on grief, a task model provides another.

## *Tasks of Mourning*

Another approach to mourning is by thinking of tasks that individuals take on rather than thinking of stages or phases. Worden (1991) believes that individuals attempt four basic tasks as they work through their grief. These tasks include accepting the reality of the loss, working through the pain of grief, adjusting to an environment without the person, and moving on with one's life.

- **Accepting the reality of the loss.** To deal with loss, individuals must accept it. If one fails to deal with the loss, then reality is denied. Keeping the room of a lost child exactly the way it was on the day he died can make it more difficult to accept the loss and can bring the bereaved person back again and again to the initial loss. On the other hand, some individuals find that they want to do this and that this feels best to them. Individuals decide on the pace at which they cope with reality, accept it, and try to make changes in their lives.

   When Terry first heard of Angela's accident, he couldn't believe it. At first he denied it, thinking it must be someone else. It just didn't make sense to him that he could lose Angela, first to Peter, and now in an accident. Talking to his friends about her, and attending Angela's funeral helped him accept what had happened.

- **Working through the pain of grief.** Grief is hurtful and distressful. Trying to deny the grief or drown it won't help. Sometimes individuals use alcohol or drugs when they are in despair. This usually makes things worse because there still is an awareness of the distress, and they can feel this physically or emotionally.

   After Terry heard of Angela's death, he just sat in his room and was numb. The next day when he returned from work, however, he was upset. He had been thinking about Angela all day and had not been able to handle some of his transactions with customers. He took a fifth of vodka from the liquor cabinet in the living room and stared to drink; he drank most of it quickly, and passed out. When he woke up, his head pounded and his mouth and throat felt like a desert and then he remembered the loss of Angela. Only some weeks later, when he talked to his friends about how much he missed Angela, even though they hadn't seen each other more than once or twice in a year and a half, was he able to talk about his hurt and to start to acknowledge the pain. His two close friends were able to understand what he was going through, although some of his coworkers wondered why he was so upset because he hadn't seen Angela in more than a year.

- **Adjusting to the environment in which the person is absent.**
  With the loss of a spouse, many roles have to be picked up by the remaining spouse. This is particularly true when there are children who need to be cared for, taken to school, fed, and so forth. Often additional tasks, such as cleaning the house or gardening have to be done, just when a person feels least like doing so.

  Because Terry had seen Angela so little in the last year and a half, it was relatively easy for him to make progress in this task. For him, the problem was not so much the actual activities that he missed, but the remembrances of her and the thoughts of the activities that they used to do together.

- **Moving on with life.**  Worden discusses emotional relocation, which refers to developing existing or new relationships so that one can continue to grow. Otherwise, one is continually living with a relationship that no longer exists. Although a new relationship will not be the same as an old one, it will allow a person to continue to have new experiences and opportunities to care for and be cared about. When a spouse dies, relationships with children can change, and they might even improve. That improvement can be threatening in some ways, because the surviving spouse might feel guilty, as if he or she is not being true to the deceased partner. Accepting the relationship helps the person move on with life.

  Terry was aware that in the past he had not given relationships with other women much of a chance. Shortly after Angela's death, he started to date a woman at work. They had two dates, and Terry was very uncomfortable. He told her that he wanted just to be friends, as that was all he was ready for at the time. Terry was trying to move on with his life, but it was harder than he thought.

Both Parkes's stage model and Worden's task approach help us understand Terry's situation. Parkes's model helps us understand the timing of Terry's reaction to the loss of Angela. Worden's approach is more active and helps to see some of the things that Terry needs to do to make progress in his life. Both models give a different view of coping with the death of a loved one. Other stage and task models provide other insights into the process, but they tend to be somewhat similar to the two just discussed.

## *Helping Others Deal with Their Grief*

Although Worden's tasks and Parkes's stages help individuals understand the bereavement process, they do not directly relate to what we can do to help others. Corr, Nabe, and Corr (2000) suggest tasks to help others who are grieving. These tasks are cognitive, affective, behavioral, and valuational tasks.

---

## *Problems and Solutions*

---

### *What can I do to help bereaved persons deal with their loss?*

- At first, provide information if appropriate.
- Help them express feelings.
- Let them talk so they can try to make sense of the loss.
- Acknowledge the significance of the loss.
- Don't be afraid of talking about the deceased person.

---

**cognitive tasks** Needing information about what has happened so that individuals can understand the details of the loss.

- **Cognitive tasks.** When faced with a loss, individuals often need information about what happened. Frequently, they want more detail than others think is necessary. For example, Terry wanted to know how fast the train was going when it hit the car, whether the engineer could see the car, if Peter was drunk, if Angela was thrown from the car, how she died, and so forth? Providing information, when possible, can be helpful to those who are first finding out about a death and are experiencing shock.

**affective tasks** Having many feelings about the loss of a loved one and a desire to express them to others.

- **Affective tasks.** One of the most important ways that people can help those who are bereaved is to help them express their feelings about the loss of the loved one. Sometimes bereaved persons are not clear about their feelings, and they don't understand what is happening. For Terry, talking with Fred was particularly helpful. Fred helped Terry talk about his strong feelings for Angela that still existed after a year and a half. Fred did not question or discount this. He also let Terry talk about his anger at Peter for taking Angela away from him and killing her. Even though Fred knew that Peter didn't kill Angela, he let Terry express his feelings, rather than challenge him.

**behavioral tasks** Doing something to recognize a loss.

- **Behavioral tasks.** Public recognition of a death is helpful and necessary for many people. The idea of a funeral ritual is to provide a means for people to publicly act out their grief by coming together and acknowledging the loss of a person. Terry found it helpful not only to attend Angela's funeral, but also to visit her gravesite every week for a month. This allowed him to express his grief through his tears.

**valuational tasks** Examining one's own values as they relate to the loss of a loved one.

- **Valuational tasks.** Trying to make sense of a death or loss is important for virtually everyone. Doing so can be very difficult. Terry continually asked why this had happened, how could it happen to Angela. How could it really happen to someone whom he cared so much about? Just the act of asking these questions, even though he could not find answers, was helpful for him. Terry would ask these questions of Fred, who was unable to answer them, and then Terry would try to answer them himself. Just talking to Fred about them was useful.

Helping people who are bereaved with cognitive, affective, behavioral, and valuation tasks is a service that often is not acknowledged at the time, but might be appreciated later. More specific suggestions about what to do and what not to do provide more structure in dealing with bereaved individuals.

Corr, Nabe, and Corr (2000) are quite specific in making suggestions about what is helpful *not* to say to people: It is not helpful to minimize a person's loss. Individuals have strong grief reactions and taking that away is likely to upset or anger the mourning person. Here are some examples of the messages the researchers say are not helpful (p. 248).

- "Now that your baby has died, you have a little angel in heaven." (But my pregnancy was not intended as a way of making heavenly angels.)
- "You're still young, you can get married again." (Yes, but will that bring back my first spouse or lessen the hurt of his or her loss in any way?)
- "After all, your grandfather was a very old man." (And perhaps, for that reason, all the more dear to me.)

As can be seen from the comments in parentheses, the speaker does not appear to understand the loss of the bereaved person. The loss is much greater than the speaker acknowledges. Another group of unhelpful statements tends to suppress the intensity of the feelings that the person experiences. These comments are cliché responses to a person's loss (p. 248).

- "Be strong," or "Keep a stiff upper lip."
- "You'll be fine," "Don't be so upset always," "Put a smile on your face."
- "You're the big man or woman of the family now."
- "What you need to do is keep busy, get back to work, forget her."

These instructions on how to deal with grief are simple and unhelpful because they don't acknowledge the significant loss that the person has experienced. Giving advice to someone experiencing a loss should only be done very carefully. One reason is that it is hard to understand a person's grief; another is that individuals often find their own ways to cope with grief as they encounter new events in their lives.

What then is helpful? Corr, Nabe, and Corr's cognitive, affective, behavioral, and valuational tasks are perhaps most helpful. To be more concrete, it is helpful to do something immediately after a death. Make phone calls, free family members from chores, or run errands. Making

**Q 10.5** If you have lost a friend, what did you find helpful that others said or did for you?

**Q 10.6** If you have lost a friend or loved one, what did you find that was *not* helpful for you?

**Q 10.7** What could you say to Terry that would be helpful to him in his loss?

**Q 10.8** What could you say to Terry that would be *not* helpful to him?

**Q 10.9** After reading this section, what might you do differently than you would have done before, in helping a friend who was mourning the loss of a loved one?

yourself available and making contact with the bereaved is often helpful. Rather than being guarded about the death of a person, it is more helpful to behave naturally, to mention the deceased person in ways that you would have done before his or her death. When bereaved people want to talk about their loss, allow them to do so, and when they don't, allow them not to talk. Giving your own religious or spiritual views is rarely helpful, unless it is asked for very specifically. Spiritual views are personal and need to be developed and discussed by the bereaved individual. Assisting a person in expressing his or her religious beliefs is helpful.

The reason that Terry found Fred to be so helpful was that Fred seemed always available. When Terry wanted to talk, they talked. When Terry wanted to shoot pool, they shot pool. Fred never forced his views on Terry or argued with Terry, even when Terry expressed views about Peter that seemed very illogical. He never said, "Oh you will find a better girlfriend some day" or "Sometime a real nice girl will come along and you will forget Angela." Rather, Fred listened, drove Terry to the funeral, and went with him to Angela's grave when asked.

# SUICIDE AND OTHER CAUSES OF DEATH IN YOUNG PEOPLE

Unlike people in other age groups, young people (ages 15–24) are far more likely to die of human-induced causes than from illness. The three major human-induced causes are accidental death, homicide, and suicide. Because there are warning signs, in many cases, of suicide and more opportunities for prevention than there are in accidental death or homicide, I will focus most attention in this section on suicide. Some individuals have myths about suicide that are inaccurate and interfere with being helpful to those who are contemplating suicide. In addition, there are warning signs of suicide and ways to take action on these signs to help prevent suicide.

## *Death among Adolescents*

In adolescence, unlike most other periods of life the three leading causes of death are brought about by human intervention. In fact, for American adolescents, more than 68 percent of deaths are the result of accidents, homicide, or suicide. Because these deaths are human-induced they are most likely associated with trauma or violence. For example, more than half of accidental deaths are caused by automobile

TABLE **10.3** **PRELIMINARY NUMBER OF DEATHS AND DEATH RATES (PER 100,000) FOR THE 10 LEADING CAUSES OF DEATH, 15–24 YEARS OF AGE, BOTH SEXES, ALL RACES: UNITED STATES, 1996**

| Rank | Cause of Death | Number | Rate |
|------|----------------|--------|------|
| ... | All Causes | 32,699 | 90.3 |
| 1 | Accidents and adverse affects | 13,872 | 38.3 |
| 2 | Homicide and legal intervention | 6,548 | 18.1 |
| 3 | Suicide | 4,369 | 12.1 |
| 4 | Malignant neoplasms | 1,642 | 4.5 |
| 5 | Diseases of the heart | 920 | 2.5 |
| 6 | Human immunodeficiency virus (HIV) infection | 420 | 1.2 |
| 7 | Congenital anomalies | 387 | 1.1 |
| 8 | Chronic obstructive pulmonary diseases and allied conditions | 230 | 0.6 |
| 9 | Pneumonia and influenza | 197 | 0.5 |
| 10 | Cerebrovascular diseases | 174 | 0.5 |
| ... | All other causes | 3,940 | 10.9 |

*Source:* Corr, Nabe, & Corr, 2000.

accidents (see Table 10.3) (Corr, Nabe, & Corr, 2000). Another cause of death is the result of the human immunodeficiency virus (HIV) infection, which is now the sixth leading cause of death among adolescents. Education and training can help reduce deaths in these categories.

Several new education programs and strategies have been developed to try to reduce adolescent death. Driver education programs try to teach skills so that adolescents will drive more safely. In addition, Mothers Against Drunk Driving (MADD) has developed educational programs that focus on the interaction of alcohol and driving. The slogan "Friends don't let friends drive drunk" is a popular one aimed at preventing the thousands of deaths caused by alcohol-related auto accidents. Peer counselors have been trained to help fellow students who are depressed or upset. The training of such peer counselors often includes recognizing signs of suicidal intent and suggestions for what to do about them. Health education classes teach about HIV and how it is contracted. Even though prevention programs help prevent adolescent death, human-induced death remains the leading cause of death in adolescents.

Among adolescents, there are great differences in death rates depending on the gender and race of the individual. Table 10.4 shows the death rate per 100,000 for males and females of five ethnic groups who are 15 to 24 years of age. This table shows some startling statistics. Young African

TABLE **10.4** PRELIMINARY NUMBER OF DEATHS AND DEATH RATES (PER 100,000),
AGES 15–24, BY RACE AND SEX: UNITED STATES, 1996

|  | Deaths | | | Death Rates | | |
|---|---|---|---|---|---|---|
|  | **Both Sexes** | **Males** | **Females** | **Both Sexes** | **Males** | **Females** |
| All races | 32,677 | 24,533 | 8,144 | 90.2 | 131.8 | 46.3 |
| Caucasian Americans | 23,135 | 17,165 | 5,970 | 80.2 | 115.1 | 42.8 |
| African Americans | 8,291 | 6,469 | 1,823 | 150.8 | 234.7 | 66.5 |
| Hispanic Americans | 4,647 | 3,755 | 892 | 93.4 | 140.3 | 38.8 |
| Asian Americans | 769 | 542 | 227 | 52.0 | 72.4 | 31.1 |
| Native Americans | 483 | 357 | 125 | 121.4 | 176.2 | 64.0 |

*Source:* Corr, Nabe, & Corr, 2000.

American men die at a far greater rate (234.7) than do young African American women (66.5), young Caucasian men (131.8) and young Caucasian females (46.3) or do those from other cultural groups. This is partly due to the higher homicide rate of young African Americans males (15.4) per 100,000 compared with young African American females (19.4), young Caucasian males (17.5), and young Caucasian females (4.1) (Corr, Nabe, & Corr, 2000). The high homicide rate among young African American men has been a concern of both politicians and community activists. It is perhaps most poignantly described by a young African American mortician, working in a high crime area who provides funeral arrangements for a disproportionately high percentage of young black males killed by gunshots.

Two corpses lie on separate tables at the Whitted and Williams funeral home in Oakland, California. Carefully picking over every detail from clothing to skin tone, Donnell Williams is getting ready for another burial. From his dark double breasted suit to the bright sincerity in his eyes, Williams is the essence of the earnest undertaker with one notable distinction: At twenty-five, he might be the youngest mortician in the United States. He is a young African American man burying young African American men in an area of Oakland that the police call "the kill zone."

"So many young men, so many, I hate to see them come in," Williams said as he caught a spot near the eye of one corpse that was not tinted quite right and called an assistant over to touch it up. "I've had mothers come in and make 'pre-need' arrangements for their children—that's when they set up a funeral in advance because they know what's probably coming. Happens all the time. Last week I had a lady come in who had one son tragically shot, and she wanted to make arrangements for her other son," Williams said. "It was like she'd given up all hope. It was heartbreaking."

Summer and Christmas vacations are boom times for morticians in East Oakland, as in other troubled urban areas. But even in off months, there is never a shortage of customers. "I'd say I do about one girl for every twenty young men ... the majority of our business is men between 16 and 25 years old. My age. Too many." Williams makes a point of hiring young men from the surrounding neighborhood, and if they tell him of some street thug they admire, Williams advice is simple. "I take them back, show them the bodies we have and they can see the holes where they were shot or stabbed and I tell them, 'You may be idolizing that person but just look at this. Remember, we buried someone just last week who was like this person you idolize'."

*Source:* Adapted from Kevin Fagan. (1994, May 11). "So many young men, so many," laments an Oakland mortician. *San Francisco Chronicle,* p. A8. © *San Francisco Chronicle.* Reprinted by permission.

Donnell William' observations bring to life the glaring statistic of the large number of homicides of African American men. Solutions for this problem are complex. One solution immediately is gun control. Because guns are often purchased illegally, and are widely available, critics have felt that this suggestion would do little to change the situation. Hudgens (1983) notes however, that the dramatic rise of suicides can be accounted for mainly by the use of hand guns to commit suicide. Programs that try to help young African American males develop educational and job opportunities and hope in their lives show some promise. Many of these are mentoring programs in which adults, often, but not always, African American males, meet regularly with young African American men who live in high-crime areas. The needless death of young people because of homicide or suicide is a tragedy that affects not only young people, but their families and communities as well.

## Suicide

As adolescents develop, certain parts of the maturation process make them vulnerable to concerns about suicide. Clearly, suicide is not an issue for many adolescents, but for some others it is. Noppe and Noppe (1996) have suggested some ways of understanding issues that adolescents face because of biological, cognitive, social, and affective changes. Because of physical growth and sexual development, adolescents can be aware not only of growth, but also of the opposite change, decline or death. Cognitively, adolescents develop the ability to think more abstractly, to think about issues such as death, and to think about their future possibilities, which might be positive or negative. Social relationships change with the family and with peers. Although such relationships can bring closeness and intimacy, they also can bring isolation. Rejection by family or friends can create a sense of alienation, which might be different than that children experience.

During adolescence, feelings about one's development and decline (eventual death) can become strong. Adolescents can have a sense of losing their own self or identity. In adolescence, changes in biology, thinking ability, social relationships, and ability to feel or emote can cause adolescents to be more aware of their mortality and thus more aware of taking control over it by ending it. Partly because of the tragic nature of suicide, suicide is not discussed frequently by many people. As a result, some myths have developed about suicide that are inaccurate.

***Myths about Suicide.*** One of the premier researchers in suicidology, Shneidman (1985), and others (Weiten & Lloyd, 2000) have described common misconceptions or myths that individuals have about suicide. I will state some of these myths and suggestions for correcting them:

- *Myth:* People who talk about suicide won't really commit suicide. *Fact:* One of the best predictors of whether someone will actually kill him or herself is whether or not he or she has talked about it before. Certainly, not everyone who talks about suicide is going to kill him or herself. When people talk about suicide, however, this talk should be considered seriously and not dismissed.
- *Myth:* Suicides take place with no notice or warning. *Fact:* About 80 percent of suicide attempts are preceded by some type of sign. Sometimes these signs are clear, such as giving away possessions. At other times, they are more vague, such as "Well, I won't have to listen to you anymore."
- *Myth:* When people attempt to kill themselves, they want to die. *Fact:* About two-thirds of suicide attempts are made to signal for help. A suicide attempt is a very dramatic call for help. Often suicidal plans are not fully thought out or developed. Less than 15 percent of suicide attempts end in the person's death.
- *Myth:* Once a person is suicidal, he or she will always be. *Fact:* For many people, suicidal thoughts and behaviors are signs of a crisis or a temporary reaction to an event. Suicidal attempts can occur at the break-up of a relationship, after a stressful semester at school, or because of difficulties on a job. Often with the help of family, friends, or a therapist, individuals can resolve a dilemma so they no longer consider killing themselves.

Warning signs that an individual is considering committing suicide differ in their strength. Often it is difficult to make judgments about the seriousness of a suicidal attempt. When someone says, "I need to tell you something, but I want you to promise that you will never tell anyone else," be very careful about agreeing to this. You might want to say, "If it is in your best interest, I might not be able to keep this secret." If someone wants you not to tell anyone that he is going to kill himself, you will be in a very difficult position. If you did promise, you might have to consider the possible gravity of keeping your word. In other words, you might have to break your promise, despite feeling very uncomfortable about doing so. Discussing warning signs with a professional such as a psychologist or counselor can be very helpful. Don't try to make judgments yourself. Here are some warning signs that indicate that an individual is considering suicide with the strongest and most powerful ones listed first.

- Giving away possessions, such as jewelry, clothing, or furniture.
- Discussion of the method and the time. If a person says, "I intend to blow my brains out tomorrow morning," that is an extremely dangerous remark because there is a specific intent, a time, and the method is extremely lethal. The more lethal the intended method is, the more severe the warning sign is.
- Extreme changes of behavior. For example, if a person stops attending classes and stops studying, this might be an indication that she is not looking ahead to the future, but instead is planning to kill herself.
- Previous suicide attempts. These indicate that a person has thought about suicide seriously before.
- Suicidal threats or statements. Whether vague or clear, these should be taken seriously.
- Depression. This is a common sign of suicidal intention. Because individuals often lose interest in their activities, they might seem extremely sad or hopeless as well as self-deprecating.
- A previously depressed person appearing to be calm or at peace. Sometimes this is an indication that a decision about killing oneself has been finalized.
- Self-depreciatory comments such as "I am worthless," "I can't do anything right."

" These comments sometimes indicate that a person is thinking about suicide.

All these signs are indications that an individual needs help. Sometimes they are signs that the individual wants to be rescued; other times they are signs that the person wants to carry out the suicide. Some

---

## Problems and Solutions

*What can I do if I think a friend might be thinking about suicide?*

- Don't promise confidentiality.
- Ask if he or she is feeling suicidal.
- Let your friend tell you how he or she feels.
- Where possible provide a sense of hope by discussing specific situations.
- Talk about how your friend coped in the past.
- Recommend talking to a counselor or friend.

---

individuals give no signs whatsoever before they kill themselves. A person might not appear distressed or upset, yet still commit suicide. Usually, however, there are signs of intent to commit suicide. What to do when these signs are recognized is the subject of the next section.

*Preventing suicide.* Shneidman (1985) gives several suggestions for helping suicidal people. One of the first things to do is to ask a person that you suspect is contemplating suicide if he or she is feeling suicidal. Not only is it appropriate to talk about suicide, but it is also helpful for individuals to see that someone else understands how they feel. In essence, a sense of isolation is being reduced. The suicidal person is also invited to share the pain and the frustration that he or she feels. Often a suicidal person sees no option other than suicide. Talking about the person's concerns and various options can help a person who has narrowed the focus of his or her thoughts. As discussion continues, you have an opportunity to give a person alternatives to suicide and a sense of hope that things could get better. A sense of hope comes from discussing specific situations rather than giving vague statements such as "I know things will get better over time." That might be true, but a depressed person will respond better to specific alternatives than to vague generalizations. Throughout the talk about suicide, it is very important to listen carefully and to allow the person to express him or herself. As people do so, remind them of ways that they have coped in the past and have changed negative situations into good ones. But perhaps the most important point is to remember not to take on a suicidal person's problems yourself. Professionals who have been trained in dealing with suicidal individuals, can help you.

To clarify how someone can help another person who is expressing suicidal concerns, it will be helpful to give an example.

Paula is twenty-four and has just learned that her parents are getting divorced. This has taken her by surprise and has come at a bad time for her. Two months ago, her husband Randy left her to move in with another woman. She was devastated by this and depressed because she did not know that Randy had been cheating on her. Now, she hears that her parents are getting divorced. Her mother had not wanted to burden Paula with this information but finally felt it necessary to do so, so that Paula would not find out from someone else. Here, Paula is talking to her friend Ramone about what has happened. She has known Ramone for three years, and they have talked after class because they both have attended the same evening courses during much of those three years.

*Paula:* Things can't go on the way they are. I'm never going to make it.

*Ramone:* What do you mean, you're not going to make it? (Ramone wants to follow up because he is worried about Paula and that she might want to kill herself.)

*Paula:* I just feel so awful, nothing seems to have any meaning for me anymore. I hate everything. Living just doesn't seem worthwhile.

*Ramone:* I wonder if you have been thinking about killing yourself. (Ramone is direct and wants to know about Paula's suicidal intent.)

*Paula:* I thought about it a lot, but haven't talked to anybody about it. When Randy left me, I wondered what I was going to do. But then I said, "Well, I've always got my parents," but now I've got nothing. My parents are separating.

*Ramone:* That news about your parents separating really has hit you hard. (Ramone wants to hear more and listen, and give Paula a chance to talk about what's happening.)

*Paula:* I always thought my parents were so close, and now I find out that they're not. Well, at least I really wanted to believe that my parents were close.

*Ramone:* I'm not sure I follow, can you tell me more? (Ramone is listening and wants to hear more about what Paula has to say about her parents.)

*Paula:* I guess I knew that they fought sometimes and didn't get along. But when I saw my cousins go through the divorce of their parents, I really didn't want that to happen to me. I really couldn't take it.

*Ramone:* You can't take what your parents are doing? (He has known Paula a while and thinks that Paula is resourceful, that she can take it.)

*Paula:* I guess I can, I mean my parents aren't going to be dead. I'll still be able to talk to them, and my mother is still here. We've always been very close. She has always encouraged me. Like when I was working in a store and thought it was a dead end. She said I could do more. Even though she couldn't help me out with school, she encouraged me. She was always there for me.

*Ramone:* Sounds like she still will be.

*Paula:* Yeah. I guess she will be, it's not like she's dead or something. But it feels in some ways, like I'm losing her, but I guess I'm really not.

Ramone is listening to Paula and helping her deal with her worries. As Paula talks, new alternatives develop. Paula realizes that she's still going to be able to be close to her mother and still talk to her. Ramone gives Paula the opportunity to look at new alternatives. He is not afraid to ask her about her suicidal concerns. When Ramone finished talking with Paula, he felt fairly confident that Paula was not going to kill herself. But just the idea that she might do so scared him. He called the counseling center at the community college where he took evening classes and spoke with someone there. He found it really helpful to be reassured that what he was doing was appropriate. The counselor asked Ramone questions so that the counselor could further assess the situation. When Paula and Ramone talked again, Paula was still very upset about her parents, but started to see some possibilities. Although she had occasional thoughts of killing herself, she had no intent.

## SUMMARY

Dealing with the death of a loved one or the possibility of one's own death can be difficult and frightening. The loss of a loved one is often followed by a period of bereavement and grief as an individual goes through the mourning process. In this chapter, I first described the dying process and stages that individuals might experience. I described four basic tasks that individuals deal with as they are dying: physical, psychological, social, and spiritual. Suggestions were given about how to help people who are dying.

The loss of a romantic partner, a family member, or a friend is usually devastating. Parkes's four phases of mourning provide a way of understanding the grief process: shock and numbness, yearning and searching,

Q 10.10 What ways do you think would be helpful to cut down on accidental automobile deaths of adolescents?

Q 10.11 Have you ever seen warning signs of suicide in a friend or relative? Explain.

Q 10.12 What do you think about the suggestions given for talking to someone who might be considering suicide? Explain.

Q 10.13 How has your view of suicide changed in the last five or six years?

disorganization and despair, and reorganization. Another helpful view of mourning is Worden's task approach: He describes the importance of accepting the reality of the loss, working through the pain of grief, adjusting to not being with the dead person, and moving on with life. Suggestions about how to help those who are mourning were given.

Suicide, accidental death, and homicide are the leading causes of death for young people. Dealing with suicidal concerns of others and helping them was a focus of this section. Understanding myths about suicide helps us to be aware of warning signs that individuals show when they are considering suicide. Suggestions for helping people who are suicidal were also given.

## RECOMMENDED READINGS

*Necessary Losses: The Loves, Illusions, Dependencies and Impossible Expectations That All of Us Have to Give Up in Order to Grow*
Viorst, J. (Ballantine/Fawcett gold medal, 1986)
> A well-known author, Judith Viorst describes loss as encompassing a broad range of experiences that include death and other losses. These include loss occurring when one is left alone, when romantic dreams are given up on, and when we no longer feel safe or powerful. Viorst emphasizes the importance of past experience and unconscious forces in our lives. She shows readers how losses and dealing with them and becoming stronger are all related to each other.

*Death and Dying: Life and Living* (3rd ed.)
Corr, C. A., Nabe, C. M., & Corr, D. M. (Brooks/Cole, 2000).
> This book describes many aspects of the dying process and the bereavement process in detail. The authors discuss ways to help people cope with the loss of a loved one. They also discuss other issues such as homicide and suicide. Information about dealing with a suicidal person is presented clearly and helpfully. This textbook is often used in courses that include substantial content on death and dying.

## RECOMMENDED WEB SITES

*The End of Life, Exploring Death in America*
http://www.npr.org.programs/death/
> Since late 1997, National Public Radio (NPR) has regularly aired a range of programs relating to death and dying as experienced in American culture. This companion Web site at NPR offers printed and audio transcripts of each program and many bibliographical and organizational resources.

*Suicide ... Read This First*
http:///www.metanoia.org/suicide/

For those thinking about or dealing with suicidal issues in themselves or others, this site speaks directly and helpfully about suicide and suicidal feelings including suggestions about good resources and links to more information.

# PERSONAL CHOICES AND SOLUTIONS

*Throughout life individuals are constantly making choices about difficult problems that confront them. One of the most profound choices that individuals can make is in their use of substances such as tobacco, alcohol, or other drugs. Chapter 11 describes problems created by substance abuse and how to confront them, whether they affect you or those close to you. Many activities (school, work, and relationships) can lead to the physical and psychological experience of stress. How to deal with stress in a variety of situations is the focus of Chapter 12. Coping strategies are provided in Chapter 13. Many of these can help you with issues that are described in the other chapters, as several examples show.*

# ABUSING SUBSTANCES

Substance use and abuse presents a considerable problem for a significant number of Americans and others throughout the world. Problems exist both with legal drugs such as cigarettes and alcohol and with illegal drugs such as marijuana and heroin. In this chapter, we will examine the extent of the problem of each drug, positive and negative effects on health, reasons for using the drug, and treatment strategies. Although a great variety of drugs are used and abused, we will discuss only the most common ones.

Because tobacco smoking and alcohol use create significant health problems—and, in the case of alcohol, psychological problems—much of the chapter will be devoted to these legalized drugs. The illegal drug that is most prevalent in the United States is marijuana (Dowciko, 1999). I will describe some of the health issues and treatment issues that pertain specifically to marijuana. For the other drugs, I will focus on physical and psychological problems that develop with abuse of these drugs. Because treatment of drug abuse is not only important, but can be difficult, I will describe treatment both for some of the specific drugs, as well as general approaches to treating drug abuse. Included in that discussion are explanations of inpatient, outpatient, and self-help groups such as Alcoholics Anonymous.

Before discussing substance abuse use and treatment, I will define six terms that will be used at different points in this chapter. Four of these terms (addiction, tolerance, dependence, and withdrawal) deal with problems that develop as a result of a continued use of drugs. Two other terms (hallucinations and psychotic reaction) are used to describe two types of adverse reactions to drug abuse.

**tolerance** Needing more and more of a drug to experience the same effect.

- **Tolerance.** When individuals need more and more of a drug to experience the same effect, they are said to have developed tolerance to the drug. The danger with increased tolerance is that an individual needs more and more of a drug, thus increasing the chances that the drug itself will cause physiological and psychological problems. For drugs like heroin, high tolerance can lead to overdose and the possibility of severe illness or death.

- **Physiological dependence.**  When the effect of some drugs on your body becomes so necessary for normal functioning that you cannot function well without the drug, you are physiologically dependent on the drug. Cocaine and heroin are two examples of drugs that become a part of the body's system, and many negative effects result when these drugs are withdrawn.

- **Withdrawal.**  When an individual becomes dependent on a drug, its removal creates stress on the body. This process of removal is referred to as withdrawal. Common symptoms of drug withdrawal are restlessness, sweating, and agitation. Drugs such as cocaine, heroin, and barbiturates can have severe withdrawal effects.

- **Addiction.**  Those drugs that produce both dependence and withdrawal are referred to as addictive drugs. The drugs described in this chapter are all addictive in that they produce dependence and withdrawal. Although symptoms of withdrawal and degree of dependence vary—for example, compare cigarettes and heroin—all these drugs are potentially addictive. If used in small quantities, a few of the drugs can have some beneficial effects, such as alcohol. Other drugs, however, such as cocaine and heroin, can become quickly addictive with minimal usage.

- **Hallucinations.**  Basically, hallucinations refer to seeing or hearing things that are not there. Although hallucinations can occur in any of the senses, such as taste and smell, they are most often associated with seeing and hearing. Hallucinogens are hallucination-causing drugs that are usually visual.

- **Psychotic reactions.**  These are reactions in which thinking and feeling are so impaired that individuals cannot maintain contact with reality. Often statements from people who are experiencing a psychotic reaction make little sense: "The rolling is running, red and blue." Often their statements are clearly illogical or inaccurate; "Next year, I will be king of the world." When individuals have a psychological disorder in which they are out of contact with reality, they are said to be psychotic, or to have psychosis.

In this chapter, I have tried to give an overview of substance abuse and its treatment. In doing so, I have tried to use as few medical and technical terms as feasible. Drugs are chemicals that have effects on our biological systems (our bodies) so this is difficult to do. For a more thorough and detailed treatment of drug use and abuse, two specific books might be helpful, *Health Psychology* by Brannon and Feist (1997), and *Concepts of*

**physiological dependence**  When the effect of the drug on the body becomes so necessary for normal functioning that the body cannot function well without the drug.

**withdrawal**  The bodily stress experienced when an individual becomes dependent on a drug, then tries to remove the drug.

**addiction**  Drugs that produce both dependence and withdrawal.

**hallucinations**  Seeing or hearing things that are not there.

**psychotic reactions**  Reactions in which thinking or feeling are so impaired that individuals cannot maintain contact with reality.

*Chemical Dependency* by Doweiko (1999). Both of these books were major sources for the development of this chapter.

## SMOKING

Since 1964, the United States government has recognized that smoking cigarettes is responsible for many major health problems. In this section, we will look at characteristics of those who smoke and changes in smoking patterns over time. Smoking presents several health risks caused by different elements of cigarettes that lead to a variety of diseases; several are explained here. Why do people start smoking, and why do they continue to smoke? Answers to these questions and some methods used to discourage people from smoking will be provided. We will also explore some of the different approaches that have met with varying success in helping people stop smoking. Information for this section has been abstracted from Brannon and Feist (1997) who provide a more detailed overview of smoking.

### *Characteristics of Smokers*

In the United States, smoking is widespread, with about 25 percent of adults currently smoking cigarettes. Another 25 percent of adults are former smokers. Since the U.S. Surgeon General described the negative effects of smoking to the American public in 1964, the amount of cigarette consumption per person has been declining. The amount of smokers in the United States has dropped from 41 percent in 1965 to 25 percent in 1995. In general, the decline of smoking for men has been greater than for women. Women appear to have a harder time stopping smoking than do men. Possible reasons why women have not stopped smoking more are that advertising has been directed toward young women, women have been concerned about weight gain if they stop smoking, and low-nicotine cigarettes are readily available.

High school students have changed smoking patterns. Smoking declined between 1975 and 1987, but then started to increase slightly. In 1993, 28 percent of European American students, 18.5 percent of Hispanic American teenagers, and about 9 percent of African American adolescents smoked at least one cigarette a day. The percentages were similar for boys and girls. In general, education level significantly affects amount of smoking. Those who have dropped out of high school are two and one half times more likely to be smokers than are those who are college graduates. In a 15-year period, the effect of education on whether or not a person smokes has become greater and greater. Overall, education level continues to be an increasingly important factor in predicting whether or not someone will smoke.

## Health and Cigarettes

Since the 1960s, when the connection between smoking and health was made public, a vast amount of research has been conducted on smoking. Approximately 400,000 deaths each year are attributed to causes related to smoking. This figure is slightly smaller than it was seven years previously because of the decline in the amount of smoking. In general, about one in every five deaths in the United States is attributed, in some part, to smoking. The following paragraphs describe some of the components of cigarettes that make smoking dangerous, and the diseases caused by cigarette smoking will be described briefly. In addition to disease, smokers are more likely to be injured or killed in a residential fire because cigarette smoking contributes to a relatively large number of residential fires.

**carcinogens** Compounds or materials that can cause cancer.

**stroke** A sudden decrease in the blood supply to part of the brain that damages parts of the body.

Although there are more than 2,550 compounds in cigarettes and more when cigarettes are burnt, we will examine three that contribute to negative health effects: nicotine, tars, and formaldehyde. As a drug, nicotine is a stimulant and affects the central and the peripheral nervous system. Tars contain a number of compounds that can cause cancer, called **carcinogens.** In general, smoking-related diseases are found less frequently when the amount of tar in the cigarettes is less. Research is difficult because the amount of tars in cigarette smoke varies in different cigarettes, and numerous other compounds beside tars can produce cancer. For example, formaldehyde has been shown to cause cellular damage. Although the effects of nicotine on health are harder to assess than those of tars and other compounds, the net effect of smoking on health has caused problems related to heart disease and **stroke,** cancer, lung disease, and other diseases as well.

**cardiovascular disease** Diseases or illnesses of the heart and the blood vessels.

- **Cardiovascular disease.** Both heart disease and strokes are cardiovascular diseases. Together, these are the leading cause of death in the United States and the major cause of cigarette-related deaths. Of the more than 850,000 people who die of cardiovascular disease, approximately one-fifth are caused by smoking. A possible reason for the large number of deaths attributed to smoking is that nicotine, which has a stimulant effect on the nervous system, increases heart rate while constricting blood vessels. By increasing heart rate and constricting blood vessels, additional strain is placed on the cardiovascular system and increases blood pressure levels.
- **Cancer.** Cancer is the second leading cause of death in the United States, and cancer deaths are highly related to smoking. Lung cancer

causes most smoking-related deaths, and, smoking also might contribute to deaths caused by cancers of the lip, mouth, esophagus, pancreas, larynx, urinary bladder, and kidney. More than 150,000 people die each year from cancers related to cigarettes; about 80 percent of them die from lung cancer.

- **Respiratory and lung diseases.** The most common diseases related to breathing are chronic bronchitis, emphysema, and asthma. About 8,500 people a year die from respiratory diseases related to smoking.
- **Attractiveness.** Although tobacco companies would have consumers believe that smoking makes one more attractive and desirable, several studies have shown that smoking causes facial wrinkles, making individuals appear older than they are, unhealthy looking, and less sexually attractive. The term "cigarette skin" in Caucasians refers to a pale, grayish, and wrinkled skin. Women are slightly more likely to develop this than men are, and smokers are two to four times more likely to develop wrinkled skin than are nonsmokers. Smoking also contributes to bad breath, and yellowing teeth and fingers.
- **Sexual impotence.** For men, smoking has been related to difficulty in maintaining an erection in sexual activity. Studies have examined men between the ages of 31 and 49. There is some evidence to suggest that male smokers are at a 50 percent greater risk for impotence than nonsmokers are. Men who had quit smoking had lower rates of sexual difficulty than did those who continued to smoke.
- **Other diseases.** Smoking is associated with ulcers, gum disease, ovarian cysts in women, frequency of colds, and bone density.

Clearly, cigarette smoking is related to health problems. In 1993, the Public Health Service estimated that $50 billion in direct costs were related to smoking. $47 billion was estimated to be indirect costs due to smoking. Because smoking is so damaging, a question arises. Does it help to quit smoking? In general, research shows that those who quit smoking, even if they have smoked a long time, reduce their chances of dying from cigarette-related diseases. Quitting smoking seems to reduce the chance that individuals will die from heart disease but has a relatively small effect on reducing the risk of dying from lung cancer. By stopping smoking "male and female smokers can reduce their risk of cardiovascular disease to that of non-smokers, although they may never completely erase their elevated risk of lung cancer" (Brannon & Feist, 1997, p. 344.) Television and newspapers continually report evidence of the connection between health-related problems and cigarette smoking. Young people, however, continue to start smoking in great numbers. Why?

## Starting Smoking

With so much information available about the dangers of smoking, adults often wonder why junior high and high school students begin smoking each year. One reason is that adolescents tend to be oriented in the present. Smoking is not seen as an immediate threat, so adolescents might not worry about it. Some research has shown that many teenage smokers believed that in five years they would no longer be smoking. Health problems caused by smoking can be seen as something that might happen to someone else, but "not to me." A second reason for smoking is tension control. Adolescents might experience some relaxation from smoking or perceive that smoking will allow them to feel less stressed. A third reason is rebelliousness; by smoking cigarettes, adolescents can assert their individuality and independence. They can make their own choice about whether or not they wish to smoke, regardless of what parents or others may say. A fourth reason, and perhaps the most important, is peer pressure. If friends smoke, teenagers might feel that they should follow suit. On the other hand, if friends don't smoke, teenagers are much less likely to smoke. One study (Ary & Biglan, 1988) showed that for every time adolescent nonsmokers were offered a cigarette, teenagers who smoked were offered cigarettes 26 times by their friends. The fifth reason for smoking that is particularly true for young women is the belief that smoking can help control weight. These attitudes about smoking present a formidable problem for public health officials and educators who want to prevent smoking.

## Preventing Smoking

There have been numerous attempts to try to deter young people from smoking, both on the broad national level and within communities. Educational approaches include informing young people about the hazards of smoking through cigarette packages, television ads, and magazine ads. Another approach is to limit the advertising that tobacco companies can do. For example, the cartoon character, Joe Camel, was believed to make smoking seem more attractive to children and adolescents. At the strong request of government officials, Joe Camel was removed from advertising campaigns. Although much effort has been put into educational programs, such as television, posters, and articles in newspapers, there is little evidence to show that they have been effective in keeping young people from smoking. Attitudes such as believing that negative consequences will happen to others, but not to you make educational programming very difficult.

Other approaches have focused on social pressures that come from peers, as well as older brothers and sisters, and parents. These programs often have several components that include ways to help individuals to develop self-esteem, increasing skills for dealing with offers to smoke, rewarding adolescent efforts to resist social pressures, and providing information about the hazards of smoking. Evans, Rozelle, Maxwell, Raines, Dill, Guthrie, Henderson, & Hill (1981) showed how films of teenagers dealing with social pressure to smoke and resisting it were helpful in reducing levels of smoking. Smoking behavior of adolescents has been reduced by using the behavioral modeling technique. Follow-up research, however, particularly after five or six years, has shown that these programs have diminishing influence. Such programming seems to have immediate effects, as well as effects lasting two to four years. This evidence suggests that social influence programming might be reinstituted for students every two to five years, so that the effects are less likely to wear off. Although the cost of social influence programs can be high, the cost of disease and potential death from smoking is even higher.

## Continuing to Smoke

Now that we have discussed why people start to smoke and ways to prevent smoking, let us look at reasons people have for continuing to smoke. Although there may be numerous reasons why a person continues to smoke, researchers can categorize these into about five different reasons. Some individuals are habitual smokers who do so because to stop would mean to experience the unpleasant effects of nicotine withdrawal. Basically, these individuals continue out of habit, even though they experience relatively little positive effects from smoking. A second category is addictive smokers, those who are aware of their smoking and when they are not smoking. For example, they are likely to know how long it has been since their last cigarette and are careful to make sure that they have cigarettes with them when they go out. A third category is those smokers who experience a feeling of relaxation or stimulation when they smoke. A fourth category are those who smoke to reduce anxiety or stress. A fifth reason, especially for women, to continue to smoke is the fear that they will gain weight if they stop. Some smokers may find other reasons that they smoke, or smoke for a combination of the reasons given here.

In my counseling with college students, I have found that one of the biggest reasons students have for not stopping smoking is that smoking reduces anxiety or distress, and they wish to reduce tension in their lives. Furthermore, to stop smoking when they are experiencing problems, would be very difficult to do. For example, Mary has recently broken up with her boyfriend and has just failed a calculus exam. Her anxiety about losing her boyfriend, and her constant sadness about not being able to spend time with him are hurting her. Smoking is serving as a way to help her relax. This is not a time in which she wants to deal with her problem of smoking, even though she knows that it is hazardous to her. For many people, smoking behavior is particularly difficult to change when they feel like they are in a crisis or in the middle of difficult problems. However, when individuals are ready to change, there are a number of strategies for stopping smoking.

## Stopping Smoking

Because so many individuals smoke and are aware of the health hazards, many have tried to quit. Some have done so on their own, by stopping smoking and not returning to it. Others have stopped and returned many times. Schachter (1982) reports that more than 60 percent of a relatively small sample of people were able to quit smoking and not return to smoking for more than 7 years. Coambs, Li, and Kozlowski (1992) found that for smokers younger than 44 years old, light smokers were able to stop more easily than heavy smokers, however the reverse was true for smokers older than 45. The authors believe that this was because older smokers quit because they had some health problems that required attention.

Although many individuals do quit smoking on their own, many seek help. The variety of approaches include pharmacological ones, such as nicotine chewing gum, nicotine patches, and nicotine inhalers. Other approaches are more psychological in nature, including hypnosis, rapid smoking, and behavior modification. These are described further here:

- **Nicotine chewing gum.** By using chewing gum that contains nicotine, former smokers find that they experience fewer cravings for cigarettes.
- **Nicotine patches.** A nicotine patch is similar to a bandage but it releases a small dose of nicotine into the body.
- **Nicotine inhalers.** A nicotine inhaler is a plastic tube filled with nicotine that smokers inhale between two and ten times a day.
- **Rapid smoking.** An aversive technique, rapid smoking requires the smoker to take a puff every 6 seconds until the smoking becomes very unpleasant. The theory is that by making smoking unpleasant, individuals will no longer want to smoke.
- **Hypnosis.** Hypnosis can be administered individually or in groups. The hypnotist gives suggestions that make smoking unpleasant or undesirable. Other activities may be emphasized instead of smoking.
- **Behavioral approaches.** Individuals can develop systems for reinforcing their nonsmoking by giving themselves an opportunity to engage in other pleasurable activities such as movies or trips. In groups designed to help people stop smoking, the group leader often provides reinforcement and develops reinforcement strategies for

**nicotine patches**  A treatment for cigarette smoking; similar to a bandage but releases a small dose of nicotine into the body.

**nicotine inhalers**  Used as a treatment for smoking; a plastic tube filled with nicotine that smokers inhale between two and ten times a day.

**rapid smoking**  An aversive technique, rapid smoking requires the smoker to take a puff every six seconds until the smoking becomes very unpleasant.

**hypnosis**  A condition somewhat similar to sleep that produces extreme suggestibility.

**behavioral approaches**  Methods used to help individuals change or modify their behavior as it relates to drugs.

---

## Problems and Solutions

---

### What are some ways to stop smoking?

- Nicotine chewing gum, patches, and inhalers
- Rapid smoking, hypnosis, and behavioral approaches
- Physician's advice and acupuncture

---

**Q 11.1** At various times in your life, you might have decided to smoke or not to smoke. What were your reasons?

**Q 11.2** Why do 14-year-olds start smoking, but 40-year-olds rarely start smoking, if they have never smoked before?

**Q 11.3** If you are a non-smoker (or smoker) what kind of difficulties occur when you are with smokers (nonsmokers)?

**Q 11.4** If you are a smoker, and wish to quit, how can others help you? If you are not a smoker, how can you best help others quit, if they wish to do so?

their clients. A contract not to smoke is frequently part of a behavioral approach.

Several studies have examined the effectiveness of these approaches and others, such as physician's advice and acupuncture. In general, the results seem to indicate that a combination of these approaches is better than any one alone. For example, one psychopharmacological approach such as nicotine gum might be combined with one or more of the psychological approaches. In planning treatment for smoking, counselors and physicians often plan what to do if relapse occurs. In general, there is a relapse, or return to smoking, for about 70 to 80 percent of individuals. Dealing with the potential of relapse helps prevent people from getting so upset with themselves about smoking again that they give up trying to quit entirely. Some individuals are able to quit once and not return, but many others might quit several times before they quit permanently. Brannan and Feist (1997) discuss the complexity of relapse, and suggest that "one is never simply a smoker or an ex-smoker" (p. 358). Smoking is indeed a complex and pervasive health problem for many individuals.

## ALCOHOL

Alcohol is a prominent part of culture in the United States. Of all adults, 40 percent describe themselves as nondrinkers, 38 percent as light drinkers, 17 percent as moderate, and 6 percent as heavy drinkers (Brannon & Feist, 1997). Although there has been a slight drop in per capita consumption of alcohol since 1980, different groups of people show different patterns of alcohol use. In general, European Americans have more positive attitudes toward alcohol and drink more than do members of other ethnic groups. Binge drinking is more common among European

**binge drinking** Having five or more drinks at one time; used as a quantitative measure for excessive drinking.

American women than among African American or Hispanic American women. **Binge drinking** refers to having five or more drinks at one time. Young and middle-aged adults tend to drink more than older people do. By the beginning of their senior year of high school, about 90 percent of adolescents have used alcohol. A common pattern with young people is that of binge drinking, however, binge drinking has declined since 1980, dropping from 41 percent to 35 percent. Possible reasons for this drop are awareness that alcohol use, and possibly other drug use, is hazardous.

Although alcohol has been used for thousands of years, information about its effect on health is quite recent. In this section, I will examine a variety of diseases that arise from heavy use of alcohol. These vary from liver damage to impaired judgment. Although alcohol in large quantities can have negative health effects, research has shown that in small quantities, there are some benefits in drinking alcohol. Ways in which alcohol can positively affect individuals' health will also be discussed; however, the major concern of this section will be alcohol abuse, and I will look at some theories about why individuals drink. Then I will examine a variety of treatments for drinking. Information for this section is taken primarily from Brannon and Feist (1997).

## Health Problems and Alcohol

Alcohol abuse can cause a wide variety of physical problems for an individual, such as liver damage and brain dysfunction. Alcohol abuse can create problems for others through alcohol usage during pregnancy, which results in problems for the child. Impaired judgment can create problems for others, causing auto accidents and other problematic situations. The following are some of the more significant problems caused by alcohol:

**cirrhosis of the liver** Chronic scarring of the liver, leading to loss of normal liver function.

- **Liver damage.** Continued drinking of more than five or six drinks a day can cause fat to accumulate in the liver. When this happens, the liver enlarges, blood flow becomes blocked, and a type of hepatitis develops. Non-functional scars form creating **cirrhosis of the liver,** which can lead to death among alcoholics. Although others can develop cirrhosis of the liver, it is particularly common among heavy alcohol users.
- **Respiratory distress.** Medical research has shown that critically ill patients were twice as likely to develop fatal respiratory problems if they had a history of alcohol abuse than were those who did not have this history.
- **Brain damage.** Those who have used alcohol heavily for a long time can develop a brain dysfunction that impairs memory for recent events, disorients the individual, and makes it difficult to learn new

information. Alcohol interferes with the brain's complex processing activities. This irreversible condition is called Wernicke-Korsakoff's Syndrome.

- **Cancer.** Because many heavy drinkers are also heavy smokers, it is difficult to isolate the relationship between alcohol and cancer. However, some evidence indicates that cancer of the throat area is related to heavy drinking.

- **Heart attacks and strokes.** Some evidence shows that drinking binges are associated with heart attacks and strokes.

**fetal alcohol syndrome**
A combination of irreversible birth abnormalities resulting from alcohol abuse by the mother during pregnancy.

- **Pregnancy.** Heavy drinking can reduce fertility because of vitamin deficiency and effects on the liver or the pituitary gland. Another complication during pregnancy is that of **fetal alcohol syndrome,** which can cause mental retardation, growth deficiencies, facial abnormalities, or other problems for the newborn child.

- **Impaired coordination and judgment.** Heavy drinking makes it difficult for the drinker to carry out complex tasks and make good decisions. When this happens, drinkers are usually not aware of it.

  Two significant areas of judgment can have tragic effects: automobile accidents and sexual decision making. Most research reports that the greater the alcohol use, the greater the chance that an individual will be fatally injured in an auto accident. Teenager and adolescent drinkers are more likely to have more sexual partners, to have sex with people that they might not ordinarily, and to have unsafe sex (for example, without a condom) than are those who do not abuse alcohol.

- **Aggression.** Individuals who are heavy drinkers are more likely to commit crimes and to be victims of crimes than are those who are not drinkers.

Alcohol use has many complications. Most physical illnesses that result from alcohol are the result of heavy drinking, usually over a period longer than five years. Much of the psychological damage that can occur, such as impaired judgment and aggression, can occur from one alcoholic binge—five drinks or more. Alcohol tolerance, the amount of alcohol needed to produce a certain effect, differs because of a number of factors. Two of the more important factors are amount of previous alcohol usage and body weight. What constitutes alcohol abuse for one person (say, three drinks), might not be alcohol abuse for another.

## Health Benefits of Alcohol

Some recent research has shown that alcohol can be helpful when used in moderation. Researchers have compared the health of nondrinkers, light drinkers (1 or 2 drinks per day), moderate drinkers (3 to 5 drinks per day), and heavy drinkers (6 drinks or more per day). Klatsky, Friedman, and Siegelaub (1981) found that light drinkers were likely to live longer than either nondrinkers or moderate drinkers, both of whom are likely to live longer than heavy drinkers. One reason for this is that light drinking seems to lower the risk of coronary heart disease. Light consumption of alcohol offers some protection against heart attack, perhaps because it guards against the formation of blood clots, thus reducing the chance of heart attack. Other research shows that light drinkers might have better mental health functioning than either those who abstain from drinking or those who drink heavily. Although much research has been done relating alcohol use and abuse to health, the findings are often complicated and require more research.

## Reasons for Drinking

Trying to explain why individuals drink very heavily, moderately, a little, or not at all is very difficult. Considerable research has been done to explain alcoholism or heavy drinking. Scientists have developed several models for the development of alcohol abuse, but there is no clear evidence for any of the models. Some of the models are listed here.

**alcohol dependency syndrome** A psychological and physiological dependence on alcohol that results in chronic disease and disruption of interpersonal and work relationships.

- **Genetic model.** This model states that drinking is inherited from parents and children of alcoholics would be likely to become alcoholics. Research (Brannon & Feist, 1997) suggests that this is not the case, and that genetics plays a relatively small role in predicting heavy drinking.
- **Disease model.** This model was developed within the medical profession and looks at **alcohol dependency syndrome** (a term preferred to alcoholism) as a disease. Symptoms of this disease are impaired control, inability to control drinking, an increased tolerance of drinking, withdrawal symptoms, and being dependent on alcohol after a period of not drinking. Critics of the disease model say that it does not consider cognitive, affective, or environmental explanations sufficiently.
- **Self-awareness model.** Hull (1987) was concerned that alcohol directly affects thought processes, making self-feedback more superficial and less negative. Thus, when people drink, they become less self-critical and less self-aware. A reason to drink, then, is to avoid self-awareness.
- **Social learning model.** According to learning theorists, individuals learn to drink for three primary reasons: First, the taste of alcohol and the effect of alcohol might be pleasurable. Second, drinking might be consistent with one's own value system. Third, individuals learn to

---

## Problems and Solutions

*How can people stop abusing alcohol?*

- Stop on their own completely (abstain)
- Reduce drinking radically but not entirely
- Join Alcoholics Anonymous or a similar group
- Get counseling
- Aversion therapy

---

drink by being around others. In essence, they learn from people who model drinking for them.

The fact that the models of drinking are so very different helps to explain why understanding drinking is so complex. Alcohol per se is not necessarily a destructive substance. It is easily abused, however, and trying to explain why some individuals can use alcohol in a way that is beneficial and others in a way that is extremely harmful, even deadly, continues to be perplexing. The fact that so many people abuse alcohol has brought about the development of many approaches to treatment.

## Treating Alcohol Abuse

Although there has been a slight decline in drinking in the United States, it is estimated that more than half a million people receive treatment for alcohol abuse each day (Weisner, Greenfield, & Room, 1995). In general, for every woman who seeks treatment, eight men seek treatment. More of those seeking treatment tend to be between 25 and 44 than from other age groups. Even though many people seek treatment, others stop or severely limit their drinking on their own, stopping without any type of treatment program. Others may go from problem drinking to light drinking to problem drinking to abstinence, to light drinking, to problem drinking, and so forth, with no consistent fluctuation.

An issue that arises in the discussion of alcohol treatment is that of abstinence versus controlled drinking. Most individuals involved in treating excessive drinking feel that the best approach is to totally abstain from drinking. However, professionals in countries outside of the United States have often found that controlled drinking is an appropriate goal. Reviewing the research on abstinence versus controlled drinking, Brannon and Feist

(1997) believe that controlled drinking can work, particularly for people who do not have a long history of problem drinking or serious physiological damage caused by drinking. Controlled drinking seems to work best for those who are under 40, are married, and whose drinking is attributed to situational factors rather than physical dependence. Some models such as Alcoholics Anonymous accept abstinence as the only appropriate goal. Some of the approaches to alcohol treatment are listed here.

**Alcoholics Anonymous** Meetings of alcoholics who are in the process of recovering from alcoholism or alcohol dependency syndrome.

- **Alcoholics Anonymous (AA).** The best known of all approaches to problem drinking, AA was founded in 1935. The AA philosophy is that alcoholics are always in the process of recovering and that they will be alcoholics for a lifetime, whether or not they take another drink. AA meetings are available in most communities throughout the country. All adhere to the 12-step-type model. Relatively little research is available on AA because of the anonymity that is offered to those who attend. Some research suggests that AA is particularly helpful for men with less education and higher needs for authoritarianism and dependence. Because of its humanitarian nature, AA provides an opportunity to give help as well as well as to receive it. This is described further on page 300.
- **Psychotherapy.** All types of psychotherapy and counseling have been used to treat alcoholism, including group and individual therapy. Success rates of psychotherapy tend to average around 20 percent, not an encouraging rate.

**Antabuse (disulfiram)** A chemical treatment used in therapy for alcoholism.

- **Chemical treatments.** Some alcohol abusers have used **Antabuse** (disulfiram). When combined with alcohol, this produces very unpleasant effects including vomiting, sweating, headaches, difficulty in breathing and decrease in blood pressure. Therefore, if individuals take Antabuse and alcohol within a few days of each other, they can become very sick. Because of the unpleasant effects of drinking while using Antabuse, many individuals do not follow through on treatment.
- **Aversion therapy.** Although Antabuse can be seen as aversion therapy, this term is more often used when describing techniques such as pairing an electric shock with alcohol use. The rationale for this process is that alcohol becomes associated with a painful condition and thus should be avoided. Research indicates that relapse rates with aversive shock therapy are relatively high.

As with cigarette smoking, the problem of relapse with alcohol treatment is significant. Most treatment programs build in follow-up programs as well as discuss the issue of relapse prevention with their clients. Because of the negative effect of alcohol abuse on spouses and children, families are often included as a part of the treatment process. Relapse concerns then become an issue for the family. For young adults, treatment for excessive drinking is likely to be because of binge drinking rather than long-term abuse. Issues that bring young adults to treatment, usually counseling or therapy, often have to do with aggression and violence. Because binge drinking is widely accepted in many colleges and communities, it becomes an issue when individuals either realize that they have done something to hurt themselves or someone else or have been arrested by law enforcement officials. A typical example of this is Barry's situation:

During the course of their relationship, Barry and Ellen have been arguing more and more. Often these arguments occurred when Barry had been drinking. He found Ellen to be extremely attractive and was very jealous of her. If he saw her talking with another man, he would become infuriated, his face would become contorted, and his veins would stick out on his forehead. Although the first six months of their relationship had been fine, Ellen was continually questioning whether or not she wanted to keep dating Barry. In the last five months, Barry's angry nature emerged when he was drinking. Ellen liked to talk to a number of guys—friends she knew from a job that she had just finished. I talked to Barry three days after this incident.

*Barry:* Ellen told me she wasn't interested in anybody else, and I saw her with somebody. He looked overly friendly, and I told her about it the next day. We were sitting on this couch watching TV. It's one of these big, red, overstuffed couches with huge pillows. I told her how mad I was at her. And she told me to get the hell out of the apartment. I said no. Then she got up and left, flying off of the sofa. I went after her and grabbed her by the arm. She pushed me away, and I hit her across the face. She started crying then ran out of the apartment. I went after her. She was in the hallway and told me to calm down and then she said, "Let's discuss it like rational people." I said "OK," leaned against the wall, and she ran inside, locked the door, and yelled at me, "Get lost." I pounded on the door, she called the police, I saw their car outside, and I left before they could get to me. They got there fast, and I wasn't expecting it.

*RS:* You certainly are hurt by this, still angry at her.

*Barry:* I'm angry at her, but I still want her back more than anything else. She didn't have to call the police, she didn't have to yell at me.

*RS:* Seems like there was no reason for her to have done what she did. (Maybe there is, and I can find out.)

*Barry:* Well, she just gets mad at me 'cause I lose my temper sometimes, and 'cause I drink a little.

*RS:* Drink a little? (I want to find out about his drinking.)

*Barry:* Yeah, just a little bit, not too much.

*RS:* How many drinks did you have the night you were with Ellen? (I want to find out more about his alcohol use.)

*Barry:* Not much. I just finished two six packs and was starting on the third.

*RS:* So you had about 13 or 14 beers. (Barry's definition of not much and my definition are different.)

*Barry:* Yeah, 14 beers I think, but it's not a problem.

*RS:* Drinking didn't affect your behavior last Sunday. (Barry is denying drinking is a problem. Denial of alcohol as a problem is very common.)

*Barry:* Well, I get angry when I'm drunk sometimes, but she should understand.

*RS:* She should tolerate your behavior and be okay about it even when you're drunk. (If I don't confront him about his drinking, we aren't going to get anywhere.)

Slowly and patiently, I worked for several weeks trying to help Barry take responsibility for his behavior and not to blame Ellen. Because this was not the first relationship that had ended this way, it was easier for Barry to see his role in the problems. He suggested that he would have no more than two beers on any evening. I asked him if he was willing to promise me that, and he agreed. For the six months that we talked, he didn't violate this agreement. How do I know? I don't. I am guessing that he didn't, because he developed another relationship with another woman rather quickly. Lying, denying, and alcohol use seem to go hand in hand. Dealing with Barry's denying that he had a problem was probably the largest obstacle we had to overcome in counseling. The fact that he took responsibility for what he had done with Ellen and was cautious in his relationship with his new girlfriend were positive signs to me.

**Q 11.5** What kind of problems have you seen with alcohol with friends or family?

**Q 11.6** Why do you think alcohol is so popular with young adults?

**Q 11.7** Do you think that information about the negative effects of alcohol, such as health effects and drunk driving, will keep someone from not drinking? Explain.

# MARIJUANA

The cannabis plant is the source of marijuana. There are a variety of these plants, and since the 1970s, the potency of marijuana has increased, as new strains of marijuana have been developed. In the United States, marijuana is the most frequently abused illicit substance. More than 68 million people, it is estimated, have used marijuana at least once in their lives (Doweiko, 1999). Approximately 9 million are considered to be using the drug at least weekly. Most often smoked, marijuana's effect is immediate, but usually starts to decline after an hour. The effects that individuals attribute to it, health problems related to marijuana and its addictive potential, and treatment are described here.

A number of effects are attributed to marijuana. In general, an individual experiences some mild anxiety, then a sense of well being, followed by a feeling of relaxation and friendliness. Those who use marijuana often anticipate that marijuana can affect their thinking ability and the way they behave. Many believe that marijuana will not only help them to relax, but also help them to interact more easily socially and to enhance sexual functioning. Some believe that marijuana changes the way they view things and helps them become more creative. Many marijuana users expect that they will become hungry or crave food when smoking. Others report having insights about significant personal ideas that they cannot put into words. Some experience more negative reactions that include anxiety or panic reactions. These reactions reported by marijuana users represent one view of the drug; another can be seen by physicians who have reported a variety of medical complications.

## Health Effects of Marijuana

Because marijuana contains more than 400 chemicals, its effects on the body are complex. When marijuana is smoked, it yields about 4 times as much tar as a comparable cigarette. Tars have been shown to contain carcinogens, contributing to cancers such as those of the mouth and throat, as well as lung cancer. Marijuana smokers tend to have a greater frequency of bronchitis and colds than nonmarijuana smokers. Another health effect has to do with the reproductive system—men might have lower sperm counts, and women can experience fertility problems as a result of using marijuana. Some research also suggests that continued marijuana use can result in damage to the hippocampus, an area in the brain that might affect short-term memory and negatively affect attention span. Those who use both marijuana and hallucinogens can experience "flashbacks," where they reexperience an hallucination or experience a brief psychotic reaction. As medical research on chronic marijuana users has been conducted, serious medical problems have been found.

Some physicians, however, have reported that marijuana has positive health effects for certain medical problems. Marijuana has been used in the treatment of multiple sclerosis, rheumatoid arthritis, and pain caused by various illnesses. Legislators have argued whether or not using marijuana for medical purposes should be legalized. A few states allow marijuana use for certain medical conditions

Relative to its addictive potential, marijuana can result in tolerance, with individuals needing a greater amount of marijuana to produce similar effects. When individuals withdraw from marijuana, they might experience negative effects such as irritability, anxiety, insomnia, loss of appetite, sweating, or vomiting. Because of these effects, many researchers consider marijuana to be an addictive drug.

## Treatment of Marijuana Addiction

When individuals seek treatment for marijuana use, several variables affect treatment. The amount of use is a significant factor: is it weekly, a few

---

## *Problems and Solutions*

---

### *How can people stop abusing marijuana?*

- Some people stop on their own
- Group therapy
- Narcotics Anonymous
- Self-help support groups
- Individual counseling that is often focused on relationship issues.

---

times a week, or daily? Smoking several times a week or daily for several months or more, a marijuana user is likely to become addicted. Marijuana is often used along with other drugs, so selection of treatment often depends on what the other drugs are. For example, is a person using alcohol, hallucinogens, or cocaine as well as marijuana? As with other drugs, for treatment or therapy to work, individuals usually must stop using all nonprescribed drugs.

Therapists take a varied approach to treatment. For example Bloodworth (1987) recommends group therapy so that marijuana smokers can deal better with peer pressures. Other suggestions include self-help support groups, Alcoholics Anonymous, or Narcotics Anonymous. Jenike (1991) believes that a major focus of therapeutic treatment is understanding problems in relationships with friends, romantic partners, and parents. In my work with Maria, personal relationships, particularly with parents and step-parents, proved to be a major focus of her therapy.

> Maria is a senior at a large Midwestern university, where she is majoring in veterinary medicine. An unusually bright student, Maria has been able to maintain almost an "A" average throughout her four years. During the last two years, she has smoked marijuana on a daily basis. Friends often marvel at how well she can do academically, while being "stoned" so much of the time. Her basic answer is that she has been smoking at night and working at her studies and her job during the day. Maria sees marijuana as a recreational activity. However, she is aware that as she has smoked more, her relationships with others have gotten worse even though her grades have been excellent.
>
> When Maria was seven, her parents divorced, and her mother moved to San Francisco. For about three years, Maria lived with her mother, but after three years she was sent to live with her father back in

Chicago. Because as a child, she often came to school hungry, dirty, and poorly dressed, school officials contacted state agencies. Social service agencies felt that Maria's mother, although not physically abusing her, was neglecting her. Because she left her at home alone when she was at work, they suggested that Maria be placed with her father. Although she lived with her father and her stepmother, she never got along with them. She felt that her stepmother was often critical of her and favored the daughter that she had with Maria's father.

Maria was terribly exasperated by her father, who she characterized as a frustrated philosophy professor. During the day he handled mail in a large Chicago post office; in the evening he would give Maria advice on world problems and talk forever. Maria had put herself through college and got very little money from either her father or her mother.

When she visited her mother on the West Coast, she felt like she was talking to a younger irresponsible sister. Maria's mother never remarried but had had many boyfriends. Always glad to see Maria when she arrived, her mother would spend a few hours with Maria, go off to work, and then return to her boyfriend. From both of her parents, Maria felt that she received no direction. When she was with her father and stepmother, she couldn't wait to leave and get back to her apartment at school. When she was with her mother, she had similar feelings. Angry at her father, step-mother, and mother, Maria became quite cynical. She felt society and her parents were of no help to her. Often when she wasn't studying, and having a feeling of accomplishment, she had a feeling of frustration and annoyance at virtually everyone. Sometimes she found herself irritable and snapping at her friends, just as she would be irritable with her family.

About two years ago, Maria started to smoke marijuana. She enjoyed the carefree feeling, relaxation, and insights that she started to have about her family. Although she appreciated the insights, she could not articulate them clearly, and they were not helpful in dealing with her family.

When I first met with Maria, she had had pneumonia for about three weeks. During that time she had not smoked. She knew that she was not only feeling weak, but also irritated at virtually everyone she met. During this time, she was aware of her loneliness in ways that she never had been before. The few friends that she had were those who she would either buy marijuana from or smoke with. She was also concerned that when she got to vet school, she would no longer be able to have the time to smoke. Her pot smoking was scaring her and she wanted to do something about it.

Maria and I talked weekly for six months. Much of what we talked about was her anger and disappointment in her parents for not being there to help her. She was angry at her father for talking and talking but never doing anything to help himself or her. She was angry at her mother for being there for her in only a minimal way. Maria recognized immediately that to feel better about herself and to improve relation-ships, she would have to stop smoking, at least for the time being.

We agreed that she would not smoke during the spring semester of her senior year, the time that I was seeing her. This took courage and perseverance on her part, as smoking marijuana had solved some problems for her, yet created others, such as her irritability and distance from people other than those she smoked with. When she was tempted to smoke, we talked about it. But mainly we talked about her frustrations with her family and her distrust of other people, feeling they would never be there for her. In fact, she was aware that her choice of veterinary medicine was related to her preference for being with and helping animals, rather than people. She had had a pet as a child, a dog, and felt closer to her dog than to her parents. Perhaps what helped Maria most during this period was her enjoyment of learning. She enjoyed her biology and animal science courses immensely. She was able to talk with her lab partners and acquaintances that she had had in her biology classes. She was able to let the friendship with three of these people develop enough so that she saw them outside of class and socialized with them. Previously she would have characterized them as "nerds" and stayed to herself. Working with me wasn't easy, as she questioned why she should trust me, or anyone else. Often we discussed this topic as well as her family and professional plans.

For Maria to stop using marijuana took insight on her part, into the distrust and anger that she felt and how it was making her life more miserable. She was able to stop smoking and enter graduate school. Her feeling at the time that our treatment stopped was that she would not smoke again. However, we talked about what might happen if she did smoke marijuana, developing strategies for this eventuality. Because Maria and I met only once a week, I could not monitor her smoking. Recovery for Maria meant that she had to take a great deal of responsibility for herself, and she did.

When individuals seek therapeutic treatment for drug abuse when they are not in a treatment program, they must take responsibility for their own lives. Therapists are unlikely to monitor patients' urine or to interrogate them about their drug usage the way counselors do in a live-in or outpatient drug and alcohol program. If individuals cannot be honest with themselves and their therapists, then inpatient or intensive outpatient drug treatment programs are preferable. This is even more true for the drugs that we are going to examine next.

# COCAINE

Cocaine is derived from the coca bush. Grown in high elevations in South America, it has been illegally exported to other countries to be used in powder form. Although sold as "free base" cocaine or "crack" cocaine in the United States, coca leaves have been chewed by native South Americans living in the high mountain areas. When chewed, coca leaves do not have as strong an effect on individuals as do the forms of cocaine used in the United States. In the United States, cocaine is sometimes snorted by sniffing powder through the nose. Other ways of using cocaine include injecting and smoking cocaine. Unlike freebase cocaine, crack is formed into solid chunks of crystals and smoked.

The psychological effects of cocaine are often quite powerful. An immediate "rush" is followed by a period of excitation. With this comes a feeling of increased competency, energy, and self confidence. This euphoria can last from a few minutes to about twenty minutes. Because of the intensely pleasurable effects, individuals are likely to want to repeat the experience.

With extended use, however, a number of problems occur. Individuals might have a hallucinatory experience, feeling bugs crawling under their skin. Other reactions are anxiety and panic attacks that might or might not stop after the drug is no longer used. Also, some individuals develop a drug-induced psychosis and sometimes become extremely suspicious of others.

Because the initial effect of cocaine is so pleasurable, it becomes addictive rather easily. The nature of the chemical reactions on the brain is such that patterns of dependency and addiction are easily established. In addition to the negative psychological effects described previously, many serious health problems come with cocaine addiction. When cocaine is smoked, individuals might experience chest pain, coughing, bronchitis, and a variety of throat problems. Heart problems often occur as a result of using cocaine. In fact, some first-time users, as well as those who have used cocaine for longer periods have suffered heart attacks. Additional research on chronic use of cocaine reveals that brain damage can occur in a variety of ways. Other possible diseases occurring from the use of cocaine include strokes and damage to the liver. Recovery from cocaine abuse is difficult. Treatment includes total abstinence from cocaine, close medical supervision, counseling, and the use of self-help groups such as Narcotics Anonymous or Cocaine Anonymous.

# HEROIN

Technically, heroin is a narcotic analgesic. Analgesics are chemicals that bring about relief of pain while a person is still conscious. Most narcotic analgesics such as heroin are derived from opium, which is a powder made from a milky sap from a poppy plant. A medication derived from opium that was used as a pain killer in military battlefields, and later in hospitals, is morphine. Around 1900 an estimated 1 percent of the United States population was addicted to opium related narcotics (Restak, 1994).

In the United States, heroin is the preferred narcotic, partly because it is more powerful than morphine. Heroin addicts experience a greater degree of euphoria from this drug than they do from morphine.

Heroin addiction continues to be a significant problem. Estimates are that there are about one million chronic heroin abusers in the United States. A considerably larger number might have briefly experimented with opiates (Doweiko, 1999). About half of the heroin addicts in the United States live in New York City. The ratio of male to female addicts is about 3 to 1. In recent years, the supply of heroin has become more plentiful and the purity of heroin has increased. This available supply has also brought the price down.

Like cocaine, heroin produces a reduction in anxiety and an increase in self-esteem. Accompanying this is a brief pleasurable sensation. Those addicted to heroin become tolerant to the sense of euphoria rather quickly, however, requiring larger and larger doses to try to reach this effect. After a relatively short time, addicts take enough heroin to prevent symptoms of withdrawal, but not enough to become "high" on heroin (Doweiko, 1999).

A number of physical complications arise from heroin usage. Sometimes it is difficult to tell whether some of these problems arise from heroin itself or from other compounds in the street drugs purchased as heroin. When used in large doses, individuals can have seizures. Heroin users can also contract HIV or other diseases from nonsterile needles. Other problems include strokes. Perhaps the most common cause of death from narcotics is overdose. Treating an opiate overdose is quite complicated and should be done in hospitals equipped for such problems. Treating of heroin addiction is extremely difficult. Current research suggests that most addicts who achieve abstinence return to chemical use within six months (Schuckit, 1989). Some research suggests that about one third of heroin addicts will eventually be heroin free (Doweiko, 1999). Treatment programs for heroin addicts are usually inpatient programs with medical treatment, group counseling, and, in some cases, individual counseling.

**Q 11.8** Why do you think individuals want to experiment with, and then become addicted to, cocaine or heroin?

## HALLUCINOGENS

More than 100 different compounds that cause hallucinations can be found in a variety of plants and mushrooms. Some of the most well-known hallucinogens are *lysergic acid diethylamide-25* (LSD), *phencyclidine* (PCP), and *Nalpha-dimethyl-1,3 Benzodioxole-t-ethanamine* (MDMA) or "ecstasy." About 5 to 10 percent of high school students admitted to using LSD at least once a year (Doweiko, 1999).

The subjective effects of LSD and other hallucinogens have some general characteristics. First, there is a sense of relaxation followed by euphoria, and sometimes crying or laughing. After this, individuals frequently experience perceptual distortions that are visual illusions or hallucinations. Another phase usually follows in which individuals experience a distorted sense of time. They might experience mood swings, feelings of panic, or feelings of depression. Sometimes, there is a loss of contact with reality, in which individuals think they can fly, or think things that in a normal state they know would be impossible. Four to six hours from the time LSD was taken, individuals start to feel episodes of feeling normal. After about 12 hours, there can be a sense of emotional numbness. Reactions to PCP are somewhat similar with disturbances of body images with moderate levels of intoxication. High levels of PCP can cause coma, psychotic reactions, or other severe complications. Individuals taking ecstasy can experience visual hallucinations and a wide variety of complications.

Some individuals have definite negative experiences referred to as "bad trips" from taking LSD (and other hallucinogens). A bad trip on LSD refers to feeling very anxious and, usually, a sense of panic. When this occurs, the LSD user is usually talked out of the panic by calm and gentle comments reassuring the person that the feelings are due to the drug and that they will go away. Another negative effect of LSD is the "flashback," which can last a few seconds, minutes, or, less frequently, many hours. A flashback refers to having an experience very similar to that felt when taking LSD, but after the drug has worn off. Sometimes flashbacks occur days, weeks, or even months after taking LSD. Occurrences of flashbacks usually decrease over a period of months, but can reoccur for as long as five years (Doweiko, 1999). Negative effects from PCP include drug-induced psychosis and unusually high blood pressure that can lead to a stroke. Users of ecstasy might also experience drug-induced psychosis, as well as anxiety attacks, feelings of rage, and insomnia. Overdoses of any of these drugs can lead to very severe problems involving kidney failure, heart problems, and visual hallucinations.

Because of the nature of the strong reaction to these drugs, individuals tend to use them experimentally and are far less likely to become addicted to them than are users of cocaine and opiates such as heroin.

## BARBITURATES

Prescribed by physicians as sedatives to help patients sleep, barbiturates are central nervous system depressants, like alcohol, and in small doses they can can produce relaxation and intoxication. Like other addictive drugs, individuals can develop tolerance and dependence. Many people use barbiturates as sleeping pills. Barbiturates have been divided into classes depending on how long lasting they are. If people find themselves taking barbiturates regularly, they can experience withdrawal effects similar to those of alcohol including tremors, vomiting, problems sleeping, and possible hallucinations. Withdrawal and abstinence can be very difficult because seizures and brain damage can result. Longer lasting barbiturates tend to have longer withdrawal periods than do shorter acting barbiturates (Doweiko, 1999).

## AMPHETAMINES

Whereas barbiturates are depressants, amphetamines are stimulants. Those who take these drugs are likely to feel more alert, better able to concentrate, and able to work long hours. Individuals can also feel anxious and jittery. Amphetamines tend to increase blood pressure, slow the heart rate, and increase respiration. Sometimes they can produce hallucinations. The effect of amphetamines tends to last several hours. Other negative effects include insomnia, anxiety, and hostility. Some evidence exists that amphetamines can cause physical damage to brain cells and can produce psychotic reactions. Some negative effects include heart problems. Although most amphetamine users do not become addicted, a number of users do, because amphetamines are potentially emotionally and physically addictive (Doweiko, 1999). Other amphetamines are sometimes used as appetite suppressants, and some users develop anorexia. Treatment of amphetamine abuse is similar to that for cocaine abuse.

## STEROIDS

Athletes have used anabolic steroids to increase muscle size and decrease body fat. Anabolic steroids also have several medical uses, such as reducing inflammation, controlling allergic reactions, and treating certain kinds of anemia. However, there are several negative side effects when steroids are abused and recommended dosage levels are exceeded. For males, this can include breast enlargement, increased frequency of erections, or continual erections. Women might experience irregular menstrual periods, reduction in breast size, or deepening of the voice. Steroid abuse can also interfere with liver and kidney function. Steroids might play a role in the development of heart disease and in strokes. Steroid abuse has been associated with the experience of some symptoms of psychosis and aggressive

**detoxification programs**
Programs that are designed to help individuals withdraw from drugs, with emphasis on medical treatment.

or violent behaviors. Treating steroid abuse requires close medical supervision to help abusers follow a gradual **detoxification program.** Withdrawing from steroids is somewhat similar to withdrawing from cocaine, and individuals can be depressed, have sleep and appetite disturbances, and experience fatigue and anorexia.

## TREATMENT OF DRUG ADDICTION

**Intervention** The process by which individuals close to a patient in need of drug or alcohol treatment make clear to him or her that treatment is needed.

Many people who are addicted to drugs will not seek treatment on their own. Frequently a process known as an **intervention,** in which individuals close to the patient make clear to him or her that treatment is needed, is used. The purpose of this is to confront the addict's denial and rationalization so that immediate treatment can be sought. Usually this intervention is supervised by a professional who works with chemical dependency patients. Involved in the intervention are family members, friends, and possibly coworkers who can contribute to helping the addict get treatment. The intervention process is planned and rehearsed so that individuals can tell about specific incidents in which the addict's behavior interfered with his or her functioning. The purpose is not to criticize the addict or to manipulate the addict, but to inform the addict that treatment is necessary and to get the addict started in treatment. Having many people involved in the intervention rather than only one is very helpful. Sometimes that is not possible, and another form of intervention is the "either/or" approach. An example is "either you stop smoking marijuana or I will fire you." When this is done, the employer needs to follow through on the threat for it to have any impact.

Treatment for chemical dependency—which includes alcohol, marijuana, cocaine, heroin, and possibly other drugs, or a variety of drugs used in combination—can be quite complex. One issue is whether or not individuals should be hospitalized (inpatient treatment) or can live at home and have treatment at a clinic (outpatient treatment). A significant problem with inpatient treatment is its cost. Costs, often covered by health plans or insurance, can exceed $1,000 a day. Although outpatient treatment is much less expensive, it does not offer the same structure and support, particularly when medical interventions are needed, that inpatient drug addiction programs do.

**therapeutic community**
A program designed to help individuals change their lifestyles, abstain from drugs, start working, and develop positive attitudes to society.

Trying to choose from inpatient treatment programs can be quite difficult, because there are several. Detoxification programs are generally designed to help individuals withdraw from drugs and are not designed to help the individual with other addiction problems. The **therapeutic community** is a program to help individuals change their life styles, abstain

---

## Problems and Solutions

---

### What treatments are available to help friends or family that are addicted to drugs?

Interventions involving several people close to the person are planned to confront the person's drug abuse and deal with denial.

Many treatment programs are available:

- Inpatient hospitalization (detoxification)
- Outpatient treatment
- Half-way houses
- Alcoholics Anonymous
- Rational Recovery
- Secular Organizations of Sobriety
- Women for Sobriety

---

from drugs, start working, and develop positive attitudes to society. Often, these programs last between one and three years (DeLeon, 1994). Hospital treatment is another approach, with some hospitals being totally devoted to drug and alcohol treatment and other hospitals devoting units for this purpose. A compromise between inpatient and outpatient is the halfway house, where individuals live for a time after inpatient treatment, while working or going to school in the community. Research about which type of program works best is not clear. Some research supports outpatient treatment for individuals who might not need medical supervision and very close monitoring.

Many people have found that self-help groups have been very important in their continued recovery from alcohol or drug abuse. By far, the most well-known and popular is that of Alcoholics Anonymous. Characteristics of AA are that it is an educational rather than a therapeutic group. Individuals who join accept responsibility for their behavior. There is an emphasis on anonymity and confidentiality in the process of sharing their experience with alcohol and their inability to control alcohol. Members work to help themselves and each other abstain from alcohol. The 12-step AA program focuses on individuals admitting that they are unable to manage their lives and are powerless over alcohol. The program has a spiritual emphasis with a reliance on prayer, meditation, and God's

**Narcotics Anonymous** A group similar to AA; open to individuals who are abusing any drugs, including alcohol.

will to provide help to become abstinent from alcohol. Those who participate in AA have sponsors who will help them maintain sobriety. When individuals feel the urge to drink, they can call on other AA members for support and help. Another group with similar goals is **Narcotics Anonymous,** which is open to individuals who might be abusing any drug or drugs including alcohol.

Other groups have been formed, partly because some individuals have objected to the emphasis that Alcoholics Anonymous has put on spiritual growth and God. Two of these groups are Rational Recovery and Secular Organizations of Sobriety. Another organization, Women for Sobriety, was formed because a number of women felt that AA programs have not emphasized the specific problems of recovering addicts who are female. The variety of inpatient, outpatient, and support group treatment that is available attests both to the significance of the problem of drug abuse and the creative ways of helping other individuals with these significant problems.

**Q 11.9** For most personal problems, an intervention by other people is often not necessary, but for alcohol and drug abuse it often is. Why do you think this is?

Because alcohol (and drug) abuse affects the family as well as the individual, other programs have been developed for family members. Al-Anon is for husbands and wives who are dealing with an alcoholic spouse. Al-A-Teen is for teenage children of alcoholics. These programs provide an opportunity for individuals to share their experiences and problems, and learn how to cope with these problems. In these groups, individuals encourage each other and provide support.

**Q 11.10** How would you feel if you were part of an intervention group that was confronting a friend or family member with drug or alcohol abuse?

## SUMMARY

Substance abuse is a significant problem for a sizeable minority of Americans. In this chapter, cigarette smoking and alcohol abuse are described in some detail. Because these two legalized drugs create a problem for a large number of Americans, and because these drugs are readily available, my focus has been on the types of problems that they create for people, as well as solutions. Both cigarettes and alcohol present considerable issues, affecting the respiratory system and the heart. Alcohol brings about changes in behavior that create problems for those who use this drug and their families and associates. Because smoking and drinking can create difficulties for individuals, I have described treatment issues specific to each of these substances.

Although not abused as frequently as cigarettes and alcohol are, marijuana, cocaine, heroin, hallucinogens, barbiturates, amphetamines and steroids can become very significant problems for people who abuse these drugs. Of all the illegal drugs, marijuana is used most frequently. Although its negative effects might not be as severe as those of cocaine and heroin, a number of psychological and physiological problems can develop. Because there is an initial rush or feeling of pleasure when using cocaine and heroin, these extremely addictive drugs are often difficult to treat, and abusers might relapse a number of times. Other drugs that are used less frequently—hallucinogens, barbiturates, amphetamines, and steroids— present their own specific health problems and treatment issues.

Treatment for drug addiction presents problems that other psychological disturbances do not. Often it is necessary to provide an "intervention" for a substance abuser, where he or she can be confronted about the substance abuse. After that, the individual can be directed to inpatient or outpatient treatment. Another useful source of assistance with drug and alcohol addiction problems are self-help groups, such as Alcoholics Anonymous.

## RECOMMENDED READINGS

*Concepts of Chemical Dependency* (4th ed.)
Doweiko, H. E. (Brooks/Cole, 1999)
> An up-to-date, very thorough description of drug usage and abuse, this book provides many facts, including details about drugs and their effects on the body and the mind. Suggestions for treatment for different types of chemical dependency are described in some detail in this book.

## RECOMMENDED WEB SITES

*Go Ask Alice!*
http://www.alice.columbia.edu/
> This is a popular source of information that was developed by the Columbia University Health Education Program and designed for undergraduate students. Alice! browsers will find direct answers to questions about relationships, sexuality and sexual health, fitness and nutrition, alcohol and drug consumption, and other topics.

*The QuitNet Community*
http://www.quitnet.org/
> Sponsored by the Boston University School of Public Health, this site is designed to help individuals who wish to quit smoking and stop using tobacco. A range of excellent resources includes an online support community that can help you stop smoking.

*National Institute of Alcohol Abuse and Alcoholism*
http://www.niaaa.nih.gov/
> The NIAAA produces a bulletin, *Alcohol Alert,* which includes topics on alcoholism. The site includes a large data base on alcoholism.

# MANAGING STRESS

**stress** Emotional or physical strain that can interfere with coping with situations.

**Stress** is the perception of pressure or strain arising from an event or events. Sometimes the effects of stress are physiological and sometimes emotional or psychological. "This is stressing me out" is a common response to different events, individuals, or situations. Although this chapter will focus on managing stress that causes problems and difficulties for individuals, stress is not necessarily negative. Without stress in our lives, there would be no challenge, just boredom. A positive example of stress is sports. Before running in a 100 meter dash, a person might experience a knot in her stomach, tightness in her shoulders, and worry about her ability to run her fastest. Such stress is common in athletic events, where individuals enjoy participating, look forward to the events, and put in many hours of difficult practice to improve their skills. Performing music is another example. Musicians often feel the "jitters" shaky, irritable, tightness in parts of their body, before they go out to perform. Yet their love for music is very strong, and they enjoy playing, performing, and listening.

Stress affects three components of how we respond to events: thoughts (cognitions), behaviors, and feelings. Stress can affect individuals so that they express thoughts, behavior, and feelings that can be categorized as depression, anxiety, and anger. Psychologists have developed methods to help individuals change. I will use examples to illustrate how therapists use these techniques to help clients, and how you can use them when you feel depressed, anxious, or angry.

## THE PRESSURES OF STRESS AND THEIR EFFECTS

Potential stressors, positive or negative, are all around us, and we can feel the effects in many varied ways. First I will discuss the external pressures, events that we experience, and then the internal pressures—how we react, such as feeling tense and frustrated. Often this frustration is due to conflicts about choices that we have. The mind and body are not two separate entities: When we react psychologically, there are often physiological effects that we may or may not notice.

### External Stress

We have many stressors in our lives—daily ones that occur at school, at work, and with relationships. Many daily stressors are predictable but others are unpredictable. School stressors include registering for courses, taking exams, finding a parking place, writing papers, finding a book in the library, and so forth. Work stressors vary depending on the job, but often include urgency to complete a task, conflict with coworkers or bosses, and pressures to produce high-quality work. Stress in relationships has been discussed in Chapter 5, as it relates to relationships with parents and family members, and in Chapter 6, with regard to friends and romantic partners. Environmental stressors are often unavoidable: air pollution, very hot or cold temperatures, snow, rain, floods, hurricanes, and so forth.

Life events—some that we predict and some that we can't—also contribute to stress as well as to enjoyment. Life events such as graduation, christenings, bar mitzvahs, and marriages are events that we plan for. Unpredictable traumatic events include automobile accidents, sudden physical illness, death of loved ones, being fired from a job, or being transferred to another city. Such unplanned transitions and crises can cause considerable stress. Generally, predictable life events have less negative impact than do unpredictable life events.

## Internal Stress

**frustration** A form of internal stress; occurs when individuals encounter interference with the pursuit of a goal.

When events happen to us, we perceive or experience them in different ways. Some common reactions to stress include feeling a sense of frustration, being in conflict, and doubting ourselves (Weiten & Lloyd, 2000). One form of internal stress is **frustration.** When individuals pursue a goal, and they encounter interference with the goal, frustration often occurs. For example, if you are in a hurry to get to work, and there is a traffic jam, your goal of getting to work has been thwarted, and you are likely to feel frustrated. If you wish to get an "A" in a course, and you get a "C–" on an exam, you are likely to feel significant frustration. When individuals don't get the jobs that they want, or the prize they want, they are likely to feel extreme frustration.

Conflict occurs when individuals have choices. These choices might be minor or very significant. Often the choices will be between more than two possibilities. For example, What courses should you take next semester? A useful way of examining choices was originally designed by Kurt Lewin (1935), who described three types of choices: approach-approach, avoidance-avoidance, and approach-avoidance conflicts.

**approach-approach conflict** A choice between two attractive goals.

- **Approach-approach conflict.** A choice between two attractive goals. Do I want to vacation in the mountains or at the beach? Do I want vanilla or chocolate ice cream? Pizza or steak? The red dress or the blue and white one? Watch a football game or a baseball game? These are only conflicts if you like both activities. If you like baseball and football, choosing between them is an approach-approach conflict. If you only like baseball, but not football, there is no conflict.

**avoidance-avoidance conflict** A choice between two unattractive goals.

- **Avoidance-avoidance conflict.** Sometimes you have to make choices between two unattractive goals. Should I stay in a job I don't like or should I leave and risk being unemployed? Should I eat snails or liver? Should I endure the pain from my bad knee, or should I endure the pain and inconvenience from the surgery that will be necessary to fix it? Clearly these types of decisions are more unpleasant than trying to resolve an approach-approach conflict.

- **Approach-avoidance conflict.** Often one goal has attractive and unattractive aspects. Should I ask out Frankie and risk being rejected? Should I buy that new television set and run up a debt on my credit card? Should I take a job that pays very well, but I have to work until 2:00 in the morning? With approach-avoidance conflicts, hesitation is natural. Decisions might be difficult, and it can be tempting to procrastinate and to put off a choice between different ways of pursuing a single goal.

When you feel frustration or conflict, you might also feel pressure. Sometimes pressure comes from other people saying "You really ought to do this or that," or "You really ought to work rather than go to school, so that you can pay off your debts." Sometimes the pressure comes from ourselves to do better at school, work longer hours to make more money, or drive a friend to the hospital so that we feel we are being helpful. Other pressures include the self criticism that can come with making decisions about stress. "I should work harder than I have at school." "I am really not working as hard as my other classmates." "I need to sell more cars this month." These pressures from ourselves often increase stress that already exists from external sources.

## Physiological Effects

When individuals experience frustration, conflict, or other emotions they are likely to experience physiological reactions as well. Common physical complaints that are caused by stress include tension and migraine headaches. Breathing is often affected as people breathe more quickly, or hyperventilate, if they are severely stressed. Sleeping can be affected: waking up frequently during the night, having difficulty falling asleep, or possibly sleeping too much. Stomach pain can result, which might include nausea, tightness, or queasiness in the stomach. Elimination problems can also result, including frequent urination, constipation, or diarrhea. Reactions to stressful events could include heart palpitations—feeling your heart beating fast. Stress can also cause heart problems such as irregular heart beat or heart disease. Physical tightness in the body is not uncommon with stress, including back pain, jaw tension, muscle cramps, and aches in the neck and shoulders. Other reactions to stress include skin problems, infectious diseases, loss of appetite, overeating, allergies, high

**approach-avoidance conflict** Choosing between attractive and unattractive aspects that are related to a goal.

**Q 12.1** What important external stressors can you identify in your life?

**Q 12.2** Give an example of how you experience internal stressors, frustration, conflict, or pressures, in your life?

**Q 12.3** How do you experience physiological stress? What types of external stressors tend to cause certain physiological reactions in you?

blood pressure, frequent colds, and sexual problems. Virtually every part of the body can be affected by stress.

Stress is not only experienced in physical ways, but it is also experienced in our thoughts, our behaviors, and our feelings. The next section will examine these in more detail.

## THE EXPERIENCE OF STRESS

Individuals experience stress in a great variety of ways. Often they have thoughts that express and sometimes aggravate stress such as, "I have to do better than that," "I can't fail," and "My parents will never forgive me if I have to leave school." Often stress is experienced in behaviors, such as snapping at someone, breathing quickly, or tightening the neck and shoulder muscles. Another behavior that seems like a nonbehavior is giving up or not reacting. For example, not taking an exam or not showing up for work is a behavior. Stress can also be experienced emotionally. Among the more common emotional reactions to stress are fear or anxiety, depression, and anger. I will discuss all of these in more detail here.

### Thoughts and Stress

**cognitive distortion**
Systematic errors in reasoning, often stemming from early childhood errors in reasoning; an indication of inaccurate or ineffective use of reasoning.

Aaron Beck (1976, 1991) has been a major contributor to our understanding of how negative thoughts can produce human problems, such as stress. Beck refers to the types of thinking that individuals do that create stress in their lives as **cognitive distortions.** Freeman (1993) has described several of these that represent errors in thinking that lead to more worry, fear, anxiety, and upset in an individual. We will examine five of these: catastrophizing, dichotomous thinking, mind reading, overgeneralizing, and labeling. Another approach to understanding the importance of thinking in creating stress is the work of Albert Ellis (1962, 1993), who has emphasized how irrational thinking can not only be a reaction to stress but can also be compounded to increase stress dramatically. Each of these concepts is described in greater detail here.

**catastrophizing**
Exaggerating events so that an individual experiences more fear or stress.

- **Catastrophizing.** Events are exaggerated, so that the individual experiences more fear or stress. For example, "I know when I meet the sales manager, I am going to say something dumb that's going to affect my job. I know I will say something that will make her not want to consider me for advancement." Thus the individual makes the meeting with the sales manager into a feared situation, rather than just a meeting that he can cope with.

---

## Problems and Solutions

*How do I know if the way I am thinking about things is causing me problems?*

- Are you catastrophizing?
- Thinking dichotomously (all or nothing)?
- Reading others' minds?
- Overgeneralizing?
- Using negative labels?
- "Musturbating"?

---

**dichotomous thinking**
Believing that something has to be exactly as we want it to be or it or we will be failures; sometimes called black and white or all-or-nothing thinking.

- **Dichotomous thinking.** By thinking that something has to be exactly as we want it to be or it is a failure, we are engaging in all-or-nothing or dichotomous thinking. This thinking puts things into two categories, all good or all bad, or black or white. For example, if you say, "Unless I get an A– on this exam, I have failed," you are engaging in dichotomous thinking. You are saying, in a sense, that grades of A-, B+, and B are failures. Focusing on learning the information, and performing well, will produce less stress than saying, "I have to get an A on the exam or I am a failure."

**mind reading** Believing that we know how another person thinks.

- **Mind reading.** When I say, "I know that she doesn't like me," I am most likely engaging in mind reading because it is virtually impossible to know how another person thinks. Another example is, "I know the professor is going to give me a D on the paper." This thought creates stress because mind reading is almost always in a negative direction—we believe that people will have negative thoughts about us.

**overgeneralization**
Taking one or two negative events and making rules based on them.

- **Overgeneralizing.** When individuals take one or two negative events and make rules based on them, they are overgeneralizing. For example, a high school student might conclude, "Because I did poorly on my first algebra exam, I can't do math." Another example is the person who thinks because "Joy and John were angry at me, all of my friends won't like me, and won't have anything to do with me." In this way a negative experience gets turned into a general rule that can affect future behavior and put stress on an individual.

**labeling** Ascribing negative qualities to oneself based on some errors or mistakes.

- **Labeling.** Somewhat similar to overgeneralizing, labeling is ascribing negative qualities to oneself based on some errors or mistakes. If I have some awkward incidences with acquaintances, I could conclude, "I am unpopular. I'm a loser," rather than say, "I felt awkward when I talked to Maggie." Labeling myself as a loser is a very broad, sweeping statement, which might make me feel that I can't do many other things. I might feel stress as a result of the helpless feeling that can develop.

**musturbation** A word coined by Albert Ellis that refers to the stress individuals put on themselves by saying they "must" or "have to" do something.

Albert Ellis bases much of his approach on how he sees individuals responding to an unpleasant event. He gives many examples of how individuals experience an event, have negative beliefs about the consequence of the event and thus experience stress. When individuals say, "I must be loved by everyone I know, I must be competent at everything I do," "Things must go the way I want them to," they are engaging in **musturbation.** By using phrases such as "must," and "have to," individuals are increasing the amount of stress that they are experiencing. Ellis shows his clients how they can change their philosophy of life and lower their stress level by changing "musts" to less demanding terms like "it would be good if."

**Q 12.4** Try to assess if you put stress on yourself through the use of cognitive distortions or irrational thoughts. Think of some recent activities and see if you can identify some of the problems in thinking that have been described.

Beck and Freeman have identified several other cognitive distortions as well, and Albert Ellis has discussed irrational thoughts in great detail. These therapists believe that one of the major ways to help people solve their problems is by helping them first understand their negative thinking. Some of the ways that these researchers use to help individuals will be discussed in a later section. Now behavioral indicators of stress will be discussed.

## Behaviors and Stress

Stress can have a negative effect on one's behaviors, the actions that people take or fail to take. For example, Baumeister (1984) has found that when individuals think too much about what they're doing, it can negatively affect their performance. Baumeister and his colleagues studied a number of situations in which athletes might have been thinking too much about what they were doing, and might have "choked under pressure," which negatively affected their performance. When individuals need to make judgments under stress, their judgments can be rash, or indecisive. Conflicts (approach-approach, avoidance-avoidance, and approach-avoidance) can create stress for individuals so that they rush too soon to make a judgment or vacillate for so long that it might be too late to make a decision. Procrastinating is an example of stressful behavior. If you are so worried about an exam that you keep putting off your studying for that exam, stress is affecting your studying behavior in a negative way.

**Q 12.5** When you are in a stressful situation, what stressful behaviors are you likely to experience? Give an example of one or two events and the stressful behavior that you experienced.

The physiological responses that individuals have because of stress are also an example of a behavioral reaction to stress. Common examples are breathing quickly, rapid heart beat, nausea or knots in your stomach, sweatiness, and headaches. Individuals who are very afraid of taking exams are likely to experience these behavioral reactions to a stressful event (the exam).

## Feelings and Stress

When individuals are experiencing stress, they are likely to feel a variety of emotions at the same time. Lazarus (1991, 1993) has identified a number of emotions that are related to stress, including disgust, envy, guilt, and jealousy. But perhaps the most common are anxiety, depression, and anger.

**anxiety** Typically an unpleasant emotional state resulting from stress or conflict.

- **Anxiety.** This is perhaps the most common reaction to a stressful event. For example, if you were in the middle of a field during a lightening storm (a stressful event), you might experience considerable anxiety. If a drunk driver is honking his horn and is following you closely in his car, fear or anxiety is likely to be a strong emotion. If the Dean of Students or an employer sends a message saying that he or she wants to see you, you might be likely to experience anxiety or fear rather than any other emotion. When we have a conflict, especially an approach-avoidance conflict, we might be likely to experience anxiety. For example, "Should I have a back operation or not?" is likely to create anxiety because great stress is produced by considering the approach alternative—have the back operation—and the avoidance alternative—put it off and wait to see if things get better.

**depression** Often characterized by anxiety, dejection, and less physical activity, depression is a common reaction to stress.

- **Depression.** Depression or similar emotions, such as dejection, grief, or sadness are likely to be due to being frustrated by stressful events. Having a potential romantic partner say that he or she is no longer interested in being with you can certainly result in sadness. A poor grade on a test might bring about dejection. Losing a job, a more severe situation, can lead to depression. Clearly, situations such as the death of a brother or mother can lead to very long lasting grief and depressed feelings.

**anger** Feelings of rage, annoyance, and irritation.

- **Anger.** Some stressful events are likely to bring about annoyance, or stronger feelings, such as, anger or rage. Having someone bump into you in a crowded store might lead to a feeling of annoyance. Being yelled at by your boss, a clearly stressful event, can lead to anger. Delays because of traffic accidents and traffic jams can bring about strong reactions of anger and rage, referred to as "road rage." Often when we experience frustration, anger follows.

Certain stressful events are likely to evoke different emotions in people. People might feel many emotions with some events, but just one with other events. For example, the death of a loved one might bring feelings of anger, anxiety, grief, and perhaps guilt. Given the same situation, people differ greatly in the type of emotions they are likely to experience.

**Q 12.6** What are your emotional reactions to stress? Describe two stressful events and how they affected you emotionally.

**Q 12.7** Are these emotions typical of your response to stress? Explain.

Some people tend to blame themselves for an event, such as doing poorly on an exam, and are likely to feel sadness or depression. Other people place the blame outside of themselves, for example, on the teacher for constructing a poor test. As a result, they are more likely to experience anger. Also, if you have recently experienced a series of stressful events, you are likely to feel heightened emotionality.

# DEALING WITH COMMON STRESS-RELATED PROBLEMS

In this section, I will examine some different methods of using techniques that psychotherapists have developed to help individuals deal with anxiety, depression, and anger. When looking at ways of handling anxiety, we will focus particularly on methods used by behavior therapists. When examining coping with depressed feelings, we will focus on cognitive techniques that Aaron Beck and Albert Ellis developed. When examining how to deal with anger, we will look at dealing with feelings, as well as cognitive and behavioral methods. Many people use approaches that will help them that have behavioral, cognitive, and affective (feeling) aspects. We will explore some common behavioral, cognitive, and affective techniques that help individuals with a variety of situations. You then will be able to see if some of these approaches would help you in dealing with stressful situations.

## Behavioral Methods for Relieving Stress

A behavioral approach to helping individuals with stress focuses on changing the actions that people take. Over many years, those who practice behavior therapy have also incorporated cognitive and affective treatment methods. In this section, however, we will focus on three important suggestions from behavior therapy for relieving stress. They include positive reinforcement, exercise, and relaxation techniques.

**positive reinforcement** Strengthening the likelihood that a given behavior will reoccur by rewarding it.

**Positive reinforcement** has been an important concept throughout the study of behavioral psychology. Made popular by Skinner (1953), positive reinforcement increases the frequency of a behavior. If you wish someone to keep performing a behavior, you do something that will be designed to have them continue this behavior. For example, if you wish a nine-year-old girl to empty waste baskets throughout the house into a trash can in the backyard, you might give her a candy bar for doing this, give her some money, or thank her in a pleasant way. Some reinforcers will work better for some individuals than others. You can also use self-reinforcers. You might say to yourself "If I successfully finish studying Chapter 12, then I can watch *The Simpsons* on television for half an hour." Another example is

---

## Problems and Solutions

---

### How can I reduce stress by relaxing?

- Reward yourself (reinforcement).
- Exercise.
- Meditate.
- Use progressive relaxation.

---

**generalization** If an individual is reinforced for one behavior, that behavior can be broadened to include other behaviors.

to say, "After I have made three calls to prospective employers, I will be through for the afternoon and can go visit a friend."

Related to the concept of reinforcement is that of **generalization.** If an individual is reinforced for one behavior, then that reinforcement can generalize to (broaden to include) other behaviors. For example, when the nine-year-old girl is thanked for emptying the waste baskets, the thanking (positive reinforcement) might generalize to other behaviors, such as picking up books in her room. Likewise, if you reinforce yourself for reading Chapter 5, it might make it easier for you to read Chapter 6, and material for other courses. The reinforcement effects will take place gradually, so that one reinforcement will not be sufficient. Over time, if you reinforce your studying behavior, you should need less and less reinforcement. In this way, you can have a sense of accomplishment. Stress and worry are reduced by reinforcing achievements. Feeling good about what has been done is often accompanied by a sense of relaxation.

Exercise can have many benefits, among them are reduction of stress and anxiety (Sacks, 1993). Research has shown that a variety of types of fitness training can lead to positive changes in mood and self-concept as well as tension reduction. Physically, exercise can improve sleeping and digestion, which can be related to stress reduction. Physical fitness, such as muscular strength, endurance, and weight control, can also be indirectly related to stress reduction. Exercise can include sports such as running, swimming, bicycling, tennis, basketball, and skiing. Also, less strenuous activities such as walking and golf can help reduce stress. A typical exercise program includes regular activity for at least 30 minutes, 3 or 4 times a week. Such activity is generally increased gradually without over-stressing one's body. Because exercise can be inconvenient or painful, self-reinforcement for participation in exercise can be helpful.

**relaxation techniques**
Methods designed to slow down bodily processes, such as breathing and heart rate.

One of the most important techniques of behavior therapy that has been applied widely to many people is that of relaxation. **Relaxation techniques** are designed to slow down many bodily processes, such as breathing and heart rate. In addition, relaxation techniques decrease muscle tension so that muscles can become less cramped and feel more comfortable. Certain activities help you relax muscles and slow your breathing and heart rate. Listening to slow music often has a relaxing effect on people. Distracting oneself from stressors by reading a magazine or novel can also serve a similar purpose. A vacation is designed to relax individuals by removing them from stressors and providing them with activity that is stimulating, yet not too stressful. There are also more formal methods of relaxation that individuals use to reduce stress in their lives.

**meditation**  A means of relaxing and seeking higher psychological or religious levels of self-development that has been used widely in Asia.

**bonpu zazen**  A basic method of meditation based on Zen Buddhism.

**Meditation** helps individuals relax. Developed in Asia as a means of seeking higher psychological or religious levels of self-development, meditation has proved to be helpful for those who wish to reduce their stress. Reynolds (1980) has effectively taken procedures from the East and Westernized them. He suggests that **bonpu zazen** is an excellent way for individuals who have not meditated before to start. Based on Zen Buddhism, bonpu zazen is the first level of Zen meditation. Reynolds recommends that meditation can be practiced in a straight-backed chair by following these instructions for 10 to 30 minutes, preferably twice a day.

> In bonpu sitting, the person concentrates on his breathing, mentally counting each breath. There are various styles of bonpu sitting, and different masters have different preferences. One can count each inhalation and exhalation up to 10, then start over; one can count only exhalations; one can extend the exhalations and the internal count as ooooone, then twoooooo, threeeee and so forth. (Reynolds, 1980, p. 97)

This method of meditation, and other similar ones, tend to help individuals clear their minds, and just focus on breathing. Walsh (1981) provides evidence that repeated meditation can give individuals a sense of peace, tranquility, and equanimity. Meditation has also been shown to reduce heart rate, breathing rate, and other physiological signs of stress.

**progressive relaxation**  A method that has individuals tense and relax muscle groups, such as arms, face, neck, to achieve deeper and deeper levels of relaxation.

Another method, called **progressive relaxation,** was first developed by Jacobson (1938). Basically this involves tensing and relaxing muscle groups, including arms, face, neck, shoulders, chest, stomach, and legs to achieve deeper and deeper levels of relaxation. Behavior therapists such as Wolpe (1990) often spend five or six sessions to teach their clients relaxation. To relax, finding a comfortable position in a quiet place is important. The individual should have a quiet attitude, focusing on relaxing and redirecting attention to relaxing when attention wanders from the exercise. Relaxation techniques can focus on the entire body all at once, but many approaches take one muscle at a time as in the following:

> Sit back as comfortably as you can. As you relax like that, tense up your right fist, feel the tension in your right fist, wrist, and forearm. Just feel the tension in your fist. Now, let go. Relax your right fist. Straighten out your fingers and allow your fist, wrist, and forearm to relax. Feel the comfortable heaviness that comes with relaxing your right fist. Just let your fist relax. And now repeat that once more. Tighten up your right fist, feel the tension in the fist, forearm, feel the tightness . . . and now, let your fist, wrist, forearm, relax.

Meditation and relaxation techniques tend to produce similar results. They bring about a sense of peace and calmness, along with physiological changes, such as a slowing of the heart rate and breathing. To use these successfully, you must practice them for some time on an almost daily basis. Audiotapes for these purposes are available commercially. Listening to these tapes, some with quiet musical backgrounds, can provide a sense of relaxation that might generalize to other daily activities.

Behavioral methods can be used with a wide variety of emotional problems and disorders. Perhaps they are best known for helping individuals who are experiencing a great deal of anxiety. Reinforcement, generalization, modeling, and relaxation methods have all been used successfully in helping people who experience anxiety in their daily life.

In the following example of Karen, I will use several methods that could help her with the anxiety that she feels in her life.

> Karen is a nineteen-year-old student, who is in her third semester at a local community college. Karen is very concerned about her classes and her grades because she very much wants to transfer to a four-year university where she can study marketing. Karen's parents own a small printing business, which they've owned for more than 25 years. Karen has worked with them and would like eventually to work full-time with them or start out on her own. She very much wants to be successful in her work.
>
> Karen is a small, slender woman, about five feet tall, weighing less than one hundred pounds. She has long, dark hair and her facial expression is earnest and concerned. As she speaks, she leans forward and speaks quickly in a high-pitched voice.
>
> *Karen:* I am really worried about what college I'm going to get into next year. It's not just a matter of sending out applications, it's everything. When I come to the parking lot here, I feel myself starting to get nervous. It's bad. When I go to classes, it's probably the worst, especially math class. When I study, it starts up again. I'm nervous when I'm studying, and math is the worst. It doesn't matter whether I'm studying at home or

at school. And I really try to study all the time. My parents are always saying, "Come on, take a break," "Karen why don't you relax a little bit." Easy for them to say, but really hard for me to do, I'm so, so worried.

*RS:* Math class seems to be really bad for you. (I want to learn more about the anxiety that she feels when her stress is particularly great.)

*Karen:* I worry walking over to that class. It's one of those new classrooms, in a new building. There are the usual tablet arm chairs, one window real high up and a huge blackboard that runs wall to wall across the room. The room isn't very big and there are only about 25 of us in the class. I usually try to get there early so that I can get the seat closest to the door. One time, I was late, I was talking to a friend, it only happened once. Then I had to sit way on the other side. I was a mess. (Karen starts to cry).

*RS:* It was one of the most difficult times for you? (I want to hear more about Karen's experience of anxiety.)

*Karen:* It was terrible. I felt flushed all over, my hands started to sweat, and I had to do everything to keep from crying. I started to breathe fast and to feel my heart beating. Just talking about it now makes me feel those same feelings all over again.

*RS:* Just take a moment now and sit back comfortably and quietly. Take in a gentle breath and let it out slowly. . . . Just let yourself relax into the chair and breathe in and out slowly and easily. Feel the comfortable relaxation as you exhale, as you let yourself relax. (I have decided to help Karen relax somewhat now so that we can talk more about her concerns. To do that, I have used a very small portion of a relaxation exercise.)

*Karen:* That feels better for now. This is such a problem for me, I want it so bad, to be able to go to a good college and get a bachelor's in marketing.

*RS:* You seem to have such strong goals for yourself, they really seem to preoccupy your thoughts. (I want to draw attention to the role of stress in Karen's life.)

*Karen:* Yes, I want this more than anything. My brother didn't do well in school and I want to. I have visions of being a successful business woman.

*RS:* There are times when wanting it so much seems to interfere with getting what you want. (I want to return to her problems with stress).

*Karen:* Yeah I wish I could be like Ginny. She gets "A's," studies some, but seems to be so calm and collected about it.

*RS:* Tell me more about how Ginny studies and does her work. (Ginny might serve as a model for good study habits without stress.)

*Karen:* She just comes to class, we talk, she always seems prepared, but she has time for her work, for her boyfriend, and seems to spend about two or three hours a day for studying. I must spend double that, easy.

*RS:* She seems to have a different view of studying than you. (I'm looking for ways that Ginny's behavior can serve as a model for Karen.)

*Karen:* She sure is different. She has more confidence, she seems to know that she'll do well, go on to a four-year school, and doesn't worry about being successful, the way I do.

*RS:* There is a calmness about her that seems to work for her. (I am pointing out some aspects of Ginny as a model for calm behavior, that may be helpful to Karen).

*Karen:* Yes, the way she comes into class. She sits down, opens her notes, looks at the teacher, smiles a lot.

*RS:* You could try that, it might work for you.

*Karen:* You know, I tried something like that once, I guess I'm a little embarrassed to talk about it, but I almost used her posture and sat down the way she did. For a few minutes, that worked for a while.

*RS:* That's great. Maybe you should try it again; it worked once. I bet it can work other times too. (I am reinforcing what was a positive experience for Karen, so that she can feel less stress in similar situations.)

*Karen:* Yes I think there are times when I can do this. Not all classes, but maybe in the easier ones like English; it would be a good start.

*RS:* That sounds great, acting calmer in English class may help you focus more on your work and what the teacher says. (Again I am reinforcing Karen's idea, and I particularly like her suggestion for acting calmer in an easier situation. This way she can gradually generalize her behavior to a more difficult situation such as math class.)

**Q 12.8** In what situations do you feel the most stress?

**Q 12.9** Choose at least one of the three methods (reinforcement, modeling, or relaxation) to show how you might be able to change a stressful situation to one that might be less stressful.

This small example shows how reinforcement and relaxation techniques can be used to help decrease stress, and more specifically, symptoms of anxiety. Of course, it's going to take more than this brief conversation with Karen to help her calm down and concentrate on her work rather than her tension, but the previous conversation shows how methods can be used that counter stress and teach calmness and relaxation.

## *Using Cognitive Methods*

Cognitive methods focus on different ways to change thinking. In a previous section, I described how negative thinking (cognitive distortions) could cause stress. Here we will look at ways for decreasing stress. Some common techniques that cognitive therapists use include decatastrophizing, challenging dichotomous thinking, challenging mind reading, challenging overgeneralizations, and reattribution. These approaches stem from the work of Aaron Beck (1976). Some similar methods have been described by Albert Ellis (1993) for challenging beliefs and disputing irrational thoughts.

**decatastrophizing**
A method of challenging an individual when he or she exaggerates a feared outcome.

- **Decatastrophizing.** When individuals catastrophize or exaggerate a feared outcome, it is helpful to challenge it. One useful approach

---

## *Problems and Solutions*

---

### *How can I change distorted thinking or irrational beliefs?*

- Decatastrophize
- Challenge dichotomous thinking
- Challenge mind reading
- Challenge generalizations
- Relabel negative thoughts
- Dispute your irrational beliefs

---

is the "what if" techniques. If someone says that he or she is very afraid that X would happen, a rejoinder is, "What if that did happen?" Here is an example.

*Joan:* If I don't make the Dean's list this semester, things will be over for me. I'll be a mess; I'll never get into law school.

*RS:* And what if you don't make the Dean's list, what would happen?

*Joan:* Well, it would be terrible, I don't know what I would do.

*RS:* Well, what would happen if you didn't make Dean's list?

*Joan:* I guess it would depend on what my grades would be. There's a big difference between getting all "Bs" and not making the Dean's list and getting all "Cs."

*RS:* And if you got all "Bs"?

*Joan:* I guess it wouldn't be so bad, I could do better the next semester.

*RS:* And if you got three "Cs" and two "Bs"?

*Joan:* That's really not likely. I'm doing much better in my classes. It might hurt my chances for law school, but I might be able to recover.

Asking "What if it did happen?" seems to help Joan examine her situation carefully, and see alternatives to handling it.

- **Challenging dichotomous thinking.** When people describe things as all or none, or all black, or all white, they are indulging in dichotomous thinking. Challenging that through **scaling** turns a dichotomy into a continuum. Thus, in the example with Joan, grades can be seen as varying in degree; Joan will respond differently to the possibility of

---

**challenging dichotomous thinking** Methods used to help individuals see that they are turning events into all good or all bad options.

**scaling** Turning a dichotomy into a continuum by using a numerical scale, such as one to ten rather than just zero and ten.

getting a 3.0 rather than a 3.25 than to the possibility of being on the Dean's list or not on the Dean's list. The discussion about "Bs" and "Cs" changes Joan's all or nothing approach to one with various points along a line.

**challenging mind read-ing** Asking individuals who assume they know what someone else is thinking, how they know this.

- **Challenging mind reading.** When individuals assume that they know what someone else is thinking, it is helpful to ask them how they know this.

*Byron:* I know Peter doesn't like me, when I saw him the other day he just ignored me.

*RS:* How do you know that he saw you?

*Byron:* Well I'm not really sure. He was talking to someone else, and we passed on the way to class.

*RS:* And if he did see you, how do you know that he was thinking that he didn't like you.

*Byron:* Well, I guess I don't.

My challenge to Byron, allows him to question his assumptions and see that they might not be correct.

**challenging generaliza-tions** Examining or ques-tioning the accuracy of absolute statements that individuals make.

- **Challenging generalizations.** When individuals generalize or make absolute statements, it is helpful to examine whether or not they are accurate. In the following examples, I challenge Molly's overgeneralizations.

*Molly:* I've been on this job about five weeks, and everyone at work is smarter than me.

*RS:* Everyone? Every single person at work is smarter than you?

*Molly:* There are a lot of people at work I don't know well at all. But my co-worker, Nicole, seems smarter; she seems to really know what's going on.

*RS:* Notice how we went from everyone at work being smarter than you to just Nicole.

*Molly:* I guess it is just Nicole. She had a lot of experience in my field and seems to know just what to do.

I have challenged Molly's belief that everyone at work is smarter than her. When we looked more closely at this belief, Molly could see that she did not have much evidence that this was true and really was focused on one person. It is natural to expect that a coworker who has worked at a place for several years is going to know more about the field than you would, if you had only worked there for five weeks.

**relabeling** Changing how individuals label them-selves in a negative way to more accurate terms.

- **Relabeling.** When individuals label themselves in a negative way, it is helpful to relabel more accurately.

TABLE **12.1** DISPUTING AND CHALLENGING IRRATIONAL BELIEFS

| Irrational Belief | Challenge and Disputation |
|---|---|
| Everything I do must be perfect. | It is reasonable to try to do your best, but expecting to be perfect is asking too much. |
| There is no need for me to suffer any pain or discomfort. | Although it is uncomfortable to be in pain, it is part of living, and it can be tolerated. |
| What might happen in the future could be very dangerous. | Getting anxious about the future will not help anything. When an event occurs then you can deal with it. |
| If I can't find the right solution to each problem, it will be terrible and awful. | You can be satisfied by using the best solution that you can find, not all problems have good solutions. |
| I must do well on the exam. | It would be nice to do well on the exam, but your life can go on if you don't do as well as you had hoped. |

*Mel:* I am such a retard. I can never do well in math.

*RS:* Calling yourself a retard doesn't seem to help. Let us look at the difficulties that you had in math and discuss them in more detail.

I am attempting to relabel Mel's label. It is better to say that he has had "difficulty with math" than to say that he is a "retard." Note also that Mel is generalizing about his math ability, and I am trying to challenge that.

- **Challenging and disputing irrational beliefs.** Albert Ellis spent more than fifty years helping people dispute and challenge irrational beliefs. Table 12.1 lists a few irrational beliefs and challenges to them.

As the examples in Table 12.1 show, for each irrational thought, there is a way to challenge the thought. By questioning ourselves, we can see that some of our assumptions are not always correct.

Although challenging irrational beliefs and thoughts can be used with many different kinds of problems, it has been applied most directly to people who are depressed and sad. They often have beliefs such as "Nobody loves me," "I can't do anything right," "Everything I do comes out badly," "I am so incompetent." All these general statements can be responded to by using cognitive techniques. Within the following example, I will show how I could challenge the beliefs of Paul, who can see no reason to go on with his life, because of some recent and not-so-recent events.

Paul has just broken up with his girlfriend of two years and has quit his partnership in a lawn-care business. Furthermore, he has found out that his parents are getting a divorce. Although he is twenty-three and has been out of high school for six years, he still is upset by school. He regrets not having done better in high school, and he regrets the fact that he did not go on for more education after high school.

*Paul:* I've been so miserable lately. Nothing in my life has gone right. I feel like everybody else is doing much better than I, and I am a failure.

**challenging and disputing irrational beliefs** A method challenging people's views that they must be perfect, that they should not suffer pain or discomfort, that the future could be dangerous, and that if they don't find a solution things will be terrible.

**Q 12.10** Can you give examples of when you catastrophize, use dichotomous thinking, mind read, overgeneralize, or label. Try to give at least one example of three of these.

**Q 12.11** For each of the examples of distorted thinking, can you show how you can use one of the methods to challenge your thinking?

**Q 12.12** Give two examples of irrational beliefs (using Ellis's ideas) and show a way to challenge each, using the examples in Table 12.1. (Hint: try using "must" or "have to" phrases in the irrational belief.)

*RS:* You seem so overwhelmed by things right now. (These are examples of overgeneralizations, catastrophizing, and dichotomous thinking, but I don't want to overwhelm him by challenging him on everything.)

*Paul:* Yes, everything is so overwhelming, and when I found out that my parents were going to get divorced after being married 28 years, that just floored me. I'll never be able to recover. It is the worst thing that could have happened to me.

*RS:* It really creates a problem for you, and it can seem unsurmountable to you. But maybe together we can see if there are some ways to deal with this. (The fact that Paul's parents are getting divorced is a very tragic event. However, Paul is making it so massively difficult that I have decided to decatastrophize it, to put it in a perspective where it can be worked on.)

*Paul:* It really is hard. Although I know I will still be able to see my parents. My father moved out of the apartment about six weeks ago and I've still been in contact with him, but I don't see him as much as I used to. My Mom is still upset, and it seems hard for me to comfort her.

*RS:* You seem to be trying to help your mother in the best way that you can. (Here I am using a behavioral technique, reinforcing Paul's action to help his mother, and acknowledging his effectiveness when he doesn't catastrophize.)

*Paul:* I know when I talk to my mother, my father doesn't like it. He thinks I'm a traitor to him, and I'm betraying him.

*RS:* How do you know that your father thinks that you're a traitor to him? (I am challenging Paul's mind reading.)

*Paul:* I don't really know what he thinks. He just has been bad mouthing my mother a lot. I really don't know what he thinks about me.

*RS:* It's helpful to reconsider your beliefs sometimes. Particularly when you feel bad. When you feel depressed, it really can color how you see things. (In a broad way, I am describing to Paul why it is not helpful to catastrophize or mind read.)

*Paul:* As much as I try to, I don't seem to be able to help my parents much. I just feel like I have failed in everything. Other people have succeeded, the people I went to high school with, the guys I hang around with. They all have good jobs. I'm a real failure.

*RS:* You seem to describe things like there are only two categories, success and failure. Everyone else is a success and you're a failure, according to your definition. (I am challenging Paul's dichotomous thinking.)

*Paul:* Sometimes it really seems that way, but really not always. I guess it isn't that clear cut. I've done pretty well in my lawn business and made a pretty good living, even though it isn't very prestigious. And some of my friends, I guess the ones I don't talk about, have had drug problems, and are really working in dumb jobs right now.

*RS:* It seems that you get a broader picture of things when you don't categorize them quite so narrowly.

*Paul:* I know it is better for me to look at things broadly, but it's really very difficult. Sometimes I just say to myself over and over again "I must be a success, I must not fail, I must not fail."

*RS:* It would be nicer if things get better, and I believe that we can work on them, so that will happen. But saying they "must" and "I have to," seem to do little more than put more pressure on you and contribute to you feeling more and more depressed. (I am challenging Paul's irrational thought that he "must" be a success, and I am helping him to take some of the pressure off of himself that he has put on.)

In these examples, I have used decatastrophizing, challenging mind reading, and dichotomous thinking to help Paul think accurately and feel less depressed. In a real situation, I would not use so many techniques so quickly. I do so here for illustration. Also, I might use some other approaches that might be behavioral. (I did use some reinforcement with him.) And I might respond more to his feeling of depression. However, the cognitive techniques that I've illustrated can be helpful for therapists to use with clients when they are depressed and they might help you when you feel depressed.

## Using Affective Methods with Stress

Although you can deal with feelings in a number of ways, one way stands out. Carl Rogers (1961, 1980) was the originator of person-centered therapy. His therapy almost wholly is oriented toward understanding the experience of the client as well as being aware of one's own experience. In discussing conditions for therapeutic change Rogers (1959) focuses on three important characteristics of a relationship: genuineness, acceptance, and empathy. These three concepts can be applied to understanding yourself and others. I will discuss these in more detail and then apply them to coping with your own anger as well as the anger of others. As a way of providing contrast to understanding awareness as an approach to anger, I will also examine some other approaches to anger. But first, let us examine Rogers's (1959, 1961, 1980) concepts of genuineness, acceptance, and empathy.

- **Genuineness.** Basically, genuineness refers to not being phony with yourself or others. To be genuine, you must know your own thoughts and feelings. By being aware of your own thoughts, you can develop genuineness in relationships with others. This does not mean an individual needs to be genuine in dealing with people in all situations. When buying a car, for example, you might have to negotiate, and being genuine would not be a good way to make a deal. Being aware

**Q 12.13** Describe two times when you have felt sad or depressed.

**Q 12.14** Give two examples of how you could use one or two of the techniques to challenge your own negative thinking or negative beliefs.

**genuineness** Being open and honest with your own thoughts and feelings. Not being phony with oneself or others.

---

### *Problems and Solutions*

---

*How can I deal with aggressive or angry emotions in myself or others?*

- Be genuine, accepting, and empathic when appropriate.
- Be aware of your feelings and physical sensations.
- Stop and slow yourself down and relax.
- Decide what to say.

---

of your own feeling of despair or the despair of someone else is an example of being genuine. Here's an example from therapy.

*Janine:* I'm lost, totally lost. I've got no direction.

*RS:* You are feeling lost and not sure where to go. I sense your despair and feel I'm here to be with you in this tough time.

In my statement, there is an openness to the client, and a genuine feeling for Janine. I'm aware of my feelings for her and want to express that to her.

**acceptance** Referring to appreciating a person and not judging that person. This can mean accepting hurtful, bizarre, or sometimes negative feelings.

- **Acceptance.** Acceptance refers to appreciating a person and not judging. To accept means to accept hurtful, bizarre, and sometimes abhorrent feelings. To accept individuals does not mean that you agree with them, but refers to caring for them. There is neither positive nor negative judgment. The individual is valued for being himself or herself. An example of accepting a person who has done an abhorrent act is given here.

*Miles:* My son is three years old and he had gone into my stamp collection, tore some stamps up, threw them all over the room, and was pouring milk on them. I got so angry that I threw him against the wall and hit him in the face with my fist, breaking his jaw.

*RS:* You were so angry with your son that you just lost your temper, and now you're very upset with yourself for having done this.

In this example, I am accepting Miles, but not agreeing with or condoning his behavior. I want to understand him as a person and express that to him. In a different situation, I could be his judge, the child's doctor, or a police officer. Here, I am in the role of caring for him rather than judging him. There are times when it is appropriate to judge yourself and others, and other times when it might be better to accept yourself or others. Rogers was particularly interested in the importance of accepting rather than judging.

**empathy** Entering a person's world to understand it without being influenced by your own values and views. Empathy, when expressed to another person, shows sensitivity and understanding.

- **Empathy.** Being empathic with someone is to enter their world and to understand it without being influenced by your own values and views. This includes being sensitive to the individual at each moment that she is talking, to be sensitive to her fear, rage, or confusion. In essence, when we are empathic, we are living his or her life and sensing the meanings of that life without making judgments. Not only do we understand that person but we communicate that understanding as well (Rogers, 1975). This is similar to the concept of acceptance, but implies understanding in addition to acceptance. It is an attitude toward the person. In the previous example, I not only accepted Miles, but I indicated that I understood his anger at his son and his upset with himself. I do not approve of what he has done, but I am trying to understand him and his experience.

**catharsis** A way to express strong feelings by getting them off "your chest." Individuals can feel better about themselves by revealing uncomfortable feelings.

Being genuine, so that you can accept and empathize with your own feelings or experience, and those of others can be considerably helpful in a number of different situations. Rogers believed these conditions were among the most important for helping people change. He felt that it was not necessary to give advice or suggestions, but by understanding and communicating understanding of people's experience, one could help them solve many emotional problems. In a similar way, Rogers felt that people's problems often developed because those around them such as parents, teachers, or friends did not provide the types of conditions that were necessary for them to feel accepted. In the following example, I will show how these three conditions can help someone who is angry. Psychoanalysts have a similar concept that they refer to as **catharsis.** A simpler term would be "getting it off your chest." By expressing feelings that are difficult to describe or to reveal, individuals can feel better about themselves when their difficulties or pain is understood.

Here, I will examine Max's anger at his girlfriend. First I will show how Rogers's approach to understanding another person can be helpful with Max. Then I will discuss some other ways to deal with anger in another individual, as well as our own anger that we have.

*Max:* I don't know what came over me. I guess the best term for it is a jealous rage. I was just furious at Gwen because I saw her at a bar with somebody else. We've been going out for three years, and we've had disagreements and things like that. But never have I seen her with someone else. I got so mad at her that I went up to her apartment. She has a two bedroom apartment that she shares with Kathy, and I walked right in. I've had a key for a couple of years so that part was easy. I just walked right into Gwen's room. I took this brass lamp that she has and I just shattered it against the wall. The light bulb broke, the shade tore, and the base was dented. I took every picture I could find on her bureau and I smashed them with what was left of the lamp. Then I dumped all of her clothes on the floor to look for letters. I went into her closet and tore her clothes off the rack looking for letters again. I didn't find anything, but any papers I saw I threw around the room. It was a miniature hurricane. I've never been that angry in my life.

*RS:* Your fury and rage were so great at Gwen, you couldn't contain yourself. You even surprised yourself. (It is difficult to find words that express Max's anger; I'll do the best I can.)

*Max:* I've never felt so much fury. My chest was ready to explode, my face was red. If Gwen were there, I probably would have torn her up too. I could have done her a lot of damage, just as I did to her room.

*RS:* You seem scared by your fury and the damage that you could have done to Gwen. (I sense a scare in Max, and I want to communicate that I understand it.)

*Max:* The scare came as I was leaving the apartment and realized what I had done. I realized how angry I was at her and how hurt I was by seeing her with that guy.

*RS:* That awareness of your anger seemed to stun you. You're still angry at her, but shocked at what you've done too. (Max is feeling several things, and I am trying to communicate my understanding of these to him.)

*Max:* I guess I didn't understand how jealous I could be. I'm really afraid of losing Gwen, and I may have by being such a stupid idiot.

*RS:* Since that incident, it sounds like you've been blaming yourself a lot. (My purpose here is not to help Max change his behavior, but understand it so that he can change it on his own.)

As Max and I talk like this, gradually over a period of weeks, Max should be able to better understand his own experience of his relationship with Gwen. He should have a better understanding of his anger at her, his insecurity about his own feelings, and his need for her. He may also start to take responsibility for his actions. If Gwen decides to return to him, I will help him understand himself in that situation. If Gwen decides to stop seeing him totally, I will help him understand his feelings about this outcome. My understanding of Max should help him to better understand and accept himself. I do this by focusing on being genuine, accepting, and empathic. My goal is not to help Max get Gwen back or to judge Max, but to show my caring and understanding of Max so that he can grow in understanding of his own feelings, behavior, and thoughts, and change accordingly.

In dealing with your own anger, some useful ideas can be taken from the person-centered approach to understanding Max's anger. One of the first things that we can do when we are angry is to be aware of our experience of anger, which can include feelings of rage, but also to be aware of a burning sense in our chest, or in our stomach, or a flushed feeling in our face, rapid breathing, or rapid heartbeat. When we are aware of these sensations, then it becomes possible to back off. There are several ways to calm yourself take deep breaths, hold onto an object, count to ten, or use a relaxation technique, such as tensing one's fists and relaxing. When we become aware of our own anger, and then calm ourselves, we can be in a position to decide how to act with another person.

Sometimes we feel angry when talking with someone else. Think of a time when you saw two people get into a physical fight, or a very loud verbal argument. How do they look? Their body postures are generally such that they are pointing toward each other. They might use fingers to point, their faces might be contorted with rage. What they are not doing is trying to understand the other person. They often will use "you" statements as in "You're a stupid moron; you never listen to me; you did this stupid thing and that stupid thing." They might try to explain their points of view while the other person is doing the same. These behaviors are good examples of what *not* to do when you wish to avoid an angry conflict. Rather, it is better to pull away slightly physically, to lower one's voice, to try to defuse the other person's anger. Letting the person express himself or herself and then responding calmly to the person can help to defuse a potentially harmful situation. Sometimes you choose to let the other person have his or her way, rather than to be involved in an argument or fight. You can focus on understanding a person's rage and reply to it only when that person has calmed down.

**Q 12.15** Think of an example of when it has been helpful to talk to someone else when you are angry. What is it that he or she did to help? How similar is it to what I did with Max?

**Q 12.16** Think of a situation in which you are angry. Describe the way you handled it. How could you have used some of the suggestions that I have given here to handle your anger?

**Q 12.17** Think of a situation like Max's. How are the two different? How did you feel at the time? How did you feel later?

## SUMMARY

Although stress is necessary and a part of living, it also creates difficult problems for individuals. External stressors that occur daily, such as those at school or at work, or traumatic events, like the death of a loved one, put us in stressful situations. When individuals experience stress, they often feel many bodily changes that affect their muscles, breathing, heart rate, and other parts of the body. Individuals also experience stress psychologically. They might do this through thoughts that they have about the situations, ways they act (behaviors), and feelings that they have. Often thoughts (or cognitions) that are reactions to stress are not helpful and can include catastrophizing, dichotomous thinking, mind reading, and overgeneralization. Also, individuals might have irrational thoughts as a result of stressful situations. How individuals respond behaviorally to stress can include impaired performance of a task, physical illness, or procrastination.

Although individuals have a number of emotional feelings when they respond to stress, the most common are anxiety, depression, and anger.

Psychotherapists have been helpful in describing ways that individuals can deal with thoughts, behaviors, and feelings. Aaron Beck devised several ways to help individuals change distortions in their thinking. Albert Ellis described ways to challenge and dispute irrational thoughts. Behavioral therapists provide some methods for helping individuals reinforce their own positive behavior, learn from modeling others, and learn how to relax. Carl Rogers has focused his therapeutic work on how individuals can improve themselves through being genuine, accepting themselves and others, and being empathic with themselves and others.

Behavioral, cognitive, and person-centered techniques were applied to a variety of personal problems. Behavioral techniques can often help reduce anxiety, and methods were described. Cognitive approaches were applied to feelings of depression and sadness. The person-centered approach was used for helping individuals understand and deal with their own anger as well as that of others. Anxiety, depression, and anger can be understood from any of these points of view: behavioral, cognitive, and person-centered. Often therapists apply a combination of behavioral, cognitive, and person-centered approaches to a great variety of problems. You can choose methods that you will find most helpful to use in working on your own problems.

## RECOMMENDED READINGS

*Love Is Never Enough*
Beck, A. T. (Harper & Row, 1988)
> This book is designed to help couples communicate mores effectively. Aaron Beck is the founder of cognitive therapy, and he shows how errors in thinking, cognitive distortions, can lead to anxiety and depression and miscommunications. Beck shows how individuals can recognize and change cognitive distortions that interfere with communication plans. To make this book practical, Beck includes questionnaires that help individuals investigate their own relationships. Actual conversations of troubled couples make this book come alive.

*How to Stubbornly Refuse to Make Yourself Miserable about Anything—Yes, Anything!*
Ellis, A. (Carroll Communications, 1988)
> By disputing irrational beliefs (see page 319), Ellis shows how individuals can use a reasoned approach to avoid depression and anxiety. This book is particularly helpful for individuals who are "hard on themselves" and are self-critical or perfectionistic. Ellis gives many practical suggestions for dealing with irrational thinking.

*Anger: The Misunderstood Emotion*
Tavris, C. (Simon & Schuster, 1989)

>Anger is a powerful emotion that creates difficulties for many people. Tavris shows how anger can be used to achieve positive goals. Anger is examined from many different angles. A popular writer, Tavris writes in a lively and humorous fashion.

# RECOMMENDED WEB SITES

*Mental Health Net*
http://www.cmhc.com/

>This is an excellent site that explores all aspects of mental health. Many psychological disorders and treatment are discussed along with professional issues. There are links to more than 8,000 mental health resources.

*The Student Counseling Virtual Pamphlet Collection*
http://uhs.bsd.uchicago.edu/scrs/vpc/virtulets.html

>The Student Counseling Office at the University of Chicago has provided links to good online information developed at many counseling centers for issues that affect college students. Concerns include love, friendship, relationships, and mental health issues

*Stress, Anxiety, Fears, and Psychosomatic Disorders*
http://www.cnhc.com/psyhelp/ch835/

>This resource is part of Clayton E. Tucker-Ladd's online text, *Psychological Self-Help*, and provides a discussion of stress and its relationship to psychological and physiological disorders.

*The Anxiety-Panic Internet Resource: Relaxation*
http://www.algy.com/anxiety/relax.html

>This site deals with anxiety, panic, and stress. Many suggestions are given for increasing one's knowledge of relaxation techniques and ability to relax.

*The Albert Ellis Institute*
http://www.rebt.org/

>Since the 1950s, Albert Ellis has written more than 750 articles and 65 books that have dealt with ways to overcome irrational beliefs. This site shows Ellis' approach to disputing irrational beliefs.

# COPING STRATEGIES

This chapter covers some important ways of dealing with future concerns that apply to almost every topic that has been covered. These ways of coping (Kleinke, 1998) include strategies that often can be applied differently to different topics.

- *Using support systems.* Different support systems can be used for a variety of activities, such as studying, career choice, dealing with stress, and family or other issues.
- *Problem solving.* Some problem-solving strategies lend themselves better to some types of situations than others. A three-step problem-solving approach can be used in several situations.
- *Maintaining emotional control.* Some topics in this book can be dealt with through thinking and planning, such as studying and choosing a career, whereas others dealing with love, family relationships, and the loss of a loved one are concerns that we relate to emotionally. How to maintain emotional control (or let go) depends on the type of situation.
- *Talking yourself through challenges.* Each of the topics in this book presents a different type of challenge. Furthermore, challenges within each of these topics tend to be unique. Dealing with the break-up with a romantic partner is different for each person and in each situation. Suggestions are made for how to talk yourself through difficult situations.
- *Sense of humor.* Although individuals can't maintain a sense of humor in every situation, there are advantages in being able to look at situations from different perspectives, including humorous ones.
- *Self-rewards.* People often take their successes for granted, but criticize themselves for difficulties. Rewarding oneself for successes can help you develop a sense of achievement and accomplishment. Methods for doing so will be described for each of the chapters.

These coping strategies are discussed in this final chapter because they can be applied differently to the many topics that have been discussed in this book. The coping strategies of using support systems, problem solving, maintaining emotional control, and rewarding yourself are applied to each of the previous 11 chapters. I will describe the strategies of talking yourself through challenges and having a sense of humor about situations.

## Support Systems

**support systems** People to whom you turn for a variety of help.

Having people that you can turn to for a variety of help (**support systems**) is one of the most important coping skills that individuals can use

(Cohen & Hoberman, 1983). Being able to know all you need to know to handle difficult life problems is an unreasonable expectation. Sometimes individuals need tangible support—help in finishing a job, fixing a car, or getting a loan. In other cases, individuals need informational support—advice or feedback on what they are doing, such as when taking a course or completing a job. In many situations, individuals need emotional support from people that they can confide in and can trust. Sometimes people want someone to lean on or to provide reassurance. People who seek emotional support from friends or loved ones look for those who care about them. When requesting tangible or informational support, a trusting relationship might be less important. Finally, another type of support is called "belonging support," in which individuals want to feel that they fit in with other people. If you are a part of a group or groups at school, then you are likely to feel a sense of belongingness. If you have ever had an experience of going to a new school, you will recognize that it usually takes a little while for that sense of "belongingness" to develop.

Support not only provides information, a sense of belonging, and help when you are in emotional stress, but it can also affect your self-esteem (Thoits, 1986). Knowing that there is support for what you are going through or what you are doing can help you develop more self-confidence when you are dealing with difficult situations. Furthermore, you are likely to learn new skills or approaches to situations that will also help you feel better about yourself. A sense of companionship or friendship often develops when individuals make a request for support. Rather than feeling dependent or needing others, asking for support can increase a person's sense of well-being.

Support systems do not develop automatically. If you are upset about a tragedy in your life, you are likely to seek someone that you have known for some time (although some crisis situations are exceptions to this). Support systems depend on the relationships that you have with people rather than on the number of individuals that you come in contact with. When you seek support, whether tangible, informational, or emotional, it helps to have reasonable expectations and attitudes. Making reasonable requests rather than unreasonable demands helps. You are likely to be the source of support for others in a variety of ways and to have a sense of when requests for support are too demanding.

The type of support that individuals need depends greatly on the situation that they are in. Table 13.1 describes in more detail the types of support systems that are useful for each of the chapters (2 through12). When you need help in dealing with a variety of situations, you might find it useful to reexamine Table 13.1.

**TABLE 13.1 SUPPORT SYSTEMS**

*Learning and Studying* (Chapter 2). Although teachers and teaching assistants are obvious sources for help with learning, there are others. Study groups, tutors, and friends can be effective support systems.

*Choosing Careers* (Chapter 3). Because choosing a career can be such a complex task, professional resources such as career counselors are often helpful. Developing a networking system of people that you know from previous work or current work, as well as friends and family can also help you learn more about a variety of careers. When you make new or different choices about your career, choose those individuals for support who are likely to go along with your choices rather than make judgments about them.

*Adjusting to Work* (Chapter 4). Coworkers and bosses are possible support systems as are former coworkers and employers.

*Family Relationships* (Chapter 5). Because of the complexity of alliances within a family, family members might not be helpful as support systems in family relationships if they have preconceived ideas about how to handle a problem. Counselors and friends who are good listeners often provide a useful support system.

*Love and Friendship* (Chapter 6). Depending on the situation, family members might be supportive in dealing with issues with romantic partners or friends, but sometimes it is helpful to seek people who are outside the situation and less likely to be judgmental, such as counselors and therapists.

*Sexuality and Intimacy* (Chapter 7). Many knowledgeable health professionals, such as physicians, nurses, marriage counselors, and organizations such as Planned Parenthood can provide support with issues relating to birth control and sexually transmitted diseases.

*Gender Roles* (Chapter 8). Those who share similar views of gender roles are likely to be supportive of you. On the other hand, it is also helpful to find individuals of both genders that you can contact with concerns about dealing with the other gender. Many individuals have found couples or marriage counseling to be useful in dealing with intimacy and gender issues.

*Cultural Diversity* (Chapter 9). Friends who are open to the value systems and beliefs of a wide variety of people are likely to offer support when you are dealing with people from a different culture than your own. Also, having a variety of people from different cultures who you can call on for informational or emotional support can be valuable.

*Dying and Living* (Chapter 10). In addition to friends and family, many professionals can help you with grieving and mourning. Clergy, pastoral counselors, staff of funeral homes, hospice staff, and psychologists and psychiatrists can provide support for a brief duration or longer. Seeking knowledgeable individuals to help you with the loss of a loved one can add to the support that your friends and family can offer.

*Abusing Substances* (Chapter 11). A wide variety of inpatient and outpatient treatments are available to individuals that have substance concerns. Organizations such as Alcoholics Anonymous and Narcotics Anonymous are easy to contact, and members often have experience serving as support for others.

*Managing Stress* (Chapter 12). When you are dealing with stressful situations, it is helpful to know whether or not you want advice or someone to listen to you, or both, so that you know what to ask for. People who have been helpful and non-judgmental in the past are likely to be supportive in the future.

# PROBLEM-SOLVING STRATEGIES

Different types of problems require different types of solutions. Some problems, as discussed in Chapter 1, do not have solutions; rather, they require a focus on emotional issues. Problems with romantic partners and family members tend to fit into this last category. Being adaptable and using different strategies for different problems can be quite helpful. Sometimes problems have unusual or unexpected solutions or strategies. Using a type of approach that you have never used before could be successful. In general, problem-solving strategies require an active approach to a problem rather than avoiding a problem or waiting for it to solve itself.

**problem solving** An active approach to coping with a problem rather than a passive or avoidant approach.

Although there are a number of **problem-solving strategies**, I will describe a relatively simple and straightforward one that works best for problems that have a solution, rather than for those that are emotionally focused (D'Zurilla & Nezu, 1982). To use a problem-solving approach, it helps if you believe that you can solve the problem and can figure out strategies that will work. Even if you are not confident, trying to approach a problem calmly and rationally with a belief that you can find a solution will help. When you can do this, then you can take four steps toward resolving a problem.

1. *Define the problem.* Examine what the problem is and how to approach it. What are the critical issues; what are the conflicts involved? If you can determine this, it is easier to make a list of your goals that you will meet by resolving the problem.
2. *List options.* Writing down different plans, as many as possible, can be helpful. You can modify and change these plans. Rather than criticize your ideas as you write them, put them down first. Then you can change, rewrite, and borrow ideas from one plan or another.
3. *Make decisions.* Weigh your possible plans or ideas. Beside each option, write the possible outcomes if that option is chosen. What seem to be the consequences of each? Which would be easiest to carry out? Which solutions could cause other problems? Can you incorporate portions of one solution into another? What will you do if your first plan doesn't work? Being flexible and making new lists if the solution doesn't work can be helpful.
4. *Try out an option.* Put a plan into action. If it does not seem to work, alter the plan or change options. Reassessing your plans creates flexibility and can lead to a more satisfactory decision. Because predicted outcomes don't always match actual outcomes, willingness to change strategies is helpful.

Renise has been working as a computer programmer for the last three years. Her company has been partially supportive of her desire to complete requirements for her bachelor's degree in computer science. At the age of 26, Renise is sole support for her 3-year-old daughter. Because of family and work demands, Renise has been taking one course per semester for the last two years. She needs seven more to finish her degree requirements. The burden of taking and studying for a course on top of all her responsibilities, has put a great deal of stress on her.

   She now has the opportunity to take three courses in the summer to reduce the time she will be spending on courses during the next few years. To do this, her supervisors have agreed to give her a leave of absence for one month and she can use her vacation time to cover the other month. Another issue is childcare. She often left her daughter, Rhonda, with her sister who has two young boys. However, her sister will be working part time this summer. Renise will have to find day care for Rhonda. Renise has finally paid off credit card debts and does not want to borrow money for day care for Rhonda and to support herself when she is not earning income.

What should she do? Renise uses the three step problem-solving method shown in Figure13.1.

Renise was able to make lists of her conflicting problems. She determined her goals (to complete 3 courses in the summer). She then made 3 lists. Each list had some problems with it. Then she integrated ideas from the three lists into a temporary plan. She was aware that the courses she chose and the assignments that were required for them might force her to change her plans.

Not all problems can be approached this way. Sometimes when you try a solution, other problems develop. With some problems, particularly conflicts with individuals, you need to be able to react to the comments, requests, or actions of others. Examine how problem-solving strategies can be applied or adapted to each of the topics covered in this book. Table 13.2 (see page 335) provides some ways of using a variety of strategies, including the one just discussed.

## MAINTAINING SELF-CONTROL

Individuals vary in the degree that they feel they have control over events that happen to them— **self-control** (Kleinke, 1998). Some individuals tend to blame others and feel that what happens to them is beyond their control. They might feel that there is little they can do to change important things in their life and that they are helpless to deal with problems. This attitude makes it difficult to make changes in one's life. Being able to take responsibility for aspects of your life that you can control can give you a sense of confidence and competence.

Trying to change passive attitudes to ones where you can control the situation can significantly affect areas of your life. For example, rather than saying "Getting a good job depends on who you know," an individual can say, "I will continue to make contacts for job interviews and increase the number of individuals that I know." The first statement is rather passive and helpless sounding; the second gives control to the job-seeker. Here's another example: "No matter what I do, some people aren't going to like me." A different approach is, "If I try to understand people, I can help them learn more about me and my positive qualities." In this way, the person can influence interactions with other people. With regard to school, here's another example: "I don't know why I get the grades that I do." Instead, you could use this: "I need to talk to my teacher to understand what I can do to improve my grade."

**Q 13.1** Describe a situation in which you can apply the problem-solving strategy discussed on p. 332.

**Q 13.2** Apply the 4-step problem-solving method to a problem.

**self-control** Taking responsibility for events and aspects of one's life.

**Q 13.3** Give an example of a helpless or passive statement and then change it to a statement in which you have control.

1. Define the problem.

I want to graduate. Critical issue: Can I financially afford to leave work temporarily to complete 3 of the 7 remaining courses? Conflicts: Supporting Rhonda and me while I finish 3 courses. 3 courses are a lot to take this summer. Can I do it? Can I find good day care for Rhonda? How much will my sister be available to care for Rhonda? Goals met by solving problem: Move 12 to 18 months closer to graduation and the salary increase that will result. Stop worrying about this problem so much.

2. List options

A
Get a part time job.
Take care of Rhonda when I'm not in school.
Try to find easy courses.

B
Get my sister to take care of Rhonda, offer to pay her.
Take evening courses.
Study during the day.

C
Take care of Rhonda myself.
Study when she's napping.
Take evening courses.

3. Make decisions

I won't make enough from a part time job to help with much of anything. Rhonda doesn't sleep long enough for me to get my work done. I will talk to my sister about paying her to take care of Rhonda. I think there will be times when I can take care of her boys and Rhonda too. I am going to have to see how my course schedule will work out and when projects and exams are due, so I can see when I will be most available to take care of Rhonda and the boys.

FIGURE **13.1**　Example of Using the First Three of the Four-Step Problem-Solving Method

## TABLE 13.2 PROBLEM-SOLVING STRATEGIES

*Learning and Studying* (Chapter 2). In one sense, studying is a form of problem solving. Many courses such as math and science require a specific method of problem solving. The 3-step problem solving strategy can help you decide what to study and for how long.

*Choosing Careers* (Chapter 3). Choosing a career is different than most other problem-solving situations in that career choice concerns can span a lifetime. Career decision-making strategies are more complex than the 3-step process because individuals must consider their personality, interests, values, and abilities, as well as environmental factors, such as the job market, when they make career decisions.

*Adjusting to Work* (Chapter 4). Solving problems at work depends on how long you have been on a job and whether the problem deals with salary, working conditions, bosses, or coworkers. Thinking through alternative actions before acting can be helpful.

*Family Relationships* (Chapter 5). Attitudes of openness, an orientation toward others, being agreeable, and being conscientious (discussed in Chapter 1) all help in solving family problems.

*Love and Friendship* (Chapter 6). Emotion-focused solutions to understanding people you are angry at or upset with can be useful. Caring for others helps you solve problems with others.

*Sexuality and Intimacy* (Chapter 7). Because there is so much inaccurate information about sexuality, it is important to gather accurate information before making decisions. Clearly, knowing your own values before being involved in a sexual situation decreases the chances of impulsive decision making. Decisions regarding sexually transmitted diseases should be considered seriously and require medical advice.

*Gender Roles* (Chapter 8). Try to understand problems and issues from the perspective of someone of a different gender. Focus on understanding communication styles rather than on rational decision making.

*Cultural Diversity* (Chapter 9). Seeing oneself from another person's point of view can help you solve problems that deal with cultural issues. Challenging your own beliefs and seeing them as culturally derived rather than as the only way of seeing things can be useful. Being compassionate with others who endure racism can help in solving problems related to cultural diversity.

*Dying and Living* (Chapter 10). Emotions and feelings are very powerful and can remain so for a very long time. For many individuals, a rational decision-making process rushes the mourning process. Being patient with those who are dying or are dealing with the death of a loved one is helpful because their rational decision-making processes can be affected by the sense of loss.

*Abusing Substances* (Chapter 11). Decision making when one is under the influence of drugs or alcohol or when one is addicted can be quite different than decision making when one is sober or non-addicted. If you are addicted, it is very important to listen to the advice of others and seek help from groups such as Alcoholics Anonymous.

*Managing Stress* (Chapter 12). When making decisions, it is important that they be thought through and not be based on catastrophizing, dichotomous thinking, overgeneralization, or negative labeling. Solutions to problems can include reinforcing yourself, modeling your behavior from someone you know, relaxing, and challenging irrational beliefs. Often problems are lessened by a caring and understanding attitude toward yourself or others.

---

**Q 13.4** What strategies are useful to you in maintaining self-control? Give an example from one of the topics in Table 13.3.

When dealing with situations that we encounter in our lives, it is helpful to assess how much control we have over such situations. By trying to get information to solve problems, individuals can start to control different events in their lives. Often by learning more about what we need to do to maintain our psychological or physical health, solutions will develop. Feeling that one is destined to be a failure or that one is doomed to bad luck takes control out of the hands of an individual. This is not to say that individuals have total control over their lives. Clearly, individuals cannot control some accidents and disasters. Once an auto accident, a fire, a flood, or tornado has occurred, nothing can be done to change that event. However, individuals can control how they deal with events and with others. Often this control takes the form of understanding your emotions, controlling them, and finding ways to respond. Table 13.3 gives some suggestions for maintaining self-control and responding to situations for each of the topics described in the book.

TABLE **13.3** MAINTAINING SELF-CONTROL

*Learning and Studying* (Chapter 2). When dealing with problems of completing a paper or preparing for an exam, it is helpful to take responsibility for the exam or the paper and see the event in perspective. Exam panic can be decreased by focusing on the exam (or paper) as one event in a series of many events in one's academic career. Sometimes students say to themselves, "This exam is going to be so tough, it won't matter whether or not I study." It will matter. Assigning the control or responsibility for the exam to the instructor only limits a student's role in preparation.

*Choosing Careers* (Chapter 3). Choosing a career is a long process taking many years for many people. Being tolerant about the length of this process can be helpful. Focusing on the process of learning about what you like and are good at rather than on the specific choice can help take the pressure off you to make a choice. Looking for a job can be a discouraging process—job hunting has been described as a series of "no's" followed by one "yes." Predicting that the job hunting experience might be slow and full of "no's" controls the discouragement that you might feel.

*Adjusting to Work* (Chapter 4). At work, you might have many daily stresses. Maintaining emotional control when dealing with customers, coworkers, and bosses can be extremely important. Telling yourself to calm down, to count to ten, to relax for a moment, to take a deep breath, all help ensure emotional control.

*Family Relationships* (Chapter 5). Not surprisingly, relationships with brothers, sisters, children, and parents are characterized by deep feelings. Identifying the feelings and controlling them helps individuals deal with anger and other feelings toward family members. Thinking of the other person and caring and empathy for others, help to maintain a sense of control because the focus is on others rather than on angry or depressed feelings that you might have.

*Love and Friendship* (Chapter 6). In intimate relationships, emotional control is frequently tested. To deal with anger and upset, it is helpful to step away and to physically calm yourself. Strategies are discussed in Chapters 5, 6, and 12.

*Sexuality and Intimacy* (Chapter 7). Because sexual situations are passionate ones, in which individuals might have difficulty maintaining control, it is useful to have clearly made decisions about values and behavior before the situation arises. Discussing birth control and STDs before being in a sexual situation helps an individual to be consistent in his or her decision making.

*Gender Roles* (Chapter 8). Understanding how someone of the other gender thinks or feels can help individuals relate more easily to the members of the other gender. Concentrating on ways that gender roles can affect communication also helps.

*Cultural Diversity* (Chapter 9). By understanding the needs and values of others, individuals can focus on how to respond to others and thus maintain control over themselves. Putting yourself in the position of someone else can help you step back from a situation and see it from a different point of view.

*Dying and Living* (Chapter 10). With grief and mourning comes the loss of emotional control. Choosing who to go to for support can be a significant decision. Providing support for those who need to let go of emotional control can itself be rewarding. Because the grieving process is often long, being tolerant of yourself and others in establishing the self-control that you previously had can be very useful.

*Abusing Substances* (Chapter 11). Being aware of the effect of substance abuse on emotions and decision making helps individuals to make decisions about using alcohol and drugs. Thinking about substances before using them helps individuals avoid being in situations where they have little self-control, such as driving drunk, arguing, or getting into physical fights.

*Managing Stress* (Chapter 12). By being aware of and catching one's negative beliefs, such as catastrophizing or overgeneralizing, people can stop stress before it starts. Being aware of irrational thoughts and how these can increase anxiety can be helpful. Slowing yourself down and identifying irrational thoughts can provide a way of controlling your feelings and behaviors.

# TALKING YOURSELF THROUGH CHALLENGES

Thinking clearly about how you're going to solve a problem and what you're going to do can be an extremely effective approach. Meichenbaum (1985) has written about strategies for confronting difficult life challenges. He suggests that people first prepare themselves to deal with a problem, then confront the problem, and then reflect on how they handled the problem.

To prepare for a challenging problem, it is helpful to think about how you will use support systems (Table 13.1), your approach to solving the problem (Table 13. 2), and how you will maintain control while dealing with the problem (Table 13.3). Thinking of a coping strategy, ways in which you've dealt with stressful events before, and how you can apply that knowledge now can all be effective. Some statements, such as the following, can help you deal with difficult situations.

> "I feel anxious now, but I've felt that way before, and I can handle the situation."
> "I can learn from the experience regardless of the outcome."
> "Upsetting myself will not help me deal with the situation."
> "I can use a particular problem-solving plan to make things work."
> "I can use relaxation strategies while confronting the problem."

Mental rehearsal is an effective approach to problem-solving. Picturing yourself dealing with the problem and how you will solve it can be particularly helpful. Athletes often picture themselves performing an event before they do it as a way of maintaining control and decreasing feelings of anxiety.

When dealing with the problem itself, it helps to reassure yourself that you have dealt with problems well in the past and can do so again. Some strategies include these:

> "Let me focus on what I have to do, and not be distracted by other pressures."
> "If I act as if I know what I'm doing, I can feel like I know what I'm doing."
> "If I start to get nervous, I can relax."
> "I've handled more difficult problems than this in the past."

As an individual works on a problem, the problem can change. If your challenge is dealing with an angry individual, that individual might change the way he or she responds in ways that you have not predicted. Being flexible and able to change focus can be very helpful.

**positive reinterpretation**
Focusing on ways to view events in a more positive way.

Another way to change focus is to interpret events in a positive way; this is called **positive reinterpretation:** Individuals recognize that their problems could be worse. You can do this by comparing your difficulties with those of others. Such comparisons often help people relax and see other solutions. Research (Park, Cohen, & Murch, 1996) shows how positive interpretation helps people solve problems and cope with difficult circumstances.

**Q 13.5** Describe what you might say to talk yourself through a specific problem that you could be dealing with soon.

After the problem is over, it is useful to think about what you have learned. You should look for ways to congratulate yourself in handling the problem, as well as for ways you can improve in the future. Appreciating the positive contributions that you made to the situation is extremely important. By reflecting on a situation, you are able to step back or distance yourself from a situation and increase the chances that you will be less emotionally involved. By doing so, you can decrease the anxiety that you experience. Another way of doing this is by maintaining a sense of humor.

## HUMOR

Having a sense of humor about what we do helps us to take ourselves less seriously and, thus, be less frightened or anxious in a variety of situations. As Frankl (1969) points out, when you laugh at yourself, you can't feel sad and dejected at the same time. Humor allows us to examine situations differently and sometimes to see new and different ways of dealing with them. Humor also is a way of saying "I make mistakes sometimes, but that's not so bad, I can manage it."

Humor is a particularly effective way for dealing with anger, sadness, and depression. If we take ourselves less seriously, then we can see a situation differently so that we can see it as less serious than it originally was. For example, if I am angry at a friend for being late for an appointment, I can think of a situation in which I was delayed for an appointment by someone who talked more quickly than anyone I had ever known. As I hear parts of that conversation in my mind, I smile about that person's ability to get more words into 30 seconds than anyone else.

The type of humor that I am describing is light and self-directed. Humor when directed at others can often be disguised anger and sarcasm. When I describe humor as being an effective way of solving a problem, I am not describing statements like this: "What garbage dump did you get that dress from?" This type of humor is mean and directed toward someone else in a negative way. I have described humor that can be directed at oneself to decrease anxiety, sadness, or other negative emotions.

**Q 13.6** Describe a situation in which you used humor to cope with a problem. Explain how it helped.

## REWARDING ONESELF

Although most people are equipped to criticize themselves and find fault with what they have done, they are less likely to reward themselves for positive achievements that they have made. I have found that relatively few individuals reward or encourage themselves when they have been successful. Many tend to focus on faults or problems that they have had in the past and ignore their successes. Some individuals are perfectionists who set themselves up for failure. In general, whatever they do is not good enough. There are some individuals who can take an "A–" average and turn it into a failure experience by focusing on how they could have done better.

**reward** A way of encouraging oneself and supporting oneself when you have been successful.

If you are able to **reward** yourself for accomplishments, then you are able to develop a sense of confidence in what you do. Rather than identify a few large tasks to be accomplished, it is better to structure an activity so that there are several smaller tasks, and time for you to reflect on successes that you have made. Rewarding yourself at various points in time builds not only a sense of accomplishment in specific tasks but also self-esteem along the way. When athletes set tasks for themselves, they usually do so in small increments so that they have time to appreciate what they have done before going on to another task. For example, figure skaters try to focus on the next item of difficulty rather than to think far ahead about their eventual goals. Although it may be helpful, thinking about being an Olympic skater is not as helpful as concentrating on each task you need to complete.

Receiving praise from others helps you build a sense of confidence. Unfortunately, who provides the praise and when depends on factors that are outside of our control. Many people tend to ignore the praise from other people and listen to their own self-criticism. Because self-criticism is so frequent, and self-praise so infrequent, I have made suggestions of ways that you can consider rewarding yourself that relate to topics covered in this book (Table 13.4). Often, my suggestions deal with the process of achieving, not necessarily just the achievement itself.

You might find yourself uncomfortable with the suggestions made in Table 13.4 or find them somewhat silly. I suspect that that is because many individuals are uncomfortable with giving themselves praise. However, self praise or positive reenforcement can lead to increased self-confidence and esteem.

**Q 13.7** Give an example of a situation that you can praise yourself for handling. What can you say to yourself?

## Conclusion

Each of the chapters has dealt with a significant area of human life. In this book, I have tried to provide information about ways of dealing with problems that you encounter in life. All these areas should be relevant to you at some time in the future. Because of this, you can view the book as being unfinished and incomplete. The pages in Appendix A will give you an opportunity to follow changes in different aspects of your life. Whether or not you choose to fill out those sections, you will be living out your life in almost every area that we have covered. I hope that the information that I have provided will assist you in some useful ways in the future.

Your choices and your solutions to personal problems do not end with this book. Be open to taking risks and trying new things. Support groups exist for all kinds of issues, such as groups for victims of rape or incest,

**TABLE 13.4 STRATEGIES FOR REWARDING ONESELF**

*Learning and Studying* (Chapter 2). Reward yourself not only for high grades, but also for learning concepts and for mastering chapters or segments of material.

*Choosing Careers* (Chapter 3). Learning about occupations and about what people do in them, how much they make, and so forth is helpful. Rewarding oneself for having job interviews and talking with prospective employers is also a worthwhile achievement. Some individuals tend to ignore these achievements and focus only on being successful in choosing a career or in getting a job.

*Adjusting to Work* (Chapter 4). For most individuals, a work day consists of accomplishing a number of tasks. Some of these are typical job duties, others are unexpected, such as dealing with an irate customer or boss. Selecting significant activities from a group of activities and praising oneself for having completed them successfully can lead to increased self-esteem.

*Family Relationships* (Chapter 5). Many family relationships can be difficult, including a number of awkward or stressful situations. Finding solutions to these problems and working them out is not easy. Appreciating your ability to do so is very worthwhile.

*Love and Friendship* (Chapter 6). Often love and friendship are activities that are taken for granted. Appreciating friends and loved ones and praising ourselves when we are helpful to others is not arrogant but, rather, creates confidence in interpersonal relationships.

*Sexuality and Intimacy* (Chapter 7). Having a clear set of sexual values and being consistent with your own values and respectful of those of others can be viewed as an accomplishment.

*Gender Roles* (Chapter 8). For centuries, authors have written of the difficulties that individuals of one gender have in understanding the feelings and actions of individuals of the other gender. Making efforts to understand others' gender roles is an accomplishment.

*Cultural Diversity* (Chapter 9). Because of the wide range of prejudice and discrimination that exists in many countries, the ability to counter these problems should not be taken lightly. Praising yourself for reducing prejudice or discrimination is certainly worthwhile.

*Dying and Living* (Chapter 10). Being helpful and compassionate to those who are dying or who have lost a loved one is often difficult. Showing caring and providing support for such individuals is something that they need and can appreciate. Sometimes it helps to put yourself in the place of others for a moment, to appreciate what you have done for them.

*Abusing Substances* (Chapter 11). If you are aware of an individual or individuals who substantially abuse drugs, you can appreciate what a significant accomplishment it is not to do so.

*Managing Stress* (Chapter 12). Often some of the most difficult situations individuals encounter are stressful ones. By praising oneself for having accomplished a difficult task, anxiety and stress can be reduced.

men's and women's groups, groups for reentering students, medical self-help groups, and drug and alcohol self-help groups. Don't hesitate to use these. Furthermore, individual and group counseling is available in virtually every community. Therapists and counselors can explain how they can help you. Often friends will provide help as you provide help to them. I wish you well in your life's choices.

# RECOMMENDED READINGS

*Asserting Yourself: A Practical Guide For Positive Change*
S. A. Bower and G. H. Bower (Addision-Wesley, 1991)
> This book describes non-assertiveness, anger, and assertive behavior. The authors show how you can act assertively in different types of situations by providing verbal scripts that are appropriate for a variety of situations. The range of situations is very broad, including dealing with a substance abuser, dealing with the silent treatment, working with people who make demands that seem unreasonable, and dealing with job situations.

*Your Perfect Right* (7th ed.)
R. E. Alberti and M. L.Emmons (Impact, 1995)

>After many editions, this book has been considered to be a classic in its field. The authors show how to differentiate assertive, aggressive, and passive behaviors. They give examples of each and show how to respond assertively in a wide variety of situations. The authors also teach individuals that they have the right to express themselves, while respecting the rights of others.

*The Psychotherapy Maze*
O. Ehrenberg and M. Ehrenberg (Aronson, 1994)

>This book describes issues to consider if you would like psychotherapy to help you in dealing with problems that are discussed in this and other chapters. The authors talk about how to select a therapist and how to help therapy work. They also give you suggestions for determining whether therapy is working for you. Important issues such as fees, health maintenance organization plans, and emergency phone calls are also discussed.

*Am I Crazy, Or Is It My Shrink?*
L. E. Beutler, B. Bongar, and J. M. Shurkin (Oxford University Press, 1998)

>Although the title sounds humorous, this is a very serious examination of issues related to psychotherapy. The authors cover issues such as choosing a therapist and asking the therapist questions and what to do if you are uncertain whether therapy is working for you. Information is provided for helping you recognize when the therapist is acting unprofessionally or unethically. The authors are experts in the field of research on the effectiveness of psychotherapy.

## RECOMMENDED WEB SITES

*How to Find Help with Life's Problems* (APA Brochure)
http://helping.apa.org/brochure/index.html

>This site, designed by the American Psychological Association, gives suggestions about seeking out different types of therapy for different types of problems.

*Mind Tools*(tm)
http://www.mindtools.com/index.html

>James Manketlow provides practical suggestions for dealing more efficiently and effectively with problems. Problem-solving and stress-reduction techniques are useful and practical.

# LIFE'S CHOICES: JOURNAL PAGES

The following pages give you an opportunity to keep a record or a journal of events that are related to Chapters 2 through 12. There are several ways to do this. You may wish to do this during the course, after it, or both. It is a way of thinking about the important areas of your life that you make choices about. When you make an entry, put the date of the entry next to it. That way you can return to it later and see how you have changed or progressed.

Be careful of what you write, in case this is seen by someone you don't want to see what you have written.

# CHAPTER 2: LEARNING AND STUDYING

1. What new material do you enjoy learning?
2. What effective studying strategies have you learned?
3. What methods have you used to work with procrastination?
4. What new subjects do you want to learn?

# CHAPTER 3: CHOOSING CAREERS

1. What are your new interests?
2. What are new values that are important to you?
3. What are new abilities or achievements that you have made?
4. What new occupations seem attractive to you and why?
5. What new networking resources do you have?

# CHAPTER 4: ADJUSTING TO WORK

1.  Date and record reactions to a new job.
2.  What have you done that contributes to feeling effective at work?
3.  What activities feel satisfying at work? Can you do more of these?
4.  What type of career crises have you had and how have you handled them?

_____

_____

_____

_____

_____

_____

_____

_____

_____

_____

_____

_____

_____

_____

_____

_____

_____

_____

_____

# CHAPTER 5: FAMILY RELATIONSHIPS

1. How do you deal with relationships with brothers and sisters?
2. What strategies work for different family problems?
3. What changes do you want to make in dealing with your family?

# CHAPTER 6: LOVE AND FRIENDSHIP

1. What changes have you noted in relationships?
2. What types of choices have you made in relationships?
3. How do you deal with relationship issues or problems?

_____

_____

_____

_____

_____

_____

_____

_____

_____

_____

_____

_____

_____

_____

_____

_____

_____

_____

_____

_____

_____

_____

_____

# CHAPTER 7: SEXUALITY AND INTIMACY

1. What are your sexual values and your views of those of others who are important to you?
2. What social pressures about sexuality concern you?
3. Are your religious and sexual values appropriately consistent? Explain.

# CHAPTER 8: GENDER ROLES

1. How are your gender views changing?
2. How do the gender views of others affect you?
3. What behaviors or changes in behaviors have you observed in yourself and others in dealing with the other gender?
4. What do you try to do to maintain a positive image of your appearance and body?

_____

_____

_____

_____

_____

_____

_____

_____

_____

_____

_____

_____

_____

_____

_____

_____

_____

_____

_____

_____

_____

# CHAPTER 9: CULTURAL DIVERSITY

1. How have your stereotypes changed?
2. How have you observed prejudice in yourself and others?
3. How have you addressed discrimination?
4. In what way do the racial identity models on page 235 apply to you now?

# CHAPTER 10: DYING AND LIVING

1.  What concerns have you about the loss of loved ones?
2.  How can you use information about stages of mourning or the tasks of mourning (pp. 255–258)?
3.  How have you dealt with the grief of others?

_____

_____

_____

_____

_____

_____

_____

_____

_____

_____

_____

_____

_____

_____

_____

_____

_____

_____

_____

_____

# CHAPTER 11: ABUSING SUBSTANCES

1. What information about substance abuse do you need?
2. If you have substance abuse concerns, how do you know that?
3. If you have substance abuse concerns, what are you doing about them?
4. Do you or others that are close to you need treatment or have concerns regarding the treatment of substance abuse? Describe.

## CHAPTER 12: MANAGING STRESS

1. What negative thoughts or irrational beliefs are contributing to your stress?
2. What strategies have you used to change these thoughts?
3. What do you do to relax?
4. What strategies do you use to reinforce yourself?
5. How do you show compassion toward yourself and others?

_____

_____

_____

_____

_____

_____

_____

_____

_____

_____

_____

_____

_____

_____

_____

_____

_____

_____

_____

_____

_____

# Glossary

**ability**  The quality of current performance, what the individual is doing now.

**acceptance**  Referring to appreciating a person and not judging that person. This can mean accepting hurtful, bizarre, or sometimes negative feelings.

**achievement**  Judgments about past performance; what the individual has done. Also, making use of one's abilities to do things that gives a sense of accomplishment; one of six work adjustment values.

**achievement motivation**  Refers to the striving for excellence. It was originally defined from an individualistic perspective, but has also been defined from a collectivist perspective.

**acquaintance rape**  Rape that occurs when someone is raped by someone she or he knows from a nonromantic situation.

**acronym**  Words that are created from the first letter of other words. They are used to help remember a series of words and are a type of mnemonic device.

**addiction**  Drugs that produce both dependence and withdrawal. Thus individuals need the drug to function and their bodies are stressed if they try to stop using the drug.

**adjustment**  Ways in which people cope with their lives, and the problems and challenges that they face; refers to all areas of life.

**affective tasks**  Having many feelings about the loss of a loved one and a desire to express them to others.

**aggressive behavior**  Insisting on one's own rights while violating other's rights. This can include making fun of, dominating, or belittling another person.

**agreeableness**  Making an effort to agree with others. Sometimes it means sharing similar opinions.

**alcohol dependency syndrome**  A psychological and physiological dependence on alcohol that results in chronic disease and disruption of interpersonal and work relationships; a term used by health professionals that is similar to but preferred to alcoholism. Some signs are frequent blackouts, delirium tremens (hallucinations, confusion, rapid heartbeat), liver disease, neurological impairment, or congestive heart failure

**Alcoholics Anonymous**  Meetings of alcoholics who are in the process of recovering from alcoholism or alcohol dependency syndrome. Abstinence from alcohol is a goal for alcoholics who participate in this program. They adhere to the 12-step-model that has a strong spiritual component. Anonymity is offered to those who attend the meetings.

**altruism**  Wishing to help others by doing things for them or getting along with them; one of six work adjustment theory values.

**androgyny**  The idea that each person has both masculine and feminine personality traits. An androgynous person scores above average on masculinity and femininity on a test of androgyny.

**anger**  Feelings of rage, annoyance, and irritation. Often these are brought about by stress. Anger can be expressed through yelling, facial expression, or physical confrontation.

**anorexia**  A life-threatening disorder in which individuals refuse to eat enough to maintain minimal weight. They starve themselves because of an intense fear of becoming obese.

**Antabuse (disulfiram)**  A chemical treatment used in therapy for alcoholism. When used with alcohol, Antabuse produces very unpleasant effects including vomiting, sweating, headaches, difficulty in breathing and decrease in blood pressure.

**anticipated events**  Events or occurrences that happen in the lifespan of most individuals, such as starting a job or retiring.

**anxiety**  Typically an unpleasant emotional state resulting from stress or conflict. When experiencing anxiety, individuals are likely to feel fear, apprehension, and physical feelings such as rapid heartbeat or fast breathing.

**anxious-ambivalent style**  An adult attachment style in which individuals might be anxious about relationships ending. As children they might have experienced inconsistent reactions from parents or care givers.

**approach-approach conflict**  A choice between two attractive goals. For example, do you want to go to the movies or to an amusement park?

**approach-avoidance conflict**  Choosing between attractive and unattractive aspects that are related to a goal. For example, should I buy a new car and then have to pay expensive car payments?

**aptitude**  Predictions about future performance; what the individual will do in the future. Aptitude tests attempt to measure possible future achievement.

**assertiveness**  A way of expressing oneself such that likes are expressed clearly; distinguished from passive and aggressive behavior.

**attachment**  An emotional bond with another person that is usually powerful and long lasting; used most often to describe the relationship between infant and mother.

**authoritarian parenting style**  Parents controlling what their children do, but being unlikely to accept their child's behavior. The attitude is perhaps best expressed by "do this because I told you to and don't ask questions."

**authoritative parenting style**  Parents having a high degree of acceptance of the child while having a high degree of control. Parents discuss standards and expectations while valuing obedience.

**autonomy**  The opportunity to work independently or on one's own, including trying out one's own ideas, being creative, and taking responsibility for one's actions. This is one of six work adjustment theory values.

**avoidance-avoidance conflict**  A choice between two unattractive goals. For example, should I clean my room or wash the dishes?

**avoidant style** An adult attachment style in which individuals are likely to have difficulty developing close and trusting relationships, especially with romantic partners.

**avoiding a problem** Not trying to solve a problem; can lead to self-destructive activities such as drinking. Other ways of avoiding a problem are by not thinking about it or by doing a neutral activity such as watching television.

**bargaining** Asking God for more time, asking for special dispensation, or asking to be spared from death. This is Kübler-Ross's third stage of dying.

**behavioral approaches** Methods used to help individuals refrain from drugs. Reinforcement (similar to reward) is used as a major behavioral technique.

**behavioral tasks** Doing something to recognize a loss. A funeral ritual is a common behavioral task.

**belonging** The need to love, to share, and to cooperate with others; defined by William Glasser.

**bereavement** Usually associated with the loss or death of a loved one; associated with loneliness, missing someone, and grief.

**binge drinking** Having five or more drinks at one time; used as a quantitative measure for excessive drinking.

**bisexuality** Being attracted to members of one's own gender as well as to members of the other gender.

**blaming oneself** Being critical of oneself for causing a problem; can make it more difficult to focus on possible actions.

**bonpu zazen** A basic method of meditation based on Zen Buddhism.

**boundaryless career** A career that might have frequent job rotations, temporary assignments, and transfers from one part of a company to another. As a result, individuals are likely to feel less security than they would if they were assigned to one task.

**bulimia** A means of trying to maintain weight control by induced vomiting or occasionally using laxatives to rid the body of food. Individuals often go through a binge-purge cycle in which they eat great amounts of food and then vomit or use laxatives.

**carcinogens** Compounds or materials that can cause cancer.

**cardiovascular disease** Diseases or illnesses of the heart and the blood vessels.

**career** An individual's work and leisure that takes place over his or her lifespan. Choices and decisions about careers are made throughout the lifespan.

**career crisis** Event that can be traumatic and can have long-lasting effects. Examples are accidents that occur at work or being fired or laid off.

**catastrophizing** Exaggerating events so that an individual experiences more fear or stress.

**catharsis** A way to express strong feelings by getting them off "your chest." Individuals can feel better about themselves by revealing uncomfortable feelings.

**challenging and disputing irrational beliefs** Method developed by Albert Ellis; used to help individuals with their problems. A method challenging people's views that they must be perfect, that they should not suffer pain or discomfort, that the future could be dangerous, and that if they don't find a solution things will be terrible.

**challenging dichotomous thinking** Methods used to help individuals see that they are turning events into all good or all bad options. A common method of challenging dichotomous thinking is scaling.

**challenging generalizations** Examing or questioning the accuracy of absolute statements that individuals make.

**challenging mind reading** Asking individuals who assume they know what someone else is thinking , how they know this.

**change** To make different or to alter; individuals have the ability to make many changes in their lives.

**child abuse** Harm to children that includes physical, sexual, and emotional activity as well as neglect. Defining what constitutes harm or abuse to children is often a decision left to social service agencies and legal institutions.

**choices** Selecting from alternatives; choices cover all areas of life.

**chronic hassles** Situations that interfere with the performance or satisfaction of a job. Examples are an unreasonable supervisor or unpleasant physical working conditions.

**cirrhosis of the liver** Chronic scarring of the liver, leading to loss of normal liver function. Symptoms are jaundice (yellow skin and eyes), hair loss, enlarged spleen, diarrhea, bleeding, and mental confusion, as well as many others.

**cognitive distortion** Systematic errors in reasoning, often stemming from early childhood errors in reasoning; an indication of inaccurate or ineffective use of reasoning.

**cognitive tasks** Needing information about what has happened so that individuals can understand the details of the loss.

**collectivist culture** A culture in which individuals learn to attend to the needs and values of others and place them above their own needs and values.

**comfort** A variety of ways in which a job can be less stressful for an individual, including being independent, being active or busy, being able to do a variety of work, being well paid, and having security. Comfort is one of six values of work adjustment theory.

**communication style** A general way of communicating to another person. Tannen believes that the male communication style is the norm to which women's style is compared.

**companionate love** Feelings of deep friendship and affection along with sexual feelings, thoughts, and concern for another person.

**confidentiality** Keeping a secret and not telling others what has been told to you in confidence. Confidentiality is important in developing a trusting relationship with others. It is particularly important for clients when discussing personal problems with psychologists, clergy, social workers, or psychiatrists.

**conscientious** Being reliable, so that one can be counted on to do what he or she says. This also includes taking pride in activities that one does. Contributing to being responsible for words and actions.

**cultural markers** Sometimes called rites of passage; signify the transition from one role to another. Graduation from high school is a cultural marker indicated by a celebration such as a graduation ceremony.

**cultural racism** When one cultural group is able to use its cultural values to define the value system for a country, then other cultural values tend to be ignored and to be considered inferior.

**cultural relativity** Understanding individuals' behavior relative to their culture, and, later, relative to its meaning for individuals, the opposite of ethnocentrism.

**cultural universals** Situations and events that virtually all people are likely to experience. Examples are education, parenting, and mourning.

**culture**  A set of attitudes, values, beliefs, and behaviors that are shared by a group of people. Culture can be experienced differently by each individual.

**curiosity**  The desire for something new or unusual; the tendency among people to explore their environment for its own sake.

**date rape**  Rape that occurs in the context of a dating, romantic relationship. Date rape can occur when a woman refuses to have sex, then a man forces her to have sexual relations with him.

**decatastrophizing**  A method of challenging an individual when he or she exaggerates a feared outcome. One way of doing this is using "what if" techniques.

**denial**  A common initial reaction to loss, Kübler-Ross's first stage reaction to hearing that an individual has been diagnosed with a terminal illness.

**depression**  A common reaction to stress that is often characterized by anxiety, dejection, and less physical activity. Other emotional responses that are consistent with depression are unhappiness, sadness, and grief.

**detoxification programs**  Programs that are designed to help individuals withdraw from drugs, with emphasis on medical treatment. Programs are usually inpatient and last several days.

**dichotomous thinking**  Believing that something has to be exactly as we want it to be or it or we will be failures; sometimes called black and white or all-or-nothing thinking.

**discrimination**  Actual behavior toward a person or persons based on belief, usually prejudice.

**discrimination (job)**  Making employment or other decisions based on people's gender, race, cultural group, age, or other such characteristics. The effects of job discrimination are seen in the lower employment and salary rates of women and minorities compared with white men.

**double bind**  Giving contradictory messages or conflicting demands that can induce stress. One example would be telling someone that you love him or her in an angry tone of voice. The tone of your voice would contradict your expression of love.

**double jeopardy**  Experiencing discrimination because of both gender and race or cultural identity.

**empathy**  Understanding another's point of view and communicating that understanding to that person. The point of view can be emotional or one that is not clearly expressed. When expressed to another person, the empathic individual shows sensitivity and understanding.

**ethnic group**  In general, national origin defines ethnic group or ethnicity. Individuals can have several different national origins.

**ethnocentrism**  Believing that the values and attitudes of one's own group is the standard by which other groups should be evaluated.

**exploration**  The act of searching for something or examining something. Curiosity is a tendency; exploration is the act of looking or searching.

**expressive style**  A style of behavior that includes expressing emotions and being sensitive to the feelings of others. Deborah Tannen describes this style as often being used by females.

**factor**  A characteristic required for successful job performance.

**family therapy**  A form of counseling or psychotherapy designed to help family members improve relationships and solve problems. Often all, or most, members of the family participate together in therapy.

**fetal alcohol syndrome** A combination of irreversible birth abnormalities resulting from alcohol abuse by the mother during pregnancy. Possible abnormalities are small head, small brain, heart defects, hip dislocation, mental retardation, learning disabilities, and many others.

**freedom** How we wish to live our lives, express ourselves, and worship; defined by William Glasser. Included also are people we associate with, what we wish to read or write, and how we wish to create or behave.

**frustration** A form of internal stress; occurs when individuals encounter interference with the pursuit of a goal.

**fun** Hobbies and things we do for amusements, such as sports, reading, collecting, laughing, and joking; defined by William Glasser.

**gender** Refers to whether one is male or female. Male and female differences can be learned or inherited.

**gender roles** Expectations about appropriate behavior for males and females. The roles that males and females are expected to play vary somewhat depending on cultural background.

**gender schema theory** Looking at how much individuals evaluate others from the perspective of gender.

**gender stereotypes** Beliefs about the skills, personalities and behaviors that are expected of males and females. The belief that women should stay home to take of children and not work is a gender stereotype.

**generalization** If an individual is reinforced for one behavior, then that behavior can be broadened to include other behaviors.

**genuineness** Being open and honest with your own thoughts and feelings. Not being phony with oneself or others.

**goal** An end that one tries to attain. Individuals set a goal and then choose behaviors that will then help them reach the goal.

**grief** The effect of loss on an individual; can be internal or external, such as crying.

**growth** A process that continues throughout one's lifetime; can be in several areas, such as physiological, emotional, and intellectual.

**hallucinations** Seeing or hearing things that are not there. Hallucinations brought about by the use of drugs are usually visual rather than auditory or olfactory (smell).

**happiness** A feeling of pleasure or satisfaction; can last an instant or months or years.

**hedges** An expression of opinion or view that is tentative or unsure. Words such as "sort of" and "kind of" are hedges.

**heterosexism** The view that being heterosexual is inherently better than being homosexual.

**heterosexuality** Sexual desires and erotic behaviors directed toward the other gender.

**Holland type** Holland describes people's personalities using six categories: Realistic, Investigative, Artistic, Social, Enterprising, and Conventional; types of personalities are matched with working environments, which are Realistic, Investigative, Artistic, Social, Enterprising, and Conventional.

**homophobia** The fear or hatred of homosexual people.

**homosexuality** Sexual desires and erotic behaviors directed toward one's own gender.

**hospice**  Programs or facilities that are designed to take care of dying people and their families and friends. Hospices provide home services so that patients can remain in their homes. Hospices can also have a facility that provides nursing care for dying people and counseling for dying people and their friends and families.

**hypnosis**  A condition somewhat similar to sleep that produces extreme suggestibility. Sometimes used as a treatment for smoking or other drugs, the hypnotist gives suggestions to a person after bringing about a hypnotic trance.

**individual racism**  Thoughts, feelings, and attitudes based on beliefs that one individual is superior to a person or people of another race.

**individualistic culture**  A culture in which the needs of an individual are more important than those of friends, family members, or neighbors.

**induction**  The beginning process of a new job or course. Change occurs depending on the commitment that has been made to the new activity.

**inner-based solution**  Changing attitudes toward events or people or learning new skills to cope with problems. Such solutions require action by the individual to change himself or herself rather than to change the environment.

**institutional racism**  Governmental or organizational policies that have discriminated against people of different races.

**instrumental style**  A style of behavior designed to achieve solutions or reach goals. Deborah Tannen uses it to describe men's behavior, in general.

**integration**  The process of being comfortable with the work and coworkers, as one becomes familiar with a job. Integration occurs when individuals feel comfortable with job duties and coworkers.

**interest**  Curiosity about or enjoyment in an activity. Interests, as they relate to careers, usually last for periods of years.

**intervention**  The process by which individuals close to a patient in need of drug or alcohol treatment make clear to him or her that treatment is needed.

**job**  A position requiring similar skills within one organization; refers to the task that a worker is asked to perform by an employer.

**labeling**  Ascribing negative qualities to oneself based on some errors or mistakes. For example, saying "I am stupid" because I did poorly on an exam.

**labor market**  The process by which the needs of citizens of a state, nation, or world are met through employment.

**life roles**  Different behaviors displayed in different types of situations.

**lifetime sports**  Less physically demanding and requiring fewer participants than other sports. They are easier for adults to participate in at various points in their lifetimes. Examples include golf, tennis, and bowling.

**loss**  Broadly used to refer to being separated from or deprived from a person, object, status, or relationship. Often it is used to refer to the death of a loved one.

**massed practice**  A technique of learning in which the lessons or periods of practice follow each other without a break; a technical description of "cramming."

**masturbation**  Producing sexual pleasure, often including orgasm, by stimulating one's own genitals.

**meditation**  A means of seeking higher psychological or religious levels of self-development that has been used widely in Asia. In the United States and Europe, meditation has been helpful in reducing physiological and emotional stress.

**menopause**  The permanent ending of menstruation. Generally, this occurs when women reach their 50s.

**menstruation**  The periodic flow, occurring about monthly, of blood from the uterus.

**mind map**  A method of outlining material by grouping information in large or small amounts on one piece of paper.

**mind reading**  Believing that we know how another person thinks. It is virtually impossible to know exactly what someone else is thinking.

**mnemonics**  Strategies to help remember information by making it more relevant. Acronyms are an example of a mnemonic device.

**monogamy**  Maintaining a sexual relationship with only one person.

**mourning**  Coping or dealing with loss and grief in one's own way. Mourning can be internal, where others cannot see it, or external, such as at a funeral.

**multiple intelligence**  A view that suggests that individuals have different learning styles or different ways of remembering material. Gardner lists seven forms of intelligence.

**musturbation**  A word coined by Albert Ellis that refers to the stress individuals put on themselves by saying they "must" or "have to" do something. Such words increase the pressure that individuals put on themselves to do things and also increases their own anxiety.

**Narcotics Anonymous**  A group similar to Alcoholics Anonymous, open to individuals who are abusing any drugs, including alcohol.

**need hierarchy**  The hierarchy of needs developed by Abraham Maslow, in which the most basic needs, such as physiological and safety needs, must be satisfied before needs for love and belonging, self-esteem, and self-actualization can be satisfied.

**nicotine inhalers**  Used as a treatment for smoking; a plastic tube filled with nicotine that smokers inhale between two and ten times a day.

**nicotine patches**  A treatment for cigarette smoking; similar to a bandage but releases a small dose of nicotine into the body.

**non-events**  Something that an individual wants to happen but never occurs. An example would be a promotion or transfer that does not happen.

**normative**  Common guidelines for social actions. Normative behavior refers to social expectations about what is correct or proper.

**object**  In object relations theory, "object" refers to relationships with anyone or anything. Typically, the object being discussed is the father or mother.

**object relations theory**  A point of view that examines the relationships between parents and children and how individuals develop to become independent.

**occupation**  Similar jobs that are found in many organizations. For example, Jane works as an accountant, that is an occupation. She works for the Atlas Company, that is a job.

**openness**  An attitude of flexibility toward solving problems or looking for new ideas. Curiosity, without preconceived judgments, is an example of openness.

**orgasm**  The point at which sexual intensity reaches its maximum strength and a discharge occurs in which heart rate, respiration rate, and blood pressure gradually decrease.

**orientation toward others**  By enjoying being around people and being cheerful, individuals indicate an interest in being with others. Many problems relate to difficulties with others, so enjoying being with people helps in dealing with problems.

**outcome expectations**  The estimate of a probability of an outcome. Estimating what will happen when you take an English exam is an example of outcome expectations.

**outer-directed solution**  Changing the behavior of others or in some way managing the environment or parts of a problem.

**overgeneralization**  Taking one or two negative events and making rules based on them. For example, concluding that because you did poorly on one test in a course, you will do poorly on all tests in the course.

**overlearning**  Going over material after you already know it; a useful technique for improving memory.

**palliative unit**  Facilities set up to care for dying patients, usually a separate ward of a hospital.

**passionate love**  Strong feelings for someone else, being infatuated, being totally absorbed or smitten by another person.

**passive behavior**  Also known as non-assertive behavior; doing what others want even when you do not wish to do so.

**permissive parenting style**  Parents having high acceptance of the child, but little control of what the child is allowed to do. Children express themselves freely and decide what activities they will participate in and how.

**personality**  Traits that describe an individual. These include thinking, feeling, and behaving.

**physical tasks**  The physical tasks that individuals perform as they're dying, including nutritional and fluid needs.

**physiological dependence**  When the effect of the drug on the body becomes so necessary for normal functioning that the body cannot function well without the drug.

**positive reinforcement**  Strengthening the likelihood that a given behavior will reoccur by rewarding it. Reinforcement increases the frequency of a behavior.

**positive reinterpretation**  Focusing on ways to view events in a more positive way. Sometimes this means recognizing that problems could be worse or that other people have difficulties that are greater.

**power**  The need to control others and be better than others; defined by William Glasser.

**prejudice**  A judgment, feeling, or attitude about a cultural or other type of group.

**primary appraisal**  Applied to problem solving, the process of determining whether there is a problem or danger.

**problem solving**  An active approach to coping with a problem rather than a passive or avoidant approach. Problems can be emotional or behavioral.

**procrastination**  Putting off doing something until later. Delaying studying for another time is an example of procrastination.

**progressive relaxation**  A method developed by Jacobson that has individuals tense and relax muscle groups, including arms, face, neck, and other areas, to achieve deeper and deeper levels of relaxation.

**proximity**  Finding people who are nearby. Proximity is an important factor in determining with whom we develop friendships or relationships.

**psychological tasks**  Changes caused by the dying process, including a different sense of security, less control over oneself, and a different experience of what it means to be alive.

**psychotic reactions**  Reactions in which thinking or feeling are so impaired that individuals cannot maintain contact with reality. Statements made by individuals experiencing psychotic reactions often make little sense or appear to be clearly illogical or inaccurate.

**race**  A physiological concept, race is related to our biological and genetic heritage. Experts disagree about the number of races that exist.

**racial identity models**  Explanations that show common stages that individuals go through in understanding their own experience and that of others as it relates to culture.

**racism**  Beliefs that one's own race is biologically superior to that of someone from a different race.

**rape**  Unwanted, forced sexual oral, anal, or vaginal intercourse with another person. Rape is seen as an expression of hostility and aggression rather than of sexuality.

**rapid smoking**  An aversive technique, rapid smoking requires the smoker to take a puff every six seconds until the smoking becomes very unpleasant.

**rapport**  Establishing relationships with others through sharing similar experiences and empathizing with others. This is a style of talking that Tannen finds is most common in women.

**reciprocity**  The tendency to like people who like us; an important factor in explaining how friendships and relationships develop.

**reformation**  The process that occurs with coworkers on a new job as individuals become more comfortable with them. Awkwardness tends to turn into familiarity as individuals get to know their coworkers.

**relabeling**  Changing how individuals label themselves in a negative way to more accurate terms. For example, "I am stupid" can be labeled as "I try hard" or "I didn't prepare for that test."

**relational theory**  Psychological theory that studies the importance of relationships for women in finding a sense of identity. The view that women's sense of self is based, to a large degree, on their ability to develop and maintain relationships.

**relaxation techniques**  Methods designed to slow down bodily processes, such as breathing and heart rate. Such techniques can decrease muscle tension so that muscles become less cramped and feel more comfortable.

**report**  Talking about what one knows and how one does things. This is a style that Tannen finds is used most frequently by men.

**reward**  A way of encouraging oneself and supporting yourself when you have been successful. This term is somewhat similar to reinforcement, but it is used to provide a means of acknowledging an achievement.

**safety**  Feeling safe or secure within a company and that one is being treated fairly; one of six work adjustment theory values.

**satisfaction**  Being satisfied with the work that you do. A feeling of accomplishment about completing an activity.

**satisfactoriness**  An employer's satisfaction with an employee's performance and assessment of the extent to which an individual adequately completes assigned work.

**scaling**  Turning a dichotomy into a continuum by using a numerical scale, such as one to ten rather than just zero and ten.

**schema**  A way of making associations that helps individuals interpret what they see. Seeing fire coming from a window is likely to evoke a "danger" schema in many individuals.

**secondary appraisal** Applied to problem solving, the process of determining the best way to deal with the problem.

**secure attachment** An adult attachment style in which individuals trust others easily, are comfortable with others, and can be relied on in long-lasting relationships.

**self-control** Taking responsibility for events and aspects of one's life. Not blaming oneself or others but changing activities or events by taking control or responsibility for them.

**self-actualization needs** A sense of fulfillment that comes from accomplishing goals for ourselves, being creative, and expressing ourselves creatively; the highest of Maslow's needs.

**self-critical beliefs** General beliefs that interfere with coping with problems. Examples are "I am worthless," "I can't do anything right."

**self-disclosure** Describing personal aspects of yourself to others.

**self-efficacy theory** People's judgments about their own ability to complete tasks. Lack of self-confidence is similar to low self-efficacy.

**self-esteem needs** Having confidence in ourselves, feeling good about ourselves, and having a sense of being worthy.

**sensate focus** A way for treating sexual concerns that teaches partners how to please each other sensuously without reaching orgasm.

**separation and individuation** The process of separating from one's parents to make one's own choices and be responsible for one's own life.

**sex** In this text, sex is used to refer to sexual behavior such as kissing or sexual intercourse.

**sexual harassment** Being subjected to unwelcome behavior that is sexual in nature. This can range from verbal remarks that are not wanted to sexual assault such as being grabbed or fondled.

**sexual orientation** A preference for individuals of the other gender or the same gender or both. Many cultures assume that individuals will have a heterosexual orientation, a preference for individuals of the other gender.

**sexual scripts** Expectations about how individuals should express themselves sexually. Sexual scripts are quite varied and differ depending on individual values and cultural and religious beliefs.

**sexually transmitted diseases (STDs)** Diseases contracted through sexual contact with another person, usually involving exchange of bodily fluids. Common STDs are pubic lice, chlamydia, gonorrhea, syphilis, herpes, genital warts, viral hepatitis, and HIV/AIDS.

**shyness** Being uncomfortable or anxious in the presence of strangers or people with whom one is not familiar. Individuals might feel flushed, be nervous, be unable to talk, and not know what to say.

**similarity** Seeking out people who are similar to ourselves. Similarity is an important factor in determining the development of friendships or relationships.

**social interest** The sharing and concern for the welfare of others that can guide people's behavior throughout their lives. This includes a sense of being part of society and taking some responsibility to improve it. Alfred Adler developed the term.

**social tasks** Referring to the dying process, these tasks deal with the importance of interpersonal relationships and dealing with social systems such as hospitals.

**spiritual tasks** Questioning the meaning of one's life, the nature of one's values, and one's religious and spiritual beliefs as part of the dying process. For some individuals, spiritual tasks are more important in the dying process than in earlier parts of their lives.

**SQ3R** Survey, Questions, Read, Recite, Review; a well known approach to studying that focuses on being able to understand material by answering questions about it.

**state shyness**  Being shy in only certain situations, such as meeting strangers or being in a large group.

**status**  Being recognized and valued for accomplishments; one of six work adjustment theory values.

**stereotypes**  Beliefs, either positive or negative, that are held by an individual about a group of people.

**stereotypes (Holland)**  People's impressions and generalizations about occupations. Holland believes these generalizations are generally accurate.

**stress**  Emotional or physical strain that can interfere with coping with situations. Examples of emotional stress are anxiety, depression, and anger.

**stroke**  A sudden decrease in the blood supply to part of the brain that damages parts of the body. Symptoms are inability to speak, inability to move part of the body, or a loss of consciousness.

**support systems**  People to whom you turn for a variety of help. Some people can offer emotional support, others informational support, and others financial support.

**tag question**  Questions added to the end of a sentence; style associated with use by women.

**therapeutic community**  A program designed to help individuals change their lifestyles, abstain from drugs, start working, and develop positive attitudes to society.

**tolerance**  Needing more and more of a drug to experience the same effect. As more of a drug is used, the chances that the drug itself will cause physiological and psychological problems is increased.

**trait**  A characteristic of an individual that can be measured through testing or observation.

**trait shyness**  Being anxious or afraid in many interpersonal situations, such as being with small groups, strangers, or relatives; at work; or dating.

**transitions**  The movement from one part of one's career to another. Transitions can be anticipated, unanticipated, "chronic hassles," and non-events.

**unanticipated transitions**  Events that are surprises or unexpected, such as being fired.

**vaginismus**  Involuntary contractions of the vagina before intercourse. This is a type of female sexual concern.

**valuational tasks**  Examining one's own values as they relate to the loss of a loved one.

**values**  Concepts and attitudes that are important to individuals. These include general values, which are religious, political, or social, as well as work-related values.

**white privileges**  Privileges that those in the majority (in Western Cultures) tend to have without being aware of them.

**withdrawal**  The bodily stress experienced when an individual becomes dependent on a drug, then tries to remove the drug.

**work**  An activity that produces something of value for other people; a general term that relates to both paid and unpaid activity.

**work adjustment theory**  A theory that focuses on the importance of values in predicting satisfaction with work. Values include achievement, comfort, status, altruism, safety, and autonomy.

# References

Abel, G., & Rouleau, J. L. (1990). The nature and extent of sexual assault. In W. Marshall, D. Laws, & H. Barbaree (Eds.,, *Handbook of sexual assault* (pp. 9–20). New York: Plenum.

Adler, A. (1964). *Social interest: A challenge to mankind.* New York: Capricorn.

Ainsworth, M. D. S., Blehar, M. C., Waters, E., & Wall, S. (1978). *Patterns of attachment.* Hillsdale, NJ: Earlbaum.

Amato, P. R. (1993). Children's adjustment to divorce: Theories, hypotheses and empirical support. *Journal of Marriage and the Family, 55,* 23–38.

Ammerman, R. T. (1990). Predisposing child factors. In R. T. Ammerman & M. Hersen (Eds.), *Children at risk: An evaluation of factors contributing to child abuse and neglect* (pp. 199–221). New York: Plenum.

Anderson, C. D., & Tomaskovic-Devey, D. (1995). Patriarchal pressures: An exploration of organizational processes that exacerbate and erode gender earnings inequality. *Work and Occupations, 22,* 328–356.

Aneshensel, C. S. (1986). Marital and employment role strain, social support and depression among adult women. In S. E. Hobfall, (Ed.), *Stress, social support and women* (pp. 99–114). New York: Hemisphere

Ansbacher, H. L., & Ansbacher, R. (Eds.). (1970). *Superiority and social interest by Alfred Adler.* Evanston, IL: Northwestern University Press.

Aron, A., & Westbay, L. (1996). Dimensions of the prototype of love. *Journal of Personality and Social Psychology, 70,* 535–551.

Ary, D. B., & Biglan, A. (1988). Longitudinal changes in adolescent cigarette smoking behavior: Onset and cessation. *Journal of Behavioral Medicine, 11,* 361–382.

Asendorpf, J. B. (1989). Shyness as a final common pathway for two different kinds of inhibition. *Journal of Personality and Social Psychology, 57,* 481–492.

Ashraf, J. (1995). The effect of race on earnings in the United States. *Applied Economic Letters, 2,* 72–75.

Atkinson, J. W. (1964). *An introduction to motivation.* Princeton, NJ: Van Nostrand Reinhold.

Axelson, J. A. (1999). *Counseling and development in a multicultural society* (3rd ed.). Pacific Grove, CA: Brooks/Cole.

Bandura, A. (1997). *Self-efficacy: The exercise of control.* San Francisco: W. H. Freeman.

Bandura, A. (1986). *Social foundations of thought and action: A social cognitive theory.* Englewood Cliffs, NJ: Prentice-Hall.

Barlow, D. H., & Durand, V. M. (1999). *Abnormal psychology* (2nd ed.). Pacific Grove, CA: Brooks/Cole.

Baumeister, R. F. (1984). Choking under pressure: Self-consciousness and paradoxical effects of incentives and skillful performance. *Journal of Personality and Social Psychology, 46,* 610–620.

Baumrind, D. (1991). Effective parenting during the early adolescent transition. In P. A. Cowan & M. Hetherington (Eds.), *Family transitions* (pp. 111–164). Hillsdale, NJ: Erlbaum.

Baumrind, D. (1989). Rearing competent children. In W. Damon (Ed.), *Child development today and tomorrow.* San Francisco: Jossey-Bass.

Baumrind, D. (1978). Parental disciplinary patterns and social competence in children. *Youth and Society, 9,* 299–276.

Baumrind, D. (1971). Current patterns of parental authority. *Developmental Psychology Monographs, 4,* (1, Part 2).

Beck, A. T. (1991). Cognitive therapy: A 30-year retrospective. *American Psychologist, 46,* 368–375.

Beck, A. T. (1976). *Cognitive therapy and the emotional disorders.* New York: International Universities Press.

Bem, S. L. (1987). Gender schema theory and the romantic tradition. In P. Shaver & C. Hendrick (Eds.), *Sex and gender* (pp. 251–271). Newbury Park, CA: Sage.

Bem, S. L. (1981). Gender schema theory: A cognitive account of sex typing. *Psychological Review, 88,* 354–364.

Bentley, K. S., & Fox, R. A. (1991). Mothers and fathers of young children: Comparison of parenting styles. *Psychological Reports, 69,* 320–322.

Berlyne, D. E. (1960). *Conflict, arousal, and curiosity.* New York: McGraw-Hill.

Berscheid, E., & Reis, H. T. (1998). Attraction and close relationships. In D. T. Gilbert, S. T. Fiske, & G. Lindzey (Eds.), *The handbook of social psychology* (Volume II). Boston: McGraw-Hill.

Betz, N. E., & Fitzgerald, L. F. (1987). *The career psychology of women.* Orlando, FL: Academic.

Bloodworth, R. C. (1987). Major problems associated with marijuana abuse. *Psychiatric Medicine, 3*(3), 173–184.

Bolles, R. N. (1999). *What color is your parachute?* (28th ed.). San Francisco: Ten Speed.

Bowlby, J. (1982). *Attachment and loss (Vol. 1): Attachment* (2nd ed.). London: Hogarth.

Bowlby, J. (1980). *Attachment and loss (Vol. 3): Loss, sadness and depression.* New York: Basic.

Brannon, L., & Feist, J. (1997). *Health psychology: An introduction to behavior and health* (3rd ed.). Pacific Grove, CA: Brooks/Cole.

Brazelton, T. B. (1992). *On becoming a family: The growth of attachment.* New York: Delacorte.

Breitman, P., Knutson, K., & Reed, P. (1987). *How to persuade your lover to use a condom . . . and why you should.* Rocklin, CA: Prima.

Broverman, I. K., Broverman, D. M., Clarkson, D., Rosenkrantz, P., & Vogel, W. (1970). Sex role stereotypes and clinical judgments of mental health counselors. *Journal of Consulting and Clinical Psychology, 34,* 1–7.

Browne, A., & Williams, K. R. (1993). Gender intimacy and lethal violence: Trends from 1976 through 1987. *Gender & Society, 7,* 78–98.

Buss, D. M. (1989). Sex differences in human mate preferences: Evolutionary hypotheses tested in 37 cultures. *Behavioral and Brain Sciences, 12,* 1–14.

Buvat, J., Buvat-Herbaut, M., Lemaire, A., & Marcolin, G. (1990). Recent developments in the clinical assessment and diagnosis of erectile dysfunction. *Annual Review of Sex Research, 1,* 265–308.

Cash, T., & Derlega, B. (1978). The matching hypotheses: Physical attractiveness among same-sex friends. *Personality and Social Psychology Bulletin, 4,* 240–243.

Cherlin, A. J. (1992). *Marriage, divorce, remarriage* (Revised and enlarged edition). Cambridge, MA: Harvard University Press.

Ciancanelli, P., & Berch, B. (1987). Gender and the GNP. In B. B. Hess & M. M. Ferree (Eds.), *Analyzing gender: A handbook of social science research* (pp. 244–266). Newbury Park, CA: Sage.

Clements, M. (1994). Sex and America today. *Parade,* August 7, 4–6.

Coambs, R. B., Li, S., & Kozlowski, L. T. (1992). Age interacts with heaviness of smoking in predicting success in cessation of smoking. *American Journal of Epidemiology, 135,* 240–246.

Cohen, S., & Hoberman, H. M. (1983). Positive events and social supports as buffers of life change stress. *Journal of Applied Social Psychology, 13,* 99–125.

Corey, G., & Corey, M. S. (1997). *I never knew I had a choice* (6th ed.). Pacific Grove, CA: Brooks/Cole.

Corr, C. A. (1992). A task-based approach to coping with dying. *Omega, 24,* 81–94.

Corr, C. A., Nabe, C. M., & Corr, D. M. (2000). *Death and dying: Life and living* (3rd ed.). Pacific Grove, CA: Brooks/Cole.

Crooks, R., & Baur, K. (1999). *Our sexuality* (7th ed.). Pacific Grove, CA: Brooks/Cole.

Culp, J., & Dunson, B. (1986). Brothers of a different color: A preliminary look at employer treatment of White and Black youth. In R. Freeman & H. Holzer (Eds.), *The Black youth employment crisis* (pp. 233–260). Chicago: University of Chicago Press

D'Zurilla, T. J., & Nezu, A. M. (1982). Social problem solving in adults. In P. C. Kendall (Ed.), *Advances in Cognitive Behavior Research and Therapy* (Vol. 1, pp. 202–274). New York: Academic.

Dawis, R. V., & Lofquist, L. H. (1984). *A psychological theory of work adjustment.* Minneapolis: University of Minnesota Press.

DeLeon, G. (1994).Therapeutic communities. In M. Galanter & H. D. Kleber (Eds.), *Textbook of substance abuse treatment.* Washington, D.C.: American Psychiatric Press.

DeLeon, G. (1989). Psychopathology and substance abuse: What is being learned from research in therapeutic communities. *Journal of Psychoactive Drugs, 21,* 177–188.

Dinklage, L. B. (1968). *Decision strategies of adolescents.* Unpublished doctoral dissertation: Harvard University: Cambridge.

Dion, K. K., Berscheid, E. & Walster, E. (1972). What is beautiful is good. *Journal of Personality and Social Psychology, 24,* 285–290.

Doweiko, H. E. (1999). *Concepts of chemical dependency* (4th ed.). Pacific Grove, CA: Brooks/Cole.

Ellis, A. (1993). *Psychotherapy and the value of a human being* (Rev. ed.). New York: Institute for Rational Emotive Therapy.

Ellis, A. (1962). *Reason and emotion in psychotherapy.* Secaucus, NJ: Lyle Stuart.

Emery, R. E., & Lauman-Billings, L. (1998). An overview of the nature, causes, and consequences of abusive family relationships: Toward differentiating maltreatment and violence. *American Psychologist, 53,* 121–135.

Erikson, E. H. (1963). *Childhood and society* (2nd ed.). New York: Norton.

Evans, R. I., Rozelle, R. M., Maxwell, S. E., Raines, B. E., Dill, C. A., Guthrie, T. J., Henderson, A. H., & Hill, D. C. (1981). Social modeling films to deter smoking in adolescents: Results of a three year field investigation. *Journal of Applied Psychology, 66,* 399–414.

Everitt, B. J., & Bancroft, J. (1991). Of rats and men: The comparative approach to male sexuality. *Annual Review of Sex Research, 2,* 77–118.

Feingold, A. (1992). Good-looking people are not what we think. *Psychological Bulletin, 111,* 304–341.

Feingold, A. (1990). Gender differences in effects of physical attractiveness on romantic attraction: A comparison across five research paradigms. *Journal of Personality and Social Psychology, 59,* 981–993.

Feiring, C., & Lewis, M. (1987). The child's social network: Sex differences from three to six years. *Sex Roles, 17,* 621–636.

Ferree, M. M. (1987). She works hard for a living: Gender and class on the job. In B. B. Hess & M. M. Ferree (Eds.), *Analyzing gender: A handbook of social science research* (pp. 322–347). Newbury Park, CA: Sage.

Fischhoff, B. (1992). Giving advice: Decision theory perspectives on sexual assault. *American Psychologist, 47,* 577–588.

Fiske, S. T., & Taylor, S. E. (1991). *Social cognition.* New York: McGraw-Hill.

Fitzgerald, L. F., & Ormerod, A. J. (1993). Breaking silence: The sexual harassment of women in academia and the work place. In F. L. Denmark and M. A. Paludi (Eds.), *Psychology of women: A handbook of issues and theories* (pp. 553–581). Westport, CT: Greenwood.

Fleming, S., & Balmer, L. (1996). Bereavement in adolescence. In C. A. Corr & D. E. Balk (Eds.), *Handbook of adolescent death and bereavement* (pp. 139–154). New York: Springer.

Frankl, V. (1997). *Viktor Frankl—Recollections: An autobiography.* New York: Plenum.

Freeman, A. (1993). A psychological approach for conceptualizing schematic development for cognitive therapy. In K. T. Kuehlwein & H. Rosen (Eds.), *Cognitive therapy in action* (pp. 54–87). San Francisco: Jossey-Bass.

Freeman, A. (1987). Cognitive therapy: An overview. In A. Freeman & B. Greenwood (Eds.), *Cognitive therapy: Applications in psychiatric and medical settings* (pp. 1935). New York: Human Science Press.

Fromm, E. (1956). *The art of loving.* New York: Harper & Row (Colophon) (paperback edition, 1974).

Gagnon, J. H., & Simon, W. (1973). *Sexual conduct: The social sources of human sexuality.* Chicago: Aldine.

Gardner, H. (1983). *Frames of mind: The theory of multiple intelligences.* New York: Basic.

Gardner, J. N., & Jewler, A. J. (1997). *Your college experience: Strategies for success* (3rd ed.). Belmont, CA: Wadsworth.

Garnets, L., & Kimmel, D. (1991). Lesbian and gay male dimensions in the psychological study of human diversity. In J. D. Goodchilds (Ed.), *Psychological perspectives on human diversity in America.* Washington, D.C.: American Psychological Association.

Gilligan, C. (1982). *In a different voice.* Cambridge, MA: Harvard University Press.

Gilligan, C. (1977). In a different voice: Women's conception of self and morality. *Harvard Educational Review, 47,* 481–517.

Gilmore, D. (1990). *Manhood in the making: Cultural components of masculinity.* New Haven, CT: Yale University Press.

Ginott, H. G. (1972). *Teacher and child: A book for parents and teachers.* New York: Macmillan.

Gladue, B. A. (1994). The biopsychology of sexual orientation. *Current Directions in Psychological Science, 3,* 150–154.

Glasser, W. (1998). *Choice theory: A new psychology of personal freedom.* New York: Harper.

Glasser, W. (1985). *Control theory: A new explanation of how we control our lives.* New York: Harper & Row.

Glasser, W. (1965). *Reality therapy: A new approach to psychiatry.* New York: Harper & Row.

Gonzales, M. H., & Meyers, S. A. (1993). "You're mother would like me": Self-presentation in the personal ads of heterosexual and homosexual men and women. *Personality and Social Psychology Bulletin, 19,*131–142.

Grambs, J. D. (1989). *Women over forty: Visions and realities.* New York: Springer.

Gutek, B. (1985). *Sex and the workplace.* San Francisco: Jossey-Bass.

Gutek, B., & Koss, M. P. (1993). Changed women and changed organizations: Consequences of and coping with sexual harassment. *Journal of Vocational Behavior, 42,* 28–48.

Hackett, G., & Betz, N. (1981). A self-efficacy approach to the career development of women. *Journal of Vocational Behavior, 18,* 326–339.

Hare-Mustin, R. T., & Marecek, J. (1988). The meaning of difference: Gender theory, post-modernism, and psychology. *American Psychologist, 43,* 445–464.

Hatcher, R. A., Trussell, J., Stewart, F., Cates, W., Jr., Stewart, G. K., Guest, F., & Kowal, D. (1994). *Contraceptive technology* (17th ed.). New York: Ardent Media.

Hazen, C., & Shaver, P. (1987). Romantic love conceptualized as an attachment process. *Journal of Personality and Social Psychology, 52,* 511–524.

Hazan, C., & Shaver, P. (1986). *Parental care giving style questionnaire.* An unpublished questionnaire.

Helms, J. E. (1995). An update on Helms's white and people of color racial identity models. In J. Ponterotto, J. M. Casas, L. A. Suzuki, & C. M. Alexander (Eds.), *Handbook of multicultural counseling* (pp. 181–198). Thousand Oaks, CA: Sage.

Herek, G. M., Gillis, J. R., Cogan, J. C., & Glunt, E. K. (1997). Hate crime victimization among lesbian, gay, and bisexual adults. *Journal of Interpersonal Violence, 12,* 195–215.

Hettich, P. I. (1992). *Learning skills for college and career.* Pacific Grove, CA: Brooks/Cole.

Hofstede, G. (1984). *Culture's consequences: International differences in work-related values.* Newbury Park, CA: Sage.

Holland, J. L. (1997). *Making vocational choices: A theory of vocational personalities and work environments.* Odessa, FL: Psychological Assessment Resources.

Holmes, T. & Rahe, R. (1967). The social readjustment rating scale. *Journal of Psychosomatic Research, 11,* 213–218.

Hopson, B., & Adams, J. D. (1977). Towards an understanding of transitions: Defining some boundaries of transition. In J. Adams, J. Hayes, & B. Hopson (Eds.), *Transition: Understanding and managing personal change* (pp. 1–19). Montclair, NJ: Allenheld & Osmun.

Hudgens, R. W. (1983). Preventing suicide. *New England Journal of Medicine, 30,* 897–898.

Hughes, L. (1996). *Beginnings & beyond: A guide for personal growth & adjustment.* Pacific Grove, CA: Brooks/Cole.

Hull, J. G. (1987). Self-awareness model. In H. T. Blane & K. E. Leonard (Eds.), *Psychological theories of drinking and alcoholism* (pp. 272–304). New York: Guilford.

Hunt, M. (1974). *Sexual behavior in the 1970s.* Chicago: Playboy Press.

Hyde, J. S. (1996). *Half the human experience: The psychology of women* (5th ed.). Lexington, MA: Heath.

Jacobson, E. (1938). *Progressive relaxation.* Chicago: University of Chicago Press.

Jakubowski, P. A. (1977). Assertion training for women. In E. I. Rawlings & D. K. Carter (Eds.), *Psychotherapy for women* (pp. 147–190). Springfield, IL: Charles C. Thomas.

Jenike, M. A. (1991). Drug abuse. In E. Rubenstein & D. D. Federman (Eds.), *Scientific American medicine.* New York: Scientific American Press.

Jones, J. M. (1997). *Prejudice and racism* (2nd ed.). New York: McGraw-Hill.

Jordaan, J. P. (1963). Exploratory behavior: The formation of self and occupational concepts. In D. Super, R. Starishevsky, N. Matlin, & J. P. Jordaan (Eds.), *Career development: Self concept theory* (pp. 42–78). New York: College Entrance Examination Board.

Jordan, J. V. (1997). *Women's growth in diversity: More writings from the Stone Center.* New York: Guilford.

Kail, R. B., & Cavanaugh, J. C. (1996). *Human development.* Pacific Grove, CA: Brooks/Cole.

Kenrick, D. T., Groth, G. E., Trost, M. R., & Sadalla, E. K. (1993). Integrating evolutionary and social exchange perspectives on relationships: Effects of gender, self-appraisal, and involvement level on mate selection criteria. *Journal of Personality and Social Psychology, 64,* 1951–1969.

Kinsey, A., Pomeroy, W., & Martin, C. (1948). *Sexual behavior in the human male.* Philadelphia: Saunders.

Klatsky, A. L., Friedman, G. D., & Siegelaub, A. B. (1981). Alcohol and mortality: A ten-year Kaiser-Permanente experience. *Annals of Internal Medicine, 95,* 139–145.

Kleinke, C. L. (1998). *Coping with life challenges* (2nd ed.). Pacific Grove, CA: Brooks/Cole.

Knussman, R., Christiansen, K., & Couwenbergs, C. (1986). Relations between sex hormone levels and sexual behavior in men. *Archives of Sexual Behavior, 15,* 429–445.

Kohlberg, L. (1981). *The philosophy of moral development: Essays on moral development* (Vols. 1–2). San Francisco: Harper & Row.

Koss, M. P. (1993). Rape: Scope, impact, interventions, and public policy. *American Psychologist, 48,* 1062–1069.

Koss, M. P., Gidycz, C. A., & Wisniewski, N. (1987). The scope of rape: Incidents and prevalence of sexual aggression and victimization in a national sample of higher education students. *Journal of Consulting and Clinical Psychology, 55,* 162–170.

Kübler-Ross, E. (1975). *Death: The final stage of growth.* Englewood Cliffs, NJ: Prentice-Hall (Spectrum).

Kübler-Ross, E. (1969). *On death and dying.* New York: Macmillan.

Lazarus, R. S. (1993). Why we should think of stress as a subset of emotion. In L. Goldberger & S. Breznitz (Eds.) *Handbook of stress: Theoretical and clinical aspects* (2nd ed.). New York: Free Press.

Lazarus, R. S. (1991). *Emotion and adaptation.* New York: Oxford University Press.

Lazarus, R. S., & Folkman, S. (1984). *Stress, appraisal, and coping.* New York: Springer.

LeFrancois, G. R. (1996). *The lifespan* (5th ed.) Pacific Grove, CA: Brooks/Cole.

Lent, R. W., Brown, S. D., & Hackett, G. (1994). Toward a unified social cognitive theory of career and academic interest, choice, and performance. *Journal of Vocational Behavior, 45,* 79–122.

Lewin, K. (1935). *A dynamic theory of personality.* New York: McGraw-Hill.

Lofquist, L. H., & Dawis, R. V. (1991). *Essentials of person-environment correspondence counseling.* Minneapolis: University of Minnesota.

Longstreth, L. E. (1970). Birth order and avoidance of dangerous activities. *Developmental Psychology, 2,* 154.

Maccoby, E. E. (1990). Gender and relationships: A developmental account. *American Psychologist, 45,* 513–520.

MacKenzie, R. A. (1997). *The time trap.* New York: AMACOM.

Maddi, S. R. (1989). *Personality theories: A comparative analysis* (5th ed.). Belmont, CA: Brooks/Cole.

Maltz, D. M., & Borker, R. A. (1983). A cultural approach to male-female miscommunication. In J. A. Gumperz (Ed.), *Language and social identity* (pp. 196–216). New York: Cambridge University Press.

Marrone, R. (1997), *Death, mourning, and caring.* Pacific Grove, CA: Brooks/Cole.

Maslach, C., & Goldberg, J. (1998). Prevention of burnout: New perspectives. *Applied and Preventive Psychology, 1,* 63–74.

Maslow, A. (1970). *Motivation and personality* (2nd ed.). New York: Harper & Row.

Masters, W. H., & Johnson, B. E. (1980). *Human sexual inadequacy* (2nd ed.). New York: Bantam.

Masters, W. H., Johnson, B. E., & Kolodny, R. C. (1994). *Heterosexuality.* New York: HarperCollins.

Matsumoto, D. (1996). *Culture and psychology.* Pacific Grove, CA: Brooks/Cole.

McIntosh, P. (1989). White privilege: Unpacking the invisible knapsack. *Peace and Freedom Journal.* July/August.

Meichenbaum, D. (1985). *Stress inoculation training.* New York: Pergamon.

Miles, M. S., & Demi, A. S. (1986). Guilt in bereaved parents. In T. A. Rando (Eds.), *Parental loss of a child* (pp. 97–118). Champaign, IL: Research Press.

Miller, J. B. (1991). The development of women's sense of self. In J. B. Jordan, A. G. Kaplan, J. B. Miller, I. P. Stiver & A. L. Surrey (Eds.), *Women's growth and connection* (pp. 11–16). New York: Guilford.

Mirvis, P. H., & Hall, B. T. (1994). Psychological success and the boundaryless career. *Journal of Organization Behavior, 15,* 365–380.

Moore, D. W. (1994, May). One in seven Americans victim of child abuse. *The Gallup Poll Monthly,* pp. 18–22.

Morrison, D. R., & Cherlin, A. J. (1995). The divorce process and young children's well-being: A prospective analysis. *Journal of Marriage and the Family, 57,* 800–812.

Morrow, L. (1993, March 29). The temping of America. *Time,* pp. 40–44, 46–47.

Myers, D. G., & Diener, E. (1997). The pursuit of happiness. *Scientific American, Special issue 7,* 40–43.

Nass, G. D., Libby, R. W., & Fisher, M. P. (1981). *Sexual choices: An introduction to human sexuality.* Monterey, CA: Brooks/Cole.

NIH (National Institute of Health) (1999). HIV/AIDS Fact Sheet. National Institute of Allergy and Infectious Diseases.

Noppe, L. D., & Noppe, I. C. (1996). Ambiguity in adolescent understandings of death. In C. A. Corr & D. E. Balk (Eds.), *Handbook of adolescent death and bereaving* (pp. 25–41). New York: Springer.

*Occupational Outlook Handbook.* (1998). Washington, D.C.: U.S. Department of Labor.

*Occupational Outlook Quarterly* (1999). U.S. Department of Commerce, Bureau of the Census, Washington, D.C., p. 40.

Ogbu, J. (1993). Differences in cultural frame of reference. *International Journal of Behavioral Development, 16,* 483–506.

Park, C. L., Cohen, L. H., & Murch, R. L. (1996). Assessment and prediction of stress-related growth. *Journal of Personality, 64,* 71–105.

Parkes, C. M. (1987). *Bereavement: Studies of grief in adult life* (2nd ed.) Madison, CT: International Universities Press.

Parsons, F. (1909). *Choosing a vocation.* Boston: Houghton Mifflin.

Peterson, G. W., Leigh, G. K., & Day, R. D, (1984). Family stress theory and the impact of divorce on children *Journal of Divorce, 7,* 1–20.

Pines, A. M. (1993). Burnout. In L. Goldberger & S. Breznitz (Eds.), *Handbook of stress: Theoretical and clinical aspects* (2nd ed.). New York: Free Press.

Pryor, F. L., & Schaffer, D. (1997, July). Wages and the university educated: A paradox resolved. *Monthly Labor Review,* 3–14.

Pryor, J. B., LaVite, C. M., & Stoller, L. M. (1993). A social psychological analysis of sexual harassment: The period situation interaction. *Journal of Vocational Behavior, 42,* 68–83.

Rapaport, K., & Burkhart, B. R. (1984). Personality and attitudinal characteristics of sexually coercive college males. *Journal of Abnormal Psychology, 93,* 216–221.

Reis, H. T., & Patrick, B. C. (1996). Attachment and intimacy: Component processes. In E. T. Higgins & A. Kruglanski (Eds.), *Social psychology: Handbook of basic principles.* New York: Guilford.

Restak, R. (1994). *Receptors.* New York: Bantam.

Reynolds, D. K. (1980). *The quiet therapies.* Honolulu: University Press of Hawaii.

Rinpoche, S. (1992). *The Tibetan book of living and dying.* New York: HarperCollins.

Robinson, F. P. (1970). *Effective study* (4th ed.). New York: HarperCollins.

Robinson, J. P., & Milkie, M. A. (1998). Back to basics: Trends in and role determinants of women's attitudes toward housework. *Journal of Marriage and the Family, 60,* 205–218.

Roe, A., & Lunneborg, P. W. (1990). Personality development and career choice. In D. Brown, L. Brooks, & Assoc. (Eds.), *Career choice and development: Applying contemporary theories to practice* (2nd ed., pp. 68–101). San Francisco: Jossey-Bass.

Rogers, C. R. (1980). *A way of being.* Boston: Houghton Mifflin.

Rogers, C. R. (1975). Empathic: An unappreciated way of being. *Counseling Psychologist, 5,* 2–10.

Rogers, C. R. (1961). *On becoming a person.* Boston: Houghton Mifflin.

Rogers, C. R. (1959). A theory of therapy, personality, and interpersonal relationships as developed in the client-centered framework. In S. Koch (Ed.), *Psychology: A study of science: Formulations of the person and the social context* (pp. 184–256). New York: McGraw-Hill.

Rosman, B. L., Minuchin, S. & Liebman, R. (1975). Family lunch session: An introduction to family therapies in anorexia nervosa. *American Journal of Orthopsychiatry, 45,* 846–853.

Russo, N. F. (1979). Overview: Sex roles, fertility, and the motherhood mandate. *Psychology of Women Quarterly, 4,* 7–15.

Sacks, M. H. (1993). Exercise for stress control. In D. Goleman & J. Gurin (Eds.), *Mind/body medicine: How to use your mind for better health.* Yonkers, NY: Consumer Reports Books.

Sanday, P. (1981). The socio-cultural context of rape: A cross-cultural study. *Journal of Social Issues, 37,* 5–27.

Schachter, S. (1982). Recidivism and self-cure of smoking and obesity. *American Psychologist, 37,* 436–444.

Schlossberg, N. K. (1984). *Counseling adults in transition.* New York: Springer.

Schuckit, M. A. (1989). *Drug and alcohol abuse: A clinical guide to diagnosis and treatment* (3rd ed.). New York: Plenum.

Sharf, R. S. (2000). *Theories of psychotherapy and counseling: Concepts and cases.* Pacific Grove, CA: Brooks/Cole.

Sharf, R. S. (1997). *Applying career development theory to counseling* (2nd ed.). Pacific Grove, CA: Brooks/Cole.

Sharf, R. S. (1993). *Occupational information overview.* Pacific Grove, CA: Brooks/Cole.

Sherwin, B. B. (1991). The psychoendocrinology of aging and female sexuality. *Annual Review of Sex Research, 2,* 181–198.

Shneidman, E. S. (1985). *Definition of suicide.* New York: Wiley.

Simon, W., & Gagnon, J. (1986). Sexual scripts: Permanence and change. *Archives of Sexual Behavior, 15,* 97–120.

Skinner, B. F. (1953). *Science and human behavior.* New York: Free Press.

Sternberg, R. J. (1988). Triangulating love. In R. J. Sternberg & M. L. Barnes (Eds.), *The psychology of love.* New Haven, CT: Yale University Press.

Sternberg, R. J. (1986). A triangular theory of love. *Psychological Review, 93,* 110–135.

Stockard, J. (1997). *Sociology: Discovering society.* Belmont, CA: Wadsworth.

Super, D. E. (1990). A life span, life space approach to career development. In D. Brown & L. Brooks (Eds.), *Career choice and development: Applying contemporary theories to practice* (2nd ed., pp. 107–261). San Francisco: Jossey-Bass.

Super, D. E. (1970). *Work Values Inventory.* Boston: Houghton Mifflin.

Super, D. E., & Nevill, D. D. (1989). *The Values Scale: Theory, research, and application.* Palo Alto, CA: Consulting Psychologists Press.

Super, D. E., Nevill, D. D. (1986). *The Salience Inventory.* Palo Alto, CA: Consulting Psychologists Press.

Surrey, J. L. (1991). The self-in-relation: A theory of women's development. In J. B. Jordaan, A. G. Kaplan, J. B. Miller, J. P. Stiver, & J. L. Surrey (Eds.), *Women's growth and connection* (pp. 51–66). New York: Guilford.

Tannen, D. (1990). *You just don't understand: Women and men in conversation.* New York: Ballantine.

The American workforce: 1992–2005. (1993). *Occupational Outlook Quarterly, 37,* 4–44.

Thoits, P. A. (1986). Social support as coping assistance. *Journal of Consulting and Clinical Psychology, 54,* 416–423.

Tice, D. M., & Baumeister, R. F. (1997). Longitudinal study of procrastination, perform-ance, stress, and health: The cost and benefits of dawdling. *Psychological Science, 8,* 454–458.

Tiedeman, D. B., & O'Hara, R. P. (1963). *Career development: Choice and adjustment.* New York: College Entrance Examination Board.

Till, F. (1980). *Sexual harassment: A report on the sexual harassment of students.* Washington, D.C.: National Advisory Council on Women's Educational Programs.

U.S. Bureau of the Census. (1995). *Statistical abstract of the United States: 1995* (115th ed.). Washington, D.C.: U.S. Government Printing Office.

U.S. Department of Labor. (1997–1998). *Occupational Outlook Quarterly.* Washington, D.C.

Ubell, E. (1984). Sex in America today. *Parade,* October 28, 11–13.

Unger, R., & Crawford, M. (1996). *Women and gender: A feminist psychology* (2nd. ed.). New York: McGraw Hill.

Walker, L. E. (1989). Psychology and violence against women. *American Psychologist, 44,* 695–702.

Wallace, P. (1975). *Pathways into work.* Lexington, MA: D. C. Heath.

Walsh, A. (1991). *The science of love: Understanding love and its effects on mind and body.* Buffalo, NY: Prometheus.

Walsh, R. (1981). Meditation. In R. J. Corsini (Ed.), *Handbook of innovative psychothera-pies* (pp. 470–488). New York: Wiley.

Walster, E., & Walster, G. (1978). *A new look at love.* Reading, MA: Addison-Wesley.

Watkins, C. E., Jr. (1992). Birth-order research and Adlerian theory: A critical review. *Individual Psychology, 48,* 357–368.

Weiner, A. B. (1976). *Women of value, men of renown: New perspectives in Trobriand exchange.* Austin: University of Texas Press.

Weisner, C., Greenfield, T., & Room, R. (1995). Trends in the treatment of alcohol prob-lems in the U.S. general population, 1979–1990. *American Journal of Public Health, 85,* 55–60.

Weiten, W., & Lloyd, M. A. (2000). *Psychology applied to modern life* (6th ed.) Pacific Grove, CA: Brooks/Cole.

Wolpe, J. (1990). *The practice of behavior therapy* (4th ed.). New York: Pergamon.

Worden, J. W. (1991). *Grief counseling and grief therapy: A handbook for the mental health practitioner* (2nd ed.). New York: Springer.

Wubbolding, R. E. (1988). *Using reality therapy.* New York: Harper & Row.

Yang, K. S. (1982). Causal attributions of academic success and failure and their affective consequences. *Chinese Journal of Psychology* [Taiwan], *24,* 65–83. (The abstract only is in English.)

Zajonc, R. B., & Mullally, P. R. (1997). Birth order: Reconciling conflicting effects. *American Psychologist, 52,* 685–699.

Zimbardo, P. G. (1990). *Shyness.* Reading, MA: Addison-Wesley.

Zimbardo, P. G. (1977). *Shyness: What it is, what to do about it.* Reading, MA: Addison-Wesley.

Zuckerman, M. (1990). Some dubious premises in research and theory on racial differ-ences. *American Psychologist, 45,* 1297–1303.

# Index